ADVENTURING WITH BOOKS

ADVENTURING WITH BOOKS

2,400 titles for pre-K–grade 8

second edition

PREPARED BY
SHELTON L. ROOT, JR.,
AND A COMMITTEE
OF THE NATIONAL
COUNCIL OF
TEACHERS OF
ENGLISH

CITATION PRESS
NEW YORK
1973

Library of Congress Catalog Card Number: 72-80622

Standard Book Number: 590-09702–4

NCTE Stock Number: 42000

Copyright © 1973 by the National Council of Teachers of English. All rights reserved.

Published by Citation Press, Library and Trade Division, Scholastic Magazines, Inc., Editorial Office: 50 West 44th St., New York, N.Y. 10036.

Printed in the U.S.A.

ACKNOWLEDGMENTS

The chairman of this committee wishes to express his appreciation to those who worked closely with Vera Petersen, who was primarily responsible for the picture-story book section: Verda Allen, Betty Jo Cramer, Nan Moreland, and Joseph B. Rubin. The most recent updating was done by members of the current Committee on Adventuring with Books, whose chairman is Patricia Cianciolo. To Carol Harpole, who worked on the final draft, her secretary Lynn C. Lester, and especially to Virginia Leland, cochairman of the committee, many thanks.

Cynthia Smith and Brenda Jarboe of NCTE headquarters prepared the manuscript for publication.

Without the cooperation of publishers, it would have been impossible to prepare this volume. The Committee on Paperbound Publishing of the Association of American Publishers was responsible for coding the paperback titles.

Finally, gratitude is due to the knowledgeable, hard-working committee members, who are listed on pages viii and ix.

Shelton L. Root, Jr.

FOREWORD

This second edition of ADVENTURING WITH BOOKS is intended to serve as a guide to any adult—be he teacher, layman, or librarian, or parent—who is interested in selecting books for children of preschool age through the eighth grade.

Though such an undertaking may be overly ambitious, it can hardly be faulted because there are literally thousands upon thousands of books available for children in this age range. Obviously, some of these titles hold greater promise for young readers than do others. We have selected for inclusion in this bibliography books that we believe combine the qualities of entertaining reading with literary merit. Certainly the particular combination of these two qualities will not be equal in every instance. Therefore, a simple arrangement of priorities has been established. To be included in this bibliography, a book must first have a high potential for reader involvement or interest. Second, the book must have a degree of literary merit that raises it above others of its type. Selection in terms of these criteria, particularly the latter, is admittedly precarious. This is especially so when one recognizes that the most important element in determining the success of book selection is the individual for whom the book is intended. So true is this fact that we, as a committee, can only offer this list with the confidence that you, the user, will apply your knowledge and understanding of individual readers' interests, tastes, purposes, and reading abilities to the process of book selection.

Successful selection of books for young readers depends not only upon one's knowledge of children in general and in particular but also in good part upon helping him become as comfortable in rejecting a suggested book as he is in accepting one. Remember that the more reluctant a child is to accept adult suggestions, the more apt he is to have had previous experiences with adults who have made it difficult for him to reject suggested books without appearing to also reject the adult who has made the suggestions. Book selection fails when it becomes a matter of an adult forcing his choice upon a young reader. Rejection of suggested books ought to be no more than an invitation to the adult to involve the reader more, to know him better, to help him feel more confident, and to continue the search for books that will prove appealing to that particular reader.

This present edition has more than 2,400 entries. Of necessity, most of them are about books of recent publication, but many older titles have been included for the user's consideration. Out-of-print titles are not included.

The table of contents shows how the books have been catagorized for annotation. The numbers concluding each bibliographic entry indicate the age range for which that book is apt to be most appropriate. Titles that were available in paperback at the time this bibliography was prepared are so indicated by the letter P, and the publisher is noted if there is only one edition. When the cost is of special importance, the user should remember that book prices change rapidly and that it would be wise to consult the individual publisher's most current catalog. Prices have been verified as of Spring 1972.

A final word. . . . It is the hope of this committee that the adults who use ADVENTURING WITH BOOKS will find it to be a most helpful tool in bringing to fruition one of the greatest of all adventures—that of bringing children and books together.

Shelton L. Root, Jr.
College of Education
University of Georgia

CONTENTS

PICTURE BOOKS
    ABC Books   1
    Counting Books   2
    Fables   4
    Folk Songs in Separate Volumes   6
    Mother Goose   7
    Story Books   9

FICTION
    Realistic   44
    Historical: United States   77
    Other Times and Places   97
    Mystery   129
    Sports   142
    Animals   144
    Science Fiction   155
    Fantasy   158

TRADITIONAL FOLK LITERATURE   175

BIOGRAPHY   196

POETRY
    Individual Collections   219
    Anthologies   228

HOLIDAYS 236

RELIGION AND HOLY DAYS 240

SOCIAL STUDIES
Transportation and Communication 255
The World's Past 259
America's Heritage 266
Other Lands and Peoples Today 279
Man and His Problems 284

BIOLOGICAL SCIENCES
Ancient Living Things 287
Animals 289
Conservation and Ecology 300
Earth Sciences 303
Human Body 306
Insects 307
Natural Resources and Products 309
Plants 311
Weather 313

PHYSICAL SCIENCES
Astronomy 315
Aeronautics and Spaces 317
Energy and Machines 319

GENERAL SCIENCES 322

SPORTS AND HOBBIES 326

ARTS, CRAFTS, MUSIC, DRAMA, DANCE 331

FOREIGN LANGUAGES 345

DIRECTORY OF PUBLISHERS 348

AUTHOR INDEX 354

TITLE INDEX 370

PICTURE BOOKS FOR YOUNG CHILDREN

ABC Books

Duvoisin, Roger. *A for the Ark,* il. by the author. Lothrop 1952. $3.95; 5–8.

To keep things in good order, Noah summons the animals into the ark alphabetically. A special feature on each page is the repetition of all previous letters up to the next one being introduced. Captivating illustrations. A happy book that closes with an extra alphabet—a reverse one of letters and animals pictured from Z to A!

Eichenberg, Fritz. *Ape in a Cape,* il. by the author. Harcourt 1952. $3.25; 4–6.

An alphabet of odd animals to set any youngster agiggle. Suburb full-page illustrations by a master artist extend the hilarious situations reported in his brief text—"Ape in a cape," "Bear in despair," "Carp with a harp," and right on through X, Y, and Z.

Falls, C. B. *ABC Book,* il. by the author. Doubleday 1923. $3.50; 2–6.

A classic among animal ABC books. Illustrations and text have been lovingly cut in wood and are reproduced with four colors on each page.

Gág, Wanda. *The ABC Bunny,* il. by the author. Coward 1933. $3.95; 3–6.

Continuity of text is provided by the activities of a young rabbit. Excellent illustrations in black and white with each succeeding letter of the alphabet introduced by an oversize capital in red. The endpapers carry music for singing the entire story.

Ipcar, Dahlov. *I Love My Anteater with an A,* il. by the author. Knopf 1964. $3.54; 5–8.

A book of 26 animals, some familiar, some strange, each described in a fantastic way with words having the same initial letter as the animal. Fascinating reading for children and adults.

Petersham, Maud and Miska. *An American ABC,* il. by the authors. Macmillan 1941. $4.95; 6–10.

An ABC book for children old enough to be interested in the history of our country. Colorfully illustrated.

Tudor, Tasha. *A Is for Annabelle,* il. by the author. Walck 1954. $3.75; 5–7.

A book for little girls—and adults interested in antiques. Alternating pages of enticing water colors and pencil drawings illustrate this alphabetical account of the possessions of Annabelle, a most winsome and exquisite antique doll.

Wildsmith, Brian. *Brian Wildsmith's ABC,* il. by the author. Watts 1963. $3.95; 3–5.

Vibrant with color are the large, effective paintings of objects and animals. The text consists of one identifying word in lower case repeated on the following line in all capitals. A distinctive volume.

Counting Books

Carle, Eric. *1,2,3 to the Zoo,* il. by the author. World 1968. $3.86; 3–6.

In this ingeniously planned counting and story book each double-spread page contains a numeral and a corresponding number of joyously colorful animals in a train car. Not only are principles of mathematics presented visually but an imaginative and alert "reader" could concoct several stories by looking carefully at the pictures in this wordless book.

Eichenberg, Fritz. *Dancing in the Moon,* il. by the author. Harcourt 1955. $3.25; 4–8.

Outlandish animals busy carrying on the antics described in the brief rhymes compel any child to count, and the counting goes from one through 20.

Françoise. *Jeanne-Marie Counts Her Sheep,* il. by the author. Scribner 1951. $3.12; 5–8.

A cumulative tale that provides easy reading because of the repetition. Number words as well as numerals up to seven are used. Colorful, bold, childlike illustrations.

Friskey, Margaret. *Chicken Little, Count to Ten,* il. by Katherine Evans. Children 1946. $2.75; 3–5.

A favorite of pre-school children. Questions and answers about how various animals drink water form the continuity. Chicken Little meets one cow, two elephants, three camels, and other animals increasing in number to ten.

Gregor, Arthur. *1 2 3 4 5,* il. with photos by Robert Doisneau. Lippincott 1956. $3.50; 4–6.

Full pages of superb photography give children experience in counting to 12. The brief text in verse is on accompanying pages.

Ipcar, Dahlov. *Brown Cow Farm,* il. by the author. Doubleday 1959. $3.50; 5–7.

A book for counting to 100. Pages of animals for counting to ten, enticing and informative text about the various animals. With springtime come new baby animals and counting by tens to 100.

Langstaff, John. *Over in the Meadow,* il. by Feodor Rojankovsky. Harcourt 1957. $3.50; 3 up.

A large, colorful counting book distinguished by the animal drawings. Music for singing is on the last page.

Merrill, Jean. *How Many Kids Are Hiding on My Block?* il. by Frances Gruse Scott. Whitman 1970. $3.75; 4–6.

Eleven children of various racial and ethnic groups play hide and seek. The last one found gets a free ice cream cone three scoops high! Easy to read.

Seiden, Art. *1 2 3 Board Book,* il. by the author. Grosset 1948. $1.95; 2–5.

Attractive and colorful objects on a white background make counting to ten inviting even for toddlers. A "tall" book for comfortable holding, thick pages for easy turning, shiny surfaces for quick cleaning.

Tudor, Tasha. *1 Is One,* il. by the author. Walck 1956. $3.75; 4–6.

For counting to 20. Gentle pictures of a timeless yesteryear that will bring pleasure to any child of today—a keepsake book.

Fables

Aesop. *Aesop's Fables,* il. by Alice and Martin Provensen. Golden 1965. $3.95; 4–10.

A Giant Golden Book profusely illustrated in full color brings meaning and delight of the fables to the very young.

————. *Aesop's Fables,* retold by Anne Terry White, il. by Helen Siegl. Random 1964. $2.95; 6–10.

Richly detailed woodcuts in a combination of golden mustard and black on cream-colored paper. An attractively designed book of 40 fables.

Brown, Marcia. *Once a Mouse,* il. by the author. Scribner 1961. $4.95; 5–8.

This version of an old Indian fable, resplendent with woodcuts in color, deserves its Caldecott Award.

Dayrell, Elphinstone. *Why the Sun and the Moon Live in the Sky: An African Folktale,* il. by Blair Lent. Houghton 1968. $3.25; 5–8.

Stylized graphics harmonize with the national origin of the text.

Domjan, Joseph. *The Little Cock,* retold by Jeanne B. Hardendorff, il. by the author. Lippincott 1969. $4.95; 4–8.

This sturdy folktale tells of a brave little cock who had his newly found diamond halfpenny taken away from him by the greedy Turkish Sultan—and how he got it back. The illustrations are works of art. They are intricately designed woodcuts printed in rich colors.

Elkin, Benjamin. *Such Is the Way of the World,* il. by Yoho Mitsuhashi. Parents 1968. $3.50; 4–8.

This volume is beautifully designed from cover to cover, well written, and artistically illustrated. The tale, passed down from ancient Ethiopia, is of Desta, who is in charge of his father's cattle for the first time. He takes the cattle to graze, with his pet monkey Jima sitting on his shoulder, and nearly loses him. Much of the credit for the book should go to the illustrator, for she has created a work of art. The endpapers are a glowing African design; the illustrations are bright and exciting.

Galdone, Paul. *The Wise Fool,* based on a tale by Francois Rabelais, il. by the author. Pantheon 1968. $3.95; 6–8.

Based on the theme, "A wise man can get good advice from a fool," this story is wittily developed. The humorous and robust illustrations are a perfect complement for the story, depicting well the atmosphere of the Parisian marketplace of an earlier time.

Hazen, Barbara. *The Sorcerer's Apprentice*, il. by Tomi Unger-er. Lancelot 1969. $3.95; 5–10.

A large picture book version of the old folktale about the sorcerer's apprentice who charms a broom to come to life and to carry water up the steep steps of the castle but doesn't know the magic words to make the broom stop.

La Fontaine, Jean de. *The Hare and the Tortoise*, il. by Brian Wildsmith. Watts 1966. $4.95; 4–8.

Illustrations vibrant with color fill each page and extend the meaning of this favorite fable.

————. *The Lion and the Rat*, il. by Brian Wildsmith. Watts 1963. $4.95; 4–8.

The old jungle fable of a rat befriending a lion trapped in a rope net fairly bursts with color and action.

————. *The North Wind and the Sun*, il. by Brian Wildsmith. Watts 1964. $4.95; 4–8.

For sheer design and color, too good to miss!

————. *The Rich Man and the Shoemaker*, il. by Brian Wildsmith. Watts 1966. $4.95; 5–9.

With pictures in opulent color the artist extends the fable so that any reader will consider whether quantities of money really do bring one joy and contentment.

Lexau, Joan M. *It All Began with a Drip, Drip, Drip . . .*, il. by Joan Sandin. McCall 1970. $4.25; 6–9.

The retelling of an Indian fable about a blundering potter whose mistakes always made him look braver or cleverer than he really is. Hilariously told and illustrated.

Perrault, Charles. *Cinderella*, il. by Marcia Brown. Scribner 1954. $3.25; 4–8.

Illustrated with all the dash and flair befitting this old French tale. A Caldecott Award winner.

————. *Puss in Boots*, il. by Marcia Brown. Scribner 1953. $3.25; 5–9.

The famous cat who goes strutting through the countryside in his little red boots has delighted children for generations. An excellent translation from the French, with lively illus-trations that reflect the mood of the story.

Rockwell, Anne. *The Wonderful Eggs of Furicchia,* il. by the author. World 1969. $3.95; 5–8.

Meet Furicchia, a good witch. Her magic hen lays magic eggs that help all manner of people. When an envious neighbor schemes to steal the secret, he is appropriately punished. This adaptation of an old Italian tale is a pleasure to read aloud. The decorative pen and water-color drawings truly serve the text by creating the feel of medieval Florence and reflecting the drollness of the legend.

Shivkumar, K. *The King's Choice,* il. by Yoko Mitsuhashi. Parents 1971. $3.95; 4–8.

A lion, a kind noble king, triumphs over the trickery of his courtiers—a fox, a leopard, and a vulture—and accepts the companionship of the loyal and good camel. This simple fable from India is exquisitely illustrated in a style suggestive of the traditional art of India.

Wildsmith, Brian. *The Miller, the Boy and the Donkey,* il. by the author. Watts 1969. $4.95; 4–8.

Wildsmith retells and pictures this La Fontaine fable in eye-appealing and humorous full color.

Yolen, Jane. *The Seventh Mandarin,* il. by Ed Young. Seabury 1970. $4.95; 5–8.

A dramatic, original fable that tells how the seventh mandarin—the simplest and youngest of the mandarins—discovers that it is folly to believe only what is written when he is forced to go beyond the palace walls to get back the giant dragon kite, carrier of the king's soul. Beautiful multicolored expressionistic paintings enhance the oriental feeling of this modern fable.

Folk Songs in Separate Illustrated Volumes

The Fox Went Out on a Chilly Night, il. by Peter Spier. Doubleday 1961. $3.50; 3 up.

As vigorous as the song itself are the handsome illustrations. In rich fall colors Mr. Spier has portrayed a New England setting for the fox and his escapades. Music included.

Frog Went A-Courtin', adapted by John Langstaff, il. by Feodor Rojankovsky. Harcourt 1955. $3.50; 4–8.

A master at drawing animals, Rojankovsky well deserves the Caldecott Award he won for these illustrations. So superbly do they extend the oft-sung romance of the frog and mouse that any child would be captivated. Music included.

I Know an Old Lady, adapted by Rose Bonne, il. by Abner Graboff. Rand 1961. $3.50; 3 up.

Hilarious illustrations complement the words, "I know an old lady who swallowed a fly . . ." Music included.

Mommy, Buy Me a China Doll, adapted by Harve Zemach, il. by Margot Zemach. Follett 1966. $3.95; 3–6.

Bright primitive pictures capture the spirit of the question-and-answer game played by a young child and her mother. The singsong rhyme is based on a children's song from the Ozarks but will delight children everywhere.

Sleep Baby Sleep, il. by Trudi Oberhansli. Atheneum 1967. $4.95; 3–6.

The old familiar cradle song is brilliantly enhanced with childlike, primitive drawings. The words are repeated with music on the last page.

Mother Goose Books

And So My Garden Grows, il. by Peter Spier. Doubleday 1969. $3.95; 4–8.

This is the fourth volume of the illustrator's Mother Goose Library. The water-color sketches are packed full of things to see and invite the viewer to look at them again and again.

Appley Dapply's Nursery Rhymes, il. by Beatrix Potter. Warne 1917. $1.50; 3–6.

See also *Cecily Parsley's Nursery Rhymes.* Both books are companion volumes in size and format to the original *The Tale of Peter Rabbit.* Few rhymes, profusely illustrated with exquisite water-color drawings.

Book of Mother Goose and Nursery Rhymes, il. by Marguerite de Angeli. Doubleday 1952. $5.95; 3–7.

No harshness invades the warmth and geniality portrayed in the large and friendly edition of these favorite rhymes.

Brian Wildsmith's Mother Goose, il. by Brian Wildsmith. Watts 1965. $5.95; 3–6.

Large, gay pictures, refreshing in their brilliance, illustrate familiar rhymes.

In a Pumpkin Shell, il. by Joan Walsh Anglund. Harcourt 1960. $2.95; 3–6.

A Mother Goose ABC book with 24 rhymes, all well known and full of fun. Charmingly illustrated in color and black and white.

Lavender's Blue, comp. by Kathleen Lines, il. by Harold Jones. Watts 1954. $7.95; 4–7.

Familiar and unfamiliar rhymes plus cradle and nursery rhyme games with instructions for playing them. Alternate pages of illustrations in black and white and in soft full color beautifully show the English countryside of bygone years.

Mother Goose, il. by Frederick Richardson. Hubbard 1962. $5.95; 3–6.

A favorite for decades. For every rhyme there is a large full-page, full-color illustration with everything pictured as old-fashioned as Mother Goose herself. Each rhyme printed within the frame of its own illustration.

Mother Goose, il. by Tasha Tudor. Walck 1944. $4.00; 3–7.

Exquisite detail in the illustrations weaves a special magic over the beloved rhymes. A beautiful book with one rhyme and its illustration on each page. Comfortable size for a young child to hold.

Mother Goose and Nursery Rhymes, il. by Philip Reed. Atheneum 1963. $4.95; 5–7.

Wood engravings in six colors are deceivingly simple and tremendously effective. The book is uncluttered in appearance; the characters have personality and verve.

Ring O'Roses, il. by L. Leslie Brooke. Warne 1923. $3.95; 3–7.

Pale-hued pictures (by today's standards) are full of action, humor, and detail. Where there are animals, Leslie Brooke gives them personality plus!

Sing Mother Goose, il. by Marjorie Torrey. Dutton 1945. $5.95; 3–7.

Each rhyme is illustrated and has music in simple arrangement for singing. Many familiar tunes.

The Tall Book of Mother Goose, il. by Feodor Rojankovsky. Harper 1942. $2.50; 3–6.

Over 100 rhymes, sometimes illustrated with Old World flavor. Solemn children in peasant clothes live in cozy, flower-bedecked cottages. Superb animal drawings. The "tall" shape of the book makes it very comfortable for little hands to hold.

The White Land, il. by Raymond Briggs. Coward 1963. $3.50; 4–7.

The colorful illustrations for this edition suggest museum masterpieces of the last century. A joy for sheer looking. By the same artist: *Ring a Ring O'Roses.*

Story Books

Alexander, Lloyd. *The King's Fountain,* il. by Ezra Jack Keats. Dutton 1971. $5.95; 4–8.

An original parable that tells how a poor man musters enough wisdom, eloquence, and courage to convince the king that the people who live in the city below will die of thirst if a great palace fountain is built. Brilliant acrylic paintings dramatically emphasize the themes of this story— "the ideas of personal responsibility and of people discovering in themselves resources they never suspected."

Aliki. *Keep You Mouth Closed, Dear,* il. by the author. Dial 1966. $3.50; 4–10.

An uproariously funny account in pictures and story of a crocodile family that accidentally solves the problem of its son, who swallows everything from his mother's mixing spoon to his father's alarm clock.

Andersen, Hans Christian. *The Emperor's New Clothes,* il. by Erik Blegvad. Harcourt 1959. $3.25 (P—Rand, $.29); 7–10.

Excellent translation of one of Andersen's beloved and well-known stories. Outstanding illustrations.

――――. *The Nightingale,* tr. by Eva Le Gallienne, il. by Nancy Ekholm Burkert. Harper 1965. $3.95; 8 up.

Double-page spreads and an oversize format provide for an unusual book. Burkert's artistry and Le Gallienne's careful translation fill all the requirements for an outstanding book.

――――. *Seven Tales,* tr. by Eva Le Gallienne, il. by Maurice Sendak. Harper 1959. $3.95; 8–10.

A distinguished collection of seven well-loved fairy tales.

――――. *The Steadfast Tin Soldier,* il. by Marcia Brown. Scribner 1953. $3.12; 7–10.

Drawings predominantly in lavender and pink add a new dimension to this engrossing tale—a tale loved by young and old around the world.

————. *The Steadfast Tin Soldier,* il. by Monika Laimgruber. Atheneum 1971. $4.95; 8–9.

A decidedly modern expressionistic interpretation of this classic fantasy. The brightly colored and action-filled illustrations in this oversized picture book aptly extend the tragic story about the stern, duty-bound soldier and the lovely dancer.

————. *Thumbelina,* tr. by R. P. Keigwin, il. by Adrienne Adams. Scribner 1961. $3.50; 8–12.

Andersen's story of a little girl only one inch high in an excellent translation. Stolen by a frog and befriended by a field mouse, she finally flies with a swallow to the land of sun, flowers, and fairies. Many dainty illustrations with gemlike colors illustrate the text. This fantasy picture book will delight young listeners in the middle to upper grades. By the same author: *It's Perfectly True; The Swineherd; Andersen's Fairy Tales.*

Anglund, Joan Walsh. *The Brave Cowboy,* il. by the author. Harcourt 1959. $2.25; 3–7.

Once there was a brave cowboy, very brave, not even afraid of ornery rustlers. He relives the excitement and perils of the wild West as he pedals his tricycle and plays in his own bedroom. The drawings of his real experiences are in black; those that are make-believe appear as an overlay in red. By the same author-artist: *Cowboy and His Friend* and *Cowboy's Secret Life.*

Ardizzone, Edward. *Tim to the Lighthouse,* il. by the author. Walck 1968. $4.00; 6–12.

In this Tim story, Tim is the leader in getting the lighthouse light turned on in time to avert a shipwreck and in capturing the villainous ship wreckers who were responsible for putting it and its tenders out of commission. The book's appeal derives from the healthy escape provided from a world restricted by adult dictates.

Asbjørnsen, P. C., and J. E. Moe. *The Three Billy Goats Gruff,* il. by Marcia Brown. Harcourt 1957. $3.50; 4–8.

Young children never tire of this beloved Norwegian tale. They chuckle over the action, the colorful words, and Marcia Brown's vigorous illustrations that extend so well the humor of it all.

Asch, Frank. *George's Store,* il. by the author. McGraw 1969. $2.95; 7–12.

Bold black and white spontaneous and crude sketches are

only part of this fun-filled picture book, which tells about the many things that George sells in his store and the many people who come there to buy. The surprise ending will delight young readers.

Belpré, Pura. *Santiago,* il. by Symeon Shimin. Warne 1969. $3.95; 5–9.

About a Puerto Rican boy in New York City who wants to show his classmates pictures of his beautiful chicken left behind in Puerto Rico. One day his teacher brings the class to Santiago's apartment so they can see the pictures.

Bemelmans, Ludwig. *Madeline,* il. by the author. Viking 1939. $3.50 (P—Viking, $.75); 4–8.

Easily the best of all the Madeline books. Madeline, a young child in a Paris boarding school, has personality plus. This story is an account of her appendectomy. Handsome drawings. As perfect a picture book as ever was made.

————. *Parsley,* il. by the author. Harper 1955. $4.50; 5–8.

This is one of Bemelmans' very best in text and pictures. Marginal drawings of alpine flowers are a bonus. The story, with huge colorful illustrations, centers on Old Parsley, a stag who most comically outwits a hunter.

Berg, Joan. *Bigger Than an Elephant,* il. by the author. Crown 1968. $3.50; 3–6.

This book will help pre-schoolers to explore size relationships. A child is pictured along with a number of animals ranging in size from a goldfish to a giraffe. In each across-the-page illustration the child is shown to be the same size as the animal. At the book's end the opening question is repeated, "What size would you like to be?" The drawings are sturdy and lifelike.

Bernadette. *Hans the Miller Man,* il. by the author. McGraw 1969. $4.50; 5–8.

Hans leaves home in search of a friend. He leaves behind a caterpillar who had tried to be a friend but had not been noticed. The search is in vain and Hans returns to his lonely mill to find a butterfly.

Bishop, Claire H. *The Five Chinese Brothers,* il. by Kurt Wiese. Coward 1938. $2.95; 5–9.

That old tale of the five brothers who look exactly alike and who each have most unique abilities—thereby saving the lives of each other—is retold with the art of a professional storyteller. The excellent drawings expand the humor of the tale.

Bolognese, Don. *A New Day,* il. by the author. Delacorte 1970. $4.50; 4–8.

A simple retelling of the Nativity, but the story takes place today in the American Southwest and the characters are migrant workers, Jose and Maria. The beautiful paintings strengthen the parallel of this contemporary interpretation of the Christmas legend.

Bond, Jean Carey. *Brown Is a Beautiful Color,* il. by Barbara Zuber. Watts 1969. $3.50; 4–8.

In rhymed couplets, this book lists a wide variety of things that are pleasantly brown. The boldly brown cartoon illustrations are full of fun.

Brown, Marcia. *Felice,* il. by the author. Scribner 1958. $4.37; 5–8.

Exquisitely drawn water colors in rich blues, black, and rose provide the Venetian setting for this story of a gondolier's son who wishes for and finally gets a cat of his own—a cat he names Felice.

Brown, Margaret Wise. *The Golden Egg Book,* il. by Leonard Weisgard. Golden 1947. $1.00; 3–6.

Flowers, animals, and the newness of spring burst from the pages of this appealing book, which gives an account of the friendship of two fuzzy young animals—a duckling and a bunny.

———. *Little Fur Family,* il. by Garth Williams. Harper 1946. $3.95 (P—Scholastic, $.75); 2–6.

Here is a happy, wholesome tale of family life in and around an old tree in the woods. A tiny book, 2 $1/4$ × 3 $1/4$ inches, bound in fur, and perfect for bedtime reading.

———. *Wait Till the Moon Is Full,* il. by Garth Williams. Harper 1948. $4.50; 4–8.

A curious young raccoon wants to see the night, but his mother tells him he will have to wait—wait while the moon is as "thin as a raccoon's whisker," wait while it is as "big as the curve of a raccoon's ear," wait till the "moon is full." Then he may join all the other creatures who love the night. The drawings of the irresistible baby and his gentle mother are in perfect harmony with the poetic text.

———. *Where Have You Been?* il. by Barbara Cooney. Hastings 1952. $2.50 (P—Scholastic, $.50); 3–6.

A cozy little book, just right for small hands. Rhythmic verses present questions and answers about familiar animals. Black-and-white drawings with a dash of red provide perfect illustrations.

Burch, Robert. *Joey's Cat,* il. by Don Freeman. Viking 1969.-
$3.50; 4–7.

A slight story about Joey's cat, a brave mother cat who
protects her kittens from a dog and a big possum. Joey and
his family are black; his father is portrayed as a policeman.
Illustrations are blue and black line and wash sketches.

Burton, Virginia Lee. *Choo Choo: The Story of a Little Engine
Who Ran Away,* il. by the author. Houghton 1937. $3.73
(P—Scholastic, $.60); 4–7.

Choo Choo, an old-fashioned black engine in search of
excitement, decides to run away and causes much trouble
and turmoil. The lively drawings and action-filled story
appeal especially to little boys.

————. *Life Story,* il. by the author. Houghton 1963. $5.50;
8–12.

Here all the world is truly on stage, and the reader can
witness the thrilling drama of natural history from its
beginning on this earth to modern times. Here are hundreds
of marginal sketches, 36 pages in full color, and a text so
excellent that children will use it not only for reference but
also for the sheer pleasure of reading.

————. *The Little House,* il. by the author. Houghton 1942.
$3.75; 5–9.

The experiences of a little house, set on a hill and surrounded by apple trees, tell vividly the story of night and
day, the four seasons, and changes that occur when urban-
ization encroaches upon quiet country life. A treasured
story. Vivacious illustrations in full color won the Caldecott
Award in 1943.

————. *Mike Mulligan and His Steam Shovel,* il. by the author.
Houghton 1939. $3.50; 4–8.

Little boys are reading the story of Mike Mulligan and his
steam shovel, Mary Ann, as enthusiastically as their fathers
did a generation ago. One of the most convincing personifi-
cations of a machine ever written. Lively pictures, dramatic
action, and a satisfying conclusion.

Byars, Betsy. *Go and Hush the Baby,* il. by Emily A. McCully.
Viking 1971. $3.50; 3–5.

An affectionately humorous and realistic account of how a
boy attempts to quiet his crying baby brother. The line and
wash drawings in two colors complement the text.

Carigiet, Alois. *The Pear Tree, the Birch Tree, and the Barberry
Bush,* il. by the author. Walck 1967. $7.00; 5–9.

So beautifully drawn are the full-page illustrations that any one of them could be matted, framed, and exhibited. The story as well as the pictures tell of a gentle Swiss family and their love for birds and trees.

Carle, Eric. *Do You Want to Be My Friend?* il. by the author. Crowell 1971. $4.50; 4–7.

Told almost entirely without words, this well-constructed suspense story is about Little Mouse who looks for and finally finds a friend. Very good for use in composing aloud, creative writing, reading readiness skills, and just plain fun.

———. *The Tiny Seed,* il. by the author. Crowell 1970. $4.50; 4–7.

Beautiful collage paintings and simple poetic text effectively tell a story that artistically dramatizes the beauty of the changing seasons and the life cycle of a flowering plant.

Caudill, Rebecca, and James Ayars. *Contrary Jenkins,* il. by Glen Rounds. Holt 1969. $3.50; 5–9.

Funny tall-tale adventures about Contrary Jenkins, a man who lived by the contrary rule among the Tennessee pioneers, are recounted. Distinctive line drawings add to the humor of each episode.

Chaucer, Geoffrey. *Chanticleer and the Fox,* il. by Barbara Cooney. Crowell 1958. $3.75; 6–9.

Handsome illustrations that earned the Caldecott Award in 1959 set this adaptation of the "Nun's Priest's Tale" from *The Canterbury Tales* apart from others.

Clark, Ann Nolan. *In My Mother's House,* il. by Velino Herrara. Viking 1941. $3.50; 7–10.

Tewa Indian children, who certainly see their world differently from their white cousins, helped write this book. They emphasized what was important to them. The rhythm of the text reflects Indian patterns of speech. Distinguished illustrations add to this meaningful and informative portrayal of life in the Tesuque pueblo.

Coatsworth, Elizabeth. *Lighthouse Island,* il. by Symeon Shimin. Norton 1968. $4.25; 7–11.

Alex's exciting vacation spent on a lighthouse island off the coast of Maine makes an appealing story. The artist's excellent illustrations create just the right mood.

D'Aulaire Ingi and Edgar P. *Leif the Lucky,* il. by the authors. Doubleday 1941. $4.50; 6–10.

Over a thousand years ago young Leif, true son of the Vikings, sailed with his father Eric the Red across the Atlantic to Greenland and later to our own continent. Good research makes this account as accurate as possible in both pictures and text, with the author-artists adding humorous detail from their own imaginations. Strong, vigorous illustrations in color fortify the story.

––––––. *The Magic Meadow*, il. by the authors. Doubleday 1958. $3.95; 7–10.
Peterli herds his grandfather's cows and goats in a flowery meadow high in the Alps. Here magic works, bringing good fortune to the boy and his grandfather. The history and the charm of the rugged Swiss people are shown in several folk tales and the legend of William Tell. There is rich detail in the colorful illustrations.

de Regniers, Beatrice Schenk. *Circus*, il. with photos by Al Giese. Viking 1966. $3.95; 5–8.
A razzle-dazzle circus story with glittering, rhythmic verses that catch the same excitement as the camera does in the brilliantly colored photographs.

––––––. *The Giant Story*, il. by Maurice Sendak. Harper 1953. $3.79; 3–6.
This imaginative account of Tommy's day as a giant will cause many a little boy to throw out his chest, test his arm muscles, and stomp about. Maurice Sendak's illustrations are as clever as the tale itself.

––––––. *A Little House of Your Own*, il. by Irene Haas. Harcourt 1954. $2.50; 4–6.
"Everyone has to have a little house of his own," begins this gem of a book. It is full of ideas that will spark the imagination of a young child and send him off to find new hiding places.

––––––. *May I Bring a Friend?* il. by Beni Montresor. Atheneum 1964. $3.95; 4–8.
A little boy brings an unusual array of "friends" to the palace when he is invited to dine with the king and queen. One of the happiest books of the decade, enhanced by Caldecott Award-winning illustrations.

Eiseman, Alberta. *Candido*, il. by Lillian Obligado. Macmillan 1965. $4.25; 7–10.
A three-year-old llama has trouble learning to do his work. The surprise ending will delight any reader. Softly sketched illustrations are intriguing and informative.

Emberley, Barbara. *Drummer Hoff*, il. by Ed Emberley. Prentice 1967. $4.25; 4–8.
All readers who look Drummer Hoff straight in the eye will find the whimsical soul of Ed Emberley, who won a Caldecott Award for this book in 1968.

Enright, Elizabeth. *Zeee,* il. by Irene Haas. Harcourt 1965. $3.50; 7–10.

"Zeee was a bad fairy and proud of it." Thus begins some marvelous humor. The full color drawings of the fairy's miniature world make it a choice volume.

Ets, Marie Hall. *Gilberto and the Wind,* il. by the author. Viking 1963. $3.00 (P—Viking, $.75); 3–6.

Young children are always fascinated by the wind—that invisible power that does amazing things. Here the simple text and expressive pictures show a Latin American child having a variety of experiences with the wind. A gem of a book.

————. *In the Forest,* il. by the author. Viking 1944. $2.50 (P—Viking, $.75); 4–6.

A little boy with a new horn and a paper hat goes for a walk in the forest. All the animals he meets on his imaginary journey want to come too. They parade, picnic, and play games until it is late, and the little boy's father comes to find him. Always a favorite among pre-schoolers.

————. *Play with Me,* il. by the author. Viking 1955. $2.75 (P—Viking, $.75); 3–6.

A tiny two-year-old attempts to make friends with the creatures in the meadow, but they all run away. When she sits quietly on a rock, perplexed by the whole matter, one by one the animals return and come to her. A sensitive story with appealing pictures.

Feinstein, Joe. *A Silly Little Kid,* il. by John Paul Richards. Steck 1969. $2.95; 4–7.

Instead of discovering that he must be like older boys to enjoy himself, little Henry finds out that it would be a drag to be like big Larry.

Fisher, Aileen. *Listen, Rabbit,* il. by Symeon Shimin. Crowell 1964. $3.95; 5–8.

Lilting rhythm tells of a boy who wants very much to bring home a little wild rabbit for a pet, but his parents will not consent. Alone the child watches "his rabbit" in various out-of-door places, through the seasons, and is finally rewarded in the spring by finding a furry nest with five newborn rabbits in it. The gentle, irresistible beauty of the drawings places this picture book among the most distinguished.

————. *Sing Little Mouse,* il. by Symeon Shimin. Crowell 1969. $3.95; 4–7.

This story in verse tells of a boy who is preoccupied with

finding a white-footed deer mouse "who is sometimes heard
to sing a song like a trilling bird."

Flack, Marjorie. *Angus and the Ducks,* il. by the author.
Doubleday 1930. $2.95; 3–6.

The antics of Angus, a Scotch terrier puppy, delight even a
three-year-old and continue to interest him when he can
read the story for himself. Rollicking words, enhanced by
lively pictures, encourage good listening among the youngest.

————. *Boats on the River,* il. by Jay Hyde Barnum. Viking
1946. $4.95; 4–7.

Excellent for the young child's beginning interest in transportation. The variety of boats vividly portrayed in the large
illustrations makes this volume a favorite among kindergarteners. Brief, informative text.

————. *The Story about Ping,* il. by Kurt Wiese. Viking
1933. $2.00; 4–7.

A beloved little duck from the yellow waters of the Yangtze
River is now holding the third generation of listeners spell-
bound. Excellent pictures.

Fleischmann, Peter, and Morton Schindel. *Alexander and the
Car with a Missing Headlight,* il. by French children. Viking
1967. $4.95; 4–7.

Vigorous paintings by Parisian kindergarteners establish the
story of a crazy old car—escapades that will delight and
intrigue the young. This volume has been adapted from a
superb color film of the same title distributed by Weston
Woods Studios in Weston, Connecticut.

Fleischman, Sid. *McBroom's Ear,* il. by Kurt Werth. Norton
1969. $4.25; 5–8.

A tall tale of the McBroom family and their efforts to keep
the grasshoppers away from the prize ear of corn they are
growing for the county fair.

Foster, Joanna. *Pete's Puddle,* il. by Beatrice Darwin. Harcourt
1969. $3.50; 3–6.

If you are Pete's age and have on your rain hat, slicker and
boots, you just might want to play in a puddle. Pete's
problem is that all the puddles seem to be unavailable.
When at last he finds one, he puts it to excellent use.

Gág, Wanda. *The Funny Thing,* il. by the author. Coward
1929. $3.00; 5–8.

The Funny Thing is an *aminal* with blue points from the top
of his head to the tip of his long curled tail. Original plot,

colorful words, and enticing black-and-white illustrations make this a perennial favorite.

————. *Millions of Cats,* il. by the author. Coward 1928. $2.95; 4–7.

A very old woman wishes for a sweet little fluffy cat, and her husband set out to find one but returns with "hundreds of cats, thousands of cats, millions and billions and trillions of cats." The charm of the book lies in the simply told, fast-moving story and the handsome black-and-white drawings.

Galdone, Paul. *Henny Penny,* il. by the author. Seabury 1968. $3.50 (P—Scholastic, $.75); 5–7.

The drawings in this book are huge and clear, humorously portraying the characters in this tale that has been heard by generations of young children. To give the story an added spark, the author has added a new character. The book is perfect for reading aloud or for use with creative dramatics.

Garelick, May. *Where Does the Butterfly Go When It Rains?* il. by Leonard Weisgard. Scott 1961. $3.75 (P—Scholastic, $.60); 4–7.

The question is not answered in this book, but the soft blue misty pictures and the lilting poetic style create a mood of mystery and a real appreciation of nature. Excellent for discussion and pondering.

The Golden Goose Book, il. by L. Leslie Brooke. Warne, n. d., $3.95; 4–8.

Profusely illustrated with inimitable full-page color drawings as well as pen-and-ink sketches. The collection includes four stories: "The Golden Goose," "The Three Bears," "The Three Pigs," and "Tom Thumb." A perennial favorite.

Goodall, John S. *The Adventures of Paddy Pork,* il. by the author. Harcourt 1968. $2.75; 3–6.

The continuity of illustration from full page to half leaf, full page to half leaf, shows the thoughts and actions of a young pig in an English countryside setting. The unique feature is that there is no text, but the very obvious tale can be quickly told by child or adult.

Goudey, Alice E. *The Day We Saw the Sun Come Up,* il. by Adrienne Adams. Scribner 1961. $3.25; 5–7.

The author and artist have again captured the child's wonder and joy in the world about him: the sunrise and sunset, spider webs laced with dew, shadows that change from large to small, clouds that hide the sun.

————. *Houses from the Sea,* il. by Adrienne Adams. Scribner 1959. $3.25; 5–8.

Lovely, lilting lines tell of two children's day at the seashore. Delicate, misty paintings describe the adventure. Accurate and enticing information should encourage children to collect and classify their own shells.

Gramatky, Hardie. *Little Toot,* il. by the author. Putnam 1939. $3.75; 4–8.

A ridiculous, lighthearted tugboat frolics through one adventure after another and finally proves himself a hero. Both the humor and the pathos are understood by young children. They love the convincing faces in the illustrations of the little tug, and they consider him a real personality.

Greenberg, Polly. *Oh Lord, I Wish I Was a Buzzard,* il. by Aliki. Macmillan 1968. $4.95; 5–8.

This frank account of two Negro children picking cotton in the hot, hot fields chants with the simplicity of a spiritual. The masterful illustrations give an impression of the endlessness of cotton to be picked.

Greene, Carla. *Animal Doctors: What Do They Do?* il. by Leonard Kessler. Harper 1967. $2.50; 6–7.

A picture of the work of a veterinarian for beginning readers. By the same author: *Doctors and Nurses: What Do They Do?*

Grieder, Walter. *The Enchanted Drum,* tr. by Doris Orgel, il. by the author. Parents 1969. $4.50; 4–8.

Bitzgi, a Swiss boy, is a drummer in the local fife and drum club that is preparing for the carnival. But he does not like to practice. The illustrations of this oversize book are exceptional. The carnival atmosphere is brilliantly represented.

Grimm, Brothers. *The Elves and the Shoemaker,* il. by Katrin Brandt. Follett 1968. $3.50; 5 up.

First published in Switzerland, this edition of the well-known tale is beautifully illustrated in color.

————. *The Four Clever Brothers,* il. by Felix Hoffmann. Harcourt 1967. $4.95; 5–9.

Four brothers, all sent out to seek their fortunes, become apprentices and learn different trades. Together they rescue a princess from a dragon's rockbound island, and each gains a fourth of the kingdom. Magnificent illustrations.

————. *Grimm's Fairy Tales,* il. by Arnold Roth. Macmillan 1963. $3.95; 8–11.

A collection of stories that are now part of our heritage. If children are good, perhaps someone will tell one of these before bedtime or at least during meals. The tales expertly mix common folk sense with uncommon happenings.

―――. *Grimm's Fairy Tales,* introduction by Frances Clarke Sayers, il. by children from 15 countries. Follett 1968. $6.95; 5 up.
The best known and loved Grimm fairy tales are compiled with authenticity into an excellent book with 50 beautiful illustrations by children from all over the world. The creativeness and ingenuity of these young artists make the book one young and old will love.

―――. *Little Red Riding Hood,* il. by Harriet Pincus. Harcourt 1968. $3.50; 5–9.
The heroine is pictured as a humorously plum child. She and her grandmother are each eaten in a single gulp but are released when the huntsman slits open the wolf.

――― *Little Red Riding Hood,* il. by Bernadette. Watts 1969. $3.95; 4–8.
One of the most enticing picture story books of that year! All sorts of detail in the vibrant double-page spreads. In this version of the tale, Little Red Riding Hood is extremely innocent, the sly wolf terribly wicked. Children will relish the wolf's well-deserved and miserable end. Truly a keepsake volume!

―――. *Nibble Nibble Mousekin: A Tale of Hansel and Gretel,* adapted and il. by Joan Walsh Anglund. Harcourt 1962. $3.25; 5–8.
The tale of Hansel and Gretel is skillfully portrayed in this version with its quaint children and forest of gnarled trees. The crafty witch in her sugary cottage is convincing but not frightening to children.

―――. *Rapunzel,* il. by Felix Hoffmann. Harcourt 1961. $4.95; 6–10.
The book is effectively illustrated in somber tones up to the point of the prince's arrival. From there on there is a warm rosy cast to all the pictures. Redemption through love is evident in the story, and the ending, which reveals the fate of the wicked witch, pleases children immensely.

―――. *The Seven Ravens,* il. by Felix Hoffmann. Harcourt 1963. $4.95; 5–8.
An old enchantment tale in which seven brothers are changed into ravens. The love and efforts of their little sister reverse the spell, and they all become human again. Handsomely illustrated.

————. *The Sleeping Beauty,* il. by Felix Hoffmann. Harcourt 1960. $4.95; 6–10.

The poignant old tale is gloriously enhanced by the Swiss artist who knows with precision when to use somber tones, when to use rich warm ones, and when to let his drawings appear without color. A book of beauty from beginning to end.

————.*Tales from Grimm,* adapted and il. by Wanda Gag. Coward 1936. $4.50; 5–10.

Beautiful in physical format as well as in the telling. Sixteen best-known tales of the brothers Grimm from "Hansel and Gretel," "Cinderella," and "The Frog Prince" to "Snow White and Rose Red." Frontispiece (in pastel colors) and all other illustrations (black and white) have the Gag benchmarks of symmetry, chiaroscuro, curved lines, and subtle humor.

————. *The Traveling Musicians,* il. by Hans Fischer. Harcourt 1953. $4.50; 4–8.

Vigorous color illustrations make this a superior edition of the tale of the Brementown musicians.

————. *The Wolf and the Seven Little Kids,* il. by Felix Hoffmann. Harcourt 1959. $4.95; 4–8.

Personality abounds in the drawings of the wolf, the mother goat, and the seven little kids. An unexcelled edition of this favorite old tale.

Hader, Berta and Elmer. *The Big Snow,* il. by the authors. Macmillan 1948. $4.50; 4–8.

The hardship of winter in the woodlands is pictured through the eyes of the wild creatures. A positive note is added in that one sees how human beings can help. Beautifully illustrated and tenderly told. A Caldecott Award winner.

————. *The Mighty Hunter,* il. by the authors. Macmillan 1943. $4.50; 5–8.

Little Brave Heart is not very big, but feeling brave he decides to skip school and go hunting on his own. With bow and arrow he encounters one animal after another, each increasing in size. When finally he is confronted by an angry mother bear, he learns an important lesson and streaks back to school. Children will be intrigued by the lively folktale quality of the story as well as the vibrant illustrations.

Hajime, Kijima. *Little White Hen,* il. by Setsuko Hane. Harcourt 1969. $3.25; 4–8.

This Japanese version of the story about a little white hen outwitting the cunning fox is well told and illustrated.

Handforth, Thomas. *Mei Li*, il. by the author. Doubleday 1938. $3.50; 6–10.

A perennial favorite is this tale of an endearing little Chinese girl. The well-written text reveals customs surrounding the celebration of the Chinese New Year. For his handsome drawings, the author-artist won the Caldecott Award in 1939.

Heide, Parry. *Sound of Sunshine, Sound of Rain*, il. by Kenneth Longtemps. Parents 1970. $3.95; 5–8.

The story of a blind boy and how he finds a friend in the park. Exquisite cut paper montage illustrations.

Hoban, Russell. *Bedtime for Frances*, il. by Garth Williams. Harper 1960. $3.50; 4–7.

Although Frances is only a young badger, she knows all the old bedtime tricks that boys and girls have been using for generations. Children see the humor in this tender family story, and they love the furry animals, drawn as only Garth Williams can draw them. By the same author: *Bread and Jam for Frances* and *A Baby Sister for Frances*, both illustrated by his wife, Lillian Hoban.

Hoff, Syd. *The Litter Knight*, il. by the author. McGraw 1970. $4.50; 4–8.

A moral tale about a knight who preferred to clear up litter rather than to joust and hunt dragons.

———. *The Horse in Harry's Room*, il. by the author. Harper 1970. $1.95; 3–7.

In simple but appropriate language, the author tells of Harry's experiences with his imaginary horse. The ending leaves the to-be-or-not-to-be matter open to Harry's desire. The line drawings reinforce the direct simplicity of the story.

Hogan, Carol G. *Eighteen Cousins*, il. by Beverly Komoda. Parents 1968. $3.50; 4–8.

A city boy goes to visit his cousins on a farm and enjoys the simplest delights of a country day. The lilting rhymes are perfectly complemented by gay cartoon-like pen and crayon drawings and each double-page spread has 18 cousins to make counting fun.

Holl, Adelaide. *Moon Mouse*, il. by Cyndy Szekeres. Random 1969. $3.50; 4–8.

Sophisticated youngsters living in this exciting space age will delight in the tale of Arthur, a baby mouse who wants to go to the moon. Arthur's curiosity can no longer be stayed so he sets out for the moon and finds it—at least he thinks he does. The story is fun and aided by fine illustrations.

Huber, Ursula. *The Nock Family Circus,* il. by Celestino Piatti. Atheneum 1968. $4.95; 5–8.

The traveling family circus, unknown to American children, has long been common in Europe but is today disappearing. Here is an account of one of the last few in existence. Everyone from the youngest child to the spirited old grandfather has his tasks and acts to perform. Excellent illustrations will lure any child who has felt the thrill of the big top to enjoy this behind-the-scenes account of a small circus.

Hutchins, Pat. *Clocks and More Clocks,* il. by the author. Macmillan 1970. $4.95; 4–8.

Mr. Higgins adds clock after clock to the rooms of his house, but they never seem to be quite in agreement. Finally the problem is solved. This is a true picture-story book. Without the illustrations, the story would not quite come off.

———. *Rosie's Walk,* il. by the author. Macmillan 1968. $3.95; 3–6.

Rosie the hen went for a walk across the yard and got back in time for supper. Unnoticed by Rosie but completely obvious to the delight of the reader is the fact that she is stalked by a hungry fox whose antics are never once mentioned in the text. Here is a broadly humorous book perfectly pictured and written in language easy enough for an advanced first-grader to read independently.

Ipcar, Dahlov. *The Cat at Night,* il. by the author. Doubleday 1969. $3.95; 4–8.

A cat on his night prowl sees everything as clear as day. Alternating pages show night scenes as humans observe them, and then the same places in glorious color as the cat sees them. A fascinating book.

———. *Stripes and Spots,* il. by the author. Doubleday 1953. $3.50; 4–7.

A jungle adventure for the young. Each page with its striped or spotted animals is brilliant with tropical color and captures the feeling of a big and wild place. A book that will be asked for over and over.

———. *The Wonderful Egg,* il. by the author. Doubleday 1958. $3.50; 5–9.

Enticing pictures and basic information about dinosaurs to lure even the youngest. Reference pages at the end provide a glossary for pronunciation and scale drawings to see the relative sizes of the dinosaurs discussed.

Iwasaki, Chihiro. *Staying Home Alone on a Rainy Day,* il. by the author. McGraw 1969. $3.95; 3–6.

Allison is left at home in charge while mother goes to the store, but suddenly there is a thunder storm and Allison is very happy when mother returns. The water color illustrations are splendid.

Jackson, Jacqueline. *Chicken Ten Thousand*, il. by Barbara Morrow. Little 1968. $3.95; 4–8.

The story of a battery chicken's escape from her crate is dramatized with verve and perception.

Jacobs, Joseph, ed. *Mr. Miacca*, il. by Evaline Ness. Holt 1967. $3.75; 5–9.

Delightful Victorian illustrations lend just the right amount of scare to this popular folktale of naughty Tommy Grimes, who is almost cooked for supper by Mr. Miacca.

Johnson, LaVerne. *Night Noises*, il. by Martha Alexander. Parents 1968. $3.50; 3–7.

This quietly reassuring book treats an old topic in a fresh manner. Pre-schoolers will want to hear and look at it over and over again.

Joslin, Sesyle. *What Do You Say, Dear?* il. by Maurice Sendak. Scott 1958. $2.95; 4–7.

"A handbook of etiquette for young ladies and gentlemen to be used as a guide for everyday social behavior." Children catch the humor of the basically serious situations and the very funny pictures. A companion volume, *What Do You Do, Dear?* relates proper conduct for all occasions and is equally amusing.

Jupo, Frank. *A Day around the World*, il. by the author. Abelard 1968. $2.95; 5–8.

This book tells about the daily journey of the earth and how it affects time; it takes the reader around the world to see what the children are doing at the very same moment in places as far apart as Brazil, West Africa, Siberia, India, and Japan. Exquisite two-color illustrations.

Kantrowitz, Mildred. *Maxie*, il. by Emily A. McCully. Parents 1970. $3.50; 4–8.

Maxie was an old lady who felt she was unneeded. One day she decided just to stay in bed, but the whole neighborhood comes to find out what is wrong with her. Maxie finds out that she is indeed needed.

Kaufmann, Alicia. *Little Is Nice*, il. by Victoria de Larren. Hawthorn 1970. $4.25; 4–7.

About a small boy who does not like being little or having to use anything that is little.

Keats, Ezra Jack. *Apt. 3*, il. by the author. Macmillan 1971.
$5.95; 6–10.

Sam and his little brother Ben hear someone in their
apartment building playing the harmonica. Eventually the
boys not only find out where the music is coming from but
they find that it is being played by a blind man who proves
to be a new and wonderful friend. Each illustration in this
oversized picture book constitutes a lovely painting in and
of itself.

———. *Goggles!* il. by the author. Macmillan 1969. $3.95
(P—Collier, $.95); 4–8.

Some big boys threaten to take away the pair of lensless
motorcycle glasses that Peter and his friend Archie find.
With the help of Willie, Peter's dachshund, the bullies are
outwitted. Collage paintings effectively help to unfold this
story told in strong, sparse words and set in the big city.

———. *A Letter to Amy*, il. by the author. Harper 1968.-
$3.95; 4–8.

The fourth of Keats' picture story books featuring Peter, an
appealing little Negro boy. He is older now than he was in
The Snowy Day. This time he is concerned about inviting
Amy to his party. The plot is slight, but the book is pleasant
enough, and the illustrations are even better than in the
earlier books.

———. *Peter's Chair*, il. by the author. Harper 1967. $3.95;
4–7.

Understanding parents help Peter, first seen in *The Snowy
Day*, resolve his feelings and accept with pride a new baby
sister. Beautiful collages by the author-artist.

———. *The Snowy Day*, il. by the author. Viking 1962. $3.50;
3–6.

Fascinating, colorful collages give a graphic account of a
black pre-school child's glorious day in deep, new snow. A
joy for all children and well deserving of the Caldecott
Award. More experiences with Peter can be found in
Whistle for Willie and *A Letter to Amy*.

Krahn, Fernando. *A Flying Saucer Full of Spaghetti*, il. by the
author. Dutton 1970. $3.95; 5–10.

Captionless cartoons create an amusing mystery story. Great
for use in composing aloud or creative writing activities.

Krum, Charlotte. *The Four Riders*, il. by Katherine Evans.
Follett 1953. $2.95; 3–6.

Here in folktale style complete with rhythm and refrain is a
short but enticing story of an old horse whose three riders,

all barnyard fowls, won't share their pleasure with a little
old man. The three get their comeuppance, and finally all
four ride along together. A big book with large print and
delightful bright pictures.

Leaf, Munro. *The Story of Ferdinand*, il. by Robert Lawson.
Viking 1936. (P—Viking, $.75); 4 up.

A gentle young bull inadvertently sits on a bumblebee. The
action that follows causes him to be chosen for the bull
fights in Madrid, but once in the ring, alas, he will not fight.
A masterpiece of humor in story and pictures.

_____. *Wee Gillis*, il. by Robert Lawson. Viking 1938. $3.50
(P—Viking, $.75); 5–8.

A Scottish boy has a difficult problem—he doesn't know
which relatives to live with. He spends a year with those on
the lowlands and then a year with those on the highlands.
During this time he develops a most powerful set of lungs
and ends up living between the two areas and playing the
world's largest bagpipe. The keenly drawn black-and-white
illustrations reflect the humor of the story.

Lewis, Claudia. *When I Go to the Moon*, il. by Leonard
Weisgard. Macmillan 1961. $4.95; 6–10.

An earth child observes his world from the moon. Marvels of
the earth and moon are factually presented through rhythmic verse and imaginatively extended by the excellent
illustrations.

Leydenfrost, Robert. *The Other Side of the Mountain*, il. by the
author. Macmillan 1968. $4.50; 4–8.

Rufus, who paints pictures of "things around him," decides
to visit the other side of the mountain. There he meets a stag,
a wild turkey, a mother porcupine with three babies, 13
rabbits, a bear, a turtle, and a great horned owl. To each he
offers a comfortable place on "his side," so all the animals go
home with him. This simple cumulative talking animal tale
will appeal to young readers who believe that they and
animals should, and naturally do, share the same world. The
"dot" pictures are appealing, and the text is nearly as
uncluttered as the illustrations.

Lindgren, Astrid. *The Tomten*, il. by Harold Wiberg. Coward
1961. $3.75; 4–8.

Adapted from a poem by Viktor Rydberg. In Sweden a dwarf
with a long, bright red stocking cap who carries on his
activities unseen by humans is called a tomten. The one in
this story is hundreds of years old, lives in a hayloft, and
comes out at night when human beings are asleep. He
converses with farm animals in tomten talk and even comes

into the house where the family is asleep and trips quietly about. There's magic and old world charm in both the retold story and its captivating moonlit illustrations. By the same author: *The Tomten and the Fox.*

Lionni, Leo. *Alexander and the Wind-Up Mouse,* il. by the author. Pantheon 1969. $3.95; 5–8.

Alexander wants to be a wind-up mouse like Willie, who is the little girl's favorite toy. A magic lizard can change him, but then he learns that Willie's key is broken and decides to turn Willie into a real mouse like himself. Illustrated with appealing bold collage representations.

———. *The Biggest House in the World,* il. by the author. Pantheon 1968. $3.95; 4–6.

Strong, glowing pictures of snails in amazing shells traveling over huge cabbage leaves and through damp woodsy places tell a story within a story of how disastrous a large shell can be for a small snail who needs to move about for his very existence.

———. *Inch by Inch,* il. by the author. Obolensky 1960. $3.95. (P—Scholastic, $.75); 3–7.

The clever inchworm, as green as an emerald, outwits the robin and all his feathered friends, humping to safety through the tall grasses. Fascinating, colorful collages.

———. *Swimmy,* il. by the author. Pantheon 1963. $3.50; 4–7.

The lesson on cooperation for survival among fishes may be overplayed, but the variety of texture, color, and design in the illustrations is not. An intriguing picture book!

———. *Tico and the Golden Wings,* il. by the author. Pantheon 1964. $3.50; 6–9.

In this touching fantasy a little bird is born without wings and must depend on his friends for survival until the day comes when a "wishingbird" grants him his only request. Then he uses his golden gift to enrich the lives of others. The illustrations, inspired by the traditional arts of India, have highly stylized designs of rich color and geometric pattern. One wishes upon completing the story that one too could have wings of gold.

Lobel, Arnold. *Giant John,* il. by the author. Harper 1964. $2.92; 4–8.

Although John is a giant bigger than the king's castle, he is loving, kind, and gentle until he is enticed into dancing by the fairies' magic music. Children are entranced by the humorous events that follow and the equally humorous illustrations.

_____. *Prince Bertram the Bad*, il. by the author. Harper 1963. $3.99; 4–8.

Richly detailed illustrations extend this hilarious story of an unmanageable child prince who is finally forced to mend his ways. Laughs galore for any youngster!

Löfgren, Ulf. *The Wonderful Tree*, il. by the author. Delacorte 1970. $4.17; 4–7.

Edward finds a furnished house in the branches of a large tree. There he lives and has several wholly satisfying small adventures. The illustrations, bright, gay, and stylized, are an indispensable part of this sturdy but dreamlike creation.

Lund, Doris Herold. *Attic of the Wind*, il. by Ati Forberg. Parents 1966. $3.50; 4–8.

Imaginative rhymes and alluring pictures show a place where young people can find and play among their lost treasures. A storehouse of beauty.

McCloskey, Robert. *Blueberries for Sal*, il. by the author. Viking 1948. $3.50 (P—Viking, $.60); 3–6.

"Kuplink, kuplank, kuplunk," go the blueberries into little Sal's pail as she and her mother and Little Bear and his mother get all mixed up on Blueberry Hill. Both text and pictures are printed in blue as juicy as the blueberries themselves. A gem of a book.

_____. *Burt Dow: Deep-Water Man*, il. by the author. Viking 1963. $4.00; 6–10.

A whale of a tale ensues when Burt Dow, a retired deep-water man, goes fishing on the Tidely-Idley and takes along his pet sea gull. Fabulous illustrations and a shipload of fun.

_____. *Make Way for Ducklings*, il. by the author. Viking 1941. $3.50 (P—Viking, $.65); 4–8.

Mrs. Mallard's concerns for her family are touching and justified as the hazards of her living in Boston's Public Gardens are graphically portrayed. Children love to count the first brown eggs in the nest, then the fuzzy ducklings as they march across the pages. A Caldecott Award winner that is already a classic.

_____. *One Morning in Maine*, il. by the author Viking 1952. $3.50; 5–8.

Little Sal's concern over the loss of her first tooth is the source of much discussion about animals and their habits. Healthy, wholesome family life combined with rollicking fun in both pictures and story. A book to be enjoyed over and over.

_____. *Time of Wonder,* il. by the author. Viking 1957. $3.95; 5 up.

"It's going to blow. We're going to have some weather," and that they do! Vividly pictured are the sky, the sea, and some islands along the coast of Maine. The awe and tension produced by the mighty storm is resolved in this excellent account of a time of wonder. A well-deserved Caldecott Award winner.

McKee, David. *Elmer: The Story of a Patchwork Elephant,* il. by the author. McGraw 1968. $4.50; 4–7.

Elmer's patchwork colors made all the other elephants laugh, and they were all happy until Elmer decided he didn't want to be different. The illustrations are big, bold and bright.

Mahy, Margaret. *A Lion in the Meadow,* il. by Jenny Williams. Watts 1969. $4.95; 5–8.

This make-believe story will delight small listeners. The bold bright illustrations enhance the fantasy.

Memling, Carl. *What's in the Dark?* il. by John E. Johnson. Parents 1971. $3.95; 3–7.

A consoling statement that what is present in the nighttime darkness is almost the same as what was there in the daytime. Warm and comfortable colorful sketches add to the sleepy and faraway feeling of this story.

Merrill, Jean. *Here I Come. Ready or Not,* il. by Frances Gruse Scott. Whitman 1970. $3.75; 4–6.

A realistic account of two children playing hide-and-seek on a farm. Easy to read.

Minarik, Else Holmelund. *Little Bear,* il. by Maurice Sendak. Harper 1957. $2.50; 6–8.

In four chapters, four endearing tales for a beginning reader to tackle for himself. By the same author: *Father Bear Comes Home; Little Bear's Friend; Little Bear's Visit; A Kiss for Little Bear.*

Mosel, Arlene. *Tikki Tikki Tembo,* il. by Blair Lent. Holt 1968. $4.50; 6–8.

Long, long ago in China, it was the custom that first-born sons were honored with very long names. This retold tale makes plain why that is no longer true! Remarkably intriguing illustrations.

Ness, Evaline. *Josephina February,* il. by the author. Scribner 1963. $3.12; 5–9.

A warm and appealing story of a little girl in Haiti who finds a baby burro on her way to market. Colorful woodcuts lend charm.

_____. *Sam, Bangs, and Moonshine,* il. by the author. Holt 1966. $3.95; 4–8.

Samantha, a fisherman's daughter with an untamed imagination, repentantly discovers a difference between moonshine and reality. The powerful yet tender drawings won the Caldecott Award.

Newberry, Clare Turlay. *Percy, Polly, and Pete,* il. by the author. Harper 1952. $3.50; 4–8.

Records the "before and after" third-birthday behavior of Shasha and its consequent effect on three young kittens. Well written and superbly illustrated.

Olschewski, Alfred. *Winterbird,* il. by the author. Houghton 1969. $3.25; 4–6.

The story of a bird, a cat, and a dog following each other in the snow is told without words.

Orgel, Doris. *The Uproar,* il. by Anita Lobel. McGraw 1970. $4.95; 5–9.

Saul Lawrence thought his mother said she was going to "the uproar" rather than "the opera." During her absence, in dreaming and wondering about *Madame Butterfly,* he constructs a world that imaginatively and logically intermingles the fanciful and the real. The large illustrations effectively extend this dream sequence.

Peet, Bill. *Fly Homer Fly,* il. by the author. Houghton 1969. $4.50; 5–8.

Homer is a simple country pigeon who gets conned by a fast-talking sparrow into moving to Mammoth City. It doesn't take Homer long to learn that city life isn't nearly as attractive as Sparky the sparrow said. But the sparrows help Homer when he is injured on his way home, and they all go to visit him in the country.

_____. *The Whingdingdilly,* il. by the author. Houghton 1970. $4.95; 5–8.

Scamp, the dog, wants to be a horse, but a well-meaning witch turns him into a Whingdingdilly with the hump of a camel, zebra's tail, giraffe's neck, elephant's front legs and ears, rhinoceros' nose, and reindeer's horns.

Pene Du Bois, William. *Lion,* il. by the author. Viking 1956.- $3.75; 4–7.

High up in the sky, this book tells us, is an animal factory where artists with wings design new animals. Distinctive illustrations and an amazing text present a fantasy on how the lion was invented.

Perrine, Mary. *Salt Boy,* il. by Leonard Weisgard. Houghton 1968. $3.50; 6–9.

Salt Boy belongs on any shelf of distinguished literature for children. This quiet, powerful story of a Navajo child's experience, enhanced with sensitive drawings, shows cultural values that few of our children have an opportunity to see.

Piatti, Celestino. *The Happy Owls,* il. by the author. Atheneum 1964. $4.95; 4–7.

The sage advice of two happy and contented owls is neither understood nor appreciated by the vain, quarrelsome barnyard fowls. Handsomely designed drawings in rich color outshine the story with their brilliance and beauty.

Politi, Leo. *Little Leo,* il. by the author. Scribner 1951. $3.25; 5–8.

Little Leo from America, complete with Indian costume, visits his grandparents in Italy. Village children are intrigued with the costume. Little Leo tells the mothers that they can use his for a pattern. Soon dozens of little Italian children are happily "playing Indian."

_____. *Song of the Swallows,* il. by the author. Scribner 1949. $3.25; 5–8.

Illustrations in gentle hues extend this story of the swallows that return every year to the Mission of San Juan Capistrano. A Caldecott Award winner. By the same author: *Juanita; Lito the Clown; A Boat for Peppe; The Butterflies Come.*

Pollack, Reginald. *The Magician and the Child,* il. by the author. Atheneum 1971. $6.50; 7–11.

A highly sophisticated verbal and visual demonstration that life continuously offers one something new and that one can and should express his own feelings about life—be this done through paintings, music, dance, or stories.

Portal, Colette. *The Life of a Queen,* il. by the author. Braziller 1964. $3.95; 4–8.

A fact-based account of the life cycle of a queen of the blue ants moves to sheer fantasy as one begins to study the gloriously colored illustrations.

Potter, Beatrix. *The Roly-Poly Pudding,* il. by the author. Warne 1908. $1.50; 5–8.

A longer tale and one of the funniest in this section. Tom Kitten on a spree of disobedience is caught by two rats, tied securely with a network of strings, buttered, and covered with pastry dough. Only in the nick of time is he saved from being cooked and eaten as a roly-poly pudding.

_____. *The Tale of Jemima Puddle-Duck*, il. by the author. Warne 1908. $1.50; 4–8.

Jemima Puddle-Duck is a simpleton. Taken in by the flattery of a fox, she helps him collect items for "their" dinner party but in the end is rescued by her wiser friends. A perfect picture story book.

_____. *The Tale of Mr. Jeremy Fisher*, il. by the author. Warne 1906. $1.50; 4–6.

A masterpiece in miniature is this tale and its illustrations of a frog's fishing expedition and his entertainment of dinner guests.

_____. *The Tale of Mr. Tod*, il. by the author. Warne 1912. $1.50; 5–8.

Children go into peals of laughter over the escapades of two woodland villans—a fox and a badger.

_____. *The Tale of Mrs. Tittlemouse*, il. by the author. Warne 1910. $1.50; 4–8.

"Mrs. Tittlemouse was a most terribly tidy particular little mouse, always sweeping and dusting . . . " Every child knows her counterpart in his own acquaintance and enjoys this tale of her anxiety with the woodland creatures who come to visit.

_____. *The Tale of Peter Rabbit*, il. by the author. Warne 1902. $1.50; 3–6.

Unexcelled in literary quality and enhanced with reproductions of the original water-color illustrations is this edition of the tale of the famous little rabbit who runs off to Mr. McGregor's garden. Sequel: *The Tale of Benjamin Bunny*, in which Peter and his cousin, Benjamin, go to Mr. McGregor's garden to retrieve the clothes from the scarecrow.

_____. *The Tale of the Flopsy Bunnies*, il. by the author. Warne 1909. $1.50; 5–8.

Magnificent vocabulary is an integral part of any Beatrix Potter tale, and this is no exception. The astute Flopsy, now married to Benjamin, saves her six little rabbits just in time from becoming a meal for Mr. and Mrs. McGregor.

_____. *The Tale of Tom Kitten*, il. by the author. Warne 1907. $1.50; 4–7.

Tom Kitten and his sisters ruin their best clothes just before guests arrive for tea. Their mother, Mrs. Tabitha Twitchet, is "affronted" and says they are not fit to be seen. Accordingly they are sent to bed, but "somehow there were very extraordinary noises overhead, which disturbed the dignity and the repose of the tea party." A gem of a book.

————. *The Tale of Two Bad Mice,* il. by the author. Warne 1904. $1.50; 4–7.

Two mischievous little mice pilfer a doll's house to equip their own. They are caught and finally make amends for what they have done. Perfectly charming illustrations and a most enticing tale. By the same author: *The Tale of Squirrel Nutkin.*

Preston, Edna Mitchell. *Pop Corn and Ma Goodness,* il. by Robert Andrew Parker. Viking 1969. $4.50; 4–9.

A rollicking good story that reads *a-clippetty-cloppetty* from beginning to end. The full page watercolors catch the folk quality of the verse.

Rand, Ann. *Sparkle and Spin: A Book about Words,* il. by Paul Rand. Harcourt 1957. $3.50; 4–8.

Brilliant in design and color, this captivating book is an adventure with words, their sounds, their meanings, and their uses. An exposure to nouns, verbs, homonyms, and onomatopoeia without so much as even mentioning their technical labels.

Raskin, Ellen. *The World's Greatest Freak Show,* il. by the author. Atheneum 1971. $4.95; 5–8.

Alastair Pflug, the magician, becomes rich and very famous but realizes that he is the richest and unhappiest freak in the whole world. The humorous illustrations, the marvelous play on words, and the surprise ending all serve to make this a pleasurable and thought-provoking reading experience.

Rees, Ennis. *Potato Talk,* il. by Stanley Mack. Pantheon 1969. $3.95; 6–9.

Not only does a potato talk, but so does a dog, a tree, a branch, a rock. Told in rhyme, this tale is cumulative in every sense of the word. The biggest laugh of all is found on the last page. The drawings are hilarious and imaginative.

Reesink, Maryke. *The Fisherman's Family,* il. by Georgette Apol. Harcourt 1968. $3.95; 5–9.

Young readers will find pleasure in the achievements of Jan, a responsible young boy. Colorful pictures and meaningful text show life in a small Dutch seaport.

Reidel, Marlene. *Jacob and the Robbers,* il. by the author Atheneum 1967. $4.95; 4–7.

Jacob is a moonwalker. When the moon shines brightly, Jacob can do marvelous things he could never do in the day or on a moonless night. Excitement is added by three robbers who must be foiled. Rich, dark illustrations enhance the mood of fantasy.

Rey, H. A. *Curious George,* il. by the author. Houghton 1941. $3.75 (P—Scholastic, $.75); 3–6.

Chucklebait for the young is found in *Curious George* and all its sequel volumes. A small but curious monkey from the jungle provides fun in his experiences in the city.

Ringi, Kjell. *The Winner,* il. by the author. Harper 1969. $3.95; 3–6.

A tale told only in pictures of the eventual consequences of one-upmanship which will spellbind pre-readers.

Rose, Mitchell. *Norman,* il. by the author. Simon 1970. $3.95; 4–8.

About Norman, the talking dog's rise to fame in "show-biz," his loss of popularity, and how he goes back to just being an ordinary dog. Bold and fresh illustrations.

Rose, Ronald. *Inoke Sails the South Seas,* il. with photos by the author. Harcourt 1966. $4.50; 7–12.

A young Fijian dreams of becoming a man of the sea—but first, in the midst of all the excitement, he must attend to his schooling. This accomplished, he begins his life at sea. Excellent color photography makes this an outstanding book, far richer than words can relate.

———. *Ngari the Hunter,* il. with photos by the author. Harcourt 1968. $3.95; 8–12.

Young Ngari proves his knowledge and fearless by going by himself on "a walkabout in the bush." Striking color photographs of villagers and their animals are combined with factual text to show the way of life among one group of Australian aborigines today.

Sawyer, Ruth. *Journey Cake, Ho!,* il. by Robert McCloskey. Viking 1953. $3.25 (P—Viking, $.75); 3–7.

A gay new version of how the Journey Cake becomes a Johnny Cake. Spirited illustrations make this a choice volume.

Scheer, Julian. *Rain Makes Applesauce,* il. by Marvin Bileck. Holiday 1964. $4.95; 4–7.

Some of the most exquisite nonsense you will ever read or see illustrated. Too good to miss.

Schick, Eleanor. *City in the Summer,* il. by the author. Macmillan 1969. $4.50; 4–8.

On the roof of his apartment house, Jerry finds an old man who becomes his friend and takes him to the beach. The illustrations outweigh the story; they are detailed, realistic, exciting, and truly capture the sense of city life.

————. *City in the Winter,* il. by the author. Macmillan 1970. $4.95; 4–8.

A snowstorm has virtually closed down the city. Jimmy won't have to go to school so he spends the day "doing things you never get around to doing." Sturdy and durable illustrations.

————. *Katie Goes to Camp,* il. by the author. Macmillan 1968. $3.50; 4–8.

Life at a summer camp: the train ride there, meeting new friends, and camp activities are described from the perspective of Katie and her doll Corrie.

Schweitzer, Byrd Baylor. *Amigo,* il. by Garth Williams. Macmillan 1963. $4.95; 5–8.

While a young Mexican boy is thinking how he could tame a prairie dog for a pet, a prairie dog considers how he could tame a boy. Both achieve their wishes in this warm and gentle story. The illustrations are some of Garth Williams' very finest.

————. *The Man Who Talked to Trees,* il. by Symeon Shimin. Dutton 1968. $4.45; 5–8.

This ballad of a cotton wood tree takes the reader back to when the cottonwood was an inch-tall seedling, transplanted to a barren hillside by an early settler. It brings together today's generation of treeclimbers and the old man "who talked to trees." The poignant story makes the past meaningful in terms of the present.

————. *One Small Blue Bead,* il. by Symeon Shimin. Macmillan 1965. $3.50; 8–11.

In these times of speculation about human life on other planets, children will be quick to appreciate the speculation of two prehistoric American Indians—an old man and a young boy—about human life beyond their horizons. While the others of the tribe scoff, the two keep faith, and their dreams prove true. A work of art, graphically and verbally.

Scott, Ann Herbert. *Sam,* il. by Symeon Shimin. McGraw 1967. $3.95; 4–7.

The black on golden brown illustrations are works of art and

will compel anyone who looks at this book to read it. Sam is
a Negro child with an everyday problem of any small boy.
His family's tender understanding provides a rewarding
experience.

Segal, Lore. *Tell Me a Mitzi,* il. by Harriet Pincus. Farrar
1970. $4.95; 4–8.

Three short fresh fun-filled stories of child life in the city.
The pictures illuminate as well as illustrate.

Sendak, Maurice. *In the Night Kitchen,* il. by the author.
Harper 1970. $4.95; 5–9.

Mickey, the hero of this dream sequence, falls out of his
clothes and into the night kitchen, is mixed into a batter by
three chefs (who all look like Oliver Hardy), frees himself
from the dough, makes an airplane from it, flies over the
Milky Way, and brings back some milk so the chefs can
proceed with their batter-beating. Words and illustrations
provide the child with imaginative reading fare and fun-
filled wonderment. (Also, *In the Night Kitchen Coloring
Book.* P—Harper, $1.95.)

_____. *Nutshell Library,* il. by the author. Harper 1962.
$3.95; 3–8.

All in a slipcase, four miniature books each $2^{1/2} \times 3^{1/2}$
inches, bound in cloth—an alphabet book, a counting book,
a book of the months, and "a cautionary tale" about ob-
streperous young Pierre. There are laughs galore from young
listeners as Pierre gets his comeuppance! (Also available in
larger, library size without slipcase.)

_____. *Where the Wild Things Are,* il. by the author. Harper
1963. $3.95 (P—Scholastic, $.95); 4–8.

Enchantment unlimited—let no child be cheated of an
experience with these renowned wild things! These superb
illustrations won the Caldecott Award.

Seredy, Kate. *Gypsy,* il. by the author. Viking 1951. $3.56;
all ages.

"Gypsy felt weary but content. She lay on a soft nest of rags,
her newborn kittens nursing within the gently curved crescent of herself. She laid her head back and began to purr. Her
purr grew loud. It was a song without words." Thus begins
one of the most sensitively written and tenderly illustrated
books on the life cycle that can be found. It can be shared
with even the youngest listeners.

Seuss, Dr. *And to Think That I Saw It on Mulberry Street,* il. by
the author. Vanguard 1937. $3.00; 5–8.

Marco, having been chided for the tall tales he tells, tries earnestly to report what he saw on the way home from school, but his account takes on preposterous proportions. A masterpiece of fun in story and pictures.

_____. *The 500 Hats of Bartholomew Cubbins,* il. by the author. Hale 1938. $3.21; 5–9.

A fast-paced and extremely funny tale of a little boy who doffs his hat in respect to the King and then discovers another hat on his head. As fast as he removes it, another comes, and another. His troubles are ended and the magic stops with the 500th hat, elegant beyond all belief, which he sells to the King for 500 pieces of gold. Too good to miss!

_____. *Horton Hatches the Egg,* il. by the author. Random 1940. $2.85; 5 up.

A truly funny book, one of Dr. Seuss' best. Horton, the elephant, is faithful one hundred percent as he carries out his promise to watch a bird's egg while she takes a rest. Hilarious illustrations and a surprise ending.

_____. *The King's Stilts,* il. by the author. Random 1939. $2.95; 6–9.

Not vocabulary controlled, this fantastic tale is full of fun. Dike trees protect the kingdom, which is lower than the surrounding sea; Nizzards fly down to enjoy the tasty roots of the trees, and Patrol Cats go into action scaring off the Nizzards. In the hubbub of events the King's stilts are stolen, but finally Eric, the page boy, retrieves them and all ends well. Perfect illustrations in red and black.

Slobodkin, Louis. *The Friendly Animals,* il. by the author. Vanguard 1944. $3.95; 3–6.

A gem of a book in simple rhyme with excellent drawings that gives brief information about common animals. A nursery favorite.

_____. *Magic Michael,* il. by the author. Macmillan 1944. $4.50; 4–7.

Imaginative Michael is seldom a brother; more often he is "something or other," a spider or a giraffe. Eventually it becomes worth his while to be a boy. There is action and fun in this fast-paced yarn. Sequel: *Clear the Track.*

Steig, William. *Amos and Boris,* il. by the author. Farrar 1971. $4.50; 4–9.

A tender, whimsical story of how two devoted friends, Amos the mouse and Boris the whale, prove to be helpful loyal mammals when each finds his friend in extreme need of rescue. Illustrations are comical, simple, and rich with feeling.

Steptoe, John. *Stevie,* il. by the author. Harper 1969. $3.50; 4–8.

This is Robert's story of Stevie, the little boy who came every day to be taken care of by Robert's mother. Stevie was always in Robert's way, but when Stevie's parents move away, Robert finds he misses him. The illustrations make the setting reassuring and give each character a clearly defined personality.

————. *Train Ride,* il. by the author. Harper 1971. $3.95; 6–10.

Bored with sitting around on the stoop in Harlem in the summer time, four boys sneak on a train. They ride to Times Square where they play the machines in a penny arcade, watch people, and look at the tall buildings and advertisements. Late in the evening they realize that they are without train fare to get back home. Told in a dialect suggestive of Harlem, and bold pastel paintings illustrate the text.

————. *Uptown,* il. by the author. Harper 1970. $3.50; 7–12.

Two black boys walk through Harlem and try to decide what they will be when they grow up. They wonder what it would be like to be the junkies, cops, Brothers, karate experts, and hippies whom they see. Bold pastel paintings illustrate the text. Told in a dialect suggestive of from Harlem.

Suba, Suzanne. *The Man with the Bushy Beard and Other Tales,* il. by the author. Viking 1969. $4.53; 5–8.

A stunning picture book consisting of five humorous thumbnail folktales from Eastern Europe.

————. *The Monkeys and the Pedlar,* il. by the author. Viking 1970. $5.63; 4–7.

The beautiful watercolor illustrations and simple text in this oversize picture book effectively retell this well-known hilarious tale about imitative and mischievous monkeys who removed a pedlar's wares from his pack while he is asleep.

Sucksdorff, Astrid Bergman. *Chendru: The Boy and the Tiger,* English version by William Sansom, il. with photos by the author. Harcourt 1960. $4.75; 8–12.

A young Indian boy of the primitive Muria tribe is given a tiger cub. His amazing friendship with this "beloved enemy" presents an unforgettable impression of life in a jungle community. Magnificent color photography.

Suzie Mariar, il. by Lois Lenski. Walck 1968. $2.75; 3–6.

For lickety-split reading by those beginning to tackle books for themselves, here in this folk rhyme, is Suzie Mariar and her outlandish escapades. Spirited illustrations intrigue listeners not yet able to read for themselves.

Tamchina, Jürgen. *Dominique and the Dragon,* tr. and adapted by Elizabeth D. Crawford, il. by Heidrun Petrides. Harcourt 1969. $4.25; 5–9.

This story of a misunderstood dragon who is helped by a little girl is told with broad humor and freshness. The illustrations invite repeated inspection.

Thomas, Dawn C. *Mira! Mira!* il. by Harold L. James. Lippincott 1970. $3.50; 5–8.

Ramon, a little boy from Puerto Rico, comes to New York and experiences for the first time an exciting plane ride, an elevator ride, and fun in the snow.

Tresselt, Alvin. *Follow the Wind,* il. by Roger Duvoisin. Lothrop 1950. $3.25; 4–7.

A poetic fantasy that children will follow to the end. Bright, colorful pictures sweep across the pages.

_____. *Rain Drop Splash,* il. by Leonard Weisgard. Lothrop 1946. $3.00; 4–8.

Raindrops dripping from shiny leaves, splashing from a bear's tail, and trickling down tree trunks form a puddle, flow into a stream, and eventually reach the sea. A factual but picturesque story of water. The outstanding illustrations blend perfectly with the atmosphere of rain as it deluges forest, farm, and city.

_____. *White Snow, Bright Snow,* il. by Roger Duvoisin. Lothrop 1947. $3.50; 4–8.

The apprehension, the coming, and the aftermath of a heavy snow. Handsome illustrations overshadow the simple story. A Caldecott Award winner.

Tudor, Tasha. *Around the Year,* il. by the author. Walck 1957. $3.75; 4–8.

A few carefully chosen words on each page tell of life in early New England. The joys of each month are painted in delicate water colors. Typical of this artist's work are the charmingly drawn oval wreaths of fruits, flowers, or nuts that surround each picture.

Turkle, Brinton. *Sky Dog,* il. by the author. Viking 1969. $3.77; 4–7.

He was there in the sky, the shaggy white dog. The boy could see him, but his mother could not. The reader can see him, though. In the end the boy gets the dog.

Udry, Janice May. *The Moon Jumpers,* il. by Maurice Sendak. Harper 1959. $4.95; 3–6.

Children who have known the joy and excitement of playing outside after nightfall will revel in the beauty of this exquisite book. Large double-page drawings stir the imagination. The enchantment and mystery of night are finally dispelled by the warmth and security of the lights of home.

Ungerer, Tomi. *The Beast of Monsieur Racine,* il. by the author. Farrar 1971. $4.95; 5–10.

A lively verbal and visual comedy that tells of the friendship between Monsieur Racine, a retired tax collector and prize-winning gardener, and a strange beast that seems to consist of nothing more than a conglomerate of living lumps. The surprise ending will delight nearly any child.

———. *Moon Man,* il. by the author. Harper 1967. $4.50; 5–8.

"On clear, starry nights the Moon Man can be seen curled up in his shimmering seat in space." He becomes curious about Earth, so with the help of a shooting star he visits our planet. After many escapades, he is glad to be blasted off with a roar of rockets and return to the moon. Children are entranced with this clever tale and its huge, vivid pictures.

——— *The Three Robbers,* il. by the author. Atheneum 1962. $4.50; 4–8.

A little orphan girl named Tiffany is delighted to meet three fierce robbers and promptly reforms them. Their blunderbuss, the pepper-blower, and the huge red axe are greatly admired by young boys. The story, dramatically told and enhanced with brilliant illustrations, is a riot of fun and color.

Van Anrooy, Frans. *The Sea Horse,* il. by Jaap Tol. Harcourt 1968. $3.75; 5–8.

Huge, uniquely beautiful double-page illustrations set the mood for a young child's dream trip to the depths of the ocean. He has exciting adventures and learns not to be afraid of the dark. A choice book.

Varner, Velma. *The Animal Frolic,* il. by Toba Sojo. Putnam 1954. $3.29; 5–8.

Based on the original 36-foot scroll attributed to Toba Sojo of 12th-century Japan, these vigorous animal drawings fairly bounce with life and humor.

Ward, Lynd. *The Biggest Bear,* il. by the author. Houghton 1952. $3.50; 4–8.

Johnny looks for the biggest bear in the woods. What he finds and takes home as a pet is only a cub, but it grows tremendously and causes trials and tribulations to the whole valley. The outcome is satisfying, and one feels impelled to start reading the story all over again just to look in more detail at the remarkable illustrations. A Caldecott Award winner. By the same author: *Nic of the Woods,* a dog's adventures in the Canadian woods.

Wildsmith, Brian. *Brian Wildsmith's Birds,* il. by the author. Watts 1967. $4.95; 5 up.
Vibrant birds burst with color, a joy for even the youngest to pore over. An added pleasure for those who can read is the nomenclature of groups of various birds—"a wedge of swans," "a congregation of plover," and "a stare of owls."

———. *Brian Wildsmith's Circus,* il. by the author. Watts 1970. $4.95; 3 up.
An all-picture book depicting the numerous elements of the circus in bold colors and dramatic style.

———. *Brian Wildsmith's Wild Animals,* il. by the author. Watts 1967. $4.95; 4 up.
A dazzling presentation of wild animals, each grouped with his own kind and so identified—"a pride of lions," "a skulk of foxes," "a troop of kangaroos." By the same author: *Brian Wildsmith's Fishes.*

Wood, Nancy. *Little Wrangler,* il. with photos by Myron Wood. Doubleday 1966. $3.25; 5–8.
Cowboy jargon and large unposed photographs invite the reader to an adventurous roundup where a determined young ranch hand, encouraged by an old-timer, faces up to a challenge.

Yamaguchi, Tohr. *Two Crabs and the Moonlight,* il. by Marianne Yamaguchi. Holt 1965. $2.96; 8–11.
A young river crab is willing to sacrifice anything to save his mother's life. As the feelings of love and loyalty develop, the sensitively drawn illustrations add further meaning to his beautiful tale.

Yashima, Taro. *Crow Boy,* il. by the author. Viking 1955. $3.50 (P—Viking, $.75); 6–10.
A young boy from the mountain area of Japan goes to school in a nearby village, where he is taunted by his classmates and feels rejected and isolated. Finally an understanding teacher helps the boy gain acceptance. The other students recognize how wrong they have been and nickname him "Crow Boy" because he can imitate the crow's calls with such perfection. Although the setting is Japan, the theme is

universal. Distinctive colored illustrations contribute to the emotional impact of the story.

_____. *Seashore Story,* il. by the author. Viking 1967. $4.95; all ages.

Magnificent illustrations transport one to a seashore where contemporary Japanese children recall the tale of fisherman Urashima and his travels on the back of a huge turtle into the depths of the sea. They ponder the tale and are left in awe by its ending. An exquisite blend of realism and fantasy.

_____. *Umbrella,* il. by the author. Viking 1958. $3.50 (P—Viking, $.75); 4–7.

Three-year-old Momo's joy in using her new umbrella and listening to the rain fall upon it is well expressed in story and illustrations by a noted Japanese artist.

Yolen, Jane H. *The Emperor and the Kite,* il. by Ed Young. World 1967. $3.95; 6–11.

Stylistic graphics sensitively reflect an old Chinese tale with universal implications.

Zemach, Harve. *The Judge,* il. by Margot Zemach. Farrar 1969. $4.50; 5–8.

The judge dispenses rough "justice" to six prisoners who appear before him in turn, each adding frightening details to the tale of the last in their plea of innocence. In the end justice is done to the judge. Told in narrative verse.

Zimelman, Nathan. *What Shall We Have for Breakfast?* il. by John Paul Richards. Steck 1969. $3.25; 4–7.

This humorous spoof describes the search by John Jasper Jones for fresh dinosaur eggs for breakfast. The illustrations are up-to-date and low key and enrich the fun.

Zion, Gene. *Harry the Dirty Dog,* il. by Margaret Bloy Graham. Harper 1956. $3.25; 3–6.

Harry, a white dog with black spots, likes everything but his bath. He runs away from home and gets into all sorts of trouble, finally returning with a scrub brush in his mouth and begging for a bath. Chuckle bait for sure!

Zolotow, Charlotte. *Do You Know What I'll Do?* il. by Garth Williams. Harper 1958. $3.79; 3–6.

A tender closeness is expressed by a little girl for her younger brother in her loving desire to share happy times with him. "When it snows, I'll make you a snowman," and from the party "I'll bring you a piece of cake with the candle still in it." The artist has caught the seriousness of this gentle child in his appealing pictures.

_____. *The New Friend,* il. by Arvis L. Stewart. Abelard 1968. $3.50; 4–8.

The first line of this book warns of impending disaster—"I had a friend . . ."—past tense. The girls walk together and pick wild flowers. They wade in the brook and do all sorts of things together that good friends do until one day the good friend finds another friend. The consequences are painful, but Zolotow helps her reader to know that the hurt will eventually go away. It is a poignant story, made even more so by the charming illustrations.

_____. *Over and Over,* il. by Garth Williams. Harper 1957. $3.95; 4–6.

A little girl, who remembers the various holidays but does not know in what order they come, keeps asking after each one is celebrated, "What comes next?" The story ends with a party, treats, paper hats, and a birthday cake. As the little girl blows out the four candles, everyone asks her, "What did you wish?" "I wished for it all to happen again," the little girl says. And of course, over and over, year after year, it does.

FICTION

Realistic

Agle, Nan Hayden. *Maple Street,* il. by Leonora E. Prince. Seabury 1970. $4.50; 8–12.

The story of a family living on a street rapidly going "downhill" and the daughter's efforts to turn the vacant lot into a playground and to get on with the new "poor white" neighbors.

Angelo, Valenti. *The Bells of Bleecker Street.* Viking 1949. $3.77; 9–12.

Set in Greenwich Village around 1944, this story shows the influence of the Catholic Chuch on the lives of the congregation. Joey Enrico learns to deal with his friends' dares and his own conscience.

Armstrong, William. *Sounder,* il. by James Barley. Harper 1969. $3.95; 12 up.

Sounder was a dog, but this is not a dog story. It is the story of a boy's tenacity for life in a black sharecropper's family 50 years ago. In a very significant way it sums up the story of the black man who, against incredibly crushing opposition, has dragged himself into the 20th century and now challenges it to recognize his manhood.

Arthur, Ruth M. *Portrait of Margarita,* il. by Margery Gill. Atheneum 1968. $4.25; 11–14.

Part English and part Jamaican, Meg faces discrimination because of her color. As she sorts out her feelings about herself, Meg develops a commitment for teaching mentally

44

disturbed children. Strong characterization of Meg and the people around her.

Atwater, Richard and Florence. *Mr. Popper's Penguins,* il. by Robert Lawson. Little 1938. $3.50; 9–12.

The Antarctic penguin sent to Mr. Popper as a gift quite revolutionizes life in his modest home. One of the most popular humorous tales of the last 30 years.

Aurembou, Renee. *Snowbound,* tr. by Authea Bell, il. by Douglas Bisset. Abelard 1965. $3.00; 8–11.

Four children are snowbound when a severe blizzard half buries their house during the absence of their parents. The story reveals the value of carrying on even when the odds seem against success. The final reunion of rescuers from the village, searchers, and the four children shows a fine sense of values and genuine concern for others.

Baldwin, Anne Norris. *The Sometime Island,* il. by Charles Robinson. Norton 1969. $3.95; 5–8.

Brian explores a peninsula that becomes an island when the tide comes in while he is there. This adventure is recounted with a sense for the wonder, self-reliance, and courage displayed by Brian.

Ball, Zachary. *Bristle Face.* Holiday 1962. $3.95 (P—Scholastic, $.60); 11–15.

A hound dog, an orphan boy, a lonely man, and fox hunting in a mountain area are brought together to make splendid reading, especially for boys.

Barne, Kitty. *Barbie.* Little 1969. $4.95; 10–13.

Barbie is a violin virtuoso whose fascinating talent changes the lives of those around her and finally rewards her with the teacher of her dreams.

Baum, Betty. *Patricia Crosses Town,* il. by Nancy Grossman. Knopf 1965. $3.50; 9–12.

Twelve-year-old Pat Marley, a Negro, is reluctant to attend the previously all white school across town. Attend she does, and as the school year progresses she and her classmates learn much about people. The problems of integration and human relationships in general are met head-on.

Beale, Will. *Seapiece,* il. by Frank Handlin. Wheelwright 1966. $3.50; 10–14.

A very unusual story of a boy who must fight uphill all the way to prove his ability as a musician. The character development is excellent.

Beam, Maurice. *Adventure in Survival,* il. by Dirk Gringhuis. Putnam 1967. $3.29; 12–14.

A Robinson Crusoe type of story with modern frills, this adventure offers some great ideas for survival.

Beatty, Patricia. *The Sea Pair,* il. by Franz Altschuler. Morrow 1970. $4.95; 8–12.

The tale of a young Quileute Indian boy who wants to go to Seattle to train to be a mechanic. Excellent treatment of the themes of wildlife protection and problems faced by remote Indian groups in their encounter with the white man's society.

Berg, Jean Horton. *Miss Kirby's Room,* il. by Alex Stein. Westminster 1966. $3.25; 7–11.

An interesting account of behavioral changes in a classroom when one of the students steals a dollar. Characters are believable and individualized; plot is well constructed and fairly fast moving. Easy to read—high interest appeal.

Binzen, Bill. *Miguel's Mountain,* photos by the author. Coward 1968. $3.29; 5–8.

Miguel and his friends played every day on a mountain of earth in the park near their homes. When the mountain's existence was threatened, Miguel took positive action and saved the day. The book conveys the sweetness, fears, and joyful triumphs of children everywhere.

Biro, Val. *Gumdrop and the Farmer's Friend,* il. by the author. Follett 1967. $3.50; 6–9.

A delightful story about an antique car and some attempts to steal it. The vocabulary is geared for the car enthusiast. Illustrations enhance the text.

Blume, Judy. *Are You There, God? It's Me, Margaret.* Bradbury 1970. $4.50; 10–14.

A perceptive story about the emotional, physical, and spiritual ups and downs experienced by 12-year-old Margaret, child of a Jewish-Protestant union.

Bonham, Frank. *Durango Street.* Dutton 1965. $3.95 (P—Scholastic, $.75); 12 up.

Plunged back into a new ghetto environment after a stint in a detention camp, Rufus Henry proves his toughness, abilities, and intelligence when he becomes the leader of a teenage gang that, with the help of a social worker, gradually begins to "cool" its activities. Realistic picture of innercity life.

———. *Viva Chicano.* Dutton 1970. $4.50; 12 up.

A well thought out story of a Mexican-American teenager's

problems with his family, police, and gang. Characterization is completely believable.

Bontemps, Arna. *Lonesome Boy,* il. by Feliks Topolski. Houghton 1955. $3.25; 10–16.

There is a lyrical and human feeling in this book. Grandpa's advice to Bubber proves to be more insightful and helpful about contemporary issues than it was considered when the story was first published. Bubber learns the hard way that compensatory behavior leaves one with funny friends.

Bova, Ben. *Escape.* Holt 1970. $3.27; 12–16.

Danny has been sent to a special reform school watched over by SPECS (Special Computer System), a benign computer system that checks every move the boys make, teaches them, answers questions, and regulates the environment. In the end, Danny is forced to make a decision between escape and loyalty to a new black friend.

Brandbury, Bianca. *The Loner,* il. by John Gretzer. Houghton 1970. $3.50; 8–12.

Jay's parents may be financially secure, but Jay has no inner security of his own. He hates his older brother and longs for a strong self-identity. Utilization of his own hidden abilities and the help of an odd assortment of people from the cleaning woman at the marina to the marina owner enable Jay to begin the exciting process of growing up.

Brent, Stuart. *Mr. Toast and the Woolly Mammoth,* il. by Lillian Obligado. Viking 1966. $3.00; 9–12.

The story of the unearthing of a mammoth at the bottom of a quarry in northern Wisconsin. A fine account is given of techniques used by paleontologists.

Brink, Carol Ryrie. *Winter Cottage.* Macmillan 1968. $4.95; 8–12.

A story of faith in family life during the Great Depression. The responsibility for the family's well-being rests with Minty, and the incidents that occur lead to a very satisfying ending.

Bulla, Clyde Robert. *The White Bird,* il. by Leonard Weisgard. Crowell 1966. $3.75; 9–12.

Luke raises the foundling, John Thomas, in a secluded wilderness. He does not allow the boy to see any other people and warns him of the dangers of the outside world. John Thomas makes a pet of a white bird and eventually runs away from Luke. He finds that people are kind and that Luke is too, in his own harsh way.

Burchardt, Nellie. *Reggie's No-Good Bird,* il. by Harold Berson. Watts 1967. $3.95; 8–12.

Ten-year-old Reggie decides to feed and care for Charley, the baby blue jay he knocked from a tree. Once the chief troublemaker of the city housing project where he lives, Reggie changes into a responsible and constructive young man. The story is fast moving and easy to read. Of special interest to boys.

Burt, Katharine Newlin. *Girl on a Broomstick,* il. by Carolyn Cather. Funk & Wagnalls 1967. $3.25; 10–14.

Camilla Devon, a self-centered and highly imaginative 13-year-old, decides that she possesses the power of witchcraft. The story of how she finally learns the truth about herself has pathos, humor, and romance.

Butterworth, William E. *Orders to Vietnam: A Novel of Helicopter Warfare.* Little 1968. $4.50; 11–14.

A West Point dropout, now a draftee, learns what it means to be responsible for men's lives. The book is much better than the author's *Helicopter Pilot.*

Calhoun, Mary. *Depend on Katie John,* il. by Paul Frame. Harper 1961. $3.50; 8–12.

In this continuation of *Katie John,* the young reader should have no difficulty identifying with Katie's trials, tribulations, and fun. Plot is simple, characters are definite, and situations are believable. Story will appeal to girls.

Campbell, Hope. *Why Not Join the Giraffes?* Norton 1968. $4.50; 6–12.

Suzie's parents are hip and her brother swings, so Suzie longs to be strictly square.

Canty, Mary. *The Green Gate,* il. by Vera Bock. McKay 1965. $3.50; 9–12.

This story of how eight-year-old Emily learns to cope with her blindness will alert the young reader to the problems that one with such a handicap probably encounters. It is brief; the plot is simple yet well developed; and descriptions are poignant and thought-provoking.

Carlson, Natalie Savage. *Ann Aurelia and Dorothy,* il. by Dale Payson. Harper 1968. $3.95 (P—Dell, $.75); 9–12.

A friendship between a Negro and a white girl in which the Negro child does not have all the problems. Ann Aurelia's mother is divorced, remarries, and leaves her with a foster parent. Dorothy's family is more stable, and the friendship grows in a natural way.

_____. *The Empty Schoolhouse,* il. by John Kaufmann. Harper 1965. $4.50 (P—Dell, $.75); 7–11.

This account of what happens to ten-year-old Lullah Royall when the parochial schools in Louisiana are desegregated will probably prove to be unforgettable reading fare. The writing style makes for easy reading, and the convincing characters are portrayed with considerable depth. The plot is skillfully developed and moves along quickly, with some unneeded sterotyping. By the same author: *The Family under the Bridge; The Tomahawk Family.*

Cavanna, Betty. *The Country Cousin.* Morrow 1967. $3.95; 12–16.

Mindy, raised on a farm, unsure of herself and bored with life, works in her aunt's dress shop for the summer. She gains in self-confidence and realizes her potential as a dress designer. Some romantic interest is included. By the same author: *Going on Sixteen; Paintbox Summer;* and others.

Clayton, Barbara. *One Special Summer,* il. by Jessica Zemsky. Funk & Wagnalls 1966. $3.25; 8–12.

A bored 11-year-old girl and an over-protected, bookish boy about the same age both learn to recognize that the other has admirable qualities. During a summer of imposed companionship, they show substantial character development and discover a valuable, long-buried Indian village. Theme emphasizes the value of persistence and patience; characterization is strong and convincing.

Cleary, Beverly. *Fifteen,* il. by Joe and Beth Krush. Morrow 1956. $3.95; 12–14.

Stan manages to prevent Sandra from pouring ink on the rug while Jane is babysitting for Sandra's parents. From this incident a friendship between Jane and Stan develops, which Jane welcomes since her latest boy friend is dull and an inch shorter than she.

_____. *Henry and the Paper Route,* il. by Louis Darling. Morrow 1957. $3.75; (P—Scholastic, $.60); 8–12.

One of Cleary's delightful Henry stories. A ten-year-old boy finds humorous and ingenious ways of proving that he is sufficiently "businesslike" to take over a paper route.

_____. *Ramona the Pest,* il. by Louis Darling. Morrow 1968. $3.75 (P—Scholastic, $.60); 8–10.

This Cleary title will have the same appeal as the Henry books. Ramona has come of age and is now in kindergarten. The book is a delight from start to finish and very true to life. By the same author: *Henry Huggins; Beezus and Ramona; Henry and Ribsy; Mitch and Amy; Emily's Runaway Imagination;* and others.

Cleaver, Vera and Bill. *Lady Ellen Grae,* il. by Ellen Raskin. Lippincott 1968. $2.95; 9–12.

A convincing account of how an imaginative character gradually moves from an uninhibited tomboy to a not-so-uninhibited young lady.

_____. *The Mimosa Tree.* Lippincott 1970. $3.95; 12–16.

A shockingly realistic story of how 14-year-old Marvella and ten-year-old Hugh care for their blind father and younger brothers in an inhospitable Chicago slum.

_____. *Where the Lilies Bloom.* Lippincott 1969. $3.95; 12 up.

This is the story of an Appalachian sharecropper's family and how the children try to manage for themselves after their widowed father dies. Their heroic efforts and noble failure are beautifully told.

Clymer, Eleanor. *My Brother Stevie.* Holt 1968. $3.50 (P—Scholastic, $.60); 10–14.

Mischief comes naturally to Annie's eight-year-old brother, but Annie is the girl to handle him.

_____. *We Lived in the Almont,* il. by David K. Stone. Dutton 1970. $3.91; 9–12.

The changing views and maturing emotions of a young girl growing up in the city are handled in a realistic and memorable way.

Cohen, Peter Zachary. *The Muskie Hook,* il. by Tom O'Sullivan. Atheneum 1969. $4.25; 8–12.

Aaron's father wants him to follow him as a guide to fishermen. Aaron wants to be a lumberman. But one day he is the only person available to guide three fishermen, and the excitement of the day arouses his interest in the Muskie search. Sketches and maps aid the reader. Particularly good for fishermen.

Collier, James. *The Teddy Bear Habit,* il. by L. Lorenz. Norton 1967. $3.95 (P—Dell, $.75); 10–14.

Funny, swinging tale of a 12-year-old loser, hooked on a teddy bear until it is stuffed with "hot ice."

Cone, Molly. *Annie Annie,* il. by Marvin Friedman. Houghton 1969. $3.50; 10–14.

Teenage Annie's liberal parents allow their children to make decisions for themselves. Finding no identity in her home, Annie takes a summer live-in job in the home of an older couple. There all the decisions are made for her. This new life appeals to her until she realizes such treatment eliminates all thought. She returns home, valuing her experience of rebellion.

———. *The Other Side of the Fence,* il. by John Gretzer. Houghton 1967. $3.50; 10–13.
A story of a black family's acceptance in a white neighborhood. Although this is a reasonably well-written novel by a recognized author of several high quality books, it is a superficial treatment of a difficult problem. Joey is a summer visitor on the street where a Negro family moves in, and his rejection of the neighbors' actions makes them ashamed of themselves.

———. *A Promise Is a Promise,* il. by John Gretzner. Houghton 1964. $3.25; 12–14.
About a Jewish girl, this book should be enjoyed by many of any religious group. Ruthy goes through the process of becoming more aware of herself, others, and the heritages of herself and others.

———. *Simon,* il. by Marvin Friedman. Houghton 1970. $3.50; 10–14.
About Simon, who withdraws from the oppressive tedium of his middle-class life. There were a junk car to which he could escape and dream, a cat, a blind man who helped show him the way, and a mentally retarded girl whose plight eventually forced him to return to reality.

Conrad, Sybil. *Believe in Spring.* Vanguard 1967. $3.95; 12–15.
The story deals with that awkward stage when an older sister has all the advantages; the course of events leads to a maturity of character on the part of Nancy that results in a happy ending.

Corbett, Scott. *The Mailbox Trick,* il. by Paul Galdone. Little 1961. $3.50; 8–11.
In this sequel to *The Lemonade Trick,* Kerby Maxwell continues to try out some of the magic potions given him by a mysterious lady. He mistakenly mails three letters, and his attempts to retrieve them are exciting and hilarious.

———. *Pippa Passes,* il. by Judith Gwyn Brown. Holt 1966. $3.75; 8–11.
This exciting adventure story, filled with intrigue and humor, centers on a famous child movie star who runs away from an aunt and uncle who exploit her talents for their own profit. The children in the story are believable, but characterization of the adults is fairly shallow.

Corcoran, Barbara. *Sam,* il. by Barbara McGee. Atheneum 1967. $4.25; 11–14.

A high school junior, Sam is attending public school for the first time after an island childhood. This is the story of her social adjustment to adults and her peers as well as the resolving of her confusion caused by some people's ideas of right and wrong. The keen competition and excitement of dog shows is of special interest.

_____. *This Is a Recording,* il. by Richard Cuffari. Atheneum 1971. $5.25; 10–14.

Fourteen-year-old Marianne is shipped out West to live with her grandmother when her parents go to Europe pending a divorce. Marianne records faithfully and with unrestricted honesty her reactions to her parents, her grandmother, her new schoolmates, and to things western. By the same author: *Long Journey; Row of Tigers; Sasha, My Friend.*

Cornish, Sam. *Your Hand in Mine,* il. by Carl Owens. Harcourt 1970. $3.25; 7–9.

Sam, a small, lonesome brown boy whose mother and father work most of the time, keeps himself company with poetry he says to himself and sometimes writes down, but he never says it *to* anyone.

Cretan, Gladys Yessayan. *All except Sammy,* il. by Symeon Shimin. Little 1966. $3.00; 7–11.

This is a simply told story of how Sammy, a good baseball player and member of a highly talented musical family, learns to value the talents he does possess. Numerous large illustrations; high interest, easy vocabulary. By the same author: *A Gift from the Bride.*

Cunningham, Julia. *Burnish Me Bright,* il. by Don Freeman. Pantheon 1970. $3.95; 10–14.

A story of a mute orphan boy and his short apprenticeship to a dying old man, once the world's greatest mime, set in a tiny village in the south of France. Two underlying themes—the perils of being different and death—are handled with poignant directness.

_____. *Dorp Dead,* il. by James Spanfeller. Pantheon 1965. $3.50; 10 up.

Gill Ground finds that peace and quiet are not as valuable as he had thought in the orphanage. Kobalt is the personification of evil, and "the hunter" is some vague allusion to good. This book has received a great deal of attention because of its unusal frankness, symbolism, and unique characterization.

De Jong, Meindert. *The Singing Hill,* il. by Maurice Sendak. Harper 1962. $3.50; 8–12.

This story helps the reader to experience the feeling of loneliness that six-year-old Ray and his mother face as they try to adjust to their new home. The father-son relationships are wholesome and admirable, and the sibling relationships are truly believable. By the same author: *Along Came a Dog; The Wheel on the School; The House of Sixty Fathers; Journey from Peppermint Street; Shadrach.*

Dick, Trella Lamson. *Burro on the Beach,* il. by Ted Lewin. Follett 1967. $3.50; 9–12.

An action-packed account of the exciting experiences of a family and newfound friends during a summer vacation on the Pacific coast. Readers learn about the violent storms that occur along a sea coast, migrating whales, a petrified skeleton of a sea lion embedded in a cavern wall, and the crippling effects of war.

Donovan, John. *Wild in the World.* Harper 1971. $3.50; 12–16.

A powerful novel about the friendship between a lonely youth, the lone survivor of a once large family who lived on a secluded farm up on Rattlesnake Mountain. This poignant tale dramatizes the theme that man is a sociable creature and at times needs companionship. It also speaks lyrically of the nature of love, trust, and self-reliance.

Drdek, Richard E. *Lefty's Boy.* Doubleday 1969. $3.95; 11–15.

A story about big city slum life and the difficulties faced by a 15-year-old boy when his alchoholic father, a one-time big-league pitcher, disappears.

Dunne, Mary Collins. *Reach Out, Ricardo.* Abelard 1971. $4.95; 10–16.

A dramatic and convincing account of what happens to a family and community when grape growers strike for recognition of a union.

Ellis, Mel. *Ironhead.* Holt 1968. $3.95 (P—Archway, $.60); 10–14.

The fascination of the Everglades lends a strong aura of adventure to a boy's struggle to help his father. A series of encounters with alligators, snakes, a wild boar, and quicksand should hold any boy's attention.

Enright, Elizabeth. *Gone-Away Lake,* il. by Beth and Joe Krush. Harcourt 1957. $3.75 (P—Harcourt, $.75); 10–12.

Portia, age 11, and her 12-year-old, nature-loving cousin, Julian, have a wonderful summer exploring the swamp lands that once were a resort lake. The story should be excellent material for family reading. By the same author: *Return to Gone-Away; The Saturdays; Thimble Summer* (Newbery Award, 1939); and others.

Erwin, Betty K. *Behind the Magic Line,* il. by Julia Iltis. Little 1969. $4.95; 9–12.

The Western family struggles to have enough to eat and to wear. But the harshness is somewhat relieved because this family has Mama. Mr. Western has gone away to look for work, and Mama is responsible for the family. She sometimes works seven days a week for white families, but she would rather do this than accept welfare. The implication is that the family's difficulties are basically the result of the Negro's status in our society.

Estes, Eleanor. *The Hundred Dresses,* il. by Louis Slobodkin. Harcourt 1944. $3.95; 10–12.

The story of Wanda Petronski, shabby child of a Polish immigrant family, and of her attempts to compensate for the thoughtless attitude of her schoolmates. A sympathetic approach to social and economic differences for younger readers. By the same author: *The Moffats; The Middle Moffat: Rufus M; Ginger Pye; Pinky Pye.*

Estrada, Doris. *Periwinkle Jones,* il. by Jo Ann Stover. Doubleday 1965. $2.75; 8–10.

Readers will find delight and excitement in this humorous story of imaginative ten-year-old Periwinkle Jones, who leads her cousin Oscar and his friend Sam in a search for "pirate treasure," an ancient Arapaho Indian, and a "prisoner" in a deserted cave.

Faulknor, Cliff. *The In-Betweener,* il. by Leonard Shortall. Little 1967. $3.95; 8–12.

With little or no effort Chad gets into serious trouble. He is sprayed by a skunk; through his carelessness two of the family's cows are poisoned; he is trapped in a tunnel and overhears three robbers as they make plans to smuggle gold bars out of the country. These are only a few of his adventures. Fast moving, suspense-filled story with flesh-and-blood characters.

Fisher, Laura. *You Were Princess Last Time,* il. by Nancy Grossman. Holt 1965. $3.50 8–12.

Susie Simpson wants badly to have long hair, and she does try to check her tomboyish behavior. This account of her progress toward achieving both objectives amounts to a very well-written story with convincing characters, realistic situations (some hilarious and others far from funny), and a fast moving plot.

Fitzhugh, Louise. *Harriet the Spy,* il. by the author. Harper 1964. $3.95; (P—Dell, $.95); 10–14.

Harriet, a sophisticated sixth-grader, aspires to be a famous writer and prepares for that ultimate goal by observing and taking notes on everything of interest to her. The consequences of her unique, uninhibited, and ingenious behavior provide reading fare at times comical and at other times fairly grim. By the same author: *The Long Secret.*

Fox, Paula. *How Many Miles to Babylon?* White 1967. $3.95 (P—Archway, $.60); 9–12.

A poignant story about a lonely Negro boy who is kidnapped by a gang of older boys and forced to participate in a dog-stealing racket. A realistic portrayal of ghetto life in Brooklyn.

_____. *The Stone-Faced Boy,* il. by Donald Mackay. Bradbury 1958. $3.95 (P—Scholastic, $.50); 9–11.

Ten-year-old Gus is called Stoneface because he does not reveal any of his emotions. Middle child in a family of five, he finds it difficult to make a place for himself. A courageous act brings him out of his introspection and helps him overcome his fears.

Friedman, Frieda. *The Janitor's Girl,* il. by Mary Stevens. Morrow 1956. $3.25 (P—Scholastic, $.60); 10–14.

The superintendent of an apartment building has different reactions about his job from his four children. The variety of people who live a typical New York City apartment building adds human interest to the story of a child's adjustment problem.

Friis-Baastad, Babbis. *Don't Take Teddy,* tr. by Lise Somme McKinnon. Scribner 1967. $3.95; 10–17.

Upper-elementary children will be given insight into the problems families face when one member is mentally retarded. The story centers on Mikkell, the youngest, who progresses to the stage where he can recognize everyone's concern for the welfare of Teddy.

Furman, A. L., ed. *Everygirls' Companion.* Lantern 1968. $3.25; 10–15.

A good selection of short stories for young girls. The variation of plots and characters should create added interest in reading for those students stopped by full-length books.

Gage, Wilson. *Big Blue Island,* il. by Glen Rounds. World 1964. $3.50; 8–12.

Darrell is sent to live with his great-uncle on a Tennessee river island. Expecting an unpleasant life, he encounters just that. Only time and mutual problems can bring about mutual understanding and perhaps even love. The reader is left with hope for this, but there is no definite assurance.

Gates, Doris. *Blue Willow,* il. by Paul Lantz. Viking 1940. $3.50 (P—Viking, $.75); 10–12.

An outstanding story of migrant workers in California. Young Janey Larkin, after years of wandering, secures a permanent home and a place to display her most cherished possession, the blue willow plate. By the same author: *Sensible Kate; The Cat and Mrs. Cary; The Elderberry Bush.*

George, Jean. *My Side of the Mountain,* il. by the author. Dutton 1959. $3.95 (P—Scholastic, $.75); 10–14.

A most unusual and fascinating book. Teenage Sam spends a year on his own, living off the land in the wooded areas of the Catskill Mountains. Young people interested in plant and animal life and the wonders of nature will find this book a stimulating experience. By the same author: *Gull 737; Hold Zero.*

Gilbert, Nan. *A Dog for Joey.* Harper 1967. $3.50; 10–14.

A lonely boy, who has just moved to town after having lived on a farm, raises a puppy for Guide Dogs for the Blind.

Graham, Lorenz B. *North Town.* Crowell 1965. $4.50; 12 up.

This candid portrayal of a southern Negro family's adjustment to life in a northern industrial city is a sequel to *South Town.*

_____. *Whose Town.* Crowell 1969. $4.50; 12 up.

Describes the complexity of life for a black family recently moved to a northern city. Beneath the exciting plot of how David, a high school senior, becomes unfairly implicated in a murder charge, the author pinpoints important social issues of the injustice and inequality faced by urban blacks. There is a wealth of ghetto characters and real life situations.

Hamilton, Virginia. *The House of Dies Drear,* il. by Eros Keith. Macmillan 1968. $4.95; 10 up.

A suspenseful story about a Negro professor's family living in a strange old mansion that was once a station on the Underground Railroad.

Hample, Stuart. *Blood for Holly Warner.* Harper 1967. $3.95; 12–14.

Realistic and blunt portrayal of the thoughts and concerns of an adolescent boy. The problems faced by members of a family when parents separate and young people live with their grandparents are depicted, and the conflicts between generations and culture groups are well interpreted.

Harmon, Lyn. *Clyde's Clam Farm,* il. by Leonard Shortall. Lippincott 1966. $3.25; 9–12.

Clyde, 11 years old and an orphan, reluctantly leaves his beloved Iowa farm to start a new life with an uncle whom he does not know, an oysterman who lives on the Atlantic seaboard. The uncle is sullen and uncommunicative; relationships between the two are strained. Eventually they learn to respect and admire each other. Strong characterization and well-developed plot.

Harris, Christie. *Confessions of a Toe-Hanger,* il. by Moira Johnston. Atheneum 1967. $4.50; 11–14.

Feeny, the younger sister of the artist in *You Have to Draw the Line Somewhere,* comes to realize that she does not need to compare herself with her brother and sister. This account of her childhood, youth, marriage, and motherhood is told humorously. By the same author: *Once upon a Totem; Raven's Cry; West with the White Chiefs.*

Harris, Marilyn. *The Peppersalt Land.* Four Winds 1970. $4.95; 10–16.

A poignant story of how two 12-year-old girls—one white and one black—learn some truths about themselves, their friendship, and the devastating effects of racial antagonism on human relationships.

Harris, Mary K. *The Bus Girls,* il. by Eileen Green. Norton 1968. $3.75; 8–12.

A believable story about a growing friendship between two girls who are in the same class and ride the same school bus. It contains some exciting episodes, and character change is convincing.

Hayes, William D. *Project: Scoop,* il. by the author. Atheneum 1966. $3.50; 8–12.

Describes a "battle" between the editor of a school newspaper and the principal. The humorous story shows that the press is a powerful vehicle and can be used to attain certain goals.

Haywood, Carolyn. *Here Comes the Bus!* il. by the author. Morrow 1963. $4.25; 5–9.

These stories about an actual schoolbus driver and his passengers are set up in open format with black-and-white drawings and simple language. They are suitable to read

aloud to five- and six-year olds or may be read independently by older children. By the same author: *B Is for Betsy;
Eddie and His Big Deals; Primrose Day; Ever-Ready Eddie;*
and others.

Hentoff, Nat. *Jazz Country.* Harper 1965. $3.50 (P—Dell,
$.50); 10–16.

Tom Curtis wants to break into the Negro jazz world and
finds discrimination against him because he is white. The
candid approach to racial attitudes and the excellent descriptions of jazz music make this a powerful story.

Hightower, Florence. *Fayerweather Forecast.* Houghton 1967.
$3.25; 10–14.

A charming family of freeloaders move in on their cheerful
aunt, changing their lives, their aunt's life, and the town for
the better.

Hinton, S. E. *The Outsiders.* Viking 1967. $3.95; 12 up.

The insight of the author into the concerns of urban youth
makes this an excellent book. Written by a teenager, it
sweeps the reader into the lives of young people with real
gusto.

Hoff, Syd. *Irving and Me.* Harper 1967. $3.95; 12–14.

A humorous and fairly exciting account of how a 13-year-old
Jewish boy, new to a Florida community, succeeds in
finding friendship.

Holman, Felice. *Elisabeth, the Treasure Hunter,* il. by Erik
Blegvad. Macmillan 1964. $3.95; 7–9.

A humorous, suspense-filled, and informative tale about a
treasure hunt on a beach. The clever clues will delight the
young naturalist. The reader learns more about the wonders
of the seashore than he does about the personalities of the
characters. A sequel to *Elisabeth, the Bird Watcher.*

———. *A Year to Grow,* il. by Emily Arnold McCully. Norton
1968. $3.95; 11–14.

An excellent story, beautifully told, of a year that brings
maturity to Julia. The unusual events will bring a new view
to many readers of the importance of life's events. Julia is a
warm and honest character.

Hooker, Ruth. *Gertrude Kloppenberg,* il. by Gloria Kamen.
Abingdon 1970. $3.50; 8–12.

Readers share Gertrude's diary for six weeks. Her daily
entries, natural in both their construction and thought flow,
reveal a shy introspective city girl emerging, as time lapses,
gradually and believably into the wider world.

Hughes, Matilda. *Headlines for Caroline.* Avalon 1967. $3.50; 12–15.

Although somewhat trite, the story moves rapidly and will make good reading for those aspiring to be librarians. It is clear that the library will be saved, but the efforts of Caroline make the story interesting.

Hunt, Irene. *Up a Road Slowly.* Follett 1966. (P—Grosset, $.75); 12 up.

After the death of her parents, seven-year-old Julia Tredling comes to live with a rather forbidding spinster aunt. During the next ten years she learns to love her aunt, to ride, and to cope with her alcoholic uncle. A published writer at 17, Julia is a wise, talented girl with perceptive understanding of herself and those around her. An excellent character study. Newbery Award, 1967.

Hunter, Edith Fisher. *Sue Ellen,* il. by Bea Holmes. Houghton 1969. $3.50; 8–12.

Sue Ellen's learning difficulties are very much the fault of her home life: a sickly mother, drunken father, and seldom enough food. She is enrolled in a special class for children with problems like hers and finds that school can be enjoyed and the lessons learned there can help her get on better at home.

Hunter, Kristin. *The Soul Brothers and Sister Lou.* Scribner 1968. $3.95; 12 up.

The complexities of ghetto life are frankly and vividly portrayed in this story of a sensitive girl's search for her identity.

Huntsberry, William. *The Big Wheels.* Lothrop 1967. $3.50 (P—Avon, $.60); 12 up.

A real picture of sex, high school boys, and the corruption that results from gang control. Makes a plea for clear thinking, courage, and respect.

Huston, Anne. *The Cat across the Way,* il. by Velma Ilsley. Seabury 1968. $3.75; 8–12.

Ten-year-old Lacey's blue-collar father must follow his job from the small town of Three Corners to Cleveland. Lacey is bewildered, hurt, and homesick. Her relationship with Rosette across the way has its ups and downs, but Lacey saves her cat's life.

————, and Jane Yolen. *Trust a City Kid.* Lothrop 1966. $3.75; 10 up.

A boy from Harlem goes to spend a summer with a Quaker

farm family. His rescue of an old horse and his discovery that courage need not mean fighting make a significant and realistic story.

Ipcar, Dahlov. *General Felice,* il. by Kenneth Longtemps. McGraw 1967. $4.50; 8–12.

An account of the fierce battle two girls wage against their enemies, caretakers of a farm in Connecticut. The book has a fascinating story line, effectively created characters, and humorous and sometimes shocking incidents.

Jackson, Jacqueline. *The Paleface Redskins,* il. by the author. Little 1968. $4.50; 10–14.

Two boys and two girls (assuming Indian names and ways) and scouts fight over the possession of a small lake surrounded by beautiful hilly land (Pleasant Lake, Wisconsin). This exciting story is full of action and fast moving, with good characterization. Recommended for reluctant readers.

_____. *The Taste of Spruce Gum.* Little 1966. $3.95; 11–14.

Libby finds it hard to adjust to a new father and the rowdy life of a Vermont logging camp.

Jackson, Jesse. *Tessie,* il. by Harold James. Harper 1968. $4.95 (P—Dell, $.75); 13–16.

The vivid characterization of Tessie helps the reader to identify readily with the conflicts and confusions of a vulnerable teenage girl attempting to reconcile her world of white friends at the exclusive Hobbe private school with her home and friends in Harlem. By the same author: *Call Me Charley: Charley Starts from Scratch.*

Johnson, Annabel and Edgar. *The Grizzly,* il. by Gilbert Riswold. Harper 1964. $3.95 (P—Scholastic, $.60); 10–14.

Eleven-year-old David and his father, who is separated from his mother, spend a tremendously exciting and tension-filled weekend together in the wild outdoors. Through a fine balance of descriptive detail and dialogue between the characters, the authors offer much insight into human relationships, especially those between father and son. By the same authors: *The Black Symbol; Wilderness Bride.*

Johnson, Burdetta. *Little Red,* il. by James R. Johnson. Follett 1966. $2.95; 9–13.

An account of the adventures of two children and their pet javelina, which they find in Hidden Canyon in Arizona. The book describes canyon country, the wilderness life there, and animal habits well.

Jones, Adrienne. *Sail, Calypso!* il. by Adolph LeMoult. Little 1968. $4.95; 9–12.

An armed truce between two boys, one black, one white, ends in close friendship as they rebuild a derelict sailboat.

Justus, May. *A New Home for Billy,* il. by Joan Balfour Payne. Hastings 1966 $3.25; 7–11.

An account of a black family's attempt to find better housing facilities in an inner city. The plot is simple and well constructed; characters are believable; situations are realistic and accurate. By the same author: *New Boy in School.*

Konigsburg, E. L. *From the Mixed-Up Files of Mrs. Basil E. Frankweiler,* il. by the author. Atheneum 1968. $3.95; 8–12.

The adventures of a sister and brother who run away from home to live in the New York Metropolitan Museum of Art. The inventiveness of the author and her attention to detail bring the characters to life in this "runaway" thriller. Newbery Award, 1968.

————. *Jennifer, Hecate, Macbeth, William McKinley, and Me, Elizabeth.* Atheneum 1967. $3.50; 8–11.

A delightfully funny yet sensitive story about two lonely girls who live in suburban New York City. Friendship develops during the time that Elizabeth serves an apprenticeship for witchcraft under the careful tutoring of Jennifer.

Koob, Theodora. *The Tacky Little Icicle Shack,* il. by Kurt Werth. Lippincott 1966. $3.50; 9–12.

When three children start a roadside ice cream stand, the complications that arise from their well-intentioned efforts and their ability to adjust to the stress caused by their father's sudden illness promise humorous and heartrending reading.

Krumgold, Joseph. *And Now Miguel,* il. by Jean Charlot. Crowell 1953. $4.50 (P—Apollo, $1.65); 10 up.

In this moving story Miguel tells of his secret wish to be accepted as a man among men. The vivid word pictures and characterization of this sheep-raising family make the book outstanding. Newbery Award, 1954. By the same author: *Onion John* (Newbery Award, 1960); *Henry Three.*

Kurkul, Edward. *Tiger in the Lake,* il. by Haris Petie. Lantern 1968. $3.25; 7–12.

A good story of a boy who yearns for a responsible place in his family. He proves he can handle himself in a crisis when a tiger escapes from the circus train.

Ladd, Elizabeth. *Treasure on Heron's Neck,* il. by George Porter. Morrow 1967. $3.75; 8–12.

Ten-year-old Marty, living with her father in a woodsy,

isolated area in Maine, wants a wild animal for a pet but eventually learns that "wild animals are better off wild." The strength of this story lies in the readily identifiable theme, picturesque setting, and suspenseful action.

La Farge, Phyllis. *The Gumdrop Necklace,* il. by Alan E. Cober. Knopf 1967. $3.25; 7–10.

A sensitive story of an impoverished boy who, when invited to a birthday party, gives his friend a gumdrop necklace that suddenly glows and sparkles like real jewels.

Lee, Mildred. *Honor Sands.* Lothrop 1966. $3.95; 10 up.

A perceptive story of the special problems and feelings that go with being 14 in a small Florida town. By the same author: *The Rock and the Willow.*

L'Engle, Madeleine. *The Young Unicorns.* Farrar 1968. $3.75; 12 up.

A girl mysteriously blind, a teenage gang, and a reformed gang member are among those involved in a frightening war between good and evil. The scene is New York City. By the same author: *Mysterious; The Moon by Night.*

Lenski, Lois. *High-Rise Secret.* Lippincott 1966. $3.50; 6–10.

The chief characters in this story about an urban renewal project are a family of five and the people they meet on the elevator and in the automatic laundry. Modern innercity living is pictured in a book that can be read aloud to primary grades but will be of interest chiefly to middle-grade readers who can identify with the children, their games, problems, and growing pains. By the same author: *San Francisco Boy; Corn Farm Boy; Strawberry Girl* (Newbery Award, 1960); *Cotton in My Sack; Shoo-Fly Girl.* These make easy reading fare.

Lewis, Richard W. *A Summer Adventure,* il. by the author. Harper 1962. $2.95; 8–12.

A quiet adventure story of how ten-year-old Ross acquires a zoo of his own and learns about the balance of nature and the effects of captivity. Only the illustrations tell the reader that Ross is black.

Lewiton, Mina. *Candita's Choice,* il. by Howard Simon. Harper 1959. $3.50; 9–12.

A Puerto Rican girl in New York refuses to speak English until she can speak it perfectly. Her struggle to accept a new way of life should help other children to make this adjustment.

Lexau, Joan M. *Striped Ice Cream,* il. by John Wilson. Lippincott 1968. $3.25 (P—Scholastic, $.60); 7–10.

Becky, the youngest in a fatherless family of five children, is about to have a birthday and wants only chicken, spaghetti, and striped ice cream. What she actually does get for her birthday and how her three sisters, brother, and mother arrange to get them for her constitute a really fine story for the young reader. Realistic picture of the ups and downs experienced by an impoverished Negro family as they attempt to make their home life pleasant and stable.

Lindquist, Jennie D. *The Golden Name Day,* il. by Garth Williams. Harper 1955. $3.95; 9 up.

A small girl's loneliness for her mother, the warmth of the ways of her Swedish-American friends, and the small happy incidents of the summer in which she finds her name day make the book as reassuring and comfortable as Mr. Williams' pictures.

Little, Jean. *Mine for Keeps,* il. by Lewis Parker. Little 1962. $3.95; 9–12.

Sally, greatly inconvenienced by leg braces, is part of a lively family that refuses to indulge her. She begins to solve her problem of adjustment partly through the love and care she gives to her dog. This well-written story should interest all readers, handicapped or not. It is notable that the young author was born blind.

———. *Spring Begins in March.* Little 1966. $3.95; 8–10.

The story of a youngest daughter, Meg, a rebellious, stormy little girl who is failing in school and resents sharing a room with her crippled sister. Just when her mother decides to give Meg a room of her own, complications arise. Problems are solved with rare understanding and help from each one of her family and from her friend Charlotte. By the same author: *Home from Far.*

Low, Alice. *Kallie's Corner.* Pantheon 1966. $4.19; 10–14.

A well-written story on the in-group versus individuality theme. It is not easy, at the age intended for reading, to face this issue in real life so the book may ease the discomfort.

McCarthy, Agnes. *Room 10.* Doubleday 1966. $2.50 (P—Doubleday, $.75); 8–10.

Here is a brief, humorous, true-to-life story of a typical American third-grade room. It follows the school year from Halloween through Christmas to spring and field trips.

McCloskey, Robert. *Homer Price,* il. by the author. Viking 1943. $3.00 (P—Scholastic, $.75); 10–14.

A blithe and happy book. Six hilarious stories of a midwestern boy to whom anything can happen and usually does. Sequel: *Centerburg Tales.*

McCord, Jean. *Deep Where the Octopi Lie.* Atheneum 1968. $3.95; 12 up.

Each short story in this collection seems to capture the frustrations of youth with unique insight. "The Cave" is as unforgettable as any short story, and the realistic conclusion will be appreciated by teen readers. "My Teacher, the Hawk" takes a boy to task for his superior attitude toward nature.

McNeill, Janet. *Goodbye, Dove Square,* il. by Mary Russon. Little 1969. $4.50; 10–14.

A sequal to *The Battle of St. George,* this story finds the children older and removed from Dove Square to a new housing development. Although the new flats are clean, compact, and convenient, the children have a nostalgic remembrance of their old homes and neighborhood. In their adventures, they show an acceptance of people with their various eccentricities plus a sense of responsibility for their fellowman.

Maddock, Reginald. *The Pit,* il. by Douglas Hall. Little 1968. $4.75; 10 up.

Tough Butch Reece goes to the wild moors to escape the taunts of his schoolmates and the beatings of his father. What happens when Butch is accused of breaking into the school and stealing money and cookies and when the real thief gets caught in the pit on the moors makes an exciting and thought-provoking story.

Mann, Peggy. *The Street of the Flower Boxes,* il. by Peter Burchard. Coward 1966. $3.29 (P—Archway, $.60); 7–10.

A group of city children try the gardening business. They sell enough window boxes to the residents of the brownstones on New York's West 94th Street to improve the appearance as well as the human relations of this little area. A good book to have in the libraries of innercity schools.

Mannheim, Grete. *The Two Friends,* photos by the author. Knopf 1968. $3.95; 4–7.

Here is an attempt to picture realistically, and within a preschool setting, an integration situation in which there is no racial discord. If it weren't quite so long, children would not get fidgety listening to this account of Jenny's first two days of kindergarten.

Martin, Patrica Miles. *Trina's Boxcar,* il. by Robert L. Jefferson. Abingdon 1967. $3.25 (P—Scholastic, $.50); 8–10.

A simple, heart-rending story of a girl's struggle to learn to read and speak in English and to find a friend of her own. Trina and her family are recent arrivals from Mexico who live in a boxcar and travel about the United States. Action is fast moving, incidents are both sad and humorous, and reading level is low. The problems portrayed are very real.

Miles, Miska. *Hoagie's Rifle-Gun,* il. by John Schoenherr. Little 1970. $3.50; 7–10.

A hauntingly realistic tale of an Appalachian family and ten-year-old Hoagie who goes out to shoot small game to round out their meager diet. He has a frustrating afternoon but hopes for better things tomorrow.

———. *Teacher's Pet,* il. by Fen H. Lasell. Little 1966. $3.25; 6–9.

Lottie has her first experience in school when her parents settle down in one location and she enters the fifth grade. Before this her family were migrant workers, and Lottie was taught at home.

———. *Uncle Fonzo's Ford,* il. by Wendy Watson. Little 1968. $3.25; 8–12.

Humorous incidents center on an unusual relative who is the outcast. Deep down no one really objects to Uncle Fonzo's trying escapades.

Molarsky, Osman. *Song of the Empty Bottles,* il. by Tom Feelings. Walck 1968. $4.25; 6–10.

Thaddeus collects empty bottles to try to earn money for a guitar. When the task seems hopeless, Mr. Anderson helps him find another way.

Morey, Walt. *Angry Waters,* il. by Richard Cuffari. Dutton 1969. $4.90; 10 up.

Fifteen-year-old Dan, on parole after being involved in a robbery, is sent to work on a small dairy farm belonging to the Edwards family. His initial lack of interest in farm life is altered as his physical competence and sense of importance increase. His security is challenged when three escaped prisoners have Dan transport them on the flooded river to Seattle. But Dan facilitates their recapture and returns to the farm.

———. *Home Is the North,* il. by Robert Shore. Dutton 1967. $4.50; 10–14.

Brad must make a new life for himself after the death of his grandmother. This is the story of a boy becoming a man and making decisions about his life. The Alaskan setting adds appeal.

Morrow, Susan Stark. *Inatuk's Friend,* il. by Ellen Raskin. Little 1968. $3.50; 5–8.

Inatuk's family decide reluctantly to leave home for the city because there is not enough to eat. The exodus means a cruel end to the life he had loved but enables Inatuk to understand the Eskimo's positive philosophy. Reinforcing the sparse style, the splendid illustrations add power and drama by their sharp contrasts of color and form.

Moskin, Marietta D. *A Paper Dragon.* Day 1968. $4.50; 12–14.

Two sisters, separated when their parents were divorced, are reunited and must get to know each other again. Stresses and strains due to a broken home and the normal teenage conflicts as well as the conflicts between generations are depicted realistically.

————. *With an Open Hand,* il. by Ann Grifalconi. Day 1967. $4.50; 9–13.

An account of how a group of preadolescents learn to share their friendships. Each character is unique and believable, and behavior is representative of the age group. The plot is well constructed, and the story is interesting and exciting. Theme: Friendship is something you cannot force; it must be bestowed.

Muehl, Lois. *The Hidden Year of Devlin Bates,* il. by John Martinez. Holiday 1967. $3.25; 9–12.

Ten-year-old Devlin Bates, unable to communicate with his peers and his father, believes he is destined to be an individualist and nonconformist. During the course of time, however, he learns when he should be a part of the group and when he should follow his own interests.

Murphy, Barbara Beasley. *Home Free.* Delacorte 1970. $3.95; 10–12.

A taut, tense tale of violence and prejudice in South Carolina in which a white boy and a black boy, two friends, encounter the reality of each other's worlds.

Murphy, Shirley Rousseau. *The Sand Ponies,* il. by Erika Weihs. Viking 1967. $3.95; 9–12.

Orphaned, Karen and Tom are sent to live with relatives who bicker constantly. To escape this unhappy situation, they strike out on their own. With the help of the "magical" sand ponies their luck changes, and a new, happy life begins.

Neff, Priscilla Holton. *Tressa's Dream,* il. by Marcia Howe. McKay 1965. $3.75; 8–11.

Tressa proves to be an enterprising, staunch child. She gradually learns to enjoy taking care of a goat and manages to earn enough money to buy a neglected-looking Shetland pony.

Nesbit, E. *The Would-Be-Goods,* il. by Arthur Buckland and
John Hassal. Coward 1931, 1947; Dover 1965. $2.75
(P—Penguin, $.95); all ages.

Each chapter constitutes a high adventure of the six Bastable
children during the summer holidays at an uncle's house in
the country. Story line is delightfully humorous at times,
grim and suspense-filled at others. Numerous references to
British children's literature may whet the appetites of the
young American readers and motivate them to read them
too. By the same author: *Railway Children; Magic World.*

Neufeld, John. *Edgar Allan.* Phillips 1968. $3.95 (P—NAL,
$.60); 10–14.

A California Protestant minister's family adopts three-
year-old Edgar Allan. Because Edgar is black and the family
is white, there are many and varied reactions to the adop-
tion, both within the family and in the community. Stark,
terse telling of a memorable event.

Neville, Emily. *It's Like This, Cat,* il. by Emil Weiss. Harper
1963. $3.95; 10–14.

This Newbery Award winner relates the story of Dave
Mitchell and his endeavors in growing up and in accepting,
as well as understanding, life. Cat is a stray tom loved and
defended by Dave in spite of adversities. Newbery Award,
1964. By the same author: *Berries Goodman; The Seven-
teenth-Street Gang.*

Nordstrom, Ursula. *The Secret Language,* il. by Mary
Chalmers. Harper 1960. $2.95; 8–11.

The interests, emotions, and behavior of most pre-
adolescent girls in this story of life in a boarding school are
portrayed realistically and with warmth. The personalities
of the main characters are believable.

Norris, Gunilla B. *A Feast of Light,* il. by Nancy Grossman.
Knopf 1967. $3.95; 9–12.

An insightful story of the problems of moving to a new
country, learning a new language, and making new friends.
The well-written story shows that friendship begins by being
a friend.

———. *Take My Waking Slow,* il. by John Gundelfinger.
Atheneum 1970. $4.25; 12–16.

Thirteen-year-old Richie learns that life will get better only
if he himself does something about it. He learns the hard
way that he cannot depend upon his alcoholic father or his
mother, who is filled with bitterness and blind faith.

O'Connor, Patrick. *South Swell.* Washburn 1967. $3.50;
9–14.

An interesting account of how a summer spent surfing helped to bring a family closer together through understanding and accepting each other. Text contains much surfing vocabulary and acquaints the reader with the mores and lore of the sport.

O'Dell, Scott. *Journey to Jericho,* il. by Leonard Weisgard. Houghton 1969. $3.75; 8–12.

David's father, a miner, leaves Big Logs after a mine accident to find work in a California lumber camp. Later he sends for David, his mother, and sister. They take a jar of Grandma's home-made pickles with them, but David drops it in the excitement of seeing his father again. No one minds because the family is so happy to be together again.

Offit, Sidney. *The Boy Who Made a Million,* il. by Mayer Drew. St. Martin 1968. $3.95; 12–14.

Fifteen-year-old Bennie Burke nurses his father's failing grocery store into a national chain of cooperative markets.

Orgel, Doris. *Next Door to Zanadu,* il. by Dale Payson. Harper 1969. $3.95; 9–12.

Told in the first person, this story reveals Patricia's search for peer acceptance and the family relationships of herself and her friend Dorothy.

_____. *On the Sand Dune,* il. by Leonard Weisgard. Harper 1968. $3.50; 9–14.

A young girl's search for, and finding of, self-confidence among her peers on the beach.

Palmer, Candida. *A Ride on High,* il. by Tom Hall. Lippincott 1966. $2.95; 5–8.

Two boys take the elevated train to the baseball game, but one loses his token for the train home. Their solution is ingenious and will impress most young readers. Excellent portrayal of transportation in large urban cities. Easy reading; fast moving and well-constructed plot; good characterization.

Parkinson, Ethelyn. *Today I Am a Ham,* il. by Ralph J. McDonald. Abingdon 1968. $3.95 (P—Archway, $.60); 10 up.

Witty story about a boy who disappoints his father because he is unable to play football but eventually impresses his family with his skill as an amateur radio ham. Illustrations add much to the clever dialogue and humorous incidents.

Pedersen, Elsa. *House upon a Rock,* il. by Charles Shaw. Atheneum 1968. $4.50; 11–14.

An account of what happens to the people living in the small coastal community of Fidelgo, Alaska, when an earthquake and tidal wave destroy the area. Thoroughly believable characters; interesting view of Alaska today.

Perrine, Mary. *Nannabah's Friend,* il. by Leonard Weisgard. Houghton 1970. $3.75; 5–8.

About a young Navajo girl who cares for her grandmother's sheep.

Pitcher, Marie Elizabeth. *Shadow of a Crow.* Doubleday 1968. $3.50; 8–12.

Willie leads an ideal life on a small farm with his sister Jessica, her husband Bill, and his father. He is anticipating summer, when he plans to catch and tame a crow. His father's marriage brings many changes in their way of living, and Willie finds these changes hard to accept. Well written from Willie's point of view; the plot is suspenseful and interesting.

Rabin, Gil. *False Start,* il. by John Gundelfinger. Harper 1969. $3.79; 10–13.

Richard has little going for him. It is the Depression, and his family is very poor, but he does have a loving stable mother and he is a champion runner. The author lets this sensitive boy describe his own life in a setting of shady neighborhood characters, bully cops, and a dehumanizing hospital clinic. He learns to rise above hatred to pity and compassion.

Raymond, Charles. *Jud.* Houghton 1968. $3.50; 9–13.

Jud finds his family's decision to move to the country completely ludicrous. Only as a new set of standards develop between Jud's parents and the boy does he begin to see the value in country living.

———. *The Trouble with Gus,* il. by Charles Liese. Follett 1968. $3.50; 9–14.

A story that tells of big city problems in social integration and the changing codes of conduct faced today by the adolescent. An accurate picture of adolescent gangs and adolescent thoughts and fears. By the same author: *Up from Appalachia.*

Richard, Adrienne. *Pistol.* Little 1969. $4.95; 12 up.

Billy Catlin grew up in Montana during the Depression. His father went bankrupt and the family was forced to move to a dam site that was providing jobs for the unemployed. Here he grows increasingly aware of his father's limitations and his own need for independence. In the end, Billy helps his family move back home and strikes out alone for Chicago.

Richardson, Grace. *Apples Every Day.* Harper 1965. $3.50; 12 up.

The discovery of freedom is one of the motifs of this lively story about young people in a progressive boarding school.

Rinkoff, Barbara. *A Guy Can Be Wrong*, il. by Harold James. Crown 1970. $3.95; 8–12.

Carlos Martinez spends two weeks with a well-to-do suburban family during the summer. This easily read book tells of the tensions that arise between Carlos and the son of the house and their eventual acceptance of each other.

———. *Member of the Gang*, il. by Harold James. Crown 1968. $3.50; 9–13.

Allegiance to the gang is the only loyalty allowed, but Woodie Jackson slowly moves toward a better value system and learns that nothing comes easy. The urban slums loom in their effect on the characters.

Robertson, Keith. *Henry Reed's Journey*, il. by Robert McCloskey. Viking 1963. $3.50 (P—Grosset, $.60); 9–12.

The clear-eyed entrepreneur of *Henry Reed, Inc.* sees America on a cross-country trip with his friend Midge and her family and continues to expose the shortcomings of the adult world in his journal. Though somewhat less inventive than the first book, this sequel has irresistibly dry humor. Also in the series: *Henry Reed's Baby Sitting Service.*

———. *The Year of the Jeep*, il. by W. T. Mars. Viking 1968. $3.77; 9–12.

The excitement of planning and working for the realization of a great dream is explicit in this excellent book. As a secondary character Wang Ling is as real and believable as Cloud Shelby, the hero of the story.

Robinson, Joan. *Charley*, il. by Prudence Seward. Coward 1969. $4.95; 8–12.

Charley, believing herself unwanted by anyone, runs away to retain her self-respect. Her experiences are wholly believable. She emerges as one who has the grit to cope, while, at the same time, being able to use her imagination to its best advantage.

Robinson, Veronica. *David in Silence,* il. by Victor Ambrus. Lippincott 1966. $3.50; 9–12.

A moving story of a boy born deaf who is rejected from games by other boys at school. This novel has special value for helping children understand the problems of a deaf child and for helping deaf children understand how hard it is for other children to understand them.

Rodman, Bella. *Lions in the Way.* Follett 1966. $3.95
(P—Avon, $.60); 10–14.

This excellent presentation of the desegregation problem is
filled with insight into the multiplicity of reactions of any
group of people to forced change. Time moves rapidly
during the first week of integration at an all-white high
school. An exciting, dramatic presentation of civil strife and
human rights.

Ropner, Pamela. *The House of the Bittern,* il. by Kathleen M.
Williams. Coward 1965, 1967. $2.86; 10–14.

An excellent account of how a group of strong-minded
people resolve a conflict about two opposing ways of life—
"man's absolute takeover of nature for his own gain versus
the complete non-disturbance of nature." The theme of this
tragic story is that one can cherish tradition but bring to it
the new and good.

Rose, Karen. *A Single Trail.* Follett 1969. $3.50; 10–14.

An absorbing, believable story about rivalry and friendship
and trouble with a teacher in a racially mixed Los Angeles
grade school.

Rumsey, Marian. *High Country Adventure,* il. by Joseph Cellini. Morrow 1967. $3.50; 10–14.

A solid story of a young man's adventure when his plane
crashes. George grows in character as he learns survival from
the bush pilot, Sam. This well-written story is directed to the
boy adventurer.

Sachs, Marilyn. *The Bears' House,* il. by Louis Glanzman.
Doubleday 1971. $3.95; 9–13.

Nine-year-old Fran Ellen lives in two houses: one is sad and
dismal and in it live her brother, sisters, and mentally ill
mother; the other is a doll's house, but it is bright, filled with
fun and laughter, and in it live a happy, well-adjusted
family.

———. *Veronica Ganz,* il. by Louis Glanzman. Doubleday
1968. $3.50 (P—Archway, $.60); 8–12.

A humorous account of how 13-year-old tomboy Veronica
learns to think and act like a young lady.

Sargent, Shirley. *Yosemite Tomboy,* il. by Victoria de Larrea.
Abelard 1967. $3.50; 9–12.

Jan Kern is the tomboy personified. She systematically
alienates all the girls in school and then must struggle to
regain a place. A well-told story that will come close to
many girls who feel similar pressures.

Schaefer, Jack. *Mavericks*, il. by Lorence Bjorklund. Houghton 1967. $3.50; 12 up.

Clever use of flashbacks to tell one man's life story and his role in preventing the disappearance of the mustangs. Excellent characterization and effective use of descriptive detail strengthen the work. By the same author: *Shane.*

Shearer, John. *I Wish I Had an Afro*, il. by the author. Cowles 1970. $3.95; 8–12.

A starkly realistic account of 11-year-old John's family, his acquaintances, his in and out of school experiences, and his hopes—all told in the first person. This powerful account of black poverty will be illuminating to middle-class white readers.

Shields, Rita. *Chris Muldoon*, il. by Ray Abel. McKay 1965. $3.75; 9–12.

This is a convincing, sometimes humorous, sometimes pathos-filled account of the involvements of forgetful and impulsive Chris Muldoon, future astronaut but currently amateur detective, star basketball player, dramatist, and talented science student.

Shortall, Leonard. *Eric in Alaska*. Morrow 1967. $3.25; 6–9.

The Alaskan salmon fisherman and his work are woven into a story line about a young boy, Eric Olson, who longs to be a fisherman like his father. The plot concerns the problems Eric has in becoming grown up enough to go with his father on a fishing trip.

Shotwell, Louisa R. *Adam Bookout*, il. by W. T. Mars. Viking 1968. $3.95; 9–12.

Adam finds a new life in New York quite different from his former home in Oklahoma. The new relationships are explored with a sincerity that will sit well with children.

―――――. *Roosevelt Grady*, il. by Peter Burchard. World 1963. $2.95 (P—Scholastic, $.60); 9–12.

Roosevelt, the son of a migrant worker, longs for the time that his family can remain in one spot. "Providence" seems nearer when they have the chance to settle during the winter. Highly recommended.

Shura, Mary Francis. *Runaway Home*, il. by James Spanfeller. Knopf 1965. $3.25; 8–12.

Eleven-year-old Mike has much difficulty adjusting when his family is forced to move to Colorado from Kansas, but all ends well for him. The behavior of each character and most of the situations are realistic enough to permit the reader's emotional identification.

Smith, Emma. *Out of Hand,* il. by Anthony Maitland. Harcourt
1963. $3.95; 7–10.

Four children come to spend the summer with happy-
go-lucky cousin Polly in an old Welsh farmhouse. When
cousin Polly breaks her leg, two maiden cousins arrive to
care for them and everything is changed. Lively summer
adventure with excellent characterization of both children
and adults. By the same author: *Emily's Voyage.*

Snyder, Zilpha Keatley. *The Egypt Game,* il. by Alton Raible.
Atheneum 1967. $3.95; 8–12.

In an abandoned storage yard a group of sixth-graders engage
in complicated and lengthy dramatizations of various aspects of ancient Egypt. Intense excitement builds when a
murderer roams the neighborhood and an oracle's predic-
tions come true.

_____. *The Velvet Room,* il. by Alton Raible. Atheneum
1965. $3.95 (P—Scholastic, $.75); 9–12.

Beset by the problems of growing up in a migrant worker's
family, Robin finds refuge from the real world in a deserted
mansion with a book-lined room and a mysterious past.
Although melodramatic, this is a valid story of a girl's
discovery of where she belongs. By the same author: *Eyes in
the Fishbowl; Season of Ponies; Black and Blue Magic.*

Sonneborn, Ruth A. *Friday Night Is Papa Night,* il. by Emily A.
McCully. Viking 1970. $2.95; 5–8.

About a Puerto Rican family whose father holds two jobs
and can only be home on Friday nights. The solidarity of
family life and the love that holds them together is warmly
portrayed without being sentimental, and the book pleads
no special case.

Sorensen, Virginia. *Lotte's Locket,* il. by F. Rocker. Harcourt
1964. $3.50; 9–12.

A compassionate story of Lotte, a charming little Danish girl
whose mother is marrying an American. A deep understanding of a Danish child's heritage makes the picture of a Danish
family's life and ways warm and authentic. Understanding
of place and human loyalties combine to make this a
significant book.

_____. *Miracles on Maple Hill,* il. by Beth and Joe Krush.
Harcourt 1956. $3.50; 9–12.

A family story emphasizing the miracles of nature around
the year in maple sugar country, as well as the miracles that
love performs in the hearts of people. Newbery Award, 1957.
By the same author: *Plain Girl.*

Southall, Ivan. *Let the Balloon Go,* il. by Ian Ribbons. St. Martin 1969. $3.95; 10–13.

A boy imagines games of confrontation that are dripping with danger, with himself the brilliant and successful James Bond. He wonders why his mother thinks he has to stay a baby till he is an old man. The author's meshing of inner and outer worlds is impressive, especially when the reader learns that John has cerebral palsy.

Speevack, Yetta. *The Spider Plant,* il. by Wendy Watson. Atheneum 1965. $3.25; 9–12.

Adjusting to New York comes hard to the Santos, a Puerto Rican family trying to contend with a treeless environment, dark apartments, slum clearance, and suspicious police. How a spider plant entangles Carmen with the law, yet helps resolve some of her unhappiness, makes a wryly amusing story.

Sterling, Dorothy. *Mary Jane,* il. by Ernest Crichlow. Doubleday 1959. $3.95 (P—Scholastic, $.75); 10–14.

Mary Jane, the first Negro in her school, discovers along with her schoolmates that to win the respect and friendship of her group is not all there is to integration. The story will be timely for a long while. By the same author: *Forever Free; Freedom Train; Cub Scout Mystery.*

Stolz, Mary. *The Bully of Barkham Street,* il. by Leonard Shortall. Harper 1968. $3.50 (P—Dell, $.75); 8–12.

Insights into a troubled young boy make this another outstanding book by Mary Stolz. Martin's problems become a focal point in this beautiful example of character development.

———. *A Dog on Barkham Street,* il. by Leonard Shortall. Harper 1960. $3.50 (P—Dell, $.75); 8–11.

Edward solves two problems—how to get a dog and how to end the bullying of the boy next door. A good story showing a ten-year-old gaining responsibility and understanding.

———. *The Dragons of the Queen,* il. by Edward Francino. Harper 1969. $3.27; 9–12.

Two middle-aged travelers from the United States are abruptly marooned in Mexico and learn about dignity from a memorable old lady.

———. *A Wonderful Terrible Time,* il. by Louis S. Glanzman. Harper 1967. $4.50 (P—Scholastic, $.75); 9–11.

Mady develops independence when she and her friend go to summer camp. A good picture of middle-class Negro life. By the same author: *The Noon Day Friends.*

Swarthout, Glendon and Kathryn. *Whichaway,* il. by Richard M. Powers. Random 1966. $3.25; 10 up.

The survival of a young cowboy depends on his ability to help himself. A very good story.

Taylor, Theodore. *The Cay.* Doubleday 1969. $3.50; 8–14.

A World War II version of *Robinson Crusoe.* The hero is an old black deckhand who survives on a raft together with a 12-year-old boy passenger after their ship is torpedoed. The boy becomes blind and totally dependent on the old man for survival on the desert island where they land.

Thompson, Wilma. *That Barbara!* il. by Barbara Seuling. Delacorte 1969. $3.95; 11 up.

Set in Tumpelo, Oregon, during the 1920's. A series of impulsive and hysterical misadventures characterize Barbara's attempts to meet the growing-up process head-on. Excellent mood sketches depict her many problems.

Thomson, Peter. *Cougar,* il. by Brendan Lynch. Follett 1968. $3.50; 10–13.

An interesting portrayal of a rancher's life. Realistic presentation of problems that occur when a couple, each of whom have a son by a previous marriage, decide to marry. Life in the wilds of the mountains emphasizes the conservationists' point of view and the theory of "nature's balance."

Turnbull, Agnes Sligh. *The White Lark,* il. by Nathan Goldstein. Houghton 1968. $3.25; 8–12.

Suzy finds someone to share a difficult time in life with the crippled Mr. Prettyford. This is a good set of short stories with an interesting method of presentation.

Turner, Gerry. *Hide-Out for a Horse,* il. by Kiyoaki Kamoda. Doubleday 1967. $2.95; 6–10.

An urban child keeps a horse in a hideout on the roof of an apartment house until danger passes.

Vroman, Mary Elizabeth. *Harlem Summer,* il. by J. Martinez. Putnam 1967. $3.49 (P—Berkley, $.60); 12 up.

There is much excitement when John comes north from Alabama to spend the summer in Harlem.

Ward, Philip. *Tony's Steamer,* il by James Armstrong. Little 1968. $4.25; 8–12.

Tony finds an abandoned steamer, explores it, and makes it his "secret place." Eventually three boys invade his private world and slowly wreck the steamer. A fire breaks out on the steamer, and all the boys work together to put it out. Good portrayal of boys from mixed races learning to work and play together.

Warren, Mary Phraner. *Walk in My Moccasins,* il. by Victor Mays. Westminster 1966. $3.50; 9–12.

In modern times, five orphaned Sioux Indian children are adopted by a Montana schoolteacher and his wife. The story not only describes the struggle for acceptance by the Indian children but also shows the basic need for acceptance in mankind.

Webster, Jean. *Daddy-Long-Legs,* il. by Edward Ardizzone. Meredith 1966. $3.95 (P—Grosset, $.60); 11–14.

The revival of this story should find wide acceptance among young girls. Written in the form of letters, characters are developed that draw together a story line based on the growing maturity of Judy.

Wersba, Barbara. *The Dream Watcher.* Atheneum 1968. $3.95; 12–16.

An account of the friendship between teenage Albert, who is at odds with himself, and Mrs. Orpha Woodfin, an old lady who imagines herself a grande dame of life and letters. The book is truly effective study of how one person finds freedom, joy, and *himself.*

West, Wallace. *The Amazing Inventor From Laurel Creek,* il. by David Hodges. Putnam 1967. $3.29; 12–14.

A somewhat fantastic story of an "All-American" boy who can do anything. The book can be enjoyable for hero-worshippers.

Wier, Esther. *The Loner,* il. by Christine Price. McKay 1963. $3.75 (P—Scholastic, $.50); 11–15.

The boy names himself David after Boss takes him into her care. On the sheep range with other people, he has a struggle finding his own identity and, at the same time, developing his social skills.

———. *The Winners,* il. by Ursula Koering. McKay 1968. $3.95; 11–15.

An exciting but somewhat contrived tale of what happens to Scrub Nolan when his father sends him to his aunt's in Florida with two greedy migrant brothers. He ends up in the heart of the Everglades with an Indian boy, the owner of a houseboat, and a pet otter. Convincing and graphic descriptions of the creatures of the swampland and the problem of poachers who illegally slaughter the wildlife. By the same author: *The Barrel; The Wind Chasers.*

Witheridge, Elizabeth. *Dead End Bluff.* Atheneum 1966. $3.95; 9–12.

Guig, 13 and blind from birth, proves his capability to himself and his over-protective father one wild summer.

Historical: United States

Adams, Samuel Hopkins. *Chingo Smith of the Erie Canal,* il. by Leonard Vosburgh. Random 1958. $3.74; 11–14.

Orphan waif Chingo Smith's rise from odd jobs to captain of a canal boat during the building of "Clinton's ditch" provides the reader with the thrill of true achievement.

Alcott, Louisa May. *Little Women,* il. by Barbara Cooney. Crowell 1955, 1965. $5.00 (many paperback editions); 10–16.

Still a cherished story of the March sisters' lives. Strong characterizations make it worthy of the label "classic." *Little Men* will be enjoyed after reading this story.

Allen, Lorenzo. *Fifer for the Union,* il. by Brian Wildsmith. Morrow 1964. $3.95; 9–12.

While 12-year-old Len experiences the grim facts of army life, he also realizes that the home problems he has run away from were of his own making. Here is an excellent characterization combined with high adventure.

Anderson, Lonzo. *Zeb,* il. by Peter Burchard. Knopf 1966. $3.84; 9–14.

An exciting story of a young boy who survives a winter in colonial America of the 1680's after his father and older brother are drowned while attempting to cross the flooded Delaware River. Left with only his dog, an axe, and his knowledge of outdoor life, he lives until help arrives.

Arntson, Herbert E. *River Boy,* il. by William Ferguson. Washburn 1969. $3.95; 10–14.

Gramps the river ferryboatman dreamed and planned for a bridge across the river. It was 1846 in the Oregon Territory, and when Gramps died his job and dream were taken over by his 14-year-old grandson Dan. Dan and his friend Pete are resourceful boys who meet obstacles and setbacks with courage. Readers will enjoy the adventure as well as increase their understanding of frontier life.

Bacmeister, Rhoda. *Voices in the Night,* il. by Ann Grifalconi. Bobbs 1965. $3.50; 9–12.

Jeanie is forced to live with a neighboring family when her widowed mother is no longer able to keep her family together. She hears strange voices in the night and finds that the home she is sharing is a station for the Underground Railway. Authentic details of the Civil War period.

Baker, Betty. *Killer-of-Death,* il. by John Kaufmann. Harper
1963. $3.95; 10–14.
The white man's destruction of the Indians' way of life is
vividly described in this story of the Apaches. When the
remnants of the tribe are moved to a reservation and Killer-
of-Death sends his son to the white man's school, it is in the
hope of peace and renewal.

Ballard, Martin. *Benjie's Portion.* World 1969. $4.25; 11–15.
After the Revolutionary War, the English rewarded slaves
who enlisted with them with their freedom and unworkable
land in Nova Scotia. The ex-slaves facing enormous problems became destitute, and many joined other ex-slaves to
settle the newly found colony of Sierra Leone, West Africa.
Benjie was an orphan boy involved in this return to Africa.
The story is based on contemporary documents and ably
conveys the hardship, endurance, and injustices of the
times.

Beatty, Patricia. *The Queen's Own Grove.* Morrow 1966.
$3.95; 9–12.
An English family experiences fun and action in early
California.

Beyer, Audrey White. *Dark Venture,* il. by Leo and Diane
Dillon. Knopf 1968. $4.50; 11–14.
This book will give black children a better understanding of
their African roots and white children a better conception of
man's inhumanity to man. The first part tells of a young
Fulani of West Africa, Demba. The boy is captured by agents
of a black merchant and is destined to be sold as a slave to
American sea traders. The other two-thirds of the book is
written from the vantage point of a New England physician;
it records the voyage of the slave ship across the Atlantic and
adjustment to life in Rhode Island.

Bonham, Barbara. *Crisis at Fort Laramie.* Meredith 1967.
$3.95; 9–12.
An account of how 13-year-old Matt Bailey helps to avert an
Indian attack on Fort Laramie in 1854. The whites are saved
from almost certain massacre through the friendship of Matt
with an Indian boy his own age.

Brink, Carol Ryrie. *Caddie Woodlawn,* il. by Kate Seredy.
Macmillan 1935. $4.95 (many paperback editions); 10–12.
Caddie was a lively tomboy who wanted to do everything
her brothers did in pioneer Wisconsin of the 1860's. An
outstanding story of family life and relationships. Newbery
Award, 1936. Sequel: *Magical Melons.*

_____. *Two Are Better Than One,* il. by Fermin Rocker. Macmillan 1968. $4.95; 9–11.

Chrystal and Cordelia, two inseparable friends, share many experiences as they pass a delightful year from childhood, with their attachment to dolls, through the trials and tribulations of growing up. The story is set in a small town during the early 1900's.

Buff, Mary and Conrad. *Hah-Nee of the Cliff Dwellers.* Houghton 1956. $3.57; 10–14.

In the Southwest before the coming of the white man. Hah-Nee realizes that he does not look like the other members of his tribe. Their eventual vengeance drives him and his family away to settle near the Rio Grande River.

Bulla, Clyde Robert. *John Billington, Friend of Squanto,* il. by Peter Burchard. Crowell 1956. $3.50; 8–11.

A boy's exciting experiences while on the *Mayflower* sailing to America and during the first year of life in the Plymouth settlement. Though written simply, the book gives a rich background for understanding life as it was lived by our courageous forefathers. By the same author: *The Sword in the Tree; Viking Adventure; Squanto.*

Burch, Robert. *Queenie Peavy,* il. by Jerry Lazare. Viking 1966. $3.50; 10–14.

An engaging account of an eighth-grade Georgia girl of the 1930's who has to endure the jibes of her schoolmates about her father, who is in prison. She learns that she alone is responsible for her life.

_____. *Tyler, Wilkin and Skee,* il. by Don Sibley. Viking 1963. $3.00; 8–12.

Three boys growing up on a Georgia farm have plenty of fun and a warm family life despite the Depression. The story has clever characterization and a pervasive dry humor. By the same author: *Skinny; D. J.'s Worst Enemy; Renfroe's Christmas.*

Burchard, Peter. *Jed,* il. by the author. Coward 1960. $3.00; 9–12.

Jed sees cruelty and kindness displayed by soldiers of both armies during the Civil War.

_____. *Stranded: A Story of New York in 1875.* Coward 1967. $4.50; 10–14.

A young Scottish ship's boy is stranded in New York when he misses the sailing time. His encounters with political bosses, street gangs, and the rawness of life in New York are told in stark terms. Some insight into the lower classes' apathy about improving their own surroundings is included.

Burt, Olive. *Jayhawker Johnny,* il. by Albert Orbaan. Day 1966. $3.49; 9–12.

In the days of the California gold rush Reverend James Brier and his family are among a group headed west. Encamped close to the Mormons at the Great Salt Lake, the family meets other wagoners and plans to travel with them. A disagreement causes the Brier family to continue alone. Based on the lives of real people; a convincing portrayal of the hardships of the journey.

Camp, Paul K. *Shanty-Boat Bill,* il. by James MacDonald. McKay 1967. $4.25; 10–14.

The story is set in the difficult and challenging time of the Depression and shows well how people handled the hardships caused by the economic depression and the flooding Mississippi River. Good characterization.

Campbell, Elizabeth A. *The Carving on the Tree,* il. by William Bock. Little 1968. $3.75; 8–11.

An exciting account of the brief life of the lost colony of Roanoke. The story offers vivid portraits of men such as Governor John White, who tried to get expeditions organized to save the small colony, and Simon Fernando, the captain who left the colonists on Roanoke Island against their own wishes.

Carleton, Barbee Oliver. *The Witches' Bridge.* Holt 1967. $3.95; 11–14.

A young boy sets out to put an end to a family curse in an exciting mystery involving secret passages, New England witchcraft, and a large black dog.

Caudill, Rebecca. *Tree of Freedom,* il. by Dorothy Morse. Viking 1949. $3.50; 10–12.

During the Revolutionary War period, Stephanie moves to the wilderness of Kentucky with her family. Each child is allowed to take one prized possession, which for Stephanie is an apple seed. This becomes her "tree of freedom" as she nurtures it through the difficult war years. By the same author: *The Far-off Land; A Certain Small Shepherd.*

Ceder, Georgiana Dorcas. *Little Thunder,* il. by Robert L. Jefferson. Abingdon 1966. $3.00; 8–12.

An Indian boy struggles with feelings of inadequacy about himself because he is not tall and strong. During the War of 1812, Cricket earns the name Little Thunder. This authentic picture of the lives of Indians gradually forced from their lands tells the reader that greater understanding can be achieved through words than through wars.

Chickering, Marjorie. *Yankee Trader: Ben Tanner-1779.* Funk & Wagnalls 1966. $3.50; 12–16.

Sixteen-year-old Ben Tanner wants to travel, but he has little hope of going far from St. Johnsbury, Vermont, during 1799. Luther Chickering is driving cattle to markets far away and needs help. A series of events allows Ben to go with Luther, but the real test of his courage occurs after the trip is over.

Christgau, Alice E. *The Laugh Peddler,* il. by Arvis L. Stewart. Scott 1968. $3.95; 10–13.

Set on a Minnesota farm in the early 1900's, this is the story of a young orphaned city boy who must move to the farm of relatives. The twice-yearly visits of Yusef the peddler become bright spots for Sidney. Yusef is unjustly charged with a crime, and Sidney sets out to prove his friend not guilty. In so doing he "proves himself" and becomes a real member of the family at last. Though listed as readable for 10- to 13-year-olds, the story line will appeal more to younger children (8 to 10) in a teacher-reading-to-the-class situation, and probably nonurban children. The illustrations do not add a great deal.

Clapp, Patricia. *Constance: A Story of Early Plymouth.* Lothrop 1968. $4.50; 12 up.

Plymouth Colony as seen through the eyes of a girl from England. The colonists are flesh-and-blood people.

Clarke, Mary Stetson. *The Iron Peacock,* il. by Robert MacLean. Viking 1966. $3.95; 11–16.

A girl in her middle teens adapts to the life of a bondservant in 17th century New England. A well-balanced view of the religious and social life of the time, which presented both difficulty and opportunity for a girl of character.

————. *The Limner's Daughter.* Viking 1967. $3.95; 11 up.

An enterprising young girl finds her long-lost relatives, her ancestral family home, and a suitor in 19th century New England.

Clarke, Tom E. *The Big Road.* Lothrop 1963. $3.95; 12 up.

The author's own recollections lend authenticity to this account of a boy's experiences as a hobo during the Depression.

Cleary, Beverly. *Emily's Runaway Imagination,* il. by Beth and Joe Krush. Morrow 1961. $3.75; 8–11.

A departure from the author's "Henry" stories, this is about small town life in Oregon in the 1920's and Emily's efforts to get a library for her town.

Coatsworth, Elizabeth. *American Adventures 1620–1945,* il. by Robert Frankenberg. Macmillan 1968. $5.50; 7–10.

A collection of seven short novels about important periods in American history, each followed by an afterword identifying the factual and fictional elements. By the same author: *Sword in the Wilderness; Bess and the Sphinx; The Sod House.*

Colver, Anne. *Bread and Butter Indian,* il. by Garth Williams. Holt 1964. $2.95; 7–10.

Barbara Baum is given a treat of bread and butter when she is good. One day when she takes her treat to a favorite secret place, she shares it with a friendly Indian. Their friendship proves to be valuable.

———. *Bread-and-Butter Journey,* il. by Garth Williams. Holt 1970. $3.59; 6–10.

A sequel to *Bread-and-Butter Indian,* this simple story tells of a journey made by two pioneering families into western Pennsylvania in 1784. They encounter danger and sickness, form friendships, and struggle to find a new life and happiness.

Constiner, Merle. *The Rebel Courier and the Redcoats.* Meredith 1968. $3.95; 9–12.

A 16-year-old student is charged with the responsibility of carrying an important message from Washington to General Gates. The story tells of his escapes from near-capture while he is delivering the message; the climax is the defeat of the British at the battle of King's Mountain.

Dahl, Mary. *Free Souls.* Houghton 1969. $3.50; 10–14.

A fictionalized account of the *Amistad* case, focusing on Antonio, a 12-year-old boy aboard that ship. Forty-three illegally enslaved Africans mutiny aboard the *Amistad* in 1840, take control of the ship, and sail for Africa. Because of treacherous navigation by a captive crew member, the ship lands in North America. The mutineers are imprisoned but eventually are released and permitted to settle in Sierra Leone.

Dalgliesh, Alice. *Adam and the Golden Cock,* il. by Leonard Weisgard. Scribner 1959. $3.12; 8–11.

Adam, a young Connecticut boy, experiences the making of history when General Rochambeau's troops spend several days in the boy's home town while on their way to join General Washington in July 1780. The illustrations greatly enhance the text.

———. *The Bears on Hemlock Mountain,* il. by Helen Sewell. Scribner 1952. $3.95; 7–9.

Jonathan has to return home from Aunt Emma's house over Hemlock Mountain after dark. What people suspect of the bears on the mountain and what Jonathan experiences combine to make an exciting story.

———. *The Courage of Sarah Noble.* Scribner 1954. $2.75; 6–10.

The arbitrary meaning of courage is given a sharp, definitive interpretation through this experience of an eight-year-old girl. Colonial times, Indians, and Sarah's great desire to help her father make this an exciting adventure.

Davis, Russell G., and Brent K. Ashabranner. *The Choctaw Code.* McGraw 1961. $3.00; 10–14.

Tom Baxter, newly arrived in Oklahoma territory, makes a friend of an Indian already condemned by his Choctaw code to die. Tom learns to understand and love the region and its forests and animals through this friendship.

Edmonds, Walter. *The Matchlock Gun,* il. by Paul Lantz. Dodd 1941. $3.50; 10–12.

Based on a true incident, the story tells of the courage of young Edward, a colonial boy, and his mother who defend their home against Indian attack. Newbery Award, 1942. By the same author: *Two Logs Crossing; John Haskell's Story.*

Fall, Thomas. *Canalboat to Freedom,* il. by Joseph Cellini. Dial 1966. $3.95 (P—Dell, $.95); 10–14.

In 1840 Ben is identured to Captain Roach and works as a towpath driver for a canalboat. He becomes involved in the Underground Railroad as he develops an understanding of the horrors of slavery.

———. *Goat Boy of Brooklyn,* il. by Fermin Rocker. Dial 1968. $3.95; 10–14.

A lively and interesting story about a 13-year-old boy who lives in Brooklyn in the early 1800's. The story is chiefly concerned with his heroism in helping his father obtain a release from debtors' prison. Interesting, too, is the fine characterization of the boy's tag-along sister.

Faulkner, Nancy. *Tomahawk Shadow.* Doubleday 1959. $3.95; 12–16.

An exciting story of a teenage apprentice who in 1675 leaves a cruel master at Plymouth and finds kinder treatment at Providence under the leadership of Roger Williams. He becomes deeply involved in King Philip's War and befriends Narragansett Indians, who helped him find his way to Providence. By the same author: *The Yellow Hat.*

Field, Rachel. *Calico Bush,* il. by Allen Lewis. Macmillan 1931, 1946, 1966. $4.50; 10–14.

In 1743 Marguerite Ledoux travels to the state of Maine with a family to whom she is bound out. Troubles plague the family in Indian country. Marguerite's resourcefulness and devotion earn her freedom, but she refuses to leave her beloved family. Newbery Award, 1930. By the same author: *Hitty, Her First Hundred Years.*

Fisher, Aileen. *The Lantern in the Window,* il. by Harper Johnson. Hale 1957. $2.95; 7–10.

Involvement in the Underground Railroad adds intrigue to this well-told story. By the same author: *My Cousin Abe.*

Fisher, Laura. *Never Try Nathaniel.* Holt 1962. $4.50; 9–13.

Realistic portrayal of farm life and rural living set in the hills of Idaho at the turn of the century. Twelve-year-old Than, youngest of a family of four, learns to cope with challenges and responsibilities.

Fleischman, Sid. *By the Great Horn Spoon,* il. by Eric von Schmidt. Little 1963. $4.50; 9–12.

The lively and frequently funny adventures of young Jack Flagg and his Aunt Arabella's enormously resourceful butler, Praiseworthy, as they head for the California gold fields via Cape Horn will appeal to readers with a taste for the satirical and for the tall tale.

_____. *Chancy and the Grand Rascal,* il. by Eric von Schmidt. Little 1966. $4.50; 8–12.

Orphaned Chancy searches for his sisters and brother. The successful trip from Ohio to Kansas includes several harrowing experiences. Uncle Will and Colonel Plugg add to the adventures. By the same author: *Ghost in the Noonday Sun; Mister Mysterious and Company.*

Flory, Jane. *Faraway Dream,* il. by the author. Houghton 1968. $3.50; 9–11.

Boys and girls will enjoy this fast moving story of redheaded, hot-tempered Maggie Mulligan, a seaman's orphan living in colonial Philadelphia, whose escapades help to make her dreams come true.

Folsom, Franklin. *Beyond the Frontier.* Harvey 1968. $3.50; 12–16.

Exciting story based on the real life experience of Horatio Jones, an 18-year-old Pennsylvania boy who was captured and adopted by the Seneca Indians during the Revolutionary War. Detailed descriptions of Indian customs are included.

Forbes, Esther. *Johnny Tremain,* il. by Lynd Ward. Houghton 1943. $3.95 (P—Dell, $.75); 12–16.

A Boston apprentice becomes deeply involved in the political events leading to the opening battles of the Revolutionary War. A talented, proud boy, he learns the price of pride when another apprentice causes an accident which nearly ends his career as a silversmith. Newbery Award, 1944.

Forman, James. *So Ends This Day.* Farrar 1970. $4.50; 12–16.

A young man witnesses the ruination of his father and comes to grips with himself as a human being during an exciting three-year voyage on a whaling ship during the pre-Civil War days when the "black gold" market was at its peak.

Franchere, Ruth. *Stampede North.* Macmillan 1969. $4.95; 10–14.

Absorbing account of the experience of a 14-year-old boy who goes on the Klondike gold rush of 1897. Bent only on finding gold, he learns—after many hardships—to understand his father's love of photography and fair dealing.

Frazier, Neta Lohnes. *The General's Boots,* il. by Stephen J. Voorhies. McKay 1965. $3.95; 10–14.

In the state of Washington, a young boy and his father plant young apple trees that the father never sees produce their first fruit. The family carries out the father's dreams after he is no longer with them to help. Life on the far western frontier is realistically revealed through the struggles and hardships that the family endures during the gold rush days.

Fritz, Jean. *Brady,* il. by Lynd Ward. Coward 1960. $4.25; 10–14.

Brady struggles to accept the responsibilities of growing up in the Civil War period. When he discovers a slave hidden in his father's church, he overcomes the desire to talk too much. Realizing that his father is helping in the Underground Railroad, Brady shows his true mettle.

_____. *The Cabin Faced West,* il. by Feodor Rojankovsky. Coward 1958. $3.50; 8–12.

Ten-year-old Ann is lonely in her new cabin home in pioneer country "across the Allegheny Mountains" from her birthplace in Gettysburg. In this wilderness, there are "only boys and babies" for companions. This story of how Ann overcomes her aversion for "the West" and its way of life is told with charm, insight into a child's life, and ever-mounting interest.

_____. *Early Thunder,* il. by Lynd Ward. Coward 1967.
$4.95; 12–14.

A boy of Revolutionary times faces difficult decisions about
his primary loyalties to ideals and family. By the same
author: *I, Adam.*

Gates, Doris. *The Elderberry Bush,* il. by L. Obligado. Viking
1967. $3.50; 6–10.

A fond look at two young girls' life in the turn-of-the-century
California. By the same author: *Sensible Kate.*

Hall, Anna Gertrude. *Cyrus Holt and the Civil War,* il. by
Dorothy Bayley Morse. Viking 1964. $2.96; 10–14.

Cyrus and his friends in upstate New York feel the impact of
the Civil War even though they are far from the scenes of
battle. The hardships as well as the excitement of war are
made real in this graphic account, which is based on events
that occurred during the boyhood of the author's father.

Hall, Elvajean. *Pilgrim Neighbors,* il. by Jon Nielsen. Rand
1964. $2.95; 9–12.

A collection of stories about the Pilgrims and their Indian
neighbors. Based on careful research, the collection of
stories gives an intimate view of life between 1621 and 1676.
An index and bibliography add depth.

Haugaard, Erik. *Orphans of the Wind,* il. by Milton Johnson.
Houghton 1966. $3.50 (P—Dell, $.75); 10–14.

The story of the Civil War is told from the viewpoint of
members of an English crew when they discover their ship is
a blockade runner. Divided in their feelings about slavery,
four attempt to join the Union Army. Haugaard's poetic
language and sensitive telling make it an outstanding book.
By the same author: *The Little Fishes.*

Holberg, Ruth Langland. *The Girl in the Witch House,* il. by
Lloyd Coe. Hastings 1966. $3.75; 11–14.

Sensitively told account of the life of ten-year-old Jennifer
Rowe, who lives through the first months of the Revolutionary War in a New England village where some of the
neighbors call her family home "The Witch House."
Through her friendliness and good sense, she overcomes
their prejudice.

Holling, Holling C. *Paddle-to-the-Sea,* il. by the author.
Houghton 1941. $4.50; 10–12.

Drama and beauty characterize this book about an Indian
boy's toy canoe, which sails thousands of miles through the
Great Lakes and the St. Lawrence River to the open sea. The
story conveys a feeling for the vastness and varied occupa-

tions of America. Beautifully illustrated in color. By the
same author: *Tree in the Trail; Seabird.*

Hunt, Irene. *Across Five Aprils,* il. by Albert John Pucci.
Follett 1964. $3.95 (P—Grosset, $.60); 10–14.

A Civil War story about a family in southern Illinois. One
son chooses to fight with the Confederacy; two others choose
the Union. As a result, the war brings great tragedy to the
family, and the youngest son must shoulder a man's responsibility.

Ish-Kishor, Sulamith. *Our Eddie.* Patheon 1969. $4.50; 12
up.

A complex story of a Jewish family and the intense emotions
that bind them together despite the apparent indifference of
the father. Set in the early years of this century and involving migration to New York from England.

Jewett, Sarah Orne. *The Country of the Pointed Firs and Other
Stories,* selected by Mary Ellen Chase, il. by Shirley Burke.
Norton 1968. $6.50; 12 up.

A handsomely illustrated new edition of an American
classic containing five stories. Mary Ellen Chase's introduction helps older children to appreciate the stories and
provides background information. A major work, *The Country of the Pointed Firs,* remains a significant piece of fiction
because of its sensitive descriptions of life on the Maine
coast in the 19th century and its insightful comments about
the people who lived there. By the same author: *The White
Heron.*

Johnson, Annabel and Edgar. *Torrie.* Harper 1960. $3.95;
10–14.

Fourteen-year-old Torrie Anders cannot understand why
her parents would leave Saint Louis to join a California
wagon train. The westward movement is seen through the
eyes of one girl. By the same authors: *The Bearcat; A Golden
Touch; Wilderness Bride.*

Johnston, Norma. *The Bridge Between.* Funk & Wagnalls
1966. $3.95; 12–16.

Portrayal of a girl's difficulties in helping her family endure
the trials of the first year of the Revolutionary War in the
"neutral ground" of New Jersey. The story shows the divided loyalties of family members and friends and her
resourcefulness in taking the place of her mentally ill
mother.

Jones, Weyman. *Edge of Two Worlds,* il. by J. C. Kocsis. Dial
1968. $3.95 (P—Dell, $.75); 10–14.

Calvin Harper is headed east with a wagon train when it is
attacked by Comanche Indians. He escapes and attempts to
find his way home. When an elderly Cherokee tries to help
him, Calvin mistrusts him and begins to betray his kindness.
The Cherokee is well-educated and has truly lived at the
edge of two worlds.

Keith, Harold. *Komanticia.* Crowell 1965. $4.50; 12 up.

A young Spanish aristocrat develops living habits similar to
those of the Comanche, the captors from whom he initially
attempts to escape.

————. *Rifles for Watie.* Crowell 1957. $4.50; 10–15.

Young Jeff Bussey volunteers for service in the Union Army
in 1861. During his service he sees inhumanity and injustice
perpetrated by Confederate and Union armies alike. Jeff
discovers that the causes of the Civil War and the people
who fought in it were the result of a complex mixture of
good and evil.

Kendall, Lace. *Rain Boat,* il. by John Kaufman. Coward 1965.
$3.75; 8–12.

A Florida flood, when the country was still a British outpost,
provides the setting for this story of Shem, who believes
himself to be another Noah. Three stranded children are
picked up by the Rain Boat and help care for the pairs of
animals that Shem has rescued from the flood.

Kroeber, Theodora. *Ishi, Last of His Tribe,* il. by Ruth Robbins.
Parnassus 1964. $4.25; 8–12.

Ishi and six other Yahi Indians conceal themselves to escape
death at the hands of gold-seeking intruders in the mountains of California. These remaining Yahi maintain their
tradition of festivals and customs. The author uses Yahi
words and authentic information about the Yahi.

Latham, Jean Lee. *This Dear-bought Land,* il. by Jacob Landau.
Harper 1957. $3.95; 10–14.

Authentic details of the early settling of the Jamestown
colony. The story of Captain John Smith and the struggles of
the colonists is told from the viewpoint of young David
Warren. By the same author: *Carry On, Mr. Bowditch.*

Lawrence, Isabelle. *Drumbeats in Williamsburg,* il. by Manning de V. Lee. Rand 1965. $4.50; 10–12.

Andy struggles with fear as he attempts to serve his country
as a drummer during the Revolutionary War. Glimpses of the
feelings of soldiers on both sides of the war are given as well
as insights on some of the famed military leaders of the time.

Lazarus, Keo Felker. *Rattlesnake Run,* il. by Ken Nisson. Follett 1968. $3.50; 10–14.

Set in the 1920's, this is an exciting, suspense-filled account of the experiences of 13-year-old Adam when he takes over a mail station in the Texas brush country. Thoroughly convincing characters, fast action, realistic situations, and good balance between dialogue and descriptive detail.

Levy, Harry. *Not Over Ten Inches High,* il. by Nancy Grossman. McGraw 1968. $3.95; 7–9.

Very good story set in early Boston. Crispus Plunkett, a young chimney sweep, finds a stray dog who becomes his constant companion. Things are rocky for the two friends as family and city attempt to split them up.

McGraw, Eloise. *Moccasin Trail,* il. by Paul Galdone. Coward 1952. $4.50; 10–14.

A young boy is torn between the ways of his own family and those of the Indians who raised him. His return to his family and his adjustment to life with them make a compelling tale.

Meader, Stephen W. *The Muddy Road to Glory,* il. by George Hughes. Harcourt 1963. $3.50; 12 up.

Depicted here is the everyday life of a young Union soldier in the Civil War. It is a life full of hardships, friendships, sufferings, disappointments, and victories. The story is based on the actual history of a Maine regiment. By the same author: *Who Rides in the Dark?; Shadow in the Pines; Jonathan Goes West; Red Horse Hill.*

Meadowcroft, Enid L. *By Secret Railway,* il. by Henry C. Pitz. Crowell 1948. $4.50; 9–12.

In 1860 a young boy befriends a Negro and becomes involved with the Underground Railroad. Authentic details and strong characterization.

Miles, Miska. *The Pieces of Home,* il. by Victor Ambrus. Little 1967. $3.25; 7–11.

This is the story of the San Francisco earthquake and fire and of two boys whose secure world is suddenly turned upside down. It tells of a family that stays together even though for a time they must live in a tent in Golden Gate Park. It is also the story of a city by an author who knows and loves it.

Monjo, F. N. *The Drinking Gourd,* il. by Fred Brenner. Harper 1970. $2.50; 4–8.

An explicit and exciting account of the Underground Railroad, which tells how some slaves proceed North to Canada and their freedom by following the drinking gourd (the Big Dipper). Effective cross-hatch sketches enhance this I-Can-Read history book.

_____. *Indian Summer*, il. by Anita Lobel. Harper 1968. $2.50; 4–8.
An exciting story of an Indian raid on an isolated family cabin in early colonial America. The book makes clear to the very young reader that alertness and the cooperation of all members of a family were necessary in guarding against such an attack.

Moore, Ruth Nulton. *Hiding the Bell*, il. by Andrew A. Snyder. Westminster 1968. $3.75; 8–12.
A fictionalized account of how the Liberty Bell was saved from a British plot. Fast moving and easy to read.

Nesbitt, Rosemary S. *The Great Rope*, il. by Douglas Gorsline. Lothrop 1968. $3.50; 10–14.
During the War of 1812, one of America's best fighting ships needs to secure a great rope for its anchor hawser. Young Jonathan Cooper plays a major role in transporting this rope through the British troops swarming the countryside. An exciting historical adventure.

North, Sterling. *So Dear to My Heart*, il. by Brad Holland. Doubleday 1968. $3.95; 10–14.
Set in southern Indiana at the turn of this century, but about sturdy mountain folk who have only recently migrated north, this is a nostalgic romance that distills out all the harshness and depicts only the goodness of the Bible-reading, God-fearing people of those days. The simple plot involves ten-year-old Jeremiah Tarleton, who establishes himself in the world by raising a rejected lamb. His Granny Kincaid raises the boy according to the Good Book and comes to grips with the obligation of telling him of his parentage and why he is an orphan. North tells his story in a lilting dialect that rings true and is unobtrusive. By the same author: *Rascal.*

Norton, André. *Ride Proud, Rebel!* World 1961. $3.75; 11 up.
A young scout for Morgan's raiders experiences the adventures of Confederate cavalry but faces the reality of a lost cause. This absorbing tale is for readers of all ages interested in the Civil War.

O'Daniel, Janet. *Garrett's Crossing.* Lippincott 1969. $3.95; 11–14.
Set in the Mohawk Valley of New York in 1778, this story of a misused apprentice seamstress who finds warmth and love is historically informative and emotionally satisfying.

O'Dell, Scott. *Island of the Blue Dolphins.* Houghton 1960. $3.50 (P—Dell, $.95); 11–14.

Karana tells the story of her survival and lonely life for 18 years on an island far off the coast of California. This exceptional tale of courage and self-reliance is based on a real experience. Newbery Award, 1961.

————. *Sing Down the Moon.* Houghton 1970. $3.75; 12–16.

The devastating results of the white man's conquest of the American Indian is told through this story about a Navajo girl who is forced with her people on the "long march" to Fort Sumner from the Canyon de Chelly in 1864.

Petry, Ann. *Tituba of Salem Village.* Crowell 1964. $4.50; 10–14.

Tituba and her husband are taken from the island of Barbados to Boston and later to Salem Village to serve the Rev. Samuel Parris and his family. She is subsequently accused of witchcraft and stands trial. Simple events are turned into treacherous evidence against her. The Pulitzer Prize-winning author develops Tituba as a strong and sympathetic character.

Philbrook, Clem. *Captured by the Abnakis,* il. by Joshua Tolford. Hastings 1966. $3.25; 9–13.

An exciting account of the capture of two white boys by Abnaki Indians. Through the courage and resourcefulness of the older boy, the two succeed in escaping. The book gives an authentic picture of the dangers of early New England frontier life and an informed view of Indian life and customs.

Randall, Janet. *Topi Forever,* il. by William Ferguson. McKay 1968. $3.50; 8–12.

Topi, who belongs to a Pacific Northwest Indian tribe, is required to develop a skill before he becomes a fully accepted member of the tribe. Only by surviving a terrible flood, living alone in a graveyard of totem poles, and returning to his family is Topi able to prove his worth.

Richter, Conrad. *Over the Blue Mountain,* il. by Herbert Danska. Knopf 1967. $3.75; 10–13.

An adventure story about the experiences of two Pennsylvania Dutch boys accompanying a young woman they think can put a hex on them from across the mountain. Includes interesting Dutch expressions and a Pennsylvania Dutch legend. By the same author: *The Light in the Forest.*

Robinson, Barbara. *Trace through the Forest.* Lothrop 1965. $3.95; 9–12.

When Colonel Zane takes a group of men to cut a trace

through the Ohio wilderness, young Jim Fraley is taken along as water boy. He hopes to find some clue to his lost father who went into the territory a year earlier to find a place for his family to settle. Danger and hardships plague the men who cut Zane's trace.

Russ, Lavinia. *Over the Hills and Far Away.* Harcourt 1968. $3.50; 10–14.

Peakie, a 12-year-old girl growing up about the time of World War I, is often embarrassed by the actions of her crusading mother. The story presents a wholesome picture of family life and mentions such social issues as labor unions and minority groups.

Sachs, Marilyn. *Amy and Laura,* il. by Tracy Sugarman. Doubleday 1966. $3.50 (P—Scholastic, $.60); 10–12.

This excellent sequel to *Amy Moves In* and *Larua's Luck,* set in the Bronx in the 1930's, tells of the return of an invalid mother after her long hospitalization. Laura encounters difficulties in adjusting to the changes in her mother.

Sandoz, Mari. *The Horsecatcher.* Westminster 1957. $3.50; 10 up.

Young Elk, a Cheyenne, "son of two great warrior families," cares more for horses than for scalptaking. Spending two years in his search for The White One, a great horse, this hero goes contrary to the stereotypes and frees the hard-won horse to warn and save his people. The book is full of adventure and of Mari Sandoz' solid knowledge of her Indian neighbors. By the same author: *The Story Catcher.*

Schneider, Benjamin. *Winter Patriot.* Chilton 1967. $3.95; 12 up.

When his father is killed at his smithy by a Hessian soldier, 16-year-old Seth Kimple soon joins his older brother and a group of patriots. In the battle of Trenton, Seth finds the cause of liberty greater than his personal desire to avenge his father's murder. An exciting story in good prose.

Sharp, Edith Lambert. *Nkwala,* il. by William Winter. Little 1958. $3.95; 10 up.

"So long as Nkwala lives, fear will never again have its way with him." So vows the Salish Indian boy who in this story seeks his totem and the proof of his worth to his tribe. He finds it as he makes peace between his people and another tribe.

Shay, Myrtle. *Two on the Trail,* il. by J. C. Kocsis. Bobbs 1967. $4.00; 8–14.

Ricky and Chub take a wagon of guns West and meet every

kind of excitement and danger. This is a very good story for those who "long for the trail."

Snyder, Zilpha Keatley. *The Changeling,* il. by Alton Raible. Atheneum 1970. $5.25; 12 up.

A fanciful, evocatively written story of the relationship between two girls; one from a good family, the other born on the wrong side of the tracks.

Speare, Elizabeth George. *Calico Captive.* Houghton 1937. $3.50; 10–14.

Romance and Indian terror combine in this story of Miriam Willard in 1754. Self-reliance and perseverance are embodied in the main characters, who are based upon real people. The facts are taken from the diary of a captive. See also Lois Lenski, *Indian Captive.*

———. *The Witch of Blackbird Pond.* Houghton 1958. $3.75; 12–16.

In 1689 16-year-old Kit Tyler leaves her home in the Barbados and goes to live with her Connecticut relatives. Here she comes into conflict with rigid Puritan beliefs and practices. The exciting tale is excellent for teenagers, but good sixth-grade readers may also gain much from it. It may also be read aloud. (Newbery Award, 1959)

Steele, William O. *The Far Frontier,* il. by Paul Galdone. Harcourt 1959. $3.25; 9–12.

Tobe is bound out to Mr Twistletree, an eccentric naturalist. Together they travel throughout the Tennessee wilderness as they pursue knowledge through suspense and danger, the boy's early rebellion gives way to respect for learning and to admiration for his guardian.

———. *The Perilous Road,* il. by Paul Galdone. Harcourt 1958. $3.25 (P—Harcourt, $.75); 9–12.

A stirring tale of a country boy and of his experiences during the Civil War. Chris learns the hard way that his father was right when he said, "War is the worst thing that can happen to folks." Children will enjoy this story and should gain much from its historical setting and its emphasis upon the real values of life.

———. *Tomahawk Border,* il. by Vernon Wooten. Holt 1966. $3.95; 11–14.

The story of a 16-year-old boy who in the early 1700's joins the Virginia rangers, with difficulty learns to become a good soldier, and finally wins the respect of the other rangers by his heroism in battle.

———. *Winter Danger.* Harcourt 1954. $3.25; 9–12.

Caje is torn between his love for his roving father and a comfortable life with his kinfolks. Strong characterization and use of the vernacular of the time make Steele's books unique. Other books by the same author: *The Lone Hunt; Wilderness Journey; The Year of the Bloody Sevens; Trail through Danger; Tomahawks and Trouble; Flaming Arrows; The Buffalo Knife.*

Stephens, Peter John. *Towappu: Puritan Renegade,* il. by William Moyers. Atheneum 1966. $4.50; 10–13.

Timothy Morris is in a position to see two sides to the conflict over land during the early settlement of our country, in 1674. He is torn by his allegiance to his Indian friends and to the Plymouth colonists. Although his life makes little difference in the events of history, Timothy's story is rich with meaning and hope.

Stockton, Frank R. *Buccaneers & Pirates of Our Coasts,* il. with prints and engravings. Macmillan 1967. $3.95; 10 up.

In this reissue of a classic favorite, the grim and precarious calling of piracy is treated with romance and excitement. The reader is informed that "Christopher Columbus was the first who practiced piracy in American waters." This book continues to provide good escape reading for whose who would dream of the derring-do of bygone times.

Taylor, Don Alonzo. *Old Sam and the Horse Thieves,* il. by Lorence F. Bjorklund. Follett 1967. $3.50; 10–14.

An exciting story about horse thieves set in the Dakota Territory in the 1880's. This easy-to-read, fast moving, action-filled account has believable characters.

Thompson, Mary Wolfe. *Wilderness Winter,* il. by Ursula Koering. McKay 1968. $3.50; 11–14.

An interesting story of two families who settle near each other in Vermont but do not discover each other until several months have passed. The story is especially fine for its details of everyday life in an early American frontier community.

Toepfer, Ray Grant. *Liberty and Corporal Kincaid.* Chilton 1968. $4.50; 12–16.

An exciting fact-based story of an American corporal's part in the guerrilla warfare against the British just before the surrender of Cornwallis at Yorktown. The climax of the story comes with Corporal Kincaid's hazardous ride to warn Governor Thomas Jefferson that a British raiding party plans to capture him and the Virginia legislature.

Twain, Mark. *Adventures of Tom Sawyer.* (Many paperback editions); 12 up.

Humor and mystery have kept this classic tale in high favor with young readers since its publication many years ago. By the same author: *Adventures of Huckleberry Finn.*

Unrau, Ruth. *Who Needs an Oil Well?* il. by Jan Gleysteen. Abingdon 1968. $4.50; 10–14.

Story of a Mennonite boy living in Oklahoma during the 1930's. Although his hopes of sudden wealth are dashed when an oil company fails to find oil on the family's farm, he finds a better way of being the first of his family to go to high school.

Van der Loeff, A. Rutgers. *Oregon at Last!* il. by Charles Geer. Morrow 1961. $3.95; 10–14.

John Sager is 13 when his parents die and leave him to care for his five sisters and one brother. Determined to carry out his father's wish, John doggedly continues their journey to Oregon.

Vlock, Laurel F., and Joel A. Levitch. *Contraband of War.* Funk & Wagnalls 1970. $5.95; 12 up.

This is based on a chronicle written by William Henry Singleton, born a slave in New Bern, North Carolina, in 1843. It tells of his life first as a slave and finally at the end of the Civil War as a first sergeant in the First North Carolina Colored Infantry.

Wallace, Barbara. *Claudia.* Follett 1969. $3.50; 10 up.

Claudia's parents disapprove of her tomboyish ways, and even her friends are becoming more ladylike. The anguish of preadolescence is believably presented, and the happy ending will reassure young readers going through a similar stage.

Walton, Elizabeth Cheatham. *Voices in the Fog,* il. by Shirley Hughes. Abelard 1968. $3.95; 9–12.

Story of twins who live in New England in the 1840's. Tammy, the dependent one, is taken from Falmouth to Martha's Vineyard when her parents move there to open a new business. There she shows her independence by helping to uncover clues that lead to the arrest of smugglers who have been stealing from her father.

Watson, Sally. *Jade.* Holt 1969. $4.50; 10–14.

Sixteen-year-old Jade's dislike of slavery and defiance of society's rules result in her virtual banishment from her home in 18th-century Virginia.

Wellman, Manly Wade. *Carolina Pirate.* Washburn 1968. $3.95; 11–15.

A story of how a 19-year-old Carolina boy is forced to join a pirate crew when they capture the ship he is navigating in 1741. During the months that follow, he learns that the captain and some of the crew are not the criminals he thought all pirates to be.

Wibberley, Leonard. *John Treegate's Musket.* Farrar 1959. $2.95; 11 up.

This book is somewhat above the level of the average upper-elementary school student, but it is so rich in humor, excitement, lively characters, and details of life in America immediately preceding the Revolution that capable readers with interest in the history of their country will find the book stimulating and rewarding. By the same author: *Treegate's Raiders; Peter Treegate's War; Sea Captain from Salem.*

Wilder, Laura Ingalls. *Little House in the Big Woods,* il. by Garth Williams. Harper 1932, 1953. $4.95 (P—Harper, $.95); 9–12.

The Ingalls family lived in the Wisconsin wilderness in 1872. Life there is vividly described in this book. Based on the author's life, the stories are authentic and warm hearted. Subsequent years are described in *Little House on the Prairie; On the Banks of Plum Creek; By the Shores of Silver Lake; Little Town on the Prairie, The Long Winter; These Happy Golden Years. Farmer Boy* describes the childhood of Almanzo Wilder, whom Laura Ingalls married. All have recently been reissued by Harper in paperback editions.

Williamson, Joanne S. *The Glorious Conspiracy.* Knopf 1961. $3.64; 11–14.

Benjamin Brown escapes to America from the miserable cotton mills of England in the 1780's. He becomes involved in Burr's conspiracy against the Federalists, which is aimed at property qualifications for voting and leads to Jefferson's presidency. An unusual point of view is presented here.

Wojciechowska, Maia. *Hey, What's Wrong with This One?* il. by Joan Sandin. Harper 1969. $3.79; 5–9.

Three brothers have a dog, a cat, their own ponies, but no mother. Unwittingly, their own inventiveness turns up a likely prospect and a promising future. Born of the boys' pragmatic approach, uproarious incidents occur. The questionnaire the youngsters use for interviewing housekeepers is hilarious.

Yates, Elizabeth. *Carolina's Courage,* il. by Nora S. Unwin. Dutton 1964. $2.95; 8–11.

Carolina's family decides to leave the rocky fields of New

Hampshire and travel west to better soil. She takes her treasured doll, Lyddy-Lou, and finds that the doll plays an important role in getting the family safely through Indian country. Carolina's courage and sacrifice are believably described.

Other Times and Places

Abrahams, Robert D. *The Bonus of Redonda,* il. by Peter Bramley. Macmillan 1969. $4.50; 8–12.

An excellent tale of how progress comes in spite of superstition and tradition. Island fishermen go through interesting adventures to learn this. Will not appeal universally because of the dialect.

Allfrey, Katherine. *Golden Island,* il. by John Kaufman. Doubleday 1966. $3.25; 9–12.

Andrula and her widowed mother live in poverty on the Greek island of Kaloaysos. After a quarrel with other children, lovely Andrula, on the pretext of taking their goat to graze, spends a joyous summer riding a friendly dolphin to the island of Heria where she makes friends with nereids, fauns, and a centaur. Beautifully written story of a child and a dolphin, mythical creatures, and the Greek islands and their people.

Almedingen, E. M. *Young Mark,* il. by Victor Ambrus. Farrar 1968. $3.75; 12–14.

A boy travels from a remote Ukrainian farm to study singing in St. Petersburg in 1742. The picture of 18th-century Russia and the boy's own appealing, strong character make the book memorable.

Anckarsvard, Karin. *Aunt Vinnie's Victorious Six,* tr. by Annabelle Macmillan, il. by Paul Galdone. Harcourt 1962. $3.25; 12–15.

This story of family relationships gives a brief glimpse of children's school life in Sweden. One element of suspense keeps it moving. The plot involves cross-cultural contacts.

————. *Doctor's Boy,* tr. by Annabelle Macmillan, il. by Fermin Rocker. Harcourt 1965. $3.25; 10–14.

Jon rides in a buggy with his father as he makes house calls. He learns about medicine and life during these visits. The development of a friendship between Jon and Rickard over comes differences in economic levels and adds the strongest element to this convincing book. Swedish setting.

_____. *Struggle at Soltuna,* tr. by Annabelle Macmillan, il. by Fermin Rocker. Harcourt 1967. $3.50; 10–14.
Set in the early 1900's in Sweden, this story reveals many of the social customs and injustices of the period. Jon, a doctor's son, through his strong friendship with Rickard, the son of a pauper, is exposed to a way of life much different from his own. Believable characterization strengthens the story.

Armstrong, Richard. *The Mutineers.* McKay 1968. $3.95; 13 up.
A group of teenage boys marooned on a tropical island demonstrate both savagery and the need for civilized society.

Arnold, Elliott. *A Secret Kind of Weapon.* Scribner 1969. $3.63; 10–14.
This story is about one link in the courageous chain of men involved in the fantastic rescue operation that saved almost the total Jewish population in Denmark, Peter's father, a newspaperman, leads a double life as an underground agent. When the long arm of the Gestapo pursues them, Peter is tested and learns that he is worthy of his father's trust. Dominating the growing suspense is the excellent relationship, sensitively handled, between the 12-year-old and his father.

Arora, Shirley L. *What Then, Raman?* il. by Hans Guggenheim. Follett 1960. $3.95; 9–14.
Raman is the first in his village to learn to read. The picture presented is one of love, knowledge and teaching, personal initiative, and hard work offering hope for the future against the grim poverty of India. By the same author: *The Left-handed Chank.*

Avery, Gillian. *Call of the Valley,* il. by David K. Stone. Holt 1968. $4.50; 10–14.
Strong characterization of a Welsh farm boy in the 1880's distinguishes this story. Sam Williams rejects his unhappy life as a bootboy in the city and finds that some of his problems follow him. As he recognizes some of his own faults, he returns to the valley to accept responsibilities that are rightfully his.

Bacon, Martha. *Sophia Scrooby Preserved,* il. by David Omar White. Little 1968. $4.95; 10 up.
In this young slave girl's "success story," Sophia is captured

in Africa at six, but through all physical dangers and misfortunes her courage, intelligence, and perseverance enable her to endure. Readers will gain an understanding of slavery and 18th-century life. The African portion is reminiscent of *Amos Fortune, Free Man.* Formal life of the period is reflected in the writing style.

Baker, Betty. *Walk the World's Rim.* Harper 1965. $3.95; 10–14.

The search for the gold of Cibola by Cabeza de Vaca provides the setting for this powerful story. Chakoh, the Indian boy who goes with the group to Mexico, comes to know the greatness of character displayed by Esteban, a slave.

Barnes, Gregory Allen. *A Wind of Change.* Lothrop 1968. $3.50; 12–15.

Joseph Konda, native student in a West African boarding school, finds himself unwillingly involved in a plot to burn several of the school's dormitories. With his whole future in jeopardy, Joseph is torn between tribal tradition and his loyalty toward innocent fellow students, between the confidence of his family and that of a teacher who has befriended him.

Barringer, D. Moreau. *And the Waters Prevailed,* il. by P. A. Hutchinson. Dutton 1956. $4.95; 10–14.

Set in prehistoric times, the tale reveals a young boy's attempts to warn his tribe of the impending danger from Gibraltar. Andor proves his manhood and spends his life trying to convince his people that Gibraltar is weakening.

Baudouy, Michel-Aime. *More Than Courage.* Harcourt 1961. $3.25 (P—Harcourt, $.60); 11–14.

Nick, who likes machinery, befriends Paulo, who cares more for books. The work of cleaning up an old shop and restoring an old motorcycle helps Nick to a better relationship with his father and helps Paulo to cope better with his problem of poverty. The story is convincing and realistic.

Baumann, Hans. *I Marched with Hannibal,* tr. by Katherine Potts, il. by Ulrik Schramm. Walck 1962. $6.00; 10–14.

The story of an elephant boy who travels with Hannibal across the Alps is skillfully interwoven with historical facts to make this a vivid and credible account. Includes chronological table and maps.

_____. *Sons of the Steppe,* tr. by Isabel and Florence McHugh, il. by Heiner Rothfuchs. Walck 1958. $6.00; 12–14.

The McHughs have succeeded in making a distinguished translation from the German of this moving novel dealing with the adventures of two brothers, grandsons of Genghis Khan, growing up on the steppes of Central Asia in the 13th century. Kublai's gentler, more humanitarian nature is in constant conflict with Arik Buka's more warlike qualities.

Beatty, John and Patricia. *The Queen's Wizard.* Macmillan 1967. $4.50; 10–14.

In England in the 1600's, belief in witchcraft is widespread and plays an important role in this story. The dialogue of the period adds authenticity but makes the book difficult reading for most elementary school children. The Elizabethan age is vividly recreated.

_____. *Witch Dog,* il. by Franz Altschuler. Morrow 1968. $3.95; 12–16.

A panoramic story of the gallant prince who led the King's cavalry against the Roundheads and of the huge white poodle who was his loyal companion. The research of the authors shows in the authentic recreation of this historic period. The plot is vigorous and fast-moving. By the same authors: *At the Seven Stars; Campion Towers.*

Beers, Lorna. *The Book of Hugh Flower,* il. by Eleanor Mill. Harper 1952. $3.27; 10 up.

There is very little quaintness and much solid substance and human nature in this story of Hugh, the young apprentice mason who built the great west window of the church of Saint Nicholas, and of Alison, who loved him. Pictures and text suggest the craftsmanship and humanity of the 15th-century people.

Behn, Harry. *The Faraway Lurs.* World 1963. $3.50 (P—Avon, $.60); 10–14.

This is a mystical story of love between two young people from opposing tribes. The setting is the Bronze Age in Denmark. Expert characterization helps us feel the tragedy of the ending.

_____. *The Two Uncles of Pablo,* il. by Mel Silverman. Harcourt 1959. $3.25; 8–12.

A well-written story contrasting farm and town life in Mexico. Pablo, eight years old, has two very different, mutually antagonistic uncles, but he learns to understand and appreciate both. The small boy's sense of honesty and responsibility, as well as his resourcefulness, makes him a most appealing hero.

Bell, Margaret. *Watch for a Tall White Sail.* Morrow 1948. $3.95 (P—Grosset, $.60); 12 up.

The unusual Alaskan background gives this novel one of its

many values. Others are a sense of family loyalty, a believable love affair, illness, and danger faced courageously.

Benary-Isbert, Margot. *The Ark*, tr. by Richard and Clara Winston. Harcourt 1953. $4.25; 10–13.

Four children and their mother in postwar Germany try to eke out an existence while waiting for their father to find his way back to them from a Russian prison camp. Rich in humor and human understanding.

———. *Rowan Farm*, tr. by Richard and Clara Winston. Harcourt 1954. $3.75; 10–15.

Dr. Lechow returns home from a prison camp and begins to make a new life for himself and his family. Sixteen-year-old Margaret is the central character, but the entire family is well described. Sequel to *The Ark*. By the same author: *Blue Mystery; The Long Way Home; Dangerous Spring; Castle at the Border.*

Berna, Paul. *The Horse without a Head*, il. by Richard Kennedy. Pantheon 1958. $3.54; 9–12.

Set in Paris, this book tells the story of ten poverty-stricken street urchins whose prized possession is mysteriously stolen and of the clever and effective means used by these extraordinary children to retrieve their apparently worthless plaything. Readers will be held by the heightening suspense of the mystery as well as by the amazing life of Gaby and his gang. By the same author: *Flood Warning; Knights of King Arthur.*

Bernhardsen, Christian. *Fight in the Mountains*, tr. by Franey Sinding. Harcourt 1968. $3.25; 10–16.

Sixteen-year-old Chris feeds his hatred for the Nazis in the last days of the 1945 Norwegian resistance. His brother's death is the final blow, and yet the underlying theme of the powerfully written book decries hatred.

Berry, Erick. *Honey of the Nile*. Viking 1938, 1963. $3.37; 10–14.

The importance of Egypt in world affairs today renews interest in this book. Honey from the nectar of the flowers along the river banks was profitable business in ancient times. There are interesting incidents, such as the escape of the queen concealed under beehives on a raft.

Bingley, Barbara. *Vicky and the Monkey People*. Abelard 1967. $3.50; 9–12.

A warm, vivid account of the children of an English family stationed in India in the early 1900's. Told in the first person by Vicky, the oldest daughter, the story reveals strong family feelings, the snobbery of certain types of Britishers, the interesting ways of the Indian servants, and the princeliness of an old priest at a monkey temple.

Bishop, Claire Huchet. *Twenty and Ten,* il. by William Pène du Bois. Viking 1952. $3.00; 10–14.

The compelling story of 20 French children hiding ten Jewish refugee children during the Second World War. Stark realism shows that war disrupts the lives of children as well as adults; yet the children are natural, sometimes humorous, always appealing. By the same author: *Pancakes Paris.*

Bloch, Marie Halun. *Two Worlds of Damyan,* il. by Robert Quackenbush. Atheneum 1966. $3.95; 8–12.

A young boy living in the Ukraine must decide between two completely contrary worlds, each of which offers him some definite temporal and spiritual advantages and disadvantages. By the same author: *Aunt America.*

Boden, Hilda. *Faraway Farm,* il. by Ursula Koering. Hale 1961. $2.71; 10 up.

The Wetherby children get away from crowded London and learn how to live on a farm in the isolated Scottish Highlands. Their courage in facing other problems, including that of finding a place to live, endears them to the community.

Bond, Ruskin. *Panther's Moon,* il. by Tom Feelings. Random 1969. $3.50; 8–10.

The panther that has been molesting livestock in the small Himalayan village is now attacking humans. After a suspense-filled narrow escape, 12-year-old Bisnu realizes that the panther must be faced. When the panther springs to attack his sister, Bisnu yells a warning and runs with his axe to face the man-eater. Black-and-white drawings add drama and excitement.

Bonzon, Paul-Jacques. *The Orphans of Simitra,* tr. by Thelma Niklaus. Criterion 1962. $3.50; 12 up.

Winner of a French prize, this book tells of great love and courage. Homeless after an earthquake, two orphans are taken from Greece to Holland. The unhappy girl flees and after a long search is found by her brother.

Bothwell, Jean. *The Holy Man's Secret,* il. by Clyde Pearson. Abelard 1968. $3.75; 9–12.

The author has woven her extensive knowledge of Indian history and culture into this fascinating adventure. Premi, a young Indian girl attending a Christian mission school, sets out to satisfy her insatiable curiosity about the Holy Man and his mysterious nightly prowls.

Bourliaguet, Léonce. *A Sword to Slice through Mountains, and Other Stories,* tr. by John Buchanan-Brown, il. by Gerald Rose. Abelard 1967. $3.00; 8 up.

These eight original stories will please young audiences who delight in folktales. All stories are brief and to the point. The book is enlivened with sometimes grotesque but often humorous illustrations.

Braenne, Berit. *Little Sister Tai Mi,* tr. by Evelyn Ramsden, il. by Borghild Reed. Harcourt 1964. $2.75; 7–10.

A Norwegian sea captain and his family are world-minded. On a trip to Korea they discover a little orphan, Tai Mi, and add her to their family. The story of child victims of the Korean War is beautifully told; excellent to help build better international understanding.

Brown, Pamela. *The Other Side of the Street,* il. by N. Brown. Follett 1967. $3.50; 10 up.

The dream of a new home in London spurs Linda to try money-making schemes. Innercity life and warm human relationships are part of the appeal of this lively book.

Buck, Pearl S. *Matthew, Mark, Luke and John,* il. by Mamoru Funai. Day 1966. $3.00; 9–12.

Matthew, abandoned by his American soldier father and his Korean mother, survives by begging and hunting scraps of food from garbage. The "home" that he builds under a bridge gradually houses Mark, Luke, and John. Matthew experiences the feeling of responsibility for those he has taken into his "home." Although the story may be propaganda for adopting a foreign orphan, it is compelling.

Bulla, Clyde. *Mika's Apple Tree,* il. by Des Asmiussen. Crowell 1968. $3.75; 6–8.

A very pleasant story of a little Finnish boy who decides what he wants to be when he grows up.

———. *Viking Adventure,* il. by Douglas Gorsline. Crowell 1963. $3.95; 8–12.

Sigurd, a Viking boy, sails to Vineland on a voyage that demands all the strength and skill his father's training has given him. This simply written but exciting story may appeal to older, slower readers. By the same author: *Sword in the Tree; Three-Dollar Mule; White Bird;* and others.

Burleson, Elizabeth. *A Man of the Family.* Follett 1965. $3.50; 10–14.

Growing to manhood is the theme that pushes Speck to tackle the many responsibilities thrust upon him in this story of ranching. It is interesting, well written, and will especially appeal to horse lovers.

Carlson, Natalie Savage. *The Happy Orpheline,* il. by Garth Williams. Harper 1957. $3.95 (P—Dell, $.75); 7–10.

A happy story about 20 orphans living in an orphanage outside Paris. Their concern is not trying to find homes and adopted parents but instead to keep from being adopted.

———. *Luigi of the Streets,* il. by Emily Arnold McCully. Harper 1967. $3.95; 8–12.

Many people live in the Street of Strangers in Marseilles. There are Arabs, Gypsies, and Corsicans like Luigi's family. There are good times and bad, but Luigi and his sister Ono make friends with many different people and have many exciting adventures. By the same author: *A Brother for the Orphelines; A Pet for the Orphelines; The Family under the Bridge.*

Castle, Frances. *The Sister's Tale.* Little 1968. $4.95; 12–16.

Set in sixth century Ireland, this historical romance combines an absorbing plot with an authentic sense of that period.

Catherall, Arthur. *Camel Caravan,* il. by Joseph Papin. Seabury 1968. $3.95; 8–12.

When a favorite camel belonging to their father gives birth to her baby the day before their salt caravan is due to start on a journey across the African desert, serious problems are created for Youba and his sister Fedada. This exciting adventure gives a realistic picture of the hardships and dangers of travel on the desert.

———. *Night of the Black Frost.* Lothrop 1968. $3.50; 12 up.

While testing his uncle's fishing boat, 16-year-old Leif Knudsen experiences extreme danger and a fight for survival during a freezing fog. Two Russian pilots have been downed in the icy sea, and their rescue depends on Leif's courage. Catherall includes a Russian who wants to defect. The Norwegians are characterized as vital and strong, the Russians as weaker.

———. *Prisoners in the Snow,* il. by Victor G. Ambrus. Lothrop 1967. $3.50; 8–12.

As a plane bursts into flames above the Austrian mountains, a pilot parachutes and lands on the Hoffman farm. An avalanche and the rescue of the pilot provide an exciting series of events central to the story. Toni and Trudi Hoffman play an important part in the events that follow.

Cawston, Vee. *Matuk, the Eskimo Boy,* il. by Haris Petie. Lantern 1965. $3.25; 6–9.

Matuk's father insists that Matuk is too young to go hunting, but Matuk earns the privilege by courageously rescuing his dog. A fine story of an Eskimo boy and his father, characteristic of their way of life.

Channel, A. R. *Jungle Rescue,* il. by D. Watkins-Pitchford. Phillips 1968. $4.95; 9–14.

Life in the forests of northern India provides one thrilling experience after another: fights with tigers, snakes, wild dogs. To add to the excitement and adventure, a young boy helps a white man find lost payroll money.

Chute, Marchette. *The Innocent Wayfaring,* il. by the author. Dutton 1943. $3.95 (P—Dutton, $1.25); 12 up.

"Not a serious book, but an accurate one," this young people's novel about the 14th century tells with humor and verve the love story of young Anne, who runs away from her aunt's convent, and clerk, Nick, who rescues her. One young reader called it "the best love story I know." By the same author: *The Wonderful Winter.*

Coatsworth, Elizabeth. *The Place,* il. by Symeon Shimin. Holt 1965. $3.50; 8–11.

Ellen is on the Isthmus of Tehauntepec in Yucatan with her archeologist father. She makes friends with Natividad and Jorge and later saves Natividad's life. In gratitude Nati and Jorge take her to an amazing cave known as "the Place" to local people. This is beautiful writing, of great interest to children with sensitivity for people of other countries.

Collins, Ruth P. *Hubba-Hubba: A Tale of the Sahara,* il. by Harold Berson. Crown 1968. $3.50; 6–10.

This simple story of a boy and his pet camel is set in the northern corner of modern day Nigeria. Musa lives in a village that has changed its ways very little over the years. The story will teach the reader something of the distinguishing characteristics of a culture different from his own, and at the same time he will come to know that basically all people have much in common.

Coolidge, Olivia. *Marathon Looks on the Sea,* il. by Erwin Schachner. Houghton 1967. $3.50; 10–16.

Historical events come to life in this story of Metiochos, son of the Greek general Miltiades, who became a favorite of the Persian King Darius and fought against the Greeks in the Battle of Marathon. Boys and girls will enjoy the characterizations and the realistic action of the period.

_____. *People in Palestine.* Houghton 1965. $3.75; 12 up.
The first 70 years of Christianity in Palestine is accurately reflected in short stories which tell of the conflicts resulting from the convergence of Jewish, Roman, and Greek peoples.

Credle, Ellis. *The Little Pest Pico,* il. by Richard F. Townsend. Nelson 1969. $3.95; 6–8.
Chico, a young Mexican boy, faces many problems in his effort to contribute to the welcoming celebration planned by the villagers for the president of Mexico. His parrot Pico makes the wrong noises but in the end saves the day by providing a stand-in rendition of the national anthem. The illustrations offer a view of Mexican life.

de Angeli, Marguerite. *Black Fox of Lorne,* il. by the author. Doubleday 1956. $3.95; 10–14.
Twin sons of a Viking chieftain make clever use of their identical appearance when shipwrecked on the Scottish coast in the lusty days of the tenth century. The author's beautiful illustrations supplement the text admirably. By the same author: *The Hole in the Wall.*

De Jong, Meindert. *Far out the Long Canal,* il. by Nancy Grossman. Harper 1964. $3.50; 8–12.
Authentic story of skating on the canals in Wierum at the edge of the North Sea, in which a nine-year-old boy, Moonta, not only learns to skate but skates with a champion. All the details of canal skating on ice, on water, in sunshine, or in rain are here as one follows small Moonta's struggle to skate like other children his age.

_____. *The House of Sixty Fathers,* il. by Maurice Sendak. Harper 1956. $3.50; 9–12.
Tien Pao, a small but courageous Chinese boy, is separated from his parents when the Japanese invade his country. He befriends an American airman and is in turn adopted by the 60 men of the flier's squadron.

Dillon, Eilis. *The Coriander,* il. by Vic Donahue. Funk & Wagnalls 1964. $3.50; 10–16.
On a small island off Ireland, the villagers delight in helping to wreck a ship so they may strip her. Pat and his friend rescue the ship's doctor and keep him hidden as he recuperates. The townspeople approve of the hostage since they have no doctor on their island.

_____. *Sea Wall,* il. by W. T. Mars. Farrar 1965. $2.95; 12–15.
A warm, easily read book that depicts one faction's strong reaction against community improvement and ways in which a more liberal group finally wins its point. A natural

disaster also shows community solidarity in spite of differing views. The book has a true flavor of life on an island off
the coast of Ireland with Irish cadence in many sentences
and some Irish vocabulary. By the same author: *The Island
of Horses; The Singing Cave; The House on the Shore; A
Family of Foxes.*

Drewery, Mary. *Hamid and the Palm Sunday Donkey,* il. by
Reginald Gray. Hastings 1967. $4.25; 9–12.

An absorbing story that captures the flavor and presents a
vivid picture of Jerusalem, Jericho, and the wilderness of
Judea. The Arab waif Hamid, his donkey Haryat, and an
English family are involved in exciting episodes affecting
the lives of all. The Palm Sunday donkey, which Hamid
carves from wood fallen from one of the precious old olive
trees in the garden of Gethsemane, becomes the talisman of
Hamid's integrity and guide to his future.

Dunn, Mary. *The Man in the Box.* McGraw 1968. $4.50;
10–14.

Chau Li was too young to help when the Viet Cong put his
father in a box and left him there to die. Now he sees an
American soldier placed in the box and knows that he must
try to rescue him. This grim war story reveals a courageous
act of humanity from a young boy who shows understanding
far beyond his years.

Eisen, Anthony Fon. *Bond of the Fire.* World 1965. $3.95
(P—Dell, $.75); 11–14.

The story, set in the Ice Age, is about a boy who, with his
dog, hunts for his people. It includes accounts of the simple
life led by the people of that era. Good characterization.

Ellis, Ella Thorp. *Roam the Wild Country,* il. by Bret Schles-
inger. Atheneum 1967. $4.25; 12–15.

Story of a boy of 13 who helps to move a herd of Arabian
horses from a drought-stricken ranch in Argentina to another
part of the pampas, where good range will save their lives.
The dangerous journey gives the boy a chance to prove that
he is a real gaucho.

Evernden, Margery. *Simon's Way,* il. by Frank Newfeld. Walck
1963. $4.00; 9–13.

A Parisian boy searches for his father in 13th-century
Norway and finds friendship and exciting adventure as he
serves the king's son. In the process he attains maturity and
self-realization.

Fartchen, Max. *The River Kings,* il. by Clyde Pearson. St.
Martin 1968. $3.75; 10–14.

The tales of the swagman, a dusty vagabond, puts the lure of the river into 13-year-old Shawn's mind. He runs away from a mean stepfather and the bleak South Australian farm to work on the river and became a man on the famous *Lady Jane,* a river workhorse fighting for her share of the river trade at the turn of the century. This rough man's world is lively and the prose pace is fast. There is hard work and sweat, laced with true hilarity, high adventure, and suspense.

Fecher, Constant. *Venture for a Crown.* Farrar 1968. $3.50; 12 up.

Well-documented fiction of England in 1647. The village blacksmith's son, Rob, is embittered over the Roundheads' execution of his older brother. Rob's story tells of a boy's decisions and actions during perilous times.

Feelings, Muriel L. *Zamani Goes to Market,* il. by Tom Feelings. Seabury 1970. $3.95; 5–8.

Zamani, an East African boy, accompanies his father to market for the first time and decides to spend the shilling his father gives him on a necklace for his mother. This slow paced book has an authentic sound and appearance.

Feld, Friedrich. *The Parrot of Isfahan,* il. by Kurt Schmischke and W. Kersley Holmes. Whitman 1966. $2.75; 7–9.

This is an amusing book to read aloud. It is humorous and at the same time teaches a sound lesson. Set in Iran, the author tells with skill how Kelat, after becoming extremely greedy for money, forgets the friend who sold him the talking parrot and how he finally meets disaster.

Finkel, George. *Watch Fires to the North.* Viking 1968. $3.95; 12–16.

Roman legions withdraw from Britain and heathen Saxons are stronger as a young nobleman grows to knighthood. Legendary characters such as Artyr, Gwenyfer, Kay, and Glahad appear in this account of wars and daily living.

Floethe, Louise Lee. *Floating Market,* il. by Richard Floethe. Farrar 1969. $4.50; 6–8.

In text and illustration, a bright, gay, and happy picture of life along the klongs or canals and the floating market near Bangkok. Two children paddle their sampan loaded with bananas, durians, and dumplings along the canal, hoping to make enough money to buy a necklace for their little sister. An over-rosy picture of life in this competitive market is presented.

Forman, James. *Ring the Judas Bell.* Farrar 1965. $3.25; 10–14.

Set in Greece just after the Nazi occupation when the

Andarte are kidnapping children. A group of children who have been kidnapped and placed in a concentration camp escape and return to their village. The grim and dramatic story has a disquieting ring of truth.

————. *The Traitors.* Farrar 1968. $3.95; 12–16.
Powerful novel dealing with the effect of the rise of Nazism and World War II on the life of people in a small Bavarian village. Frank portrayal of the horrors of war and anti-Semitism is shown. Differing philosophies and ways in which people react to change and tragedy are vividly presented in the characters of Pastor Eichorn and his two sons, Kurt and Paul.

Frere, Maud. *Nicole, a Little French School Girl,* il. by Nadine Forter. Random 1966. $2.95; 7–9.
Humorous colorful illustrations enhance this picture book of Nicky's first days at school, her friendship with Arlette, her devotion to her teacher, Miss Hélène, and everyday events of her life.

Garlan, Patricia Wallace, and Maryjane Dunstan. *The Boy Who Played Tiger,* il. by John Pimlott. Viking 1968. $3.95; 7–10.
Excellent portrayal of life in a modern Burmese village, with lively black-and-white illustrations. By the same author and beautifully illustrated in appropriate Burmese colors: *Orange-Robed Boy.*

Godden, Rumer. *The Kitchen Madonna,* il. by Carol Baker. Viking 1967. $3.75; 8–11.
Two English children let nothing deter them from making an icon for their homesick Ukrainian maid. Their picture becomes the "kitchen madonna."

————. *Little Plum,* il. by Jean Primrose. Viking 1963. $3.50; 8–10.
Belinda and Gem, the new girl next door, find their way from antagonism to friendship through Little Plum, Gem's Japanese doll. The author's earlier Miss Happiness and Miss Flower (from the book of that title) appear again in this story. By the same author: *The Mousewife; Impunity Jane.*

————. *Miss Happiness and Miss Flower,* il. by Jean Primrose. Viking 1961. $3.25; 8–10.
Frightened Nona is drawn out of her shell by the gift of two Japanese dolls. The author characterizes Nona and her jealous cousin well. Directions for making a Japanese doll add to the interest.

Graham, Lorenz. *Momolu,* il. by John Biggers. Crowell 1966. $4.00; 10–16.

A village boy offers his own liberty to save his father from the city prison. A good picture of changing Liberia is presented.

Gray, Elizabeth Janet. *Adam of the Road,* il. by Robert Lawson. Viking 1942. $4.50; 12 up.

Adam becomes separated from both his father and his dog and sets about earning his way along the highroads of England as a minstrel. Excellent background for 13th century England. Newbery Award, 1943.

———. *The Cheerful Heart,* il. by Kazue Mizumura. Viking 1959. $3.50; 9–12.

A story of modern Japan and the part played by a courageous and cheerful 11-year-old girl in the rebuilding of the family home following the bombings of war. Mrs. Vining's first-hand knowledge of the Japanese people, coupled with her delightful style of writing, makes this a most interesting book.

———. *I Will Adventure,* il. by Corydon Bell. Viking 1962. $4.00; 12–14.

When runaway Andrew tries to join William Shakespeare's company, the playwright advises him to seek education and accomplishment in the real world instead. The 12-year-old, heedless and quick-tempered but warm-hearted and resourceful, is depicted realistically, and the way of life in Elizabethan times is evoked in vivid detail.

Greenleaf, Margery F. *Banner over Me,* il. by Charles Mikolaycak. Follett 1968. $4.95; 12 up.

This well-told tale of the Norman Conquest is full of battles, intrigue, and high adventure. An exciting historical novel.

Guillot, René. *The Troubadour,* il. by Laszlo Acs. McGraw 1967. $3.75; 12–14.

An excellent story of life in 13-century France. Aubrey, Knight of the Red Cross, had once been saved by Lord Oliver. Now Oliver himself is in grave trouble. Aubrey, in the guise of a troubadour, with ten-year-old Marjolaine and her pet fox to assist him, comes to Oliver's rescue. How they succeed makes a thrilling story. By the same author: *The Elephants of Sargabel; Grishka and the Bear;* and others.

Hagon, Priscilla. *Cruising to Danger,* il. by William Plummer. World 1966. $3.75; 12–14.

A young girl in search of adventure becomes involved in international intrigue when she takes a job as companion to two children on a Mediterranean cruise.

Hamilton, Virginia. *The Time-Ago Tales of Jahdu,* il. by Nonny Hogrogian. Macmillan 1969. $4.50; 7–12.

Four tales take Jahdu from Africa, where he uses his magic to help small animals, to the streets of Manhattan, where he finds his true self.

Hámori, László. *Flight to the Promised Land,* tr. by Annabelle Macmillan, il. by Mel Silverman. Harcourt 1963. $3.50; 11 up.

A 13-year-old Yemenite Jewish boy, abruptly transplanted from a Middle Ages culture, struggles to come to terms with the modern ways of 20th-century Israel. This fine adventure story, sensitively told, may help young Americans understand one kind of problem in creating a new country.

Harris, Christie. *Forbidden Frontier,* il. by E. Carey Kenney. Atheneum 1968. $4.50; 10–14.

A realistic interpretation of the conflicts faced by people of mixed racial background, in this case children born of white and Indian parents. A good picture of the Alaskan gold rush period.

_____. *Raven's Cry,* il. by Bill Reid. Atheneum 1966. $3.95; 10–14.

The Haida Indians were once lords of the western waters of Canada. Their culture and art suggest a highly civilized society. This well-documented story portrays the Indian in a much kinder way than do most books.

Haugaard, Erik. *Hakon of Rogen's Saga.* Houghton 1963. $3.00; 10–14.

Young Hakon, a Viking, inherits his father's island domain and is then driven into exile by his own kinsmen. How Hakon wins back his birthright makes this book and its sequel, *A Slave's Tale,* powerful reading.

_____. *The Little Fishes,* il. by Milton Johnson. Houghton 1967. $3.50; 11 up.

This is the story of three children and their journey from Naples to Cassino in 1943. It is a grim unhappy tale told with strength and sensitivity that recreates the impact of the war on the lives of the children.

_____. *The Rider and His Horse,* il. by Leo and Diane Dillon. Houghton 1968. $3.95; 12 up.

Powerfully written story of David ben Joseph, a wealthy Jewish boy from Tyre, who in 70 A. D. escapes from bandits to safety in Jerusalem and then runs away to join the defenders of the Masada. When the Romans are just about to take the fortress, David is chosen to live and not die with the defenders, in order to write their story for posterity.

Havrevold, Finn. *Undertow,* il. by Cathy Babcock Curry. Atheneum 1968. $4.25; 10 up.

A teenager's struggle for independence from his family and his search for identity are portrayed. Sailing and the Norwegian coast provide the background for a young man's struggle with values that have universal appeal.

Henry, Marguerite. *White Stallion of Lipizza,* il. by Wesley Dennis. Rand 1964. $3.95; 9–12.

The beauty and technique of the highly trained Lipizzaner horses of the Spanish Riding School in Vienna capture the reader as does the hero. The author has done her usual competent writing. This historically factual story for horse lovers will appeal to general readers also. By the same author: *Misty of Chincoteague; King of the Wind; Stormy, Misty's Foal.*

Hilbert, Peter Paul. *Zoo on the First Floor,* il. by Leonard Shortall. Coward 1966. $3.29; 8–12.

Two boys contract to collect wildlife of Brazil for various zoos and to house it until arrangements can be made for transport overseas. Humorous, fast paced story.

Horne, Richard Henry. *Memoirs of a London Doll,* ed. by Margery Fisher, il. by Margaret Gilles and Richard Shirley Smith. Macmillan 1967. $3.50; 8–11.

The reissue of an old book, with comments by Fisher. The first-person adventures of a doll in Victorian London make for most interesting reading.

Houston, James. *Akavak: An Eskimo Journey,* il. by the author. Harcourt 1968. $3.25; 9–12.

A young Eskimo boy, Akavak, is taking his aging grandfather to a neighboring village, but the grandfather dies as they near the end of the journey. True Eskimo character is revealed in the forceful writing. By the same author: *The White Archer; Tikta 'Liktak.*

Hoyt, Edwin P. *Swan of the East: The Life and Death of the German Cruiser* Emden *in World War I.* Macmillan 1968. $4.95; 10 up.

Exciting style and a true sea story combine to make absorbing reading for youth who want to learn more about the problems of war and the attitudes of the men involved.

Hunter, Mollie. *A Pistol in Greenyards.* Funk & Wagnalls 1968. $3.95; 12–14.

The vivid and suspenseful story of a 15-year-old boy and his involvement in the problems of the Scottish Highland tenant farmer.

———. *The Spanish Letters.* Funk & Wagnalls 1964. $3.50; 12–16.

A graphic story relating how some Scottish nobles, allied with Spain, conspire to take King James prisoner to pave the way for a Spanish invasion of England in 1589. Intrigue and excitement are created through the use of secret codes, traps, hidden tunnels, narrow escapes, chases, rooftop chases, and poisoned wine.

Ik, Kim Young. *The Shoes from Yang San Valley,* il. by Park Minja. Doubleday 1970. $2.95; 11 up.

A tale of love, tragedy, heartbreak, and reunion during the Korean War. Only a callous reader will be dry-eyed when he finishes.

Ishii, Momoko. *The Doll's Day for Yoshiko,* il. by Mamoru Funai. Follett 1966. $3.50; 8–10.

Yoshiko's wish for a set of china dolls to celebrate Doll's Day, an annual festival important to all girls in Japan, prompts Yoshiko's mother to make a special gift to her. The delicate illustrations are characteristic of Japan and have a simplicity that will appeal to third-and fourth-graders who read this warm story of modern Japan.

Ish-Kishor, Sulamith. *Boy of Old Prague,* il. by Ben Shahn. Pantheon 1963. $4.29; 10–14.

A powerful story of prejudice and superstition in feudal days. An estate near Prague and a Jewish ghetto are the settings for a young boy's examination of his own misconceptions about Jews.

Joutsen, Britta-Lisa. *Lingonberries in the Snow,* il. by Anthony Saris. Follett 1968. $3.50; 10–14.

Susie's father wins a Fulbright scholarship and the family spends a year in Finland. They go with many fears and biases about life in another country and return to the United States with a much better understanding of the Finnish people and their customs. A friendship between Susie and Laila, a Finn, provides the means for understanding.

Kassil, Ley. *Brother of the Hero,* Braziller 1968. $3.95; 12 up.

Geshka, a Russian orphan boy, lives in a dream world in which he claims Klimenti Cheremish, a famous Russian flier, as his brother since they both have the same last name. When Klimenti comes to town, Geshka's fabrications put him in a difficult situation.

Kay, Helen. *Henri's Hands for Pablo Picasso,* il. by Victor Ambrus. Abelard 1965. $2.95; 6–10.

The author follows the adventures of Henri, a baker's son who wants to be an artist like Picasso. This lively, authentic story will interest many children, especially those who like to do things with their hands. Valuable treatment of Picasso.

Kingman, Lee. *Secret Journey of the Silver Reindeer,* il. by Lynd Ward. Doubleday 1968. $3.50; 9–12.

A 15-year-old Lapp orphan must prove his ability to care for his younger brothers and sisters and for his family's herd of silver reindeer.

Knight, Eric. *Lassie Come Home,* il. by Cyrus Leroy Baldridge. Holt 1940. $3.95; 10 up.

Classic story of boy and dog devotion. Lassie, the collie, is sold when the family goes on the dole. Her escape and 400-mile trip home make an adventure in the atmosphere of prewar Great Britain.

Krumgold, Joseph. *The Most Terrible Turk,* il. by Michael Hampshire. Crowell 1969. $3.75; 6–8.

This humorous story focuses on the conflict of the old and the new in Turkey. Proud Uncle Mustafa takes revenge in a most unusual way on the many young Turks who are threatening his old way of life. His nephew Ali finds an unique plan to thwart his uncle's purpose. The black-and-white drawings give brief glimpses of the cultural background.

Lattimore, Eleanor France. *Little Pear and the Rabbits,* il. by the author. Morrow 1956. $3.50; 7–9.

Written 25 years after the original Little Pear book. A charming story of a delightful and mischievous small Chinese boy and his family. Illustrations are most interesting. By the same author: *Little Pear* and *Little Pear and His Friends.*

Lyon, Elinor. *Cathie Runs Wild,* il. by Greta Elgaard. Follett 1968. $2.95; 10–12.

After spending most of her life in an orphanage, Cathie Gull is reveling in her new-found freedom, the love of her aunt and cousin, and the companionship of two good friends. This precious security is threatened when Aunt Jean arrives from Edinburgh determined to send her niece to a boarding school to acquire culture.

———. *The Dream Hunters,* il. by Mary Dinsdale. Follett 1967. $2.95; 9–12.

A humorous adventure story that relates how a venturesome Scottish boy "rescues" a bored and lonesome girl from a boat on which she is supposedly held captive. Numerous misadventures occur before each of the children returns home.

_____. *Green Grow the Rushes,* il. by Graham Byfield. Follett 1964. $2.95; 10 up.

An exciting adventure story of how a group of curious children find an ancient Roman road among the cliffs along the coast of Wales.

McGraw, Eloise Jarvis. *The Golden Goblet.* Coward 1961. $4.95; 11–14.

A golden goblet, "more beautiful than the sun," is stolen from the Pharaoh's tomb. Orphaned Ranofer, who suspects his evil half-brother, pursues the grave robbers. This believable story gives many details of the goldsmith's craft and of ancient Egyptian life. By the same author: *Mara, Daughter of the Nile.*

MacIntyre, Elizabeth. *Ninji's Magic,* il. by Mamoru Funai. Knopf 1966. $3.50; 8–10.

Like many small boys everywhere, Ninji has trouble being a good student, getting along with other children, and pleasing his family. How he solves his problems with the help of his new friend, Alobeu, when he is looking after his small brother at the hospital, is vividly told.

Macken, Walter. *The Flight of the Doves.* Macmillan 1968. $4.50 (P—Macmillan, $.95); 8–12.

Exciting account of the experiences of 12-year-old Finn Dove and his seven-year-old sister Dervae as they make their way to their grandmother's home in Ireland after running away from their stepfather. The story is filled with intriguing mystery, fast adventure, and strong characters.

McNeill, Janet. *The Battle of St. George Without,* il. by Mary Russom. Little 1968. $4.50; 10–14.

The war-damaged church of St. George Without is the scene of this English story. Matt McGinley and his gang are put to a test when thieves attempt to carry away valuable parts of the church. This well-developed tale has an unusual setting and many fine characterizations of adults and children. By the same author: *Goodbye, Dove Square.*

MacOrlan, Pierre. *The Anchor of Mercy,* il. by David K. Stone. Pantheon 1967. $3.95; 12 up.

1777 is an exciting year for 16-year-old Yves-Marie Morgat, son of a wealthy ship chandler, as he finds himself involved in espionage, murder, and piracy when the French navy prepares to defend Brest against the British fleet.

Maiden, Cecil. *The Borrowed Crown.* Viking 1968. $3.95; 8–12.

A peasant boy impersonates a prince in this story based on a true incident from the War of the Roses.

Mark, Polly. *Tani,* il. by Ursula Koering. McKay 1964. $3.44; 8–11.

Tani, a girl of Borneo, is urged to attend mission school and then is unfairly accused of stealing a pair of earrings. Her saving the life of the headmistress forces the latter and others at the school to uncover the truth and give Tani the recognition due her.

Martin, Patricia Miles. *Little Two and the Peachtree,* il. by Joan Berg. Atheneum 1963. $2.75; 7–10.

Peach Blossom's paintings help a neighbor understand the need for opening the canal to release water onto the dry rice fields. The book is notable for the singing quality of the story and the delicacy of its sketches.

Matsuno, Masako. *Taro and the Tofu,* il. by Kazue Mizumura. World 1962. $3.41; 5–8.

Taro is a boy in modern Japan, but the temptation he meets to keep what is not his is universal. The story has charm and significance matched by the pictures.

Melnikoff, Pamela. *The Star and the Sword,* il. by Hans Schwarz. Crown 1965. $3.50; 10–14.

A vital account of how two Jewish children, ages ten and twelve, are befriended by Robin Hood and his men and assist a returned crusader deliver money for the ransom of Richard the Lion-Hearted. The book deals sensitively with the problem of prejudice in an age of persecution of Jews.

Meyers, Susan. *The Cabin on the Fjord,* il. by Trina Schart Hyman. Doubleday 1969. $3.50; 7–10.

Set in Norway, the book has universal appeal: the theme of competition between two sisters. Reidunn envies her older sister's talent, beauty, and poise, always finding herself less appealing and clever. In an attempt to please visiting grandparents, Reidunn takes a dreadful chance with her life to obtain some rare wild berries she has heard about in a troll story.

Mirsky, Reba Paeff. *Nomusa and the New Magic.* Follett 1962. $3.78; 10–14.

An authentic description of life in a Zulu village is presented without undue emphasis or apology. This look in depth at another culture is comparable in quality to the author's *Thirty-one Brothers and Sisters* and *Seven Grandmothers.*

Mitchison, Naomi. *Friends and Enemies,* il. by Caroline Sasoon. Day 1968. $4.50; 10–14.

Petrus lives in South Africa and feels some of the cruelty of white men. He is forced to flee across the border after his schoolteacher brother is arrested. Living in a rural area is a difficult adjustment for Petrus, but he grows to understand the life and his own role as a man in a free country.

Morrison, Lucile. *The Lost Queen of Egypt,* il. by Franz Geritz. Lippincott 1937. $4.75; 12 up.

The life of Ankhsenamen, wife of Tutankhamen, is chronicled from earliest childhood until the death of her husband. Old Egypt comes to life in this accurate and absorbing tale.

Norris, Gunilla B. *Lillian,* il. by N. Swanberg. Atheneum 1968. $3.95; 9–12.

In postwar Sweden, Lillian becomes worried that her mother will stop loving her after she and Lillian's father are divorced. The story is told with perception of a ten-year-old girl's problems.

O'Dell, Scott. *The Black Pearl,* il. by Milton Johnson. Houghton 1967. $3.75; 10 up.

How the discovery of the Pearl of Heaven shapes the life of its finder, Ramon, is the theme of this excellent book. Superstition, personal drives, and religious beliefs play a great part. Newbery Award Honor Book, 1968.

O'Neill, Mary. *Ali,* il. by Juan C. Barberis. Atheneum 1968. $3.95; 10–14.

Modern ways of living come to an Arab village at the edge of the desert and bring many changes to Ali, who thinks he is already a man who has no need to learn at school. When he finally gets what he wants, he realizes that he has really grown up.

Ottley, Reginald. *The Bates Family.* Harcourt 1969. $3.95; 12 up.

This story tells of a family of itinerant Australian drovers and the difficulties they encounter when a drought is followed by torrential rains. It is based on a real family, and readers will closely identify with this unusual way of life.

———. *Giselle.* Harcourt 1968. $3.25; 12 up.

Set in New Caledonia in times hardly past, this is a day-by-day story of a girl of French ancestry who knows, loves, and reveres the people around her. Giselle can understand the anguish of her uncle who was once a powerful man, now smitten by a crippling disease that makes him an invalid. She can take her mother's debilitating headaches in stride.

She can accept and love her father who works in the mines by day and "shines" deer by night. Best of all, she can take herself as she is and ask for nothing more than to help earn money for the "cure" that will make her uncle well again. Because this is a simple story, simply told, the reader will even accept the tragedy that comes at the very end. By the same author: *Boy Alone.*

Panova, Vera. *On Faraway Street,* tr. by Rya Gabel, ed. by Anne Terry White. Braziller 1968. $3.95; 12–15.

The tale of a boy who has many problems to face in growing up: a stepfather, friends who concoct mischief, and a new home. How all of this happens in modern Russia makes a good story.

Peterson, Hans. *Magnus in the Harbor* and *Magnus and the Wagon Horse,* il. by Ilon Wiland. Pantheon 1961. $2.95 each; 6–10.

These two charming stories of the everyday adventures of seven-year-old Magnus and his friends in Gothenburg, Sweden, are part of the popular series of Magnus stories being filmed for Swedish television. They reveal typical adventures of a small boy anywhere, but the Gothenburg setting is authentic. By the same author: *Magnus and the Ship's Mascot; Magnus in Danger.*

Peyton, K. M. *Flambards,* il. by Victor Ambrus. World 1968. $3.95; 12 up.

A young heiress becomes part of the fox-hunting household dominated by her cruel uncle.

Phipson, Joan. *The Boundary Riders,* il. by Margaret Horder. Harcourt 1963. $3.50; 8–12.

Three children who set out to ride the boundaries of their family's cattle ranch and inspect the fences venture too far and are lost in a blinding mist. They suffer hunger, cold, and danger for three terror-filled days. The setting, the sparsely settled country of southeastern Australia, is a perfect background for this story of courage and resourcefulness.

_____. *The Family Conspiracy,* il. by Margaret Horder. Harcourt 1964. $3.75 (P—Harcourt, $.65); 9–12.

Alarmed by their mother's illness, her need for an operation, and the family's lack of money, the four middle children of the Barker family work to earn money to help without the knowledge of their parents. The authentic picture of Australian ranch life, the vivid characterization, and the sense of family unity make this noteworthy.

_____. *Good Luck to the Rider.* Harcourt 1968. $3.50; 9–12.

Barbara Trevor finds a wild black foal and works hard at

breaking and training him. As the colt develops, so do Barbara's personal strength and courage. Set in Australia.

_____. *Peter and Butch*. Harcourt 1969. $4.50; 11 up.

Set in a small Australian town, this story describes how Peter, an adolescent boy without a father, learns that masculinity is not synonymous with toughness, and that a real man not only thinks before he acts but also accepts his own limitations.

_____. *Threat to the Barkers,* il. by Margaret Horder. Harcourt 1965. $3.50; 9–12.

Another story of the resourceful Barker family of Australia. Sheep thieves threaten Jack's new flock of stud sheep, and Edward becomes involved in a situation too difficult for a boy to handle. Mystery, adventure, and a boy's courage, with fine human relations and knowledge and love of animals, are combined in this well-written novel of ranch and family life. By the same author: *Cross Currents.*

Picard, Barbara L. *Lost John,* il. by Charles Keeping. Criterion 1963. $3.50; 10–14.

John sets out to avenge his father's death during the reign of King Richard. The search brings him much more than the knowledge of his father's killer.

_____. *One Is One.* Holt 1966. $3.95; 11–14.

Stephen learns the hard way that there is more than one kind of strength. Set in 14th-century England. By the same author: *The Lady of the Linden Tree; Ransom for a Knight.*

Pilgrim, Anne. *Selina's New Family,* il. by Graham Byfield. Abelard 1967. $4.50; 10–14.

Selina's mother decides to remarry ten years after her husband's death. Since this will mean a move to Ireland, Selina objects to the move and the marriage. Resentment and stubborn refusal to like anything about Ireland characterize Selina's first days there, but she gradually accepts the new country and the new family.

Plowman, Stephanie. *My Kingdom for a Grave.* Houghton 1971. $4.95; 12–16.

An account of the Russian Revolution and the fall of the Russian czars. A fast paced, authentic, and intriguing story written from a personal point of view. Companion volume to *Three Lives of the Czar.*

Polland, Madeleine A. *Beorn the Proud,* il. by William Stobbs. Holt 1962. $3.27; 9–12.

Beorn, a ninth-century Viking who is heir to his father's

throne, overcomes his arrogant attitude with the help of an older warrior. Ness, a captive from Ireland, proves to be a true friend interested in Beorn's feelings and conversion to Christianity.

_____. *To Tell My People,* il. by R. M. Powers. Holt 1968. $4.50; 10–14.

Lumna is taken from prehistoric Britain to Rome as a slave. Her experiences there are entirely different from her background.

_____. *The White Twilight,* il. by Alan Cober. Holt 1965. $3.50; 10–14.

In the white twilight of the long summer evenings in 16th-century Denmark, Hanne attempts to unravel a disturbing mystery. In doing so, she not only comes to a better understanding of herself but also opens the eyes of her friend Carl Adam to a wider and wiser view of the adult world. By the same author: *Queen without a Crown; Town Across Water; Deirdre.*

Potter, Bronson. *Antonio,* il. by Ann Grifalconi. Atheneum 1968. $3.50; 7–11.

Simply written story of a Portuguese fishing village and the ox boy with the crippled hand who saves the fishing fleet in a severe storm. The story shows that there is always something that one can do well.

Prishvin, Mikhail. *Treasure Trove of the Sun,* tr. by Tatiana Balkoff-Drowne, il. by Feodor Rojankovsky. Viking 1952. $4.50; 9–12.

The very first pictures of young Anna "with freckles like a million gold pieces" and of her stalwart ten-year-old brother Peterkin invite young readers to share their dangerous adventure with a wise old hound and a wolf "doomed to destruction because of his own hatred." Set in Russia after World War II.

Rankin, Louise S. *Daughter of the Mountains,* il. by Kurt Wiese. Viking 1948. $3.50 (P—Archway, $.75); 9 up.

Like youngsters who enjoyed this book when it was new, today's young reader will find that he, too, "has a friend in Tibet." The adventures of young Momo, leaving her Tibetan mountain home to regain her stolen red-gold terrier, involve robbers, a kidnapper, jungles, a ride on an Indian train, and the swirling, unfamiliar life of Calcutta.

Reboul, Antoine. *Thou Shalt Not Kill,* tr. by Stephanie Craig. Phillips 1969. $4.95; 12–16.

An Egyptian boy and an Israeli girl are both wounded and

lost in the Sinai desert in the aftermath of the 1967 Arab-Israeli war. Their struggle against and conquest of the hostile elements and their own hostility for each other make an exciting and moving story.

Reeves, James. *Rhyming Will,* il. by Edward Ardizzone. McGraw 1968. $3.50; 5–8.

A seven-year-old boy who speaks only in rhyme loses that ability at what seems to be a most undesirable time. The setting is England.

Reggiani, Renee. *The Sun Train.* Coward 1966. $3.95; 14–17.

The La Rosa family find adjusting to their new life in a large city difficult when they move from a Sicilian plantation to the mainland. Living in an apartment, going to school, and finding a suitable job for their father and a husband for Agata make this a suspenseful story.

Richter, Hans Peter. *Friedrich,* tr. by Edite Kroll. Holt 1970. $3.97; 12–16.

A moving story of an ill-fated friendship between a young boy and his Jewish friend. Set in Germany in 1929, in the early days of Nazism.

Rinkoff, Barbara. *The Pretzel Hero: A Story of Old Vienna,* il. by Charles Mikolaycak. Parents 1970. $3.95; 7–10.

Legend has it that during the seige of Vienna by the Turks in 1529 a baker's apprentice helped to save the city from capture. In her account, the author creates the exciting fiction of a boy hero whose quick thinking and resolute action saved the day for everyone but the Turks.

Robbins, Ruth. *The Emperor and the Drummer Boy,* il. by Nicolas Sidjakov. Parnassus 1962. $3.50; 9–12.

Two drummer boys, Jean and Armand, demonstrate their loyalty and courage in this exciting story focused on Napoleon's visit to Boulogne in 1804. The striking line drawings are similar in style to *Baboushka and the Three Kings,* a Caldecott Award winner of 1960. The background may enrich the history of the period for older readers. A French edition is entitled *L' Empereur et le Tambour.*

Ropner, Pamela. *The Guardian Angel,* il. by Sheila Bewley. Coward 1967. $3.29; 8–12.

Gabriella spends the summer at her grandmother's Scottish estate and becomes entangled in a web of fantasy and reality difficult to separate. The reader is never certain about what actually happens and what appears to Gabriella as dreamlike experiences, but the high suspense makes that decision unimportant.

Schatz, Letta. *Bola and the Oba's Drummers*, il. by Tom Feelings. McGraw 1967. $4.50; 10–12.

Iban, Nigeria, is the setting for this tale of Bola, a farmer's son whose skill wins him a place with the king's musicians. Lucid text, above-average writing style, and excellent characterization.

Schnack, Friedrich. *Click and the Toyshop*, tr. by Eileen Rapoport, il. by Erich Holle. Abelard 1967. $3.50; 9–12.

A young lad in modern Germany has a variety of friends: the keeper of a pet shop, the manager of a toy shop, and a sea captain. His lottery ticket brings him luck.

Seed, Jenny. *Tombi's Song*, il. by Dugald MacDougal. Rand 1966. $2.95; 7–10.

A little Zulu girl in Africa does the everyday things little girls usually do, such as going to the store on an errand for her mother. On the way she has many adventures.

Seeger, Martin L. *The Day of the Earthquake*, il. by Marilyn Miller. Lothrop 1967. $3.95; 10–14.

Life in Antioch is recreated, and events are described from the viewpoint of young Gaius, who becomes involved in secret plots and the intrigue of war. The spread of Christianity provides an authentic background for the story.

Seredy, Kate. *The Good Master*, il. by the author. Viking 1935. $4.00 (P—Dell, $.75); 10–12.

Small hoyden Kate is a problem to her gentle father until a visit to her uncle's ranch and the lively company of cousin Jancsi prove a steadying influence. Popular story with a pre-war Hungary setting. Sequel: *The Singing Tree*.

_____. *The White Stag*, il. by the author. Viking 1937. $3.00; 12 up.

The Hungarian epic about Attila and his sons is beautifully written. By the same author: *Philomena*.

Sholokhov, Mikhail. *Fierce and Gentle Warriors*, tr. by Miriam Morton, il. by Milton Glaser. Doubleday 1967. $3.95; 12 up.

Three short stories by the winner of the 1965 Nobel Prize for Literature make up this remarkable book. All deal with human beings caught in the agonies of war and revolution and show that in the midst of great trouble people act nobly and gently.

Sindall, Marjorie. *Three Cheers for Charlie*, il. by Margery Gill. Criterion 1968. $2.95; 6–10.

Charlie is a disadvantaged boy from London who is taken for

a two-week vacation to a chicken farm. Although he is eight years old, he looks frail beside robust eight-year-old Sally, who lives on the farm. Sally thinks Charlie is a coward and "too little" to do anything that she dares him to do. In an attempt to prove Sally wrong, Charlie saves the family from a disaster.

Speare, Elizabeth George. *The Bronze Bow.* Houghton 1961. $3.50; 11–14.

Young Daniel hates the conquering Romans and joins a guerilla band, but he learns that some problems are better solved by love than might. This is a moving story of young people in the time when Jesus emerged as leader and teacher. (Newbery Award, 1962.) By the same author: *Calico Captive.*

Sperry, Armstrong. *Call it Courage,* il. by the author. Macmillan 1940. $3.50; 10–12.

Sailing away to a desert island, Mafatu, the chief's son, lives in solitude until he can conquer fear. This is a distinguished tale of a boy of the South Seas. Newbery Award, 1941.

Stevenson, William. *The Bushbabies,* il. by Victor Ambrus. Houghton 1965. $3.50; 9–12.

Lacking a game permit to take her pet galago (bushbaby) home to England, Jackie stays by herself in Kenya when her family sails. With the bushbaby and an elderly African hunter, she travels over miles of wild country. An exciting narrative of Kenya, which the author knows well—the country, the people, the animals, and especially bushbabies.

Stinetorf, Louise A. *A Charm for Paco's Mother,* il. by Joseph Escourido. Day 1965. $3.86; 8–11.

A moving story of a small boy's devotion to his blind mother and his desire to help her recover her sight. Together they make a living selling cacti to tourists in Mexico. Excellent for dramatizing. The action is not lively, but children will become involved.

Stolz, Mary. *Juan,* il. by Louis S. Glanzman. Harper 1970. $3.95; 8–11.

An absorbing tale of children in a Mexican orphanage and their particular longings and desires. Told without sentimentality.

Stuart, Morna. *Marassa and Midnight,* il. by Alvin Smith. McGraw 1966. $3.75; 9–12.

Twin Negro boys born in Haiti in the 1790's are separated, with Marassa going to Paris with the Marquis and Midnight joining the slave revolt and going underground. Eventually the boys are reunited after heartbreaking experiences.

Sutcliff, Rosemary. *Beowulf,* il. by C. Keeping. Dutton 1962. $3.50; 12 up.
An excellent retelling of the Old English epic. The pictures are appropriately powerful.

————. *Dawn Wind.* Walck 1962. $5.50; 12 up.
A fine book about early English history. Owain, sole survivor of the Britons in a battle with the Saxons, returns the lost Regina to her Saxon people. Sold by the enemy, Owain finally is reunited with the girl and they start a new life.

————. *Warrior Scarlet,* il. by Charles Keeping. Walck 1958. $5.50; 12 up.
Drem, who lives in Bronze Age Britain, is told that he can never earn the scarlet cloak of a warrior because he has a useless spear arm. How he makes three friends, faces hunting wolves, and finds himself at last among the New Spears of his tribe is bibliotherapy and much more: a taut, strong, warm book. The dark, brooding pictures provide an appropriate background. By the same author: *The Shield Ring; The Eagle of the Ninth; The Lantern Bearers; The Silver Branch.*

Taylor, Elizabeth. *Mossy Trotter,* il. by Laszlo Acs. Harcourt 1967. $3.25; 10–12.
Riding in his grandfather's red sports car and inspecting the rubbish dumps are more to Mossy's liking than being page boy in a London wedding. The author, who is known for her adult novels and many short stories for *The New Yorker,* has written a charming first book for children.

Tooze, Ruth. *The Dragon Tree,* il. by Joseph Escourido. Day 1969. $3.49; 8–10.
The stories of four young boys who lived on the island of Tenerife at different times are recounted. The narrator is the 3,000-year-old dragon tree who tells what has passed beneath him. Particularly good for reading aloud.

Townsend, John R. *Goodbye to the Jungle.* Lippincott 1967. $3.75; 12–15.
This realistic presentation of an innercity family in England is probably valid for such a family in any locale: the shiftless father, the irregular family relationships, the endless involvement with the law, and the futile efforts of the children to break the pattern they recognize as shameful. The picture is presented with candor and yet with such warmth that the reader realizes that the characters are human beings.

————. *Pirate's Island.* Lippincott 1968. $3.75; 9–12.
Gordon Dobbs and Sheila, two lonely children, begin a

search for a lost treasure but become involved with a real
treasure hunt in an English setting. By the same author:
Trouble in the Jungle.

Trease, Geoffrey. *Message to Hadrian.* Vanguard 1955. $3.50;
11 up.

A thrilling historical novel for more able readers in the fifth
and sixth grade. Paul carries a message from Britain in revolt
to the court of Emperor Hadrian in Rome. It is a long journey
filled with adventure.

Treece, Henry. *The Dream Time,* il. by Charles Keeping.
Meredith 1968. $3.95; all ages.

A beautifully evocative story of harsh Stone Age life and a
boy's desire to make beautiful things rather than fight and
kill. This is a very special book and the last novel of Henry
Treece, who has again used his poet's gift for simple, telling
words that express depths of experience and feeling.

————. *The Last Viking,* il. by Charles Keeping. Pantheon
1966. $3.75; 11–15.

An exciting story of Harald Hardrada, who was killed in a
battle against the English in 1066. It covers many of his
adventures as a young Viking king, including his travels to
lands now known as Norway, Russia, and Turkey. By the
same author: *Viking's Dawn; Centurion; A Windswept City;*
and others.

Tunis, John R. *His Enemy, His Friend.* Morrow 1967. $3.95
(P—Avon, $.75); 12–16.

Conflict arises during World War II when Feldwebel pre-
sides over the execution of Jean-Paul's father. Twenty
years later a soccer field is the scene of conflict for the two.
By the same author: *Silence over Dunkerque; Schoolboy
Johnson.*

Van Der Loeff, A. Rutgers. *Avalanche,* il. by Gustav Schrotter.
Morrow 1958. $3.95; 12 up.

A powerful, well-written story showing the tragedy brought
into the lives of people in a small Swiss village when
avalanches bury their homes and loved ones. Very realistic
and thought-provoking for older children. By the same
author: *Great Day in Holland; The Skating Race.*

————. *Vassilis on the Run,* il. by George Mocniak. Follett
1969. $3.95; 10–14.

From the time Vassilis and his family return to Greece from
Albania where they have been political prisoners, until they
are settled in the refugee settlement, Vassilis is literally "on
the run." He is daring, a quick thinker, and able to elude
officials until his innocence is finally proved. The back

ground of life in Greece is convincingly depicted in this exciting story.

Van Iterson, Siny R. *Pulga,* tr. by Alexander and Alison Gode. Morrow 1970. $4.95; 12–16.

A compassionate account of a 15-year-old street urchin struggling to escape the slums of Bogota, Colombia.

van Rhijn, Aleid. *The Tide in the Attic,* il. by Marjorie Gill. Criterion 1962. $3.50; 11–14.

The reader sees the disastrous 1953 Dutch flood through the eyes of young Kees. The courage of the boy and his family in facing the future makes a touching story, honestly told.

Van Stockum, Hilda. *Mogo's Flute,* il. by Robin Jaques. Viking 1966. $3.50; 8–11.

Everyone says a tabu was put upon Mogo when he was a baby. He has to prove his worth to the villagers, and the one thing he can do well is play the flute. A beautifully told story with the authentic flavor of the village people of Kenya.

_____. *The Winged Watchman,* il. by the author. Farrar 1962. $3.25; 8–12.

The quiet courage of the Hollanders during the German occupation is symbolized in this novel's title. Despite tragedy, the warmth and even humor of a united and loyal family give a wholesome tone to a fine story.

Vaughan-Jackson, Genevieve. *Carramore,* il. by the author. Hastings 1968. $3.95; 9–12.

Based on the author's own childhood in Ireland, this is the absorbing story of an 11-year-old girl living in the Irish countryside during the 1920's as the Civil War intrudes more and more on her quiet life. Most of the people and events are real. The details of Irish farm life are vivid. The story is unforgettable.

Vavra, Robert. *Felipe the Bullfighter,* by the author. Harcourt 1968. $3.50; 8–12.

Felipe, a real Spanish boy, comes from a long line of matadors. They say that someday he will be the world's bravest matador. When the chance comes for him to fight a young bull, he is fearful though well practiced and proves himself ready. Vibrant full-color photographs catch the atmosphere of southern Spain.

_____. *Pizorro,* photos by the author. Harcourt 1968. $3.95; 7–11.

Pizorro lives on a rancho north of Mexico City. He is only eight years old, but he works hard each day helping his father provide for their large family. The surprise gift of a baby burro for Pizorro, its getting lost, and its subsequently being found, add zest to the story. Magnificent color photographs show life in the rural community and the city.

Verne, Jules. *A Long Vacation,* tr. by Olga Marx. Holt 1967.- $3.50; 12–15.

This modern version of Robinson Crusoe tells the story of 15 boys marooned on an island in the Pacific after a stormy voyage from Australia in a ship inadvertently set adrift.

Walsh, Jill Paton. *Fireweed.* Farrar 1970. $3.95; 11–14.

Bill and Julie, two teenagers, meet by chance during the London blitz and combine forces in an unusual symbiotic relationship that solves the immense problems of daily survival plus those deeper ones of loneliness and fear. The story of their life together told in the first person many years later by Bill.

Walton, Bryce. *Harpoon Gunner.* Crowell 1968. $3.75; 11 up.

At 16, Erik Nordall is a frustrated orphan who has run away from his uncle's farm to earn his rightful heritage left by his father who, before his death, was a king gunner of whales. His long quest ends in Antarctica; he learns about life on a factory ship and also, as he decodes his father's log book, the location of the fabled hidden sea of the blue whales. Can he ever excuse himself for revealing the location and thereby hastening the extinction of the blues? Disaster intervenes to give Erik a second chance. A tightly constructed novel filled with tension, mystery, and intrigue. It is packed with facts that lend credibility but may at times turn the reader's stomach. But it is a tale that once begun will go unfinished by few.

Watson, Sally. *The Mukhtar's Children.* Holt 1968. $4.50; 10 up.

Exciting story of suspense and adventure as Jasmin and Khalil, twins of the Mukhtar, cause fighting between the Arab village and the Jewish kibbutz as well as a reconciliation.

Weaver, Stella. *A Poppy in the Corn.* Pantheon 1961. $4.29; 11–14.

Teresa, a war orphan adopted into a Cornish family, doesn't feel she belongs. Her running away brings into the open the conflicts among the four children involved. The atmosphere and human relationships are authentic.

Westwood, Gwen. *Narni of the Desert,* il. by Peter Warner. Rand 1967. $3.50; 6–9.

Narni, son of a Bushman in South Africa, longs to become a hunter like his father. How he helps his mother find food during the long drought and how he finally takes part in a great hunt make a charming story. The illustrations are particularly good.

Willard, Barbara. *Storm from the West,* il. by Douglas Hall. Harcourt 1963. $3.50; 13–16.

Excellent for understanding the adjustments required of two families of teenage children united by a second marriage. The peculiarities of Americans as seen by British teenagers are well treated. Set in Scotland.

Williams, Jay. *The Horn of Roland,* il. by Sean Morrison. Crowell 1968. $3.95; 9–14.

A vigorous story of the exciting and heroic life of Roland. Especially featured are the enduring friendship of Roland and Oliver and the heroism of the two during the defense of the pass of Roncesvalles.

Williams, Susan. *Elephant Boy,* il. by Peter Chadwick. McKay 1964. $3.75; 9–12.

A realistic story of an elephant boy in Burma during the Second World War begins with a vivid account of the birth of the boy, Ba Tu, followed by as vivid an account of the baby elephant, Po Seiu. Their amazing understanding of each other carries them through the horrors of war in the jungle. This authentic story describes wartime Burma and the role elephants play there.

Williamson, Joanne S. *To Dream upon a Crown,* il. by Jacob Landau. Knopf 1967. $4.95; 12 up.

A dramatic telling of England's War of the Roses, using dialogue taken primarily from Shakespeare's trilogy on King Henry VI, gives a vivid picture of a bloodthirsty period in history.

Wojciechowska, Maia. *Shadow of a Bull,* il. by Alvin Smith. Atheneum 1964. $3.50; 10–13.

This perceptive story concerns the son of a great Spanish matador who is expected to follow his father's career. A fascinating setting, and the boy's moral and physical dilemma are realistically portrayed. Newbery Award, 1965.

———. *A Single Light.* Harper 1968. $3.95; 12 up.

The beautiful story of a girl in Spain, born deaf, who is rejected by her family and ridiculed by the people, but who longs desperately to find something to love. She finds a hidden statue of the Christ Child, which brings understand ing and changes the lives of many people. By the same author: *Turned Out.*

Zei, Alki. *Wildcat Under Glass,* tr. by Edward Fenton. Holt 1968. $4.50; 9–12.

Although set in Greece and written by a Greek, this book was first published in Russia and has not yet been published in Greece. It tells of the effect on one family of the approaching dictatorship that was proclaimed in August of 1936. Those were exciting times, and this book mirrors them beautifully. Along with adventure there is plenty of gaiety, humor, and warm family life.

Mystery

Adrian, Mary. *The Indian Horse Mystery,* il. by Lloyd Coe. Hastings 1966. $3.50; 9 up.

Indian Jim Hawk, Hap Miller, and his cousin Kathie discover that rustlers are responsible for setting dangerous grass fires and unnecessarily slaughtering cattle during their process of stealing calves. Good characterization, fair suspense, and accurate and interesting nature notes.

Allan, Mabel E. *Mystery of the Ski Slopes.* Criterion 1966. $3.50; 12–14.

Perdita goes in disguise to a Swiss pension searching for her cousin. She encounters adventure, romance, and danger.

Angier, Bradford, and Jeanne Dixon. *The Ghost of Spirit River,* il. by Kenney E. Carey. Atheneum 1968. $4.25; 9–13.

After a freak horse-van accident city-bred Perry finds himself involved in a search for the once wild horses that escaped from the van. The Alcan trail provides a picturesque setting for an exciting chase, mysterious encounters, and moments of despair.

Arthur, Robert. *Mystery and More Mystery,* il. by Saul Lambert. Random 1966. $2.95; 11 up.

These ten stories (several published in *Ellery Queen's Mystery Magazine*) are suitable for older elementary readers. Themes range from buried treasure through the prim antics of spinster sleuths to feats of dark magic and Holmesian sleuthing. Humor, blackmail, espionage, acrostics, ciphers, and codes appear. Excellent craftsmanship and deft characterization. Background and action are skillfully blended. By the same author: *Thrillers and More Thrillers; Spies and More Spies.*

Arthur, Ruth M. *A Candle in Her Room,* il. by Margery Gill. Atheneum 1967. $3.95; 12–16.

A remarkable story in which the enduring power of love and witchcraft combine to produce a tender, sad story that may help girls with the bewildering pains of adolescence to find answers to their own problems. A discarded doll found in the attic ties three generations together.

Bacon, Peggy. *The Ghost of Opalina,* il. by the author. Little 1967. $4.95; 10–15.

As Opalina, a ghostly cat with a personality all her own, relates her nine lives, children can see changes that take place over the years. Each story (life) is well written and contains a separate plot; however, it would be very easy to stop reading at the end of any chapter.

Baudouy, Michel-Aimé. *Secret of the Hidden Painting,* il. by Anne Carter. Harcourt 1962. $3.75; 10–12.

Two puzzles fire the ready imaginations of the children of a Parisian family, who spend a strange summer in the coastal Breton home of genteelly impoverished friends. Newspaper accounts of some stolen paintings and a game cock are parts of the major puzzle. Extremely well written.

Bawden, Nina. *The White Horse Gang,* il. by Kenneth Longtemps. Lippincott 1966. $3.50; 9–11.

Trouble plagues the "gang": Sam, Rose, and Abe. To find money for Rose's return to America, they kidnap spoiled Percy, who enjoys himself but is the cause of real danger for the older boys. Modern English village life is depicted through children's eyes. Illustrations set the climactic mood of Gibbett Wood.

―――――. *The Witch's Daughter.* Lippincott 1966. $3.50; 9–12.

Perdita lives on the Scottish island of Skua with a strange foster mother locally known as a witch. Tim and Janey Hogart make friends with her, and together they help uncover a secret precious stone business. Perdita finds a rare, important flower.

Berna, Paul. *The Clue of the Black Cat,* tr. by John Buchanan-Brown. Pantheon 1964. $3.50 (P—Random, $.75); 12 up.

This is perhaps Paul Berna's best mystery for young people. The Thiriets' move into much-needed new living quarters is interrupted by a cruel confidence trick. Tracking down the thieves tests the ingenuity of Bobby Thiriet and his friends.

The story is suspenseful and witty. A disappearing cat provides the link that helps clear up the mystery.

————. *The Secret of the Missing Boat,* Pantheon 1967. $3.50; 10–14.

An exciting mystery story that eventually explains why numerous people are anxious to recover a boat lost among the islands of the Morbihan in Brittany. The setting is beautifully described.

Bonham, Frank. *Mystery of the Fat Cat,* il. by A. Smith. Dutton 1968. $3.95; 10–14.

The Dogtown Boys' Club is the residual heir of a huge estate being enjoyed by a large tomcat. Another good book set in the same ghetto locale as *The Nitty Gritty.* By the same author: *Mystery in Little Tokyo; Durango Street.*

Bonsall, Crosby. *The Case of the Hungry Stranger.* Harper 1963. $2.50 (P—Scholastic, $.60); 5–10.

Wizard, the sleuth, helps his friends Tubby, Snitch, and Skinny find a culprit with a deep, blue smile. This is a logical mystery, easy enough for a beginner to read yet well enough plotted so that his story sense is not insulted. Rollicking illustrations depict a theme not mentioned in the text—a Negro boy can share a clubhouse with other six-year-olds in perfect joy and ease. By the same author: *The Mystery of the Cat's Meow.*

Bonzon, P. J. *Pursuit,* tr. by Thelma Niklaus, il. by Margery Gill. Lothrop 1962. $3.50; 10–14.

This suspenseful and intriguing story tells of the summer when Vincent is alone at his home in the French Alps. He becomes involved in a theft case and finds his own life in danger.

Borhegyi, Suzanne de. *The Secret of the Sacred Lake,* il. by David K. Stone. Holt 1967. $4.50; 10–12.

Myth and fact blend during one Guatemalan summer for three American children on the shores of a volcanic lake. Involved in an archeological search for a Mayan idol lost in 1200 A.D., they find terror, compassion, beauty, excitement, and satisfaction.

Boston, L. M. *An Enemy at Green Knowe,* il. by Peter Boston. Harcourt 1964. $3.50; 9–12.

Melanie Powers' black magic wafted from 1630 threatens Tolly, Chinese Ping, Granny, and Green Knowe itself. The loveliness of the English countryside is contrasted with the malevolence that materialized and hurt blind 18th-century

Susan. Elegant writing is enhanced by pen-and-ink drawings. By the same author: *The Children of Green Knowe; Treasure of Green Knowe; The River at Green Knowe; A Stranger at Green Knowe.*

Bower, Louise, and Ethel Tigue. *Packy,* il. by Herbert McClure. Abingdon 1967. $3.75; 8–12.

Interesting account of activities of river scouts as well as an exciting mystery story centering on an *objet d'art*—a peacock made of old gold coins and some rare silver and copper. Much information is included about American Indians. Theme: Life is a paradox.

Brecht, Edith. *The Mystery at the Old Forge,* il. by Charlotte Erickson. Viking 1966. $3.50; 6–9.

Unusual in the high quality of background, style, and characterization. City-bred Timothy learns to love the snowy country winters of the northeastern United States as he solves a 50-year-old mystery. Exquisite line drawings and blue color washes.

Byers, Irene. *Mystery at Mappins,* il. by Victor Ambrus. Scribner 1964. $3.95; 10–12.

Enterprising Leonie and her brothers find a job for her country-loving father as an estate manager at Mappins, whose new owner is a crippled, crotchety major. The three children face the question of who is sabotaging the major and the country people. This family story has Agatha Christie touches.

Carter, Bruce. *The Airfield Man.* Coward 1965. $3.95; 12–15.

Two boys, one American and one British, learn to fly a plane and at the same time unravel the mystery connected with an abandoned flying field used in World War II.

Castex, Pierre. *The Uranium Pirates,* tr. by Michael Heron. Abelard 1968. $3.95; 10–14.

Fourteen-year-old Nic spends the summer with his grandparents in a little French town. He renews acquaintance with a gang of boys he knew two summers earlier and becomes involved in some unusual adventures. Intrigue and strong characterization are the primary strengths of the book. Translation from the French results in a few unfamiliar expressions, but the text flows smoothly.

Clapp, Patricia. *Jane-Emily.* Lothrop 1969. $3.75; 10–14.

A story full of uncanny and nerve-tingling incidents occurring during a summer visit to Jane's grandmother's home. Readers will find it difficult to put down.

Clark, Margaret Goff. *Mystery of the Missing Stamps,* il. by Vic
Donahue. Funk & Wagnalls 1967. $3.25; 8–12.

Mrs. Clark uses the stamp collector's vocabulary and knowledge to build suspense. While upholding the virtues of his
friend, Ben, who is falsely accused of theft, Mark Baxter
learns that a stepfather may be loved. Innkeeping provides a
different background. By the same author: *Adirondack
Mountain Mystery.*

Corbett, Scott. *The Cave above Delphi,* il. by Gioia Fiammenghi. Holt 1965. $3.50; 10–12.

A deceivingly bright boy follows his usual speculation about
people while he and his family accompany their professor
father to Delphi. Mountain climbing, a ring in a cave,
thieving Papadopoulos, a museum, and others generate
excitement.

————. *Cutlass Island,* il. by Leonard Shortall. Little 1962.
$3.95; 11–15.

Exciting story of two teenage boys who assist in the capture
of narcotics smugglers. The climax of the story features a
battle in which the boys and their friends, using Civil War
weapons, hold the smugglers at bay until the Coast Guard
arrives.

————. *Dead Man's Light,* il. by Leonard Shortall. Little
1960. $3.75; 9–14.

Tommy is an orphan who goes to live with his uncle, the
head keeper of Dead Man's Light. Not only is a 50-year-old
mystery solved, but Tommy also manages to acquire a
permanent home. By the same author: *The Case of the Gone
Goose.*

Crary, Margaret. *Secret of the Unknown Fifteen,* il. by Vic
Donahue. Funk & Wagnalls 1966. $3.25; 9–13.

Fifteen graves are found on the wrong side of the river,
historically speaking. Burial artifacts point to either mass
murder or epidemic illness. Careful reading by teenage
protagonists of journals written by early settlers helps reveal
the truth. Well plotted with better than average characterization.

DeJong, Dola. *House on Charlton Street,* il. by Gilbert Riswold.
Scribner 1962. $3.12; 11–15.

Interesting story of a New York family of five who move into
an old house and discover its exciting past. Much of what is
learned is due to the research of the youngest member of the
family, an 11-year-old boy. By the same author: *The Level
Land.*

Derleth, August. *The Beast in Holger's Woods,* il. by Susan Bennett. Crowell 1968. $3.95; 10 up.

A skilled writer for adults turns to children's mystery. By the same author: *The House by the River; The Prince Goes West; The Irregulars Strike Again.*

Doyle, Sir Arthur Conan. *The Adventures of Sherlock Holmes.* Parents 1966. $2.95 (P—Scholastic, $.75); 12 up.

These two full-length novels and four short stories introduce the adolescent to the famous Sherlock Holmes and his equally famous partner, Dr. Watson. Doyle gives small space to criminal doings but rather emphasizes deduction and solution.

Estes, Eleanor. *The Alley,* il. by Edward Ardizzone. Harcourt 1964. $3.75; 8–12.

Ten-year-old Connie and her friends who live along the Alley gather enough clues to solve two burglaries. Plot and characterization are definitely original and interesting.

Farjeon, Annabel. *Maria Lupin,* il. by James Hunt. Abelard 1967. $3.95; 10–15.

In a London suburb Maria Lupin and her mother live together but are separated emotionally by what is a tragic mystery to Maria—what has happened to her father? Circumstances work out happily for all in this well-constructed plot.

Faulkner, Nancy. *Mystery at Long Barrow House,* il. by C. Walter Rodgers. Doubleday 1960. $3.95; 8–13.

Three American children in England, with their tutor, solve the mystery of their great-aunt's house and also make an important archeological find. Setting and characterization add value.

Fenton, Edward. *The Phantom of Walkaway Hill,* il. by Jo Ann Stover. Doubleday 1961. $3.95 (P—Archway, $.60); 9–12.

James spends a snowed-in weekend with his cousins in the country. The frenzied barking of a lonely collie leads the children to a startling discovery. By the same author: *The Riddle of the Red Whale.*

Francis, Dorothy Brenner. *Mystery of the Forgotten Map,* il. by Jerry Lazare. Follett 1968. $3.95; 9–12.

A treasure map plot with an unusual twist. In trying to find lost emeralds on their grandmother's Iowa farm, Tom and Julie discover novel riches. Suspense is sustained until the end of the story. Believable character development adds rich dimension.

Gág, Flavia. *The Melon Patch Mystery,* il. by Wanda Gág. McKay 1964. $3.95; 8–12.

Pokey Plunkett aims to win a prize for the best watermelon by improving his "Seedless-Wonder-Ball." Mystery and consternation strike with the savage pilfering of Pokey's melon patch. A pet raccoon adds humor to events that are broadcast nationwide. Amiable illustrations by the author's sister.

Garfield, Leon. *Mister Corbett's Ghost.* Pantheon 1968. $3.50; 9–12.

Outstanding ghost story in the grand tradition. Set in Hempstead in the early days of Long Island, the eerie tale will keep readers guessing. The archaic language adds to the authenticity of the setting. By the same author: *Devil-in-the-Fog.*

Goolden, Barbara. *Trouble for the Tabors.* Washburn 1966. $4.50; 12–16.

A family with teenagers lives in a small village in England where exciting things begin to happen; belongings disappear in rapid succession without a clue to the thief. Finally the youngsters unravel the mystery, but the reader is left guessing to the very end.

Gottlieb, Robin. *Mystery aboard the Ocean Princess,* il. by Mimi Korach. Funk & Wagnalls 1967. $3.25; 8–12.

An amusing and suspense-filled account of how 12-year-old Jill Washburn and her cousin Connie aid in the recovery of three valuable paintings, which were stolen and smuggled on board a transatlantic liner.

———. *Mystery of the Jittery Dog-Walker,* il. by Mimi Korach. Funk & Wagnalls 1966. $3.25; 7–11.

Gail's father is a professional dog-walker in New York City. His assistant, giant-size Rupert, enchants Gail and her friends by telling Greek myths until the disappearance of four valuable Greek statues belonging to a client, Mrs. Tottle, adds complications. Charming line illustrations of New York sustain the light touch. By the same author: *Secret of the Unicorn.*

Grant, Elisabeth. *No Sleep for Angus.* Abelard 1970. $3.95; 12–16.

Sinister black-and-white illustrations set the delightfully chilling tone of this novel set in London's dockland. Angus and the gang of boys and girls with whom he eventually becomes friends are caught up in a bank robbery. Humor offsets terror in good balance.

Hall, Marjory. *Mystery at Lion's Gate,* il. by Mimi Korach. Funk & Wagnalls 1967. $3.25; 8–12.

A family legend, hidden treasure, an old diary, and a missing stone lion engage the interest of 12-year-old Courtney Dane and her new neighbor Barbie. Novel adaptation of an old plot includes the need of a young girl to find her own bearings in life without parents.

Herbst, Dean Finley. *Flight to Afghanistan,* Steck 1969. $2.95; 10–16.

Vicki, an embassy child, travels to meet her parents who are stationed in Kabul, Afghanistan, and becomes involved in foreign intrigue. The experiences that befall Vicki seem to come out of newspaper headlines; it is surprising this isn't a true story for it is so convincing.

Hitchcock, Alfred, ed. *Alfred Hitchcock's Sinister Spies,* il. by Paul Spina. Random 1966. $3.95; 10 up.

From Doyle to Sheckley, these exciting tales are chosen to entertain young people in the same genre that entertains, amuses, and intrigues them on TV. As anthologies go, this collection is above average and represents good writers of today and yesterday. By the same editor: *Spellbinders in Suspense; Monster Museum.*

Holman, Felice. *Elisabeth and the Marsh Mystery,* il. by Erik Blegvad. Macmillan 1966. $3.95; 5–8.

A plea for conservation encapsuled in a poetic vignette of child and bird life near the marshes. Humorous, delightful, informative, fine-spun mystery. The Blegvad illustrations and map endpapers add flavor. By the same author: *A Year to Grow; Professor Diggins' Dragons; Elisabeth, the Bird Watcher.*

Jane, Mary C. *Mystery on Nine-mile Marsh,* il. by Raymond Abel. Lippincott 1967. $2.95; 10–12.

The author of more than a dozen mystery books for preadolescents sets a mood for loneliness, artistry, and possible espionage in the Atlantic coastal salt marshes. Legatee Arnold Lindsay is a complete stranger to the townspeople as well as the widow who left Moody's Island to him. Lucille and Brent Pierce enjoy animal-loving Mr. Lindsay until they make a horrifying discovery.

Jeffries, Roderic. *Patrol Car.* Harper 1967. $3.50; 10 up.

A policeman uses scientific methods of crime detection to capture thieves. The realistic story will be appreciated by young readers. By the same author: *Against Time.*

Kingman, Lee. *The Saturday Gang,* il. by Burt Silverman. Doubleday 1961. $3.25 (P—Doubleday, $.75); 9–11.

A group of ten- and eleven-year-old boys help get their Massachusetts town selected as the site of a TV series. They solve a mystery and accept Sunny Silva, a boy who is different.

Leighton, Margaret. *A Hole in the Hedge.* Farrar 1968. $3.50; 12 up.

When the three Field children are left in the care of Mrs. Kiley, queer things begin to happen. A neighbor acts strange, Paula is apprehensive about confiding in her friend, and one of the brothers receives a 20-foot inflatable balloon.

McGregor, R. J. *The Young Detectives,* il. by William Grimmond. 1934.   (P—Penguin, $.75); 8 up.

Family summer adventures in an English seaside mansion, smugglers, secret passages in a cliff, a priest's hole, customs men, and an army colonel who depends on three boys and their sisters for clues in solving the mystery make this an exciting story. Juvenile mystery buffs with a penchant for collecting books that merit rereading might well start with this.

MacKellar, William. *The Secret of the Dark Tower.* McKay 1967. $3.95; 12–16.

Two boys, Ken Taylor and Ricky Snider, travel from America to Switzerland to study for a year at the Ecole Romande. Their involvement with diamond smugglers leads to a rather complicated mystery.

Mahon, Julia C. *Mystery at Old Sturbridge Village,* il. by Sidney Rafinson. A. Whitman 1964. $2.95; 9–12.

A new twist to the theme of the too well-hidden will. Nancy finds that the solution of the mystery hinges on knowledge of the reconstruction of a model 18th-century New England village. Easy to read; high interest.

Manley, Seon, and Gogo Lewis, eds. *Suspense: A Treasury for Young Adults.* Funk & Wagnalls 1966. $4.95; 12 up.

"The good writer of suspense literature knows that it is his role to keep you on the edge of your chair, to explore with you an unknown world that—as always with the unknown—prickles your scalp, taunts your brain, stimulates your emotions." Thus in the preface the anthologists invite young people to come along and read the best. The list of contributors reads like a Who's Who in Mystery Writing from the early 18th century until today.

Martin, Fredic. *The Mystery at Monkey Run,* il. by Ned Butterfield. Little 1966. $3.50; 9–13.

Skin diving, foreign students, college researchers, and mistaken identities combine to make a different kind of mystery about sunken treasure and valuable coins. During a summer vacation two adventurous boys experience a Fourth of July disappearance, an encounter with bats in a cave, and a wild car ride with the thief through a woods.

Mendoza, George. *The Crack in the Wall and Other Terrible Weird Tales,* il. by Mercer Mayer. Dial 1968. $3.95; 7–11.
An old quarry in Vermont is the setting for these charming stories that will scare but not frighten.

Moyes, Patricia. *Helter-Skelter.* Holt 1968. $4.50 (P—Archway, $.60); 12 up.
Mod 18-year-old Felicity ("Cat") Bell is ecstatic when neighboring Dick and Tim Malley name their homemade sailboat "Cat." Espionage and a surprise ending give zing to the always interesting, sometimes hilarious, occasionally slow-moving story line.

Nash, Mary. *Mrs. Coverlet's Detectives,* il. by Garrett Price. Little 1965. $3.75; 8–12.
The three Persever children are hilariously involved in the successful search for a kidnapped cat. This is a good story for the juvenile reader who likes mystery combined with slapstick and sharply identified characters with mild adventure.

Nielsen, Jean. *The Phantom Palomino,* il. by Vic Donahue. Funk & Wagnalls 1966. $3.25; 7–11.
A neatly plotted mystery involving horses, ghost riders, and hidden treasure. Unusual background of California history makes this more than a good horse story or mystery. Realistic treatment of mental vagaries and the limitations caused by diabetes add a thoughtful tone to the book.

Pease, Howard. *The Black Tanker.* Doubleday 1941. $3.95 (P—Dell $.60); 12 up.
Rance Warren works his way across the Pacific in the engine room of a tanker. He becomes involved in many troubles on the ship and faces danger along the way. The danger and intrigue will interest many teenagers. By the same author: *Heart of Danger; Secret Cargo; Tattooed Man.*

Pène, Du Bois William. *The Alligator Case,* il. by the author. Harper 1965. $3.27; 9–12.
Three dastardly thieves use a small-town circus as a cover for their crimes, but Boy Detective carefully follows clues that reveal the culprits. The author-artist has fun with the plot and word plays.

_____. *The Horse in the Camel Suit,* il. by the author. Harper 1967. $3.95; 5–10.

A young detective attempts to prove that a police officer was justified in locking up a troupe of performers. This story offers the author's usual wit.

Perez, Norah A. *Strange Summer in Stratford,* il. by Robert Ihrig. Little 1968. $4.75; 11–14.

Jenny has an unexpected summer with her father at Stratford, Ontario, while he prepares his book on the modern Shakespearean theatre. A pleasant family, a rebellious teenager, a mystery, eccentric and amusing minor characters, and good Stratford atmosphere make the book readable and more.

Peyton, K. M. *Thunder in the Sky,* il. by Victor G. Ambrus. World 1967. $3.75; 12 up.

During the First World War, the three Goodchild brothers became involved in a mystery that points toward one of them as a spy. Danger, mystery, and private dilemmas combine to make a tale that is frank, real, and revealing of life as it was and is. By the same author: *Plan for Birdsmarsh; The Maplin Bird.*

Poe, Edgar Allen. *The Purloined Letter and the Murders in the Rue Morgue,* il. by Rick Schreiter. Watts 1966. $3.95; 12 up.

An attractive edition of two stories that have maintained their originality for over 100 years.

Poole, Josephine. *Moon Eyes,* il. by Trina Schart Hyman. Little 1965. $4.25; 10–14.

High artistry leads the reader to the brink of terror when Kate and her small brother Thomas are threatened during their father's absence. Not even washday-real Mrs. Beer can keep Aunt Rhoda from taking over the household. Kate struggles to protect Thomas from Moon Eyes, the hound of evil, who is whistled up by Aunt Rhoda. This beautiful and unusual allegory has its realistic moments.

Raskin, Ellen. *The Mysterious Disappearance of Leon (I Mean Noel),* il. by the author. Dutton 1971. $4.95; 9–12.

A wonderfully clever mystery story (and game about names) about the many years that Caroline Carillon searches for her husband Leon (Noel) Carillon.

Robertson, Keith. *The Money Machine,* il. by George Porter. Viking 1969. $4.53; 10–14.

Neil Lambert and Swede Larsen, the proprietors of the Carson Street Detective Agency, set out to uncover a counterfeiting ring that is headquartered somewhere near their hometown. After tracking down a good many false leads, their suspicions finally focus on a kindly old retired engraver and printer. The same heroes are featured in *The Crow and the Castle* and *Three Stuffed Owls* by the same author.

Rydberg, Ernie. *The Dark of the Cave,* il. by Carl Kidwell. McKay 1965. $2.95; 9–13.

Ronnie learns true human values before an operation restores his sight and shows him that his best friend is a black boy, Gar. The boys enlist their fathers' aid in freeing other boys trapped in a cave as well as in solving the mystery of a stolen watch. Believable characters and incidents.

St. John, Wylly Folk. *The Secrets of Hidden Creek,* il. by Paul Galdone. Viking 1966. $3.75; 7–11.

Based on a historical incident involving Confederate gold hidden in Georgia, three children turn a boring summer with grandparents into a time of excitement and new friendship. A geographical quirk hides the creek, which in turn holds the treasure. A tumbledown mansion with people needing help completes the ingredients with which children identify. The Galdone illustrations are invigorating.

Sobol, Donald J. *Encyclopedia Brown: Boy Detective,* il. by Leonard Shortall. Nelson 1963. $2.95 (P—Scholastic, $.50); 8–12.

Leroy Brown earns his nickname by applying his encyclopedic learning to community mysteries. The reader is asked to anticipate solutions before checking them in the back of the book. Useful with reluctant readers. By the same author: *Encyclopedia Brown Finds the Clues; Encyclopedia Brown Solves Them All.*

Stauffer, Dwight G. *Mystery at Blackstone Lake,* il. by Ernest Kurt Barth. Funk & Wagnalls 1967. $3.25; 10–14.

A geologist father takes his family on a summer exploratory trek to Blackstone Lake in the Canadian wilds. Steve is barely saved from drowning by his friend Chip. Mysterious men try to capture the boys who, while playing detective, have found a buried chest and a trail of bullet shells. Suspense piles on suspense with skillfully blended background and believable characterization. Surprise ending.

Stevenson, Robert Louis. *The Strange Case of Dr. Jekyll and Mr. Hyde,* il. by Rick Schreiter. Watts 1967. $3.95; 12 up.

An attractive edition of Stevenson's classic tale of the doctor turned monster.

Storr, Catherine. *Lucy,* il. by Victoria de Larrea. Prentice 1968. $3.95; 6–11.

A small girl, who wants to be a boy, becomes a real detective.

Trease, Geoffrey. *No Boats on Bannermere,* il. by Richard Kennedy. Norton 1965. $3.95; 10–14.

An inherited cottage in England's north country involves young Bill Mellbury with a local squire in a deepening mystery. A variation on the buried treasure plot, this first-person narrative, steeped in English idiom, gives a delightful view of an English family.

Walton, Bryce. *Cave of Danger.* Crowell 1967. $4.50; 11–14.
Matt loses interest in caves after he panics on one of his explorations. His friend's bravery in attempting to retain Matt's findings brings him back to his avocation.

Ware, Leon. *The Mystery of 22 East.* Westminster 1966. $3.50 (P—Grosset, $.50); 12 up.
This winner of the 1966 Edgar Allan Poe Award meets all the criteria for adventure, mystery, and intrigue that capture the imagination of modern youth. Befriending a stowaway, a mysterious package in the hero's cabin, and inquisitive strangers combine to keep interest high and the plot moving swiftly to its inevitable conclusion.

Warner, Gertrude Chandler. *Houseboat Mystery,* il. by David Cunningham. A. Whitman 1967. $2.95; 8–12.
The "Boxcar" children involve Grandfather Alden in another of their detective adventures. The thieves this time are caught on the houseboat of many names. Pleasant, easy reading on the theme of escape with which most children will identify. Useful with reluctant readers.

Wees, Frances Shelley. *Mystery in Newfoundland,* il. by Douglas Bisset. Abelard 1965. $3.50; 9–12.
Fog, marsh, and seaside caverns around St. John City are the atmosphere and locale of Spanish buried treasure. The visiting Patterson children and their mother nearly lose their lives as they relive history and legend while their geologist father is in Labrador. This strong plot has an authentic background. Sequel to *The Treasure of Echo Valley.*

Weil, Ann. *Red Sails to Capri,* il. by C. B. Falls. Viking 1952. $2.75; 9–12.
A French writer, an English painter, and a Danish philosopher bring excitement with them to the island of Capri in 1826. Their adventures lead to the discovery of a beautiful cave, which has been considered a place of evil by the natives.

Zapf, Marjorie A. *The Mystery of the Great Swamp,* il. by Carl Kidwell. Atheneum 1967. $3.95 (P—Scholastic, $.60); 8–12.
Jeb and his dog Mac explore the Okefenokee Swamp and discover an island that was once occupied by Indian

mound-builders. Characters are believable, and the action is suspenseful and fast moving.

Sports

Bowen, Robert Sidney. *Lightning Southpaw.* Lothrop 1967. $3.50; 10–14.

Very exciting look at the life of an ex-GI suffering from loss of memory. The author has skillfully developed an interesting personality through conversation. The only physical tie the main character has with his past is a baseball skill. What happens to him in the process of regaining his memory is the real story.

Christopher, Matt. *Long Shot for Paul,* il. by Foster Caddell. Little 1966. $2.95; 9–12.

The educable retarded child is many times forced to live on the outer fringes of a normal society, but not in this story. Many readers will envy the picture of the warm family relationship presented. A wise teacher could successfully read this book aloud. Group discussion is certain to follow.

———. *The Year Mom Won the Pennant,* il. by Foster Caddell. Little 1968. $3.50; 9–12.

When none of the fathers have time to coach the Thunderballs, one of the mothers volunteers and adds much sparkle to the game. See also E. L. Konigsburg, *About the B'nai Bagels.* By the same author: *The Counterfeit Tackle; Sink It, Rusty.*

Fenner, Phyllis R., ed. *Quick Pivot: Stories of Basketball.* Knopf 1965. $3.50; 10–15.

Excellent collection of basketball fiction. The tall tale, "How Basketball Began" by Legrand, is most unusual. The stories contain enough conversation and action to encourage teachers to read them aloud.

Friendlich, Dick. *Touchdown Maker.* Doubleday 1966. $3.50; 12–14.

Russ, after being criticized for his play in a championship game, is compelled to join the team in the new school he attends later. Inner doubts cause his conflict with his new teammates.

Heuman, William. *Horace Higby and the Scientific Pitch,* il. by William Moyers. Dodd 1968. $3.50; 12–14.

A funny story about Horace Higby, who replaces the pitcher

on a baseball team. His unorthodox methods of playing and the humorous illustrations make this an enjoyable book.

Jackson, C. P. *Junior High Freestyle Swimmer,* il. by Frank Kramer. Hastings 1965. $3.25; 10–14.

A new team member finds an early friend, and they join against the team's bad guy. Achieving success as a team brings about eventual understanding and friendship. The author uses skill in selecting incidents, developing relationships, and establishing realistic solutions.

————. *Midget League Catcher.* Follett 1966. $2.95; 8–10.

Simple plot of a boy who wants to become a catcher on a neighborhood team and makes it. The author holds the action to the diamond, avoids subplot traps and does a good job of showing that uninterested parents do not necessarily spell failure for their child. Built into the story are many good skill and sportsmanship pointers. By the same author: *Little Major Leaguer; Little League Tournament; Pro Hockey Comeback; World Series Rookie.*

Konigsburg, E. L. *About the B'nai Bagels,* il. by the author. Atheneum 1967. $4.25; 8–12.

A little league baseball team in a middle-class suburban neighborhood is featured. One family encourages their growing son to become increasingly aware of himself and the people around him.

Lee, Robert C. *The Iron Arm of Michael Glenn,* il. by Al Fiorentino. Little 1965. $3.75; 9–12.

Fantasy is applied to the baseball field and mystery, suspense, and humor are skillfully blended. Complete with a foreign scientist, this will make a delightful read-aloud book.

Lipsyte, Robert. *The Contender.* Harper 1967. $3.50; 12 up.

A Harlem boxing center provides relief from outside pressures for a Negro dropout. The story is strong and moving.

Lord, Beman. *Bats and Balls,* il. by Arnold Spilka. Walck 1962. $3.75; 8–12.

Irresistible to baseball enthusiasts of Little League age. The description is exceptional, coupled with slapstick humor that resolves the plot. Useful with reluctant readers.

————. *Rough Ice,* il. by Arnold Spilka. Walck 1963. $3.75; 8–14.

This story of a boy who yearns to excel in a sport because his father was a champion holds quiet significance for many families involved in organized sports for youth. The lively illustrations are appropriate. Easy reading.

McPherson, Margaret. *The Shinty Boys,* il. by Shirley Hughes. Harcourt 1963. $3.95; 12 up.

This is a well-paced, absorbing story, the kind all children enjoy, though the Scottish atmosphere, including a brogue, and the culture patterns may puzzle some American children. The use of the first person is particularly effective.

Renick, Marion. *The Big Basketball Prize,* il. by Paul Galdone. Scribner 1963. $3.25; 8–12.

If there must be sports stories about prizes, this is as good as any; it is subtly humorous and accurate about basketball facts. No mention is made of organized team sports for children of this age.

_____. *Ricky in the World of Sport,* il. by Nancy Grossman. Seabury 1967. $3.75; 9–12.

An inner city child gets a part-time job in a sports arena. His friendship with a local newspaper reporter and his own skill combine to help Ricky take his first step towards becoming a champion athlete. Illustrations are excellent; there is beauty in every face. Useful with reluctant readers. By the same author: *Football Boys* and others.

Ullman, James R. *Banner in the Sky.* Lippincott 1954. $4.50 (P—Archway, $.60); 12–14.

The lure of the unconquered mountain proves irresistible to 16-year-old Rudi, whose burning desire to scale the Citadel prompts him to overcome family resistance and his own fear of the unknown heights to accomplish his goal. Young people will thrill to the spirit of exploration, dangerous heights, and the boy's final decision to give up his dream to save a man's life.

Wells, Robert, *Five- Yard Fuller and the Unlikely Knights,* il. by Howard Eldridge. Putnam 1967. $3.29; 10–14.

One tall tale after another. Playing against all the great teams of professional football, the fanciful team members from Rock Creek in Coonskin County appear as a cross between Li'l Abner and Paul Bunyan. Straight oral reading by the classroom teacher will bring howls of laughter from the children.

Animals

Angelo, Valenti. *The Tale of a Donkey,* il. by the author. Viking 1966. $3.00; 8–11.

A stone-cutter, a wood-cutter, and a farmer pool their

resources to buy a little donkey. Each abuses him until he
runs away. Carlo finds him and nurses him back to health.
Pictures and story reveal the author's love of the Italian
countryside and of small Italian donkeys. A fine story about
fairness as well as kindness to animals.

Annixter, Jane and Paul. *Vikan the Mighty.* Holiday 1969.
$3.95; 12–16.

Two interesting stories, fatefully intertwined, of a whale and
a boy who simultaneously grow to maturity.

Bianki, Vitali. *Galinka, the Wild Goose,* tr. by S. K. Lederer, il.
by Barbara Domroe. Braziller 1963. $3.50; 7–12.

In this story by a Russian naturalist, a barnacle goose,
captured near the Gulf of Finland, winters as a pet in a
faraway village. When spring comes, she flies off to rejoin
her kind on the Great Sea Route to the Arctic. With them she
encounters and survives foxes in the lakeshore reeds and
falcons in the air, and finally she nests on the edge of the
cold ocean.

Binns, Archie. *Sea Pup,* il. by Robert Candy. Duell 1954.
$3.50; 9–12.

After raising a seal from infancy on Puget Sound, Clint
encounters problems that challenge his future companionship with his pet. He decides in the end to send the seal to a
zoo. Not only is this a heartwarming story that will appeal to
children, but it also contains much information on marine
life.

Bishop, Ann. *Noah Riddle?* il. by Jerry Warshaw. Whitman
1970. $2.50; 7–12.

A delightful collection of teasers and animal riddles. The
illustrations aptly extend Noah's puzzlement and the spirit
of the riddles.

Boston, Lucy. *A Stranger at Green Knowe,* il. by Peter Boston.
Harcourt 1961. $3.25; 9–11.

A Chinese boy spending the summer at Green Knowe tries to
hide a gorilla he was first attracted to at the London zoo. The
deep, wordless attachment of the lonely boy and the unhappy animal makes a sensitive and unusual story.

Burnford, Sheila. *The Incredible Journey,* il. by Carl Burger.
Little 1961. $4.95; 9 up.

Three animals—a Siamese cat, an English bull terrier, and a
Labrador retriever—travel through the Canadian wilderness
to return to their home. Each animal has a realistic personality since Miss Burnford characterizes them after her own
pets. An excellent adventure story.

Byars, Betsy C. *Midnight Fox,* il. by Ann Grifalconi. Viking 1968. $4.50 (P—Viking, $.75); 8–12.

While visiting his cousin's farm, Tom commits himself to saving a black fox from being shot. Interwoven is the story of a boy who comes to realize that many of his personal problems are caused by his interactions with people.

————. *Rama the Gypsy Cat,* il. by Peggy Bacon. Viking 1966. $3.50; 7–11.

A vivid account of the expeditions of a cat. Storyline is very well constructed, fast moving, and exciting.

Carlson, Natalie Savage. *Chalou,* il. by George Loh. Harper 1967. $3.27; 7–11.

Chalou, a big guard dog, makes a long and laborious trek home after having been swept miles down the river on an ice floe. Chalou displays a strong sense of loyalty yet proves he can be devoted to more than one master.

Catherall, Arthur. *Lone Seal Pup,* il. by John Kaufman. Dutton 1965. $3.50; 7–11.

Authentic life cycle story of a seal called Ah Leek from birth to becoming part of the group of independent seals. The plot involves friendship with an Eskimo boy, who saves Ah Leek's life by killing the polar bear attacking him. The life of Eskimo hunters is well portrayed as is the terrific struggle for survival by the bears, seals, whales, and fishes of the Arctic waters.

————. *A Zebra Came to Drink.* Dutton 1967. $3.50; 8–12.

A dramatic story of the dangers that face Zaabi and her newborn zebra foal in the wilds of modern Africa as they attempt to reach their grazing plain. This intensely absorbing story shows the friends and enemies of wild animals. Fascinating descriptions of animal behavior.

Clark, Ann Nolan. *Blue Canyon Horse,* il. by Allan Houser. Viking 1954. $3.50; 9–12.

A beautiful book with the story told in verse. A mare runs away from her canyon home to go with the wild herd, but in the spring she returns with her colt to her master.

Cleary, Beverly. *Ribsy,* il. by Louis Darling. Morrow 1964. $3.75; 8–12.

Henry Huggins' dog copes philosophically with the misadventures of being lost. This is a story full of chuckles.

Clymer, Eleanor. *Horatio,* il. by R. Quackenbush. Atheneum 1968. $3.25; 5–9.

A crotchety tomcat is adopted by two needy kittens.

Cone, Molly. *Mishmash,* il. by Leonard Shortall. Houghton
1962. $3.00 (P—Archway, $.60); 7 up.

A boy, new in town, acquires a dog that becomes a community problem. Pete's experiences with Mishmash and his
desire to give his teacher a gift make a hilarious story. By the
same author: *Mishmash and the Substitute Teacher; Mishmash and the Sauerkraut Mystery; Mishmash and Uncle
Looney.*

Corbett, Scott. *The Turnabout Trick,* il. by Paul Galdone. Little
1967. $3.50; 8–12.

A prissy cat is the victim of morbid cataclysm (feline
amnesia) and barks delicately. Kerby falls victim to the
amnesia too and meows plaintively. The beloved Mrs.
Graymalkin peps up her old car with a magical chemical
compound, and bank robbers are captured. All this adds up
to a humorous, fast-paced mystery story. By the same author:
*The Lemonade Trick; The Mailbox Trick; The Disappearing
Dog Trick; The Baseball Trick; The Limerick Trick.*

Daly, Maureen. *Ginger Horse,* il. by Wesley Dennis. Dodd
1964. $3.50; 11–14.

Rob and Katie attempt to free the ginger horse and become
lost in caves of the forbidden black rock. This story of
Scottish village life highlights the adventures and personality of a young motherless boy.

D'Aulaire, Ingri and Edgar. *Foxie the Singing Dog,* il. by the
authors. Doubleday 1969. $3.95; 5–8.

Foxie is injured, saved by a man who trains her to sing, and
then reunited with her first master. Reissue in color of the
1949 edition.

De Jong, Meindert. *A Horse Came Running,* il. by Paul Slag-
soorian. Macmillan 1970. $4.95; 9–14.

An exciting story, set in the Midwest, about a boy, his horse,
and a tornado that changes everything.

Dillon, Eilis. *Island of Horses.* Funk & Wagnalls 1957. $3.95;
12 up.

Danny and Pat decide to visit the Isle of Horses off the coast
of Ireland. There they find a horse Pat wants to catch for his
brother. The story is marked by suspense and adventure.

Dobrin, Arnold. *Taro and the Sea Turtles,* il. by the author.
Coward 1966. $3.50; 5–8.

A beautifully told and illustrated story of a boy who lives by
the sea and helps to free two giant sea turtles. Later his life is
saved by a large turtle.

Dumas, Gerald. *Rabbits Rafferty,* il. by Wallace Tripp. Houghton 1968. $3.25; 8–12.

The animals who participate in this story could be people living in many small and middle-sized cities. Well written and interesting but controversial, with real sociological overtones.

Farley, Walter. *The Great Dane Thor.* Random 1966. $3.95; 10 up.

Excellent dog story by a well-known author of horse stories. Thor and Lars become great friends after an ominous beginning. The book is full of the adventure of nature. By the same author: *Man O'War; Little Black, a Pony; The Black Stallion;* and others.

Fenner, Carol. *Lagalág, the Wanderer,* il. by the author. Harcourt 1968. $3.25; 5–9.

This story, set in the Philippines, of a colt whose curiosity causes him to wander away from home, rings with authenticity. Small children will identify with Lagalág in his adventure.

Geisert, Arthur. *The Orange Scarf,* il. by Thomas Di Grazia. Simon 1970. $3.95; 4–7.

A quiet story about the birth of a calf during a spring snow storm, and how the farmer's son tied his scarf around its neck so it would not get lost in the snow.

Georgiou, Constantine. *Proserpina, the Duck that Came to School,* il. by Bernard Lipscomb. Harvey 1968. $3.50; 6–9.

A well-written story that should encourage children to explore the joys of the animal world. It combines Greek mythology and modern times. Handsome pictures.

––––––. *Rani, Queen of the Jungle,* il. by Joan Sandin. Prentice 1970. $3.95; 4–8.

A beautifully told story of a small Indian boy who raises an orphaned tiger cub so she can return to the jungle. The enchantment is enhanced by the accurate and vivid illustrations.

Gipson, Fred. *Old Yeller,* il. by C. Burger. Harper 1956. $3.50; 12 up.

Travis is in charge of the household while his father is away during the summer of 1860. An old yellow dog becomes attached to the family and proves to be a tremendous help. Sequel: *Savage Sam.*

Griffiths, Helen. *Leon,* il. by V. G. Ambrus. Doubleday 1968. $3.95; 12 up.

A part-German shepherd named Leon is rescued from death as a puppy and is again rescued by his master when cruelty and neglect drive the animal to kill. By the same author: *The Greyhound.*

Henry, Marguerite. *Gaudienzia: Pride of the Palio,* il. by Lynd Ward. Rand 1960. $4.95; 11–14.

Giorgio, a peasant boy, rides a half-Arabian mare to victory in the Palio, a race held in Siena, Italy, since the Middle Ages. The exciting tale also gives a history of the Palio.

———. *King of the Wind,* il. by Wesley Dennis. Rand 1948. $3.95 (P—Rand, $1.50); 10–12.

Exciting tale of the wanderings of Sham, an ancestor of Man O'War, who was intended as a gift from the Sultan of Morocco to the French king but fell on hard times until he reached a horse racing farm in England. Newbery Award, 1949.

———. *Stormy, Misty's Foal,* il. by Wesley Dennis. Rand 1963. $4.95 (P—Rand, $1.50); 8–11.

A fine story presenting some of the ferocities of life. The natural events of life, death, and nursing motherhood are handled with integrity and dignity. Although Grandpa's dialect becomes annoying and the illustrations are over-rated, this book is a worthy successor to *Misty of Chincoteague.* By the same author: *Brighty of Grand Canyon; Justin Morgan Had a Horse; White Stallion of Lipizza.*

Hightower, Florence. *Dark Horse of Woodfield,* il. by Joshua Tolford. Houghton 1962. $3.50; 9–12.

This humorous story involves characters who have distinct roles. Though it is basically a horse story, good family relations, some mystery, and a love story are also interwoven in the plot set in Depression years.

Holling, Holling C. *Pagoo.* Houghton 1957. $5.00; 8–12.

Authentic informative story of habits and habitats and the competition for life among sea creatures, told through the eyes of Pagoo, the hermit crab. Beautiful and authentic pictures.

Johnson, James Ralph. *Blackie, the Gorilla,* il. by the author. McKay 1968. $3.95; 11–13.

Blackie becomes such a believable, lovable, and realistically delineated young gorilla that it is hard to accept the fact that this is fiction.

———. *Ringtail,* il. by the author. McKay 1968. $4.50; 10–15.

The adventures of Ringtail make a fine story. Readers who like natural science and conservation will find this absorbing and informative.

Jones, Liza. *Kolo the Panda,* il. by the author. Norton 1969. $4.25; 4–7.

What could the miserable little panda do to escape his intolerable captivity? He and his friends in the zoo plan to flee, and they do. By the time Kolo has regained the peace of his home in Tibet, he has faced the cost of freedom and reaped the rewards of friendship.

Kalnay, Francis. *Chúcaro, Wild Pony of the Pampa,* il. by Julian DeMiskey. Harcourt 1958. $2.95; 8–12.

A beautifully written story of a boy, a fine horse, and a big-hearted gaucho. The setting is the Argentine pampas. The reader will be deeply impressed by the fine description of the land and its people.

Keith, Eros. *Rrra-ah,* il. by the author. Bradbury 1969. $4.95; 4–7.

Written from a toad's viewpoint, this story describes his experiences and horror at being captured and taken home by some children. Their mother eventually orders his release because he is always jumping around the house, and Rrra-ah is happy to return to nature.

Kingman, Lee. *The Year of the Raccoon.* Houghton 1966. $3.50; 12–14.

Joey feels crowded out by his dynamic family until a pet raccoon helps him learn to cope with his world.

Kjelgaard, James Arthur. *Big Red,* il. by Bob Kuhn. Holiday 1956. $3.95 (P—Scholastic, $.60); 12–14.

Danny and the Irish setter experience a series of adventures including tracking down a bear. The quality, excitement, and insight of this story provide entertaining reading.

———. *Outlaw Red: Son of Big Red.* Holiday 1953. $3.95 (P—Scholastic, $.50); 12–14.

One of many dog stories by Kjelgaard that appeal to youngsters. Sean, son of Big Red, becomes wrongly classed as an outlaw and suffers injustices. By the same author: *Irish Red; Fire Hunter; Lion Hound; Desert Dog; Boomerang Hunter.*

Klose, Norma Cline. *Benny: The Biography of a Horse,* il. by Gloria Gaulke. Lothrop 1965. $3.95; 9–12.

A story unforgettable for any girl who has a horse or dreams of owning one. Benny is 17 before he and Norma Jean, an

11-year-old, meet each other and form a bond of friendship that lasts until Benny dies. Here real joy, pathos, and humor blend into a life-size story of how a young girl learns responsibility for herself and others by caring for Benny and allowing him to care for her.

Knight, Ruth A. *Halfway to Heaven: The Story of the St. Bernard,* il. by Wesley Dennis. McGraw 1952. $3.95; 13 up.

Combining history, biography, and dog story, the author gives an entertaining account of the Swiss hospice of St. Bernard. In 1799 Joseph joins the order and later becomes trainer of the most famous of the dogs.

Lasell, Fen. *Michael Grows a Wish,* il. by the author. Houghton 1962. $3.25; 5–9.

Michael wants a horse for his birthday. After being told that he must make his wish come true, Michael builds a sawhorse and later finds it has been replaced by a real horse. The following year his sister tries the same method, and it works equally well.

Lauber, Patricia. *Clarence Turns Sea Dog,* il. by Leonard Shortall. Random 1959. $2.95; 9–12.

An amusing account of the adventures of a friendly, fun-loving dog during a visit with his young masters to Cape Cod. This easy-to-read, high interest book has a fast moving plot with many humorous incidents.

Lawson, Robert. *Mr. Revere and I,* il. by the author. Little 1953. $3.95; 10–12.

History from horseback. A wonderful tongue-in-cheek spoofing of American history. The high-flown 18th-century style is good for this type of story, written from the point of view of Paul Revere's horse. By the same author: *Ben and Me.*

———. *Rabbit Hill,* il. by the author. Viking 1944. $3.50 (P—Dell, $.75); 9–12.

Humorous and appealing tale of the wild animals, large and small, who live on Rabbit Hill and their concern as to whether the "new people" coming into the Big House will be kind and generous. Newbery Award, 1945.

———. *The Tough Winter,* il. by the author. Viking 1954. $3.75; (P—Dell, $.65); 9–12.

Here is another Rabbit Hill story as delightful as the original one. When the "folks" go south for the winter and the caretaker arrives with a "mean and ornery" dog, the small animals experience a tough winter that is made bearable by the spirit of friendliness among them.

London, Jack. *Call of the Wild.* (many paperback editions); 9–12.

A part St. Bernard, part Scotch shepherd dog returns to the wild as the leader of a wolf pack after a series of adventures during the Alaskan Gold Rush. By the same author: *The Sea Wolf; White Fang.*

MacKellar, William. *A Very Small Miracle,* il. by W. T. Mars. Crown 1969. $3.50; 8–12.

Jamie's trust in bitter, lonely Murdo brings about a small miracle, not only in replacing his much-loved old dog, but in changing the character of Murdo.

————. *Wee Joseph,* il. by Ezra Jack Keats. McGraw 1957. $2.95; 8–12.

Davie is a small Scotch boy who owns a scrawny pup. When his father orders the dog destroyed, Davie prays for a small miracle to save his beloved Joseph. The tale of the answer to the child's prayer makes a story that will warm the heart.

Miles, Miska. *Mississippi Possum,* il. by John Schoenherr. Little 1965. $3.50; 7–11.

The beautiful format and the vivid woodcuts match a significant story, perfectly told. A fearful young possum, who must leave his hollow log for higher ground when the Mississippi floods its banks, creeps into the tent of a family of other refugees and sleeps beside the children. The country Negro family is indigenous to the river banks as is the possum himself. The story is a fine picture of a close-knit family with room in their hearts for a scared little wild creature.

Morey, Walter. *Gentle Ben,* il. by John Schoenherr. Dutton 1965. $3.95 (P—Scholastic, $.75); 10–14.

Mark is forced to give up his pet bear, but he and his family are later able to find him when they move to the island where Ben was taken. Not to be confused with the TV series of the same name. By the same author: *Home Is the North.*

Mukerji, Gopal. *Gay-Neck,* il. by Boris Artzybasheff. Dutton 1927. $4.50; 9–15.

A prize-winning adventure story about a remarkable pigeon in World War I. Much of the story takes place in India. A well-written, tightly constructed tale. (Newbery Award, 1928.)

O'Brien, John Sherman. *Silver Chief: Dog of the North,* il. by Kurt Wiese. Grosset 1933. $2.50; 12 up.

The adventures of a beautiful wolf dog and his master, a Canadian Mountie.

Ottley, Reginald. *Boy Alone,* il. by Clyde Pearson. Harcourt 1966. $3.75; 8 up.

A moving story set in Australia. Boy runs away with a dog to prevent the dog's owner from putting it with the pack.

————. *The Roan Colt.* Harcourt 1967. $3.50; 10–14.

Continuation of the adventures of Boy. Here he defies authority to save a lame colt on an Australian ranch. Next in the series: *Rain Comes to Yambroorah.*

Peyton, K. M. *Fly-by-Night,* il. by the author. World 1969. $3.86; 9–11.

This is a convincing account of the fulfillment of a lifelong desire that brings to Ruth a pony she laboriously trains.

Reynolds, Marjorie. *Ride the Wild Storm,* il. by Lorence F. Bjorklund. Macmillan 1969. $4.95; 9–12.

David is sent to spend the summer with the Macy family after his parents are separated. He regains his self-confidence and strength in various outdoor adventures and is finally able to get Salty, the horse he loves, for his own.

Rockwell, Norman and Molly. *Willie Was Different: The Tale of an Ugly Thrushling,* il. by Norman Rockwell. Funk 1969. $3.95; 8 up.

Willie's appearance and behavior were enough to make him a family outcast at an early age. Undaunted, his genius forced him on. He sang his own songs composed by himself, and this music led to his fame and subsequent adventures. The illustrations are perfectly wed to the text, combining quaintness, robustness, humor, and dignity.

Rounds, Glen. *Blind Colt,* il. by the author. Holiday 1941, 1960. $3.95; 9–12.

The story of Whitey and his fight to save his blind colt, who survives a winter on the range, is not "et by wolves," and finally convinces even Uncle Torwal that he'll make "a good Sunday horse." It is beautiful in a strong gentle way that even a small boy can understand. Mr. Rounds' authentic drawings match his words.

————. *Lone Muskrat,* il. by the author. Holiday 1953. $3.50; 9–12.

The green world of the muskrats is almost palpable in Mr. Rounds' pictures. For young readers it is also made exciting by his story of the muskrat's narrow escapes from eagle, weasel, owl, bobcat, and spring flood.

Salten, Felix. *Bambi,* il. by Kurt Wiese. Grosset 1931. $2.95 (P—Grosset, $.50); 10–12.

In this life story of a deer, details of forest life with its fears, struggles, and pleasures are simply and beautifully told. Sequel: *Bambi's Children.*

Smith, Emma. *Emily's Voyage,* il. by Irene Haas. Harcourt 1966. $3.25; 6–11.

Emily, an intrepid guinea pig, satisfies her wanderlust on a sea voyage with a crew of seasick rabbits and a cargo of safety pins and fireworks.

Street, James. *Good-bye, My Lady.* Lippincott 1954. $5.95; 9–14.

This exceptional story tells of Skeeter, an orphan living with his illiterate but wise uncle, and a dog from the swamp who laughs and cries instead of barking. Skeeter and the dog become loving and trusting companions when Skeeter is faced with the decision of whether to return the dog to its owner.

Thiele, Colin. *Storm Boy,* il. by John Bailey. Rand 1963. $2.95; 9–12.

This brief, well-told story of a boy's devotion to a bird reminds one of Charlton Ogburn's *White Falcon.* Here also, the loss of the bird marks the time of the boy's real growing up. Sensitive writing and characterization.

Turkle, Brinton. *Thy Friend, Obadiah,* il. by the author. Viking 1969. $3.77; 5–8.

Obadiah, a young Quaker boy, feels self-conscious about the loyal friendship he receives from a certain gull. It always follows him. Then for several days it is missing. Obadiah finds the gull in trouble and removes a rusty fishhook from its beak.

Unkelbach, Kurt. *The Dog Who Never Knew.* Four Winds 1968. $3.50; 12–16.

An animal-loving family whose daughter trains a puppy, who lost an eye in an accident, to become an obedience dog. Interesting, humorous, fast moving story.

Warren, Billy. *Black Lobo,* il. by Bernard Garbutt. Golden Gate 1967. $3.95; 10–14.

A fast-moving story about raising a wolf as a pet. The frustration of attempting to train Black Lobo will make exciting reading.

White, Anne Terry. *Junket,* il. by Robert McCloskey. Viking 1955. $3.50 (P—Viking, $.75); 11 up.

This very funny book tells how a wire-haired terrier brings a city family around to appreciating country life.

Young, Patrick. *Old Abe: The Eagle Hero*, il. by John Kaufmann. Prentice 1965. $3.75; 7–9.

An Indian boy tames and trains a baby bald eagle. When the Civil War breaks out, a company of Wisconsin farmers take him as a mascot. Young readers will get an introduction to Civil War times through the text and pictures.

Science Fiction

Ballou, Arthur W. *Marooned in Orbit*. Little 1968. $4.50; 12–14.

Ground controllers, scientists, computers, and the rescue pilot attempt to save two men aboard a spacecraft whose motor has become disabled by a tiny meteorite. The author has written the story as it might actually occur in the near future. Many principles of space travel are involved, which will satisfy the space curious but saturate the not-so-curious.

Brink, Carol Ryrie. *Andy Buckram's Tin Men*, il. by W. T. Mars. Viking 1966. $3.50 (P—Grosset, $.50); 9–12.

All sorts of things happen when four tin can robots assembled by a 12-year-old boy are electrified during a thunder storm and come "alive."

Brinley, Bertrand R. *The Mad Scientists' Club*, il. by Charles Geer. Macrae 1964. $3.75 (P—Scholastic, $.75); 8–10.

Dinky Poore and the other members of the Mad Scientists' Club invent many fantastic tales to surprise the citizens of Mammoth Falls. The trouble and the fun come when they have to do something to prove that their fantastic tales are true (or almost true).

Cameron, Eleanor. *Stowaway to the Mushroom Planet*, il. by Robert Henneberger. Little 1956. $3.95; 9–12.

Exciting, well-written tale about space travel. By the same author: *The Wonderful Flight to the Mushroom Planet*.

Christopher, John. *The Pool of Fire*. Macmillan 1968. $4.25 (P—Macmillan, $.95); 10–14.

The last volume in this superior trilogy set in the 21st century when our planet is conquered by the Tripods, interstellar creatures who plan total domination. If human habitation of earth is to continue, the great cities of the Tripods must be penetrated and destroyed by a small band of men who survive. This is the basis of the story: the effort to make the world habitable for free men. The first two books, *The White Mountain* and *The City of Gold and Lead,* are equally sound and intriguing.

_____. *Prince in Waiting.* Macmillan 1970. $4.95; 10–16.

The story takes place after volcanic disaster apparently has destroyed technology and portrays a future primitive society that is suggestive of the Arthurian legend.

Erwin, Betty K. *The Summer Sleigh Ride,* il. by Paul E. Kennedy. Little 1966. $3.75; 8–12.

An exciting mystery story. Four girls, 11 or 12 years old, are kidnapped and travel from the year 1933 to 2322 by time machine. A clever bit of conjecture on what man will be able to accomplish through scientific discoveries.

Heinlein, Robert. *Time for the Stars.* Scribner 1956. $3.63; 11 up.

An experiment involving twins, Tom and Pat Bartlett, is conducted in which one is sent on a space ship and the other is kept on earth. When Tom returns to earth, he is still in his 20s and Pat has aged and is a great-grandfather.

_____. *Tunnel in the Sky,* il. by P. A. Hutchinson. Scribner 1955. $3.63; 10–14.

An exciting story that opens with a high school class preparing for a test in survival. By the same author: *Between Planets; Farmer in the Sky; Starship Troopers.*

Key, Alexander. *Escape to Witch Mountain,* il. by L. B. Wisdom. Westminster 1968. $3.75; 10–12.

Two young refugees from outer space are searching for their missing companions. Their unusual abilities and inabilities hinder their search and cause them great distress. The setting is in the Blue Ridge Mountains. By the same author: *The Forgotten Door.*

Knott, William C. *Journey across the Third Planet.* Chilton 1969. $4.25; 12–16.

A boy from outer space finds himself abandoned on earth and forms a relationship with an earthling. This relationship and their struggle to cross the United States awakens each boy to the possibilities of communication through understanding and friendship. A social comment on tolerance, ecology, and the need to end violence.

L'Engle, Madeleine. *A Wrinkle in Time.* Farrar 1962. $3.25; 10–14.

Meg ventures into space and time to find her father, who, in the interest of scientific experimentation, has been missing for four years. The experience of life in space is developed in great detail. Newbery Award, 1963. By the same author: *The Arm of the Starfish.*

Lightner, A. M. *The Space Olympics.* Norton 1967. $4.50; 10–14.

Tyros Vann leaves on the spaceship *Cluster Queen* with three other young athletes to go to the planet Arcadia and the Olympic Games. The events that happened there are not as pleasant as they had anticipated.

MacGregor, Ellen. *Miss Pickerell Goes Undersea,* il. by Paul Galdone. McGraw 1953. $3.95 (P—Scholastic, $.60); 10–14.

Interesting science fiction that combines facts with fancy in a way to challenge young readers to find out more. By the same author: *Miss Pickerell Goes to Mars; Miss Pickerell Goes to the Arctic; Miss Pickerell and the Geiger Counter.*

Norton, André. *Operation Time Search.* Harcourt 1967. $3.95; 12–16.

Shifted back in time to the era of Atlantis, Ray finds himself involved in a conflict between the inhabitants of Atlantis and those of Mu. He joins the Murians, whom he believes to be just in their cause. At length he decides not to return to the 20th century.

———. *The Zero Stone.* Viking 1968. $4.50; 10–14.

A gem trader, Murdoc Jern, gains possession of a mysterious stone only to find that it has led him to the center of a web of intrigue and murder. Seeking the source of the stone and having the companionship of a catlike animal, Eet, who has E.S.P. powers, lead to thrilling adventures. By the same author: *Moon of Three Rings; Quest Crosstime; Steel Magic; Ordeal in Otherwhere; Uncharted Stars;* and many others.

Nourse, Alan E. *Universe Between.* McKay 1965. $3.95; 12 up.

This exciting novel is set in the year 2017 with the main character living in parallel worlds.

O'Brien, Robert C. *The Silver Crown,* il. by Dale Payson. Atheneum 1968. $4.95; 9–13.

Relatively uncomplicated tale about the effect of a period of control and training on subjects (boys, girls, and adults) who are then removed from the influence of the Hieronymus Machine (a thinking machine), a malignite crown, and a silver crown.

Slobodkin, Louis. *Round Trip Space Ship.* Macmillan 1968. $4.50; 8–10.

Marty "invites" his friend, Eddie Blow, to go with him to

visit his home planet, Martinea. They blast off together with a goat, a goose, a kangaroo, and other animals that Marty has frozen with his powerful cryogenetic ray epectorator. A wonderful trip ensues. By the same author: *Spaceship under the Apple Tree.*

Verne, Jules. *Twenty Thousand Leagues under the Sea.* Scribner 1925. $6.00 (P—Scholastic, $.75); 12 up.

An adventurous and exciting account of Captain Nemo and his submarine. By the same author: *A Long Vacation* and many others.

Williams, Jay, and Raymond Abrashkin. *Danny Dunn and the Weather Machine,* il. by Jack Keats. McGraw 1959. $3.25; 8–12.

An amusing adventure of two boys involved in a space ship flight into interplanetary space. For reluctant readers. By the same author: *Danny Dunn and the Anti-Gravity Paint; Danny Dunn and the Homework Machine; Danny Dunn on a Desert Island.*

Wrightston, Patricia. *Down to Earth,* il. by Margaret Horder. Harcourt 1965. $3.75; 9–12.

A strange boy is found in a deserted house in Australia by other children. Martin the Martian, as the children call him, turns out to be exactly that. The children later rescue him from the authorities just in time for him to return to his home planet.

Fantasy

Aiken, Joan. *Armitage, Armitage, Fly Away Home,* il. by Betty Fraser. Doubleday 1968. $3.95; 7–12.

Magic, ghosts, charms, and wands make this book a delightful escape into a special world. Good for oral reading.

———. *Nightbirds on Nantucket,* il. by Robin Jacques. Doubleday 1966. $3.50 (P—Dell, $.75); 10–14.

Upon awakening from unconsciousness, Dido finds herself aboard a whaler. The captain, obsessed with finding a pink whale, sends Dido with his niece to Nantucket, where she will live with Aunt Tribulation. Later there is an attempt to assassinate the King of England and the pink whale provides help. A wild spoof of melodramatic historical fiction.

———. *The Whispering Mountain.* Doubleday 1969. $3.95; 10–14.

A fast moving adventure-fantasy-melodrama set in Wales deals with a race of small folk and an ancient, long-missing harp.

———. *The Wolves of Willoughby Chase,* il. by Pat Marriott. Doubleday 1963. $3.95 (P—Dell, $.75); 9–14.
Written as a melodrama, this story burlesques the Victorian novel. Sylvia comes to stay with Bonnie while her mother is recuperating, and a wicked governess takes over. Bonnie and Sylvia are sent to an orphanage where they are attacked by large packs of wolves. Strongly stereotyped characters are amusing. By the same author: *Black Hearts in Battersea.*

Alexander, Lloyd. *The Book of Three.* Holt 1964. $3.95 (P—Dell, $.95); 10–14.
An adventure tale set in the imaginary kingdom of Prydain. Taran, the Assistant Pig Keeper, goes forth to overcome the evil Horned King. He picks up companions along the way who add to the intrigue and legendary quality of the story. Sequels are *The Black Cauldron; Coll and His White Pig* (about the same characters); *The Castle of Llyr; Taran Wanderer; The High King.* No finer sustained writing has ever been achieved by any other American author of books for children. To complete the reading experience, one must also read *The Truthful Harp.*

———. *The High King.* Holt 1968. $4.50; 9–14.
The last of the chronicles of Prydain, and perhaps the best of this magnificent series. This will be a classic. Some really great writing clothes a wonderful tale. Newbery Award, 1969.

———. *The Marvelous Misadventures of Sebastian.* Dutton 1970. $5.95; 9 up.
A buoyant comic opera, reflecting a time when the petty rulers and aristocrats of Europe had turned to bickering and conniving among themselves as a vocation and to patronizing the arts as an avocation. Sebastian, a teenage fiddler, gets involved in court intrigue and muddles his way to eventual success in ousting a cruel usurper from the throne.

———. *Time Cat.* Holt 1963. $3.50 (P—Avon, $.60); 9–12.
A boy and a cat are able to talk to each other during their journeys into nine historical periods. Though this is fantasy, the author does not allow the characters to change history or to go beyond personal capacities.

Bailey, Carolyn S. *Miss Hickory.* Viking 1946. $3.25 (P—Viking, $.65); 7–10.
This Newbery Award winner still holds the charm and grace that made it outstanding when it was originally published.

Miss Hickory, a doll with a hickory nut head, was left behind by her family and spent a winter alone but with enough adventure to hold the interest of most children.

Baker, Margaret J. *Porterhouse Major,* il. by Shirley Hughes. Prentice 1967. $3.95; 8–12.

Rory, an imaginative boy, produces a concoction that causes his cat to grow very large and behave like a highly intelligent human being. The cat takes over the receptionist's duties in Rory's father's dental office and is responsible for interesting episodes in the household in which he lives. Action filled, humorous story; interesting characters.

Barrie, J. M. *Peter Pan,* il. by Nora Unwin. Scribner 1954. $3.95 (many paperback editions); 10–12.

Tens of thousands of children have enjoyed this story and will continue to do so. By the same author: *Peter and Wendy.*

Beatty, Jerome, Jr. *Sheriff Stonehead and the Teenage Termites,* il. by Gene Holtan. Scott 1970. $3.95; 9–12.

In this broadly humorous, easy-to-read story, the theme of adult heavy-handedness is given light-hearted handling. Sheriff Stonehead tries to clear up some harmless pranks, but the young heroes show him he is just an alarmist.

Bennett, Anna Elizabeth. *Little Witch,* il. by Helen Stone. Lippincott 1953. $2.63 (P—Scholastic, $.60); 9–12.

Miniken does not want to be a witch even though she can perform all kinds of exciting and unusual feats. She only wants to be like all other girls and to go to school.

Bennett, Richard. *Shawneen and the Gander,* il. by the author. Doubleday 1932, 1962. $2.95; 6–12.

A boy, a bugle, a leprechaun, and a gander make a modern tale in the Irish tradition. Revised from the 1932 edition with new pictures.

Bond, Michael. *Here Comes Thursday,* il. by Daphne Rowles. Lothrop 1966. $3.25; 8–12.

A compilation of delightful episodes involving mouse number 1397869 (later named Thursday) after he escapes from the Home for Waif-Mice and Stray-Mice and lives with a resourceful family of mice whose home is in an organ-loft cupboard. Humorous, simple bits of fantasy stress the importance of uniqueness in personalities.

———. *Paddington at Work,* il. by Peggy Fortnum. Houghton 1967. $3.25; 6–10.

Humorous episodes about a lovable bear named Paddington. He dabbles in the stock exchange, works as a barber, joins a ballet company, and thoroughly entertains his readers in the process. Clever whimsical sketches add to the charm of the stories. By the same author: *A Bear Called Paddington; Paddington Goes to Town.*

Boston, Lucy M. *The River at Green Knowe,* il. by Peter Boston. Harcourt 1959. $3.25 (P—Harcourt, $.60); 9–12.

A story of an old house where mystery and magic abound. The Green Knowe books have become modern classics.

_____. *The Sea Egg.* Harcourt 1967. $2.75; 7–10.

The exultation of two boys who discover a Triton and become a part of his underwater world. Scuba diving gives the book contemporary interest, and the creative style makes it unique.

_____. *Treasure of Green Knowe,* il. by Peter Boston. Harcourt 1958. $3.00; 9–12.

When Tolly visits his great-grandmother in her ancestral home, he learns about the other children who grew up in that house many, many years ago. The stories are so real and so absorbing that Tolly feels these children of long ago are part of the present. This book sustains the interest of the reader in its frequent transitions from reality to fantasy. By the same author: *A Stranger at Green Knowe; An Enemy at Green Knowe.*

Brand, Christianna. *Nurse Matilda Goes to Town,* il. by Edward Ardizzone. Dutton 1967. $3.50; 7–11.

The terribly naughty Brown children are sent to London to stay with Great-aunt Adelaide while their parents take a vacation. Nurse Matilda goes along and changes them from incorrigible brats into somewhat civilized human beings. The story has some similarity to Mary Poppins. By the same author: *Nurse Matilda.*

Broun, Heywood. *The Fifty-first Dragon,* il. by Ed Emberley. Prentice 1968. $3.95; 7–12.

A delightful tongue-in-cheek tale about a timid knight who slays dragons with the help of magic. In the process, he finds self-confidence.

Butterworth, Oliver. *The Enormous Egg,* il. by Louis Darling. Little 1956. $4.25 (P—Scholastic, $.75); 9–12.

Nate Twitchell cares for an oversize egg and hatches a dinosaur. The anachronism of a medieval animal in modern times sets the stage for a very funny story. By the same author: *The Trouble with Jenny's Ear.*

Cameron, Eleanor. *The Terrible Churnadryne,* il. by Beth and Joe Krush. Little 1959. $3.95; 9–12.

Tom and Jennifer see a huge and mysterious monster roaming about in the fog and mist in a California coastal town. Few people believe them, but they eventually organize to trap the monster.

Carlsen, Ruth Christoffer. *Sam Bottleby*, il. by Wallace Tripp. Houghton 1968. $3.50; 9–12.

A delightful romp through New York with a fairy godfather brings all kinds of magic, fun, and adventure. Good for oral reading.

Carroll, Lewis. *Alice's Adventures in Wonderland* and *Through the Looking Glass*, il. by Sir John Tenniel. Macmillan 1923. $3.95 (P—Airmont, $.50); 10–12.

This fantasy, written by a professor of mathematics to entertain a little girl, is one of the most quoted books in the English language. Every child should be introduced to *Alice*, though the books' appeal will not be universal. Other editions include the Illustrated Junior Library, Grosset; and Rainbow Classic, World.

Clarke, Pauline. *The Return of the Twelves*, il. by Bernarda Bryson. Coward 1963. $4.50; 10–14.

Story of the discovery of the 12 wooden soldiers once owned by the Brontë children. The soldiers are returned to the museum in the Brontë home largely through the efforts of an 11-year-old English boy whose fondness for the soldiers helps them to come alive in his presence. The story is touching and well written.

Cleary, Beverly. *Runaway Ralph*, il. by Louis Darling. Morrow 1970. $3.95; 8–12.

This sequal to *The Mouse and the Motorcycle* tells of the hazards faced by Ralph, a mouse, when he runs away to escape adult domination. His grave situation is handled with humor that is enhanced by the illustrations.

Corbett, Scott. *Ever Ride a Dinosaur?* il. by Mircea Vasiliu. Holt 1969. $3.59; 8–11.

Bronson, the talking brontosaurus, had an I.Q. of 1500. He desparately wanted to visit the dinosaur section of the Museum of Natural History in New York. How he cons middle-aged Casper Milquetoast into a accompanying him (and their experiences en route) is the substance of this dizzy fantasy.

Craig, M. Jean. *The Dragon in the Clock Box*, il. by K. Oechsli. Norton 1962. $3.95; 7–9.

An extraordinarily perceptive story about a young child's imagination. The reader will be delighted that the young hero never does reveal his secret to the adults. (Is there a dragon in the clock box?)

Danska, Herbert. *The Street Kids,* il. by the author. Knopf 1970. $4.50; 10–14.

The sometimes humorous, sometimes tragic tale of old Hannibal Servatius Serendipity, first an apartment house superintendent and later a flower-growing watchman at a building site.

Davis, Robert. *Padre Porko: The Gentlemanly Pig,* il. by Fritz Eichenberg. Holiday 1948. $3.95; 9–12.

The hero is a consultant to every animal with problems. His humorous methods of solution will arouse interest in readers and listeners.

de Saint-Exupéry, Antoine. *The Little Prince,* tr. by Katherine Woods. Harcourt 1943. $4.25 (P—Harcourt, $.75); 8 up.

A classic tale that goes far beyond the story of the little prince and his desert-stranded airplane pilot, this book tells much about life and philosophy. Especially suited for oral reading.

Druon, Maurice. *Tistou of the Green Thumb,* tr. by Humphrey Hare, il. by Jacqueline Duheme. Scribner 1958. $3.50; 9–12.

"Flowers can prevent evil things from happening." Young gardeners can identify with the story of the boy whose green thumb magically brightens hospitals and prisons and even stops wars until at last he leaves the world on a ladder of flowers. Appropriately dainty pictures with unexpected bits of humor.

Eager, Edward. *Half-Magic,* il. by N. M. Bodecker. Harcourt 1954. $4.50; 9 up.

"Sir Kath from Toledo" and her brother and sisters use their half-magic coin and some simple arithmetic to wish for a trip to King Arthur's England and other exciting places. Their adventures are natural, surprising, and hilarious.

———. *The Time Garden.* Harcourt 1958. $3.75; 9 up.

The story of the Natterjack, a small cockney monster who allows four children to scamper through time to Elizabethan London. By the same author: *Magic by the Lake.*

Enright, Elizabeth. *Tatsinda.* Harcourt 1963. $3.50; 9–12.

Because she is different from all the other silver-haired children of Tatrajan, Tatsinda is carried away by the horrible giant Johrgong. By the same author: *Zeee.*

Farjeon, Eleanor. *The Little Bookroom,* il. by Edward Ardizzone. Walck 1956. $6.50; 9 up.

A gentle spirit, touches of pathos, country pleasures, and
musical words make these brief fanciful tales almost a
modern match for Hans Christian Andersen.

————. *The Silver Curlew,* il. by Ernest H. Shepard. Viking
1954. $3.75; 9–12.

Unless she can guess the Spindle-Imp's name, the young
queen will lose her beautiful baby. Eleanor Farjeon adds
sturdy country folk and guardian animals to the old *Tom Tit
Tot* story framework.

Fleming, Ian. *Chitty-Chitty-Bang-Bang: The Magical Car,* il. by
John Burningham. Random 1964. $3.95 (P—Scholastic,
$.75); 5–10.

The Pott family has many adventures in store when they buy
and repair an old broken-down car. The renovated automo-
bile, Chitty-Chitty-Bang-Bang, may be converted into an
airplane, hovercraft, and motorboat. This lively story is not
to be confused with the motion picture of the same name.

Foster, Elizabeth Vincent. *Lyrico, The Only Horse of His Kind,*
il. by Joy Buba. Gambit 1970. $5.95; 12–16.

Lyrico is an exceptional horse; he has wings. This is a
fantasy that will certainly subtly challenge American values
towards conservation and pollution.

Gage, Wilson. *Mike's Toads,* il. by Glenn Rounds. World
1970. $4.50; 8–12.

A simply written tale of how Mike's summer holiday became complicated by his offer to look after a friend's toads.
Warm family relations and a respect for others underlie the
story.

Garner, Alan. *Elidor.* Walck 1967. $4.25; 10–14.

Three children wander around the rubble and empty buildings at the edge of the demolition area and find themselves
in another dimension. This is an exciting account of danger,
beauty, and courage. Advanced comprehension level. By the
same author: *The Moon of Gomrath; Owl Service.*

Gordon, John. *The Giant under the Snow,* il. by Rocco Negri.
Harper 1970. $3.95; 12–16.

A suspense-filled mystery about the terrifying adventures of
three teenagers who find an ancient talisman.

Grahame, Kenneth. *The Wind in the Willows,* il. by Ernest H.
Shepard. Scribner 1954. $6.00 (P—Scribner, $1.65); 10 up.

One of the best-loved books of all time. A distinguished
edition. Other handsome volumes illustrated by Arthur

Rackham and Tasha Tudor. By the same author: *The Reluctant Dragon* and others.

Harris, Rosemary. *The Shadow on the Sun* Macmillan 1970. $4.95; 12–16.

Set just after the Flood, this tale of young love, court intrigue, and spine-chilling adventure in the evil land of Punt will keep readers absorbed from beginning to end. Plot and subplot are suspensefully interwoven.

Hollander, John. *The Quest of the Gole,* il. by Reginald Pollack. Atheneum 1966. $3.95; 12 up.

The reader will experience the same feeling that Strengal did when he came across the magic Bleeding Book of Ballydon. Quality literature is like the Bleeding Book in that it tells you things about yourself that you usually don't want to find out. This lyrical retelling of the quest perpetuates the searching desire within us all.

Holm, Anne. *Peter,* il. by L. W. Kingsland. Harcourt 1968. $3.75; 12 up.

The boy in a portrait shows a young Danish lad that a thread runs through all history, be it the struggles of Spartans against the people of Thebes or of the Saxons against the Normans. Time does not count so much in making history as do people. By the same author: *North to Freedom,* a realistic masterpiece.

Holman, Felice. *The Cricket Winter,* il. by Ralph Pinto. Norton 1967. $3.95; 7–11.

Tale of a wise sensitive boy and the friendship he develops with a cricket who lives beneath the floor boards in his bedroom. The cricket learns the Morse code as Simon is tapping it out, so communication becomes possible.

Hunter, Mollie. *The Walking Stones,* il. by Trina Schart Hyman. Harper 1970. $3.95; 10–14.

This mystical and haunting story set in the Scottish Highlands is about how a boy's friendship with an old man leads him to the secret of the Walking Stones.

Jansson, Tove. *Comet in Moominland,* tr. by Elizabeth Portch, il. by the author. Walck 1968. $4.00; 7 up.

This Scandinavian import, one of a series, has a delightful premise about the adventures of some very unusual creatures. The author is a Hans Christian Andersen Award winner.

Jarrell, Randall. *The Animal Family,* il. by Maurice Sendak. Pantheon 1965. $3.50; 10–14.

Sensitive writing depicts a lonely hunter who gradually

develops a family from a strange assortment of creatures: a mermaid, a bear, a lynx, and a boy. Symbolism and strong characterization make this haunting story believable.

Johnson, Elizabeth. *Stuck with Luck,* il. by Trina Schart Hyman. Little 1967. $3.50; 8–12.

This delightful little fantasy about the experiences of young Tom, a leprechaun named Magruder McGillicuddy O'Toole, and a recently acquired Irish terrier called Mike serves as a good introduction to the world of magic. Easy to read and a fast paced story.

Kästner, Erich. *The Little Man,* tr. by James Kirkup. Knopf 1966. $3.95; 8–11.

This charming fantasy, translated from the German, about a two-inch tall circus performer and his devoted friend Professor Hokus von Pokus, a world-famous conjurer, shows all aspects of circus life and is filled with excitement as Maxie gets in and out of thrilling predicaments. The flavor is German; the humor and rare imagination give it a special distinction. By the same author: *Emil and the Detectives.*

Kendall, Carol. *The Gammage Cup,* il. by Erik Blegvad. Harcourt 1959. $3.50 (P—Harcourt, $.65); 8–12.

Highly imaginative fantasy details the lives of a new race of little people known as the Minnipins. A rare and distinguished piece of literature. Sequel: *The Whisper of Glocken.*

Kenny, Herbert A. *Dear Dolphin,* il. by Kelly Oechsli. Pantheon 1967. $3.95; 8–12.

A humorous book with a touch of *Alice.* Ann searches for the lost city of Atlantis. Children will enjoy her many adventures.

Kesselman, Wendy Ann. *Franz Tovey and the Rare Animals,* il. by Elenore Schmid. Quist 1968. $3.25; 5–9.

Brief narrative of a lonely boy who lives in a castle in a big park, with accompanying exquisite photographs of a small boy and his imaginary animal companions. Finally a real cat, who is a rare animal, goes back through the meadows with the boy to sleep with him in the castle.

Kipling, Rudyard. *The Elephant's Child,* il. by Leonard Weisgard. Walker 1971. $4.50; 8–12.

A fine example of one of Kipling's greatest classics. Weisgard's use of bold color and form makes one feel that he is in the jungle.

_____. *Jungle Book,* il. by Kurt Wiese. Doubleday 1952. $3.50 (many paperback editions); 12 up.

Classic tales of Mowgli, the man-cub whom the wolves

adopted, Kotik the white seal, Rikki-Tikki the mongoose, and other jungle animals.

Lagerlof, Selma. *The Wonderful Adventures of Nils,* tr. by Velma Swanston Howard, il. by Hans Baumhauer. Pantheon 1947. $5.95; 9–12.

This edition includes *The Further Adventures of Nils* and has to its credit the most satisfying pictures yet. A classic in Scandinavia, this book will be read and reread.

Lamorisse, Albert. *The Red Balloon,* il. with photographs. Doubleday 1957. $3.50; 12–15.

A red balloon in Paris turns out to be magic. The superb photographs were taken during the filming of the French movie of the same name.

Langton, Jane. *The Diamond in the Window,* il. by Erik Blegvad. Harper 1962. $3.95; 10 up.

The New England of Thoreau, Emerson, and Louisa May Alcott flowers again in this delightful 20th-century spoof. Historical and storybook characters wander in and out of the pages as the children search the fourth dimension to find answers to a family secret involving Aunt Lily's lost love. This book is for a whimsical child who reads well or for reading aloud to a group.

Lawrence, Harriet. *H. Philip Birdsong's ESP,* il. by Sandy Huffaker. Scott 1969. $4.50; 12–16.

A humorous fantasy about a boy who inherits a flute from a sorcerer ancestor and finds that he is able to communicate with animals.

Lawson, John. *The Spring Rider.* Crowell 1968. $3.95; 12–16.

A story of strange occurrences on a Civil War battlefield. A boy and his sister are visited by a Yankee bugler boy, a Southern cavalry leader, and the spring rider, Lincoln himself. The spring rider persuades the bugler to blow taps so that the ghosts of the battlefield dead may sleep.

————. *You Better Come Home with Me,* il. by Arnold Spilka. Crowell 1966. $3.50; 9 up.

Read this book aloud! A lost boy finds a hospitable scarecrow, a witch who makes crash landings, a red fox who bakes crisp pancakes, and many more friends. A joyous, sad story with the smells and sights of blue mountains and the sound of a fiddle tune. Arnold Spilka's scraggly blue and green pictures are appropriate.

Leichman, Seymour. *The Boy Who Could Sing Pictures,* il. by the author. Doubleday 1968. $3.50; 7–12.

This book about a remarkable boy who lived in the Middle

Ages is a rather special delight. The premise demands that the book be read aloud.

Levine, Rhoda. *The Herbert Situation,* il. by Larry Ross. Quist 1970. $4.25; 4 up.

A drolly told spoof about happiness and how best to find it. Better suited for older children.

Lewis, C. S. *The Last Battle,* il. by Pauline Baynes. Macmillan 1956. $4.50 (P—Macmillan, $.65); 9–12.

The seventh and concluding volume of the powerful Chronicles of Narnia, the mysterious land inhabited by men and talking beasts and ruled over by the great lion Aslan. When young King Tirian is enslaved, the children of the land beyond world's end (our world) battle fiercely for the last time in the Narnia the children know. Thereafter, the new Narnia foretold by Aslan emerges. By the same author: *The Lion, The Witch and the Wardrobe; Prince Caspian; The Voyage of the "Dawn Treader"; The Silver Chair; The Horse and His Boy; The Magician's Nephew.*

Lindgren, Astrid. *Pippi Longstocking,* tr. by Florence Lamborn, il. by Louis S. Glanzman. Viking 1950. $3.00 (P—Viking, $.75); 9–11.

Living only with a monkey and horse, Pippi is one of the liveliest and most unpredictable tomboys in children's literature. A Swedish story.

Little, Jane. *Sneaker Hill,* il. by Nancy Grossman. Atheneum 1967. $3.95; 9–12.

A muddle-headed apprentice is saved from disaster by two children, a wise owl, and the young rat, Rufus.

Lofting, Hugh. *The Twilight of Magic,* il. by Lois Lenski. Lippincott 1967. $3.95; 10–13.

A boy and girl have mystical experiences which center on the possession of the Whispering Shell. This is a reissue of a tale of magic and superstition, castles, knights, kings, princesses, and peasants.

———. *The Voyages of Doctor Dolittle.* Lippincott 1922. $3.95 (P—Dell, $.60); 9–12.

Chronicle of the famous doctor's voyage to Spidermonkey Island with careful attention given to the detail that children appreciate. Sequel to *The Story of Doctor Dolittle.*

MacDonald, George. *The Light Princess,* il. by William Pène Du Bois. Crowell 1962. $4.50; 6–10.

Having no gravity and no weight, the little princess is always in danger of floating away. The Du Bois pictures give her personality if not weight.

Maddock, Reginald. *The Dragon in the Garden.* Little 1969. $4.50; 10–14.

An English story of an unlikely hero who takes the leadership in overthrowing the school bully and his gang.

Mayne. William. *Earthfasts.* Dutton 1967. $3.95; 11–13.

The relativity of time is the basis for an unusual and well-written story about the friendship between two modern Yorkshire lads and an 18th century drummer boy. By the same author: *Underground Alley; A Grass Rope; Sand; Swarm in May; A Pig in the Middle.*

Mendoza, George. *The Good Luck Spider and Other Bad Luck Stories,* il. by Gahan Wilson. Doubleday 1970. $3.50; 6–11.

These three stories of superstition constitute hilariously funny bad luck tales. Grisly cartoon-type illustrations quite suitably accompany each macabre tale.

Merrill, Jean. *The Pushcart War,* il. by Ronni Solbert. Scott 1964. $3.95; 10–14.

The day finally comes when the New York City streets are completely clogged by truck traffic. Only through the alliance between children and pushcart peddlers is the condition finally alleviated. Here is much truth, humor, and action.

———. *The Superlative Horse,* il. by Ronni Solbert. Scott 1961. $3.75 (P—Scholastic, $.60); 8–11.

This story, suggested by a Taoist tale of 350 B.C., concerns a humble stable boy who rises to fame after finding the "superlative" horse. The attractive drawings are in the early Chinese manner.

Milne, A. A. *Winnie the Pooh,* il. by Ernest H. Shepard. Dutton 1926. $3.50 (P—Dell, $.75); 7–10.

Modern classic full of wit and tenderness containing jokes one weeps over, not knowing why they are so funny. Kanga and Baby Roo, Piglet, Pooh, and Christopher Robin are characters no child should miss. By the same author: *The House at Pooh Corner.*

Moon, Sheila. *Knee-Deep in Thunder,* il. by Peter Parnall. Atheneum 1967. $4.95; 12–16.

A 13-year-old girl and her odd companions, a beetle, a butterfly, a spider, an ant, and others, meet demonic beasts, perform fearsome tasks, and experience great moments of sorrow and revelation. This lengthy fantasy, told in the spirit of Navajo mythology, has thought-provoking messages for the mature, careful reader.

Nickless, Will. *Owlglass,* il. by the author. Day 1966. $3.95;
8–11.

A charming animal fantasy, rather reminiscent of *Wind in
the Willows,* of a group of field and forest animals who fear
the hawk and the owl and ultimately find a way to keep
them as friends. Delightful tales related by various animals
enliven club meetings.

Norton, Mary. *The Borrowers,* il. by Beth and Joe Krush.
Harcourt 1953. $3.50 (P—Harcourt, $.75); 9–12.

One of the most delightful tales ever constructed for children, this is the story of the tiny people who live in the walls
of a fortunate home and borrow things. Norton creates a
wonderful world of fancy. Sequels: *The Borrowers Aloft;
The Borrowers Afield; The Borrowers Afloat.*

Ormondroyd, Edward. *Time at the Top,* il. by Peggie Bach.
Parnassus 1963. $3.75; 10–14.

In this engaging mixture of fantasy and reality many a young
reader will recognize with amusement some similarity to his
own daydreams. Susan makes several trips between past and
present to persuade her widowed father to join her in the
1880's. She has found there not only flower-bordered lanes,
lace-curtained houses, hooped skirts, and high-button shoes
but also a family that exactly complements her own.

Pearce, A. Philippa. *Tom's Midnight Garden,* il. by Susan
Einzig. Lippincott 1958. $4.25; 10–13.

Daytime life for Tom at his aunt's home in England is dull,
but each night he participates through fantasy in the lives of
the former inhabitants of the interesting old house in which
he is spending an enforced vacation. The book is British in
setting and atmosphere. The element of mystery is well
sustained, and the reader is left to make his own interpretation of the reality of the story. By the same author: *A Dog So
Small; Minnow Leads to Treasure.*

Peet, Bill. *The Wump World,* il. by the author. Houghton
1970. $3.95; 6–12.

A gently told satire in which the beautiful Wump world is
invaded by Pollutians from Pullutus who spoil everything
with factories and concrete and then abandon it for the
Wumps to put together again.

Pène, Du Bois William. *Call me Bandicoot,* il. by the author.
Harper 1970. $3.95; 10–15.

A nearly irresistable young con-artist, Ermine Bandicoot, is
the hero of this tall tale, which purports to explain how New
York Harbor became tobacco brown.

———. *The Great Geppy,* il. by the author. Viking 1940. $3.00; 10–12.

How Great Geppy, the only horse of his kind in the world, solves the Bott Circus mystery.

———. *The Twenty-one Balloons.* Viking 1947. $3.50 (P—Dell, $.75); 8–12.

A transitional reading experience for the young generation to prepare them for space exploration. The fanciful three-week trip by Professor Sherman blends comedy, fancy, and fact into an adventure anyone may have without orbiting the world.

Randall, Florence E. *The Almost Year.* Atheneum 1971. $5.95; 10–15.

A young black girl reluctantly spending the school year with a white family is suspected of being responsible for strange, unaccountable occurrences. This story is a sensitive portrayal of people reacting to their racial differences and to a poltergeist.

Raskin, Ellen. *Spectacles,* il. by the author. Atheneum 1968. $3.50; 5–9.

Iris Fogel didn't always wear glasses. Before she got them, her visual world was a highly entertaining one. The book has pairs of illustrations: the first shows in greyed outline what Iris saw, the second reveals a clear picture. Eventually she sees the world as others do when she wears glasses.

Rinkoff, Barbara. *Elbert, the Mind Reader,* il. by Paul Galdone. Lothrop 1967. $3.25 (P—Scholastic, $.60); 8–12.

After Elbert has a new filling put in his tooth, he is able to hear people's thoughts. He uses his mind-reading talents to impress the football coach, and, even though he is really too small for football, he finally is allowed to substitute. His filling is chipped and the reception is gone, but Elbert still manages to make a touchdown. Delightfully humorous, action-filled story.

Ruck-Pauquet, Gina. *Fourteen Cases of Dynamite,* il. by Lilo Fromm. Delacorte 1968. $3.50; 8–12.

Lots of fun with a zany inventor and the adventures of his friends. This good escape fiction pokes gentle fun at technology.

Sandburg, Carl. *Rootabaga Stories,* il. by Maud and Miska Petersham. Harcourt 1922. $4.50; 9–15.

A classic in children's literature. A collection of American tales in the Sandburg tradition. Great fun with words.

Sauer, Julia. *Fog Magic*, il. by Lynd Ward. Viking 1943. $3.50; 9–12.

Greta, who loves the fog, finds that she can walk through it to a community of people who lived in her Nova Scotia neighborhood a generation before her. With them she shares danger and adventure and quiet joy in a finely written story that is almost too real for fantasy. The pictures are magically appropriate.

Sawyer, Ruth. *The Enchanted Schoolhouse*, il. by Hugh Troy. Viking 1956. $3.50; 9–12.

Wanting to have something Irish to take with him to America, Brian Boru captures a leprechaun.

Scheer, George F. *Cherokee Animal Tales*, il. by Robert Frankenberg. Holiday 1968. $3.50; 8–11.

These 14 "why" stories about American animals, accompanied by a fine introduction about the Cherokee people, are reminiscent of the *Just So Stories.*

Schweitzer, Byrd Baylor. *The Chinese Bug*, il. by Beatrice Darwin. Houghton 1968. $3.50; 5–8.

A charming tale of a boy and his dream to dig to China. While he doesn't make it, the end is so pleasing that no one really cares.

Sharp, Margery. *Miss Bianca: A Fantasy*, il. by Garth Williams. Little 1962. $4.50; 8–12.

An English blend of lavish imagery, fairytale happenings, and beautiful prose, this fantasy has an underlying satire directed to adults. The child reader is too busy following the tortuous windings of the plot to be aware of it. By the same author: *The Rescuers; The Turret.*

Snyder, Zilpha K. *The Headless Cupid*, il. by Alton Raible. Atheneum 1971. $4.95; 8–12.

A family of four children and their stepsister experience encounters with the occult, a seance, and an old house occupied by a poltergeist.

Spearing, Judith. *The Museum House Ghosts*, il. by Marvin Glass. Atheneum 1969. $4.75; 8–12.

An old house that is being converted into a museum is populated with a family of ghosts who can materialize at will. The two high-spirited ghost sons get themselves into hilarious situations, which are described in the broad type of humor that children enjoy so much.

Stapp, Arthur D. *The Fabulous Earthworm Deal*, il. by George Porter. Viking 1969. $4.13; 9–12.

Once Marsh, an ambitious fellow with great determination, decides to go into the business of selling worms, he is not to be daunted. Difficulties beset him: first too many worms, then too few. In each extremity, J.T., his indispensible idea man, comes up with original solutions. What might have been disaster is turned into "earthworm gold."

Steele, Mary Q. *Journey Outside,* il. by Rocco Negri. Viking 1969. $4.50; 10 up.

The author has chosen the parable form to present her view of youth's search for identity and understanding of self. The result is a sensitive, powerful allegory. On the surface it relates a fascinating adventure that young people may enjoy simply at that level. However, most readers will sense the underlying theme and be encouraged in their own search for the answers. The powerful woodcuts are a perfect complement to the mystical mood of the story.

Steig, William. *Sylvester and the Magic Pebble,* il. by the author. Simon 1969. $4.95; 6–10.

This talking animal farce is about a young jackass, Sylvester, who is accidentally turned into a stone. Just as accidentally his parents find him, and he is turned back to his true self. Illustrated with amusing cartoons. The Caldecott Award Winner for 1970.

Stockton, Frank R. *The Storyteller's Pack,* il. by Bernarda Bryson. Scribner 1968. $5.95; all ages.

Another generation is having the delightful opportunity to discover the storytelling skill of Frank Stockton. A must for those who enjoy a well-told short story. By the same author: *The Griffin and the Minor Canon.*

Taylor, Mark. *Henry Explores the Jungle,* il. by Graham Booth. Atheneum 1968. $5.95; 3–7.

Readers first met Henry and his dog, Laird Angus McTavish, in *Henry the Explorer.* The two of them are back in an even better story. Henry, with a little help from Angus, catches an honest-to-goodness tiger in a way that will seem quite probable. Taylor's prose is disarmingly simple and matter-of-fact; the illustrations are just as honest and completely childlike.

Teal, Mildred. *The Flight of the Kite Merriweather,* il. by Valli Van de Bovenkamp. Atheneum 1968. $3.50; 7–10.

A delightful world of all kinds and sorts of kites. The adventures will appeal to boys especially.

Thurber, James. *Many Moons,* il. by Louis Slobodkin. Harcourt 1943. $3.50; 5 up.

The court jester is the only one wise enough to find a way to give the moon to Princess Lenore. Excellent illustrations. Caldecott Award winner in 1944.

Tolkien, J. R. R. *The Hobbit.* Houghton 1938. $3.95 (P—Ballantine, $.95); 9 up.

For the hobbit and his dwarf companions there can be no turning back until the dragon Smaug is slain. Tolkien's comfortable yet adventurous small people have delighted and involved their readers for decades. For adults, the story is continued in the Lord of the Rings trilogy.

Travers, Pamela. *Mary Poppins,* il. by Mary Shepard. Harcourt 1934. $3.75; 10–12.

Mary Poppins blows in with the east wind to be nursemaid to Jane and Michael and leads them through a series of incredible adventures. This popular imaginative series includes *Mary Poppins Comes Back; Mary Poppins Opens the Door; Mary Poppins in the Park.*

Turkle, Brinton. *The Fiddler of High Lonesome.* Viking 1968. $3.50; 8 up.

A great tall tale with delightful illustrations and characterizations. The Fogle clan is as spiteful and murderous a group of scalawags as ever lived. That Bochamp is their kin is as hard to believe as the events that occur on High Lonesome.

Waber, Bernard. *A Firefly Named Torchy,* il. by the author. Houghton 1970. $4.95; 5–8.

About an over-illuminated firefly who visits Broadway. Gaily whimsical and illustrated with bold bright splotches of color.

White, E. B. *Charlotte's Web,* il. by Garth Williams. Harper 1952. $3.95 (P—Dell, $.95); 10–12.

A wise, beautiful, and satisfying story of a spider and her friends. By the same author: *Stuart Little.*

Yolen, Jane. *Greyling,* il. by William Stobbs. World 1968. $3.95; 6–10.

Greyling is a selchie (a man-seal) found as a seal pup by a lonely fisherman and his wife and miraculously changed into a human baby. He grows up cherished as their adopted son, unknowing of his origin until, in the crisis of a storm to rescue his drowning foster-father, he changes forever his human form for that of a seal. Rich water colors done in hues hinting of impending tragedy enhance the drama.

TRADITIONAL FOLK LITERATURE

Almedingen, E. M. *The Treasure of Siegfried,* il. by Charles Keeping. Lippincott 1965. $3.75; 12–14.

The reader meets the beautiful Princess Kriemhild who sends him back to the 11th century, or perhaps even the fourth, for the great German epic. The story is more than heroic events; it is also a chronicle of human involvement with life and fantasy.

Anderson, Poul. *The Fox, the Dog, and the Griffin,* il. by Laszlo Kubinyi. Doubleday 1966. $2.75; 5–8.

The wise griffin in this folktale is able to bring happiness to the cat, reward the dog, and treat the fox to a slippery humorous trick.

Arbuthnot, May Hill. *Time for Fairy Tales, Old and New,* il. by John Averill. Scott 1961. $7.50; 5–12.

A classic collection of folktales, myths, and fairy tales for storytelling and reading aloud.

Arkhurst, Joyce Cooper. *The Adventures of Spider,* il. by Jerry Pinkney. Little 1964. $3.50; 7–11.

Presented here are tales from West Africa, gathered by a librarian who went to the home of her ancestors, sat in the circle of villagers to listen to the professional storytellers, and wrote her notes by moonlight.

Asbjornsen, Peter C., and Jorgen Moe. *Norwegian Folk Tales,* tr. by P. S. Iversen and C. Norman, il. by E. Werenskiold and T. Kittelsen. Viking 1961. $5.00; 8–11.

Thirty-five tales in a fine translation are excellent for reading aloud.

Baker, Laura Nelson. *O Children of the Wind and Pines,* il. by Inez Storer. Lippincott 1967. $2.95; 9–11.

Atastaze, a forlorn and wistful Huron Indian girl, receives the continent's first Christmas carol from a French priest. The pictures might have been painted on birch bark.

Barbeau, Marius. *The Golden Phoenix and Other French-Canadian Fairy Tales,* retold by Michael Hornyansky, il. by Arthur Price. Walck 1963. $4.00; 9–12.

Eight European tales that have been told and retold by French Canadians. A clever prince tricks a thief, a woodcutter, and a mysterious sultan.

Barlow, Genevieve. *Latin American Tales,* il. by William M. Hutchinson. Rand 1966. $3.50; 10 up.

A delightful collection of 19 Latin American folktales, from Argentinian to Mexican. Useful for those who are endeavoring to understand the culture and history of our Latin neighbors.

Belting, Natalia. *The Earth Is on a Fish's Back,* il. by Esta Nesbitt. Holt 1965. $3.50; 9–12.

Some things identified and described by ancient storytellers remain more beautiful than the current excitement over space flight. Belting has preserved the beauty from the past here. Distinguished design.

———. *The Sun Is a Golden Earring,* il. by Bernarda Bryson. Holt 1962. $3.50; 8–12.

A poetic view of the sun, from the folklore around the world. By the same author and artist: *The Stars Are Silver Reindeer; Calendar Moon.*

Benson, Sally. *Stories of the Gods and Heroes,* il. by Steele Savage. Dial 1940. $3.95; 9–12.

A fine collection of Greek myths based on Bulfinch's *Age of Fable,* some edited and others entirely rewritten.

Berger, Terry. *Black Fairy Tales,* il. by David Omar White. Atheneum 1969. $4.75; 8–12.

These ten South African fairy and folktales come from three different cultures. The style of telling is awesome, light, pompous, or fearsome as the intent of each story demands. The motifs of the stories are universal ones.

Bierhorst, John, ed. *The Ring in the Prairie: A Shawnee Legend,* il. by Leo and Dianne Dillon. Dial 1970. $4.50; 4–9.

This lovely legend of a renowned hunter who marries a fairy maid and is later turned into a white hawk is exquisitely illustrated with cut-paper collages.

Brown, Marcia. *Backbone of the King: The Story of Paka'a and His Son Ku.* Scribner 1966. $4.50; 10–14.

A retelling of an ancient Hawaiian legend illustrated with stunning linoleum block prints that match the drama and poetry of the tale.

Bryson, Bernarda. *Gilgamesh: Man's First Story,* il. by the author. Holt 1967. $4.95; 6–11.

A Sumerian tale presented so vigorously that the hero should be remembered.

Buck, Pearl S. *Fairy Tales of the Orient,* il. by Jeanyee Wong. Simon 1965. $5.95; 10–14.

These are spacious tales, wide as the plains and mountains of the Orient and as varied as the landscape. Excellent drama, adventure, and excitement are in the collection as are a wicked magician, events of terror, and subdued beauty.

Bulla, Clyde Robert. *Jonah and the Great Fish,* il. by Helga Aichinger. Crowell 1970. $4.50; 5–10.

A skillful and unsophisticated retelling of an Old Testament story about Jonah and how he learned to understand and to accept God's love. The illustrations are highly expressionistic and add considerable dramatic effect to the story.

_____. *Joseph the Dreamer,* il. by Gordon Laite. Crowell 1971. $4.95; 6–10.

The Old Testament story about Joseph, the dreamer, who is sold to traders by his brothers, then taken to Egypt where he eventually becomes an interpreter of dreams and a rich and powerful leader, is retold with dramatic and exquisite visual and verbal skill.

Burton, Richard. *The Flying Carpet,* adapted and il. by Marcia Brown. Scribner 1956. $3.63; 6–9.

Here the Arabian Nights story of the magic carpet speaks eloquently to young readers. Decorative illustrations are captivatingly Persian in flavor. A distinguished picture-story book.

Calhoun, Mary. *The Thieving Dwarfs,* il. by Janet McCaffery. Morrow 1967. $3.50; 8–10.

This lively, fast moving tale based on German legend shows that honesty is the best policy. The little dwarfs are appealing; illustrations are well drawn.

Campbell, Camilla. *Star Mountain,* il. by Frederic Marvin. McGraw 1968. $4.75; 8–12.

Mexican folktales worthy of reading, interpreted, however, in limited graphics.

Carlson, Natalie Savage. *The Talking Cat and Other Stories of French Canada*, il. by Roger Duvoisin. Harper 1952. $3.50; 8–12.

A collection of folktales handed down to the author by her French-Canadian great-great-uncle. Enthusiasm and humor characterize the author's style, and the illustrations stimulate interest. By the same author: *Alphonse, That Bearded One; Sashes Red and Sashes Blue.*

Chafetz, Henry. *Chanticleer*, il. by Robert Nadler. Pantheon 1968. $3.50; 9–11.

A skillful retelling of the French story by Rostand. Chanticleer comes alive again and will enchant the readers. Illustrations and format are exciting.

Chase, Richard. *Grandfather Tales*, il. by Berkeley Williams. Houghton 1948. $5.00; 9 up.

Mr. Chase brings together a family of mountain storytellers to celebrate Old Christmas (Twelfth Night). They act a mummers' play, sing homespun carols, and tell many a good yarn. Like the *Jack Tales*, these stories are tremendously tellable. The sketches have gusto.

———. *The Jack Tales.* Houghton 1943. $3.95; 8–12.

These tales were repeated orally for generations in western North Carolina. Even though they are written down, they still retain the oral freshness and a language deeply rooted in the Anglo-Saxon tradition.

Clarke, Mollie. *Aldar the Trickster*, il. by Margaret Belsky. Follett 1965. $1.95; 5–8.

Aldar prided himself on his ability to deceive people. The goat man vowed he couldn't be deceived but, of course, he hadn't reckoned with the Trickster's tactics. The Finnish folktale repeats the noodle theme in an easy-to-read form.

———. *Momotàro*, il. by Grace Huxtable. Follett 1963. $1.95; 5–8.

A Japanese folktale in which a childless woodcutter and his wife are made happy by finding a baby boy in a peach. The child grows up to be strong and brave and important to his people.

Colum, Padraic. *The Children's Homer: The Adventures of Odysseus and the Tales of Troy*, il. by Willy Pogany. Macmillan 1965. $4.95; 10–12.

Adults and children enjoy this accurate retelling of Homer's epic.

———. *The Girl Who Sat by the Ashes,* il. by Imero Gobbato. Macmillan 1968. $3.95; 9–12.

Irish turns of speech make the Cinderella story fresh. The pictures in this edition are appropriately romantic.

———. *The Six Who Were Left in a Shoe,* il. by Joseph Schindelman. McGraw 1968. $3.95; 5–9.

Mother Gabble, the goose, says the appropriate words: "Let me speak, these tales are worth telling."

———. *The Stone of Victory and Other Tales,* il. by Judith Gwyn Brown. McGraw 1966. $3.95; 8 up.

This delightful selection from the poet's tales contains many favorite stories. By the same adaptor: *Arabian Nights: Tales of Wonder and Magnificence; The Golden Fleece and the Heroes Who Lived before Ulysses.*

Courlander, Harold. *Olode the Hunter and Other Tales from Nigeria,* il. by Enrico Arno. Harcourt 1968. $3.75; 9–12.

Stories from the Yoruba, Ibo, and Hausa peoples told by a well-known folklorist.

———. *The Piece of Fire and Other Haitian Tales,* il. by Beth and Joe Krush. Harcourt 1964. $3.25; 9–12.

There is a drought in Haiti; the streams and wells are dry. The animals meet to discuss the situation and decide to ask God for help. How God helps them and how they then get further into trouble provide insight into the characteristics of animals and men.

———. *The Tiger's Whisker and Other Tales and Legends from Asia and the Pacific,* il. by Enrico Arno. Harcourt 1959. $3.25; 9–12.

These 31 robust stories from the Far East are a welcome addition to a growing body of literature from too little known areas. A section, "Notes on the Stories," adds to the usefulness of this volume. By the same author: *The Cow-Tail Switch and Other West African Stories; Ride with the Sun; The Hatshaking Dance and Other Tales from Ghana.*

Curry, Jane Louise. *Down from the Lonely Mountain,* il. by Enrico Arno. Harcourt 1965. $3.25; 9–12.

Just how much of these stories comes from the California Indian and what belongs to the storytelling skill of Jane Louise Curry, even the author probably couldn't say for sure. These renditions have a simplicity and color that make them distinctive.

D'Aulnoy, Mme. La Comtesse. *The White Cat and Other Old*

French Fairy Tales, arr. by Rachel Field, il. by E. MacKin-
stry. Macmillan 1967. $4.95; 8–11.

Seventeenth-century French fairy tales with humor and a
sense of life. The words and pictures make the book a "land
of joy," a "palace of peaceful pleasures."

de la Iglesia, Maria Elena. *The Cat and the Mouse and Other
Spanish Tales,* il. by Joseph Low. Pantheon 1966. $3.50;
7–10.

Sixteen fables and folktales retold with an ear for their
particular turn of dry wit and humor.

de la Mare, Walter. *Tales Told Again,* il. by Alan Howard.
Knopf 1959. $3.89; 9–12.

First published in 1927 as *Told Again,* this edition adds
much humor and sparkle to the favorite tales.

de Regniers, Beatrice Schenk. *The Giant Book,* il. by William
L. Cummings. Atheneum 1966. $4.75; 9–12.

Jack the Giant-Killer, Gulliver, Goliath, and Paul Bunyan are
among the fine company presented here.

Deutsch, Babette, and Avrahm Yarmolinsky. *More Tales of
Faraway Folk,* il. by Janina Domanska. Harper 1964. $2.95;
8–14.

Skillfully retold, these folktales from northern Asia are a
companion volume to *Tales of Faraway Folk.* Brief notes
give the settings, and most of the tales illustrate universal
themes.

Dorliae, Peter G. *Animals Mourn for Da Leopard,* il. by S. Irein
Wangboje. Bobbs 1970. $4.50; 10 up.

Ten West African folktales told with delightful sparkling
freshness. They reveal the humor, the beliefs, the wisdom,
and the wiliness of their West African originators. The
linoleum block prints add charm to the content and appearance.

Du Mond, Frank. *Tall Tales of the Catskills,* il. by Peter
Parnall. Atheneum 1968. $4.95; 8–12.

An excellent collection of tall tales from a master storyteller,
this will make for hours of good oral reading.

Durham, Mae, ed. *Tit for Tat and Other Latvian Folk Tales,* tr.
by Rubene-Koo Skaidrite, il. by Harriet Pincus. Harcourt
1967. $3.25; 8–10.

God and the devil plow the same field in one of these
humorous stories from the Baltic region.

Emrich, Duncan, comp. *The Book of Wishes and Wishmaking,*
il. by Hilary Knight. American Heritage 1971. $2.95; 6–12.

A compilation of wishmaking formulas that have come down through generations from American, England, Scotland, Ireland, and elsewhere. Wishes are linked to such things as the first whippoorwill of spring, to a first star and falling stars, to the first snowflake of winter, and so on.

Feagles, Anita. *Thor and the Giants,* il. by Gertrude Barrer-Russell. Scott 1968. $3.95; 6–9.

Light, life, beauty, and meaning for contemporary times are provided in this retelling and graphic presentation of an old Norse legend. See also the version by Dorothy Hosford.

Felton, Harold W. *New Tall Tales of Pecos Bill,* il. by William Moyers. Prentice 1958. $4.50; 9–12.

Hitherto untold "how" tales of one of American children's favorite cowpunchers of the Old West.

_____. *True Tall Tales of Stormalong,* il. by Joan Sandin. Prentice 1968. $4.95; 8–12.

Stormalong, the magnificent sailor of years ago, is the subject for this delightful collection of tales. Great humor and wonderful illustrations make this a must for storytellers. Reader and hearer need not accept the "truth" of the tales to enjoy them. By the same author: *Fire-fightin' Mose; John Henry and His Hammer; Pecos Bill, Cowpuncher.*

Fillmore, Parker. *The Shepherd's Nosegay: Stories from Finland and Czechoslovakia,* il. by Enrico Arno. Harcourt 1958. $3.00; 9–12.

A selection of favorite folktales chosen from three of the author's earlier books. Many children's old favorites are included. By the same author: *Mighty Mikko; Czechoslovak Fairy Tales; The Shoemaker's Apron.*

Finger, Charles J. *Tales from Silver Lands.* Doubleday 1924. $3.95; 10–12.

Every child should have the opportunity to wander with Charles J. Finger. These folktales meander in and out of Spanish-American countries, each bringing a tone and color that show the people to be deeply imaginative.

Glasgow, Aline. *The Journey of Akbar,* il. by J. C. Kocsis. Dial 1967. $3.50; 10–14.

An unusual allegory, using a rich background of the nature, tradition, and folklore of India.

Graves, Robert. *Greek Gods and Heroes,* il. by Dimitri Davis. Doubleday 1960. $3.95; 10 up.

The ancient tales of gods and men are retold in a poet's prose. The "laughing, loving, and eternally quarrelsome" gods and goddesses and their earthly prototypes are brought vividly to life.

_____. *The Siege and Fall of Troy,* il. by C. Walter Hodges. Doubleday 1963. $3.50 (P—Dell, $.50); 11 up.

Greek deities interfere incessantly in the earthly lives of an innumerable cast, confusing the plot and the line between fact and fiction in this complicated yet lovely retelling of Troy's fall.

Harman, Humphrey. *Tales Told near a Crocodile,* il. by George Ford. Viking 1962. $3.95; 9–12.

Folktales collected in the African country of Nyanza contain a variety of subjects, some animal, others human. Mr. Harman has a good storytelling technique and has retained much of the oral feeling.

Harris, Joel Chandler. *The Favorite Uncle Remus,* ed. by George Van Santvoord and Archibald C. Coolidge, il. by A. B. Frost. Houghton 1948. $4.50; 9–14.

A collection of 60 of Mr. Harris' delightful stories selected from seven volumes. The dialect of the original stories has not been lost.

Haviland, Virginia. *Favorite Fairy Tales Told in Czecho-slovakia,* il. by Trina Schart Hyman. Little 1966. $3.25; 8–11.

Once upon a time there was a collector who maintained the integrity and beauty of the past and added new visions and love for the future—Virginia Haviland. One should consider that all of her *Told in . . .* books have been far superior to other series: beautiful in illustration and format, and typical of the fairy lore of the lands represented. By the same author: *Favorite   Fairy   Tales   Told   in   Italy; . . . Scotland; . . . Sweden; . . . Spain; . . . Poland; . . . France.*

Heady, Eleanor B. *When the Stones Were Soft: East African Fireside Tales,* il. by Tom Feelings. Funk & Wagnalls 1968. $3.50; 9–12.

A collection of 16 popular stories from East Africa explaining the nature and behavior of men and animals. Black-and-white illustrations are the appropriate complement for these interesting tales.

Hieatt, Constance. *The Knight of the Lion,* il. by Joseph Low. Crowell 1968. $3.95; 9 up.

Joseph Low's graphics dominate the story and far surpass the verbal message. An English legend of the King Arthur period.

_____. *Sir Gawain and the Green Knight,* il. by Walter Lorraine. Crowell 1967. $3.50; 12 up.

Sir Gawain plays a deadly Christmas game with the enormous green-haired, green-armored Green Knight. A medievalist tells this 600-year-old best of the stories of King Arthur's knights as she has told it to her daughters. Grotesque and often comic pictures.

Hodges, Elizabeth Jamison. *Serendipity Tales,* il. by June Atkin Corwin. Atheneum 1966. $3.95; 9–12.

"Serendipity . . . the gift of finding valuable or agreeable things not sought for" is the theme of these seven mysterious tales woven with magic, fate, sorcery, and fantasy. These lovely stories, dating from the fifth century A.D., have their roots in Persia, India, and Ceylon. By the same author: *Three Princes of Serendip.*

Hodges, Margaret. *The Wave,* il. by Blair Lent. Houghton 1964. $3.50; 7–10.

Adapted from Lafcadio Hearn's *Gleanings in Buddha-Fields,* this Japanese folktale tells how Ojiisan saves his village from destruction by a tidal wave. The book is well written for reading aloud and is beautifully illustrated.

Hoge, Dorothy. *The Black Heart of Indri,* il. by Janina Domanska. Scribner 1966. $3.50; 5–9.

How the love of a virtuous maiden transforms an ugly toad into a fine young man.

Holding, James. *The Sky-Eater and Other South Sea Tales,* il. by Charles Keeping. Abelard 1965. $3.25; 5–9.

Fascinating tales of South Sea islanders' captivating folk explanations of why things are as they are. "Luno the Sky-Eater" tells why it is possible to give a proper surname to the man in the moon. "The Hermit with Two Heads" demonstrates that two heads aren't better than one, even if they do have black and red eyes.

Hosford, Dorothy. *Thunder of the Gods,* il. by Claire and George Louden. Holt 1952. $2.92; 9–12.

A retelling of 15 Norse myths. The style is simple and dignified, in keeping with the subject. The storyteller will find them an excellent introduction to Norse literature. By the same author: *By His Own Might.*

Houston, James. *Eagle Mask: A West Coast Indian Tale,* il. by the author. Harcourt 1966. $3.25; 7–11.

The story of the trials of endurance, the rituals, and the celebrations that Skemshan, a young prince of the Eagle clan of the Northwest Indians, faces in his coming of age. Houston's excellent style and knowledge of customs add to the quality.

_____. *Tiktá'Liktak,* il. by the author. Harcourt 1965. $3.25; 10–14.

One lives each of Tiktá 'Liktak's thrilling experiences with him as he survives a winter alone on an ice floe. The entire book—text, graphics, and layout—unfolds a compelling saga of human strength and adaptability.

_____. *The White Archer: An Eskimo Legend.* Harcourt 1967. $3.50; 8–12.

The story of Kungo is fast moving, and the setting is unusual. An excellent addition to collections of folktales and legends. By the same author: *Akavak: An Eskimo Journey.*

Htin Aung, Maung, and Helen G. Trager. *A Kingdom Lost for a Drop of Honey and Other Burmese Folktales,* il. by Paw Oo Thet. Parents 1968. $3.95; 9–12.

Text and pictures in this handsome book catch the authentic flavor of Burmese life.

Jablow, Alta and Carl. *The Man in the Moon: Sky Tales from Many Lands,* il. by Peggy Withers. Holt 1969. $3.97; 8–12.

Three sections recount folktales dealing with the moon, while the fourth is devoted to folktales dealing with the sun, thunder, lightning, and the stars. The stylized black-and-white illustrations add much to the handsome appearance.

Jacobs, Joseph. *The Book of Wonder Voyages,* il. by John Batten. Putnam 1967. $3.50; 8–12.

This classic book is rich in Norse, Nordic, Greek, and Arabian mythology. The imaginations of many children can be stimulated by reading these richly illustrated stories.

_____. *Hudden and Dudden and Donald O'Neary,* il. by Doris Burn. Coward 1968. $2.86; 5–9.

Amusing retelling of Celtic folktales. Wily Donald O'Neary outwits two greedy neighbors, Hudden and Dudden, so that he lives happily ever after with plenty of sheep and fat cattle. Black-and-white illustrations are witty and characteristically Irish. By the same illustrator: *English Folk and Fairy Tales; European Folk and Fairy Tales.*

Janeway, Elizabeth. *Ivanov Seven,* il. by Eros Keith. Harper 1968. $4.95; 10 up.

Even war needs a touch of humor, and this Russian folk character provides it.

Jewett, Eleanore Myers. *Which Was Witch? Tales of Ghosts and Magic from Korea,* il. by Taro Yashima. Viking 1953. $3.50; 9–12.

A lively, tellable collection for Halloween or any other time when children may care to hear of "The Man Who Feared Nothing," "The Snake Woman," or "The Statue That Sneezed." Droll and sympathetic black-and-white pictures, a helpful note on source material, and the collector's friendly attitude toward the "gentle, lovable" people of Korea all make this a good book.

Keats, Ezra Jack. *John Henry,* il. by the author. Pantheon 1965. $3.50; 5–9.

The unevenness of both the text and graphics of this important American legend about a strong man who wielded a mighty sledge hammer makes the book less than perfect. However, many of the illustrations are superb.

Kelsey, Alice Geer. *Once the Hodja,* il. by Frank Dobias. McKay 1943. $3.59; 9 up.

"For five centuries the people of Turkey and of all the Near East have been laughing" at the tales of the wise, foolish old man, the Hodja. With the help of the clear Kelsey words and the comic Dobias pictures, American children can now share the fun.

Kimishima, Hisako. *Ma Lien and the Magic Brush,* il. by Kei Wakana. Parents 1968. $3.50; 4–8.

An ancient Chinese folktale about Ma Lien, a poor peasant boy whose talent and desire to paint suffer from lack of a paint brush. One night a wizard comes to him and gives him a magic brush that makes everything he paints become real. The striking illustrations have a touch of oriental stylization while giving the illusion of perspective.

Kingsley, Charles. *The Heroes.* Macmillan 1909. $3.95 (P—Schocken, $1.95); 9–12.

A collection of myths about Perseus, Theseus, and Jason, which should inform children about these great stories.

Lang, Andrew, ed. *Arabian Nights.* Children 1968. $4.50; 10 up.

This unabridged, large-type edition will be helpful for partially-sighted children.

————. *The Red Fairy Book,* il. by J. J. Ford and Lancelot Speed. McKay 1948. $3.95 (P—Dover, $2.00); 9–12.

First published in 1890, this book includes a wide assortment of fairy tales from French, Scandinavian, German, and Rumanian folklore sources, including tales of the Brothers

Grimm and Madame d'Aulnoy. Accompanying the 37 stories are 100 line drawings. By the same editor: *The Blue Fairy Book* and many others.

Larson, Jean Russell. *The Silkspinners*, il. by Uri Shulevitz. Scribner 1968.　$3.95; 7–12.

Li Po's odyssey in search of the lost silkspinners of China, delightfully told and harmoniously illustrated.

Leach, Maria. *How the People Sang the Mountains Up*, il. by Glen Rounds. Viking 1967.　$3.75; 9–12.

Thanks to Maria Leach and Glen Rounds for this collection of how and why traditional tales. Her knowledgeable versions of the tales and his decorations make the book appealing.

_____. *Noodles, Nitwits, and Numskulls*, il. by Kurt Werth. World 1961.　$3.50; 7–12.

Here are tales, riddles, sayings, and foolish answers to delight the children, as well as documentation to intrigue the folklorist and prove that most modern jokes have ancient origins.

_____. *The Rainbow Book of American Folk Tales and Legends*, il. by Marc Simont. World 1958.　$5.95; 12–14.

This collection, which lives up to its title, serves as a good introduction to folk literature. Various sections contain remarks on the form of folktales developed. List of sources and bibliography.

Lifton, Betty Jean. *Kap and the Wicked Monkey*, il. by Eiichi Mitsui. Norton 1968.　$3.75; 8–12.

Kap, a Japanese folk character, is the basis for this lovely story. The book is full of tricks, good fun, and excellent illustrations done in a delicate wash technique.

McGovern, Ann. *Robin Hood of Sherwood Forest*, il. by Arnold Spilka. Crowell 1968.　$3.95 (P—Scholastic, $.60); 12 up.

The print is particularly good, the illustrations excellent. The language has the flavor but not the difficulty of English of the period.

McKenzie, Ellen Kindt. *Taash and the Jesters*, il. by Alan Cober. Holt 1968. $4.50; 10–14.

A tale of magic, witches, spells, and charms that may well be in the classic tradition, with something of the flavor of Tolkien.

Malcolmson, Anne. *The Song of Robin Hood*, music arranged by Grace Castagnetta, il. by Virginia Lee Burton. Houghton 1947.　$8.00; 9 up.

The hearty, jovial words, which contradict the TV stereotype of stealing from the rich and giving to the poor, and the designs, which are sturdy as oaks and delicate as wild strawberry leaves, make this book one of the great ones of our time.

———. *Yankee Doodle's Cousins,* il. by Robert McCloskey. Houghton 1941. $4.50; 9–12.

Comprehensive collection of 28 American tall tales about such heroes as Pecos Bill, Paul Bunyan, and Johnny Appleseed. Strong illustrations add to the hearty enjoyment of these tales.

Masey, Mary Lou. *Stories of the Steppes,* il. by Helen Basilevsky. McKay 1968. $3.95; 8–12.

Readers who enjoy folk motifs and comparing different versions should be attracted to this Russian collection.

Mehdevi, Anne Sinclair. *Persian Folk and Fairy Tales,* il. by Paul E. Kennedy. Knopf 1965. $3.50; 8–12.

Persian or American, these 11 colorful folktales will delight all. Some are reminiscent of the Arabian Nights; others are about animals. Drawings have an appropriate Near Eastern flavor.

Merrill, Jean. *High, Wide and Handsome,* il. by Ronni Solbert. Scott 1964. $3.50; 5–9.

Line drawings over sunset colors, rose and orange, illustrate this adaptation of a folk story from the Far East. The tales-within-a-tale technique is skillfully handled.

Minnton, Janyce L. *Legends of King Arthur,* il. by Bruno Frost. Hart 1965. $1.95; 9–13.

A fine edition of the King Arthur legends. The stories are written smoothly, and every character, even Sir Ector, retains the esteem which time and beliefs have bestowed on the Malory tales.

Nahmed, H. M. *The Peasant and the Donkey: Tales of the Near and Middle East,* il. by William Papas. Walck 1968. $5.00; 9–12.

Colored drawings accompany 34 Persian, Armenian, Turkish, Arabic, and Hebrew tales.

Ness, Evaline. *Mr. Miacca: An English Folk Tale,* il. by the author. Holt 1967. $3.75; 6–8.

An exciting story of Dickens' London and Tommy, who could not always be good. Beautiful colored pictures enhance every page.

Newman, Robert. *Grettir the Strong,* il. by John Gretzer. Crowell 1968. $3.95; 10–14.

An ancient saga of a strong warrior in a land of strong men, which tells of his combats with many antagonists (including a gigantic ghost), his strength in all sorts of competitions, his evil temper, his feuds, and his attempts to obtain justice for himself before the All-Thing, the democratic assembly of Iceland. This retelling of an old Norse tale gives a good background of the wild life of the Vikings with their feuds, superstitions, battles, and violence. Newman has created verses of his own in the retelling of the saga. The format is pleasing, with strong black-and-white drawings.

Nic Leodhas, Sorche. *Claymore and Kilt,* il. by Leo and Diane Dillon. Holt 1967. $3.95; 9–12.

Dramatic tales of Scottish heroes and kings from 211 to 1611 A.D. with beautiful black-and-white illustrations. These are fun for reading aloud or telling.

————. *Ghosts Go Haunting,* il. by Nonny Hogrogian. Holt 1965. $3.75; 9–12.

A person may not believe in ghosts until he reads this collection of haunting facts. Sorche Nic Leodhas, with information gathered from a Gaelic clan, presents ten stories, one for each finger. They'll provide one-to-one company when you're walking clockwise around graveyards and empty houses. By the same author: *Gaelic Ghosts; Kellyburn Braes; Sea Spell and Moor Magic, Tales of the Western Isles; Thistle and Thyme; Heather and Broom.*

Nyblom, Helena. *The Witch of the Woods: Fairy Tales from Sweden,* tr. by Holger Lundbergh, il. by N. Hald. Knopf 1968. $4.50; 8–11.

A first English translation of stories by a contemporary of Hans Christian Andersen.

Parker, K. Langloh. *Australian Legendary Tales,* il. by Elizabeth Durack. Viking 1966. $4.13; 12 up.

After reading a few of these legends, the reader will be haunted by the magic and superstition of the aborigines. This is a new edition, which keeps alive a masterful collection.

Perrault, Charles. *The Sleeping Beauty,* adap. and il. by Warren Chappell. Knopf 1961. $2.95; 5–9.

Fresh, imaginative illustrations and Tchaikovsky themes add to this version of the old tale.

Pollack, Merrill. *Phaethon,* il. by William Hofmann. Lippincott 1966. $3.50; 10–12.

A retelling of the Greek myth about the son of the sun god and a tree dryad who tried to drive his chariot to the sun, despite the warning of his friend Cygnus. One will always remember the thunderbolt aimed by Zeus to save the earth from the folly of Phaethon.

Pyle, Howard. *Story of King Arthur and His Knights,* il. by the author. Scribner 1903. $6.00 (P—Dover, $2.50); 12 up.

Popular legend of Arthur who gained his birthright as king of Britain by drawing his sword from an anvil. This edition is an American classic.

――――. *The Wonder Clock,* il. by the author. Harper 1887, 1915. $4.50 (P—Dover, $2.00); 8–12.

Pyle adapted tales from Grimm and other legends in his own lively and humorous way. By the same author-artist: *Merry Adventures of Robin Hood.*

Ransome, Arthur. *The Fool of the World and the Flying Ship,* il. by Uri Shulevitz. Farrar 1968. $4.95; 8–10.

This Russian folktale was first published in 1916 in a collection of retold tales by Ransome entitled *Old Peter's Russian Tales.* It follows the classic pattern of the foolish but friendly youngest son who sets out to accomplish a task at which his two older brothers have failed. It is a long story, with far more text than is usual in this sort of book. Illustrations are brightly colored and have an oriental quality. The Caldecott Award winner in 1969.

Reed, Gwendolyn. *The Talkative Beasts: Myths, Fables and Poems of India,* photos by Stella Snead. Lothrop 1969. $4.95; 8–12.

This appealing volume brings the young child closer to a concept of the family of man and the ancient culture of India. Poems and prose pieces are highly readable and carefully organized. Photos of temple wall bas-reliefs dazzle and intrigue the eye.

Reeves, James. *The Cold Flame,* il. by Charles Keeping. Meredith 1969. $3.95; 10 up.

A sad and bitter ex-soldier, sheltered by a witch, becomes the unexpected owner of an enchanted blue flame and consequently the master of the spirit it contains. Using his new-found power for questionable purposes, almost led by it to his own undoing, the soldier is ultimately saved by his own intrinsic integrity. Boys who might ordinarily turn away from fairy tales will respond to this masculine thriller.

_____. *The Secret Shoemakers and Other Stories,* il. by Edward Ardizzone. Abelard 1967. $3.25; 6–9.

A good collection of classic tales retold for oral reading. Most selections are of an European heritage but fit American needs very well. Mr. Reeves is a distinguished contemporary poet.

Ritchie, Alice. *The Treasure of Li-Po,* il. by T. Ritchie. Harcourt 1949. $2.95; 10 up.

The happy wisdom of these Chinese tales is developed in such ingenious plots and peopled with such appealing characters that no one can object to the inculcation of faithfulness or generosity or other values. The unobtrusive pictures quietly emphasize these tellable tales.

Robbins, Ruth. *Taliesin and King Arthur,* il. by the author. Parnassus 1970. $3.75; 7–11.

An exquisitely beautiful verbal and visual version of how Taliesin, a famous poet in Welsh legend, came to the city of Caerelon and sang for King Arthur and his Round Table.

Robertson, Dorothy Lewis. *Fairy Tales from Viet Nam,* il. by W. T. Mars. Dodd 1968. $3.50; 8–12.

The character, imagination, and troubled history of the Vietnamese are reflected in these stories.

Ross, Eulalie S. *The Blue Rose: A Collection of Stories for Girls,* il. by Enrico Arno. Harcourt 1966. $3.75; 9–12.

A storyteller's selection of 13 fairy tales chosen for their special appeal to girls.

_____. *The Lost Half-Hour,* il. by Enrico Arno. Harcourt 1963. $3.50; 7–10.

This volume contains a rich variety of stories, selected with taste and with a knowledge of the many needs such a collection can meet. Characters range from giants to simpletons, from delightful and wicked animals to princesses and witches. Appended is a brief but excellent discussion of storytelling.

Rudolph, Marguerita. *I Am Your Misfortune,* il. by Imero Gobbato. Seabury 1968. $3.50; 5–8.

A droll and dramatic Lithuanian folktale of Misfortune, who makes a generous poor brother rich and his stingy rich brother poor. In the Gobbato illustrations, Misfortune is an endearingly chubby monster who could not possibly terrify a child. Pictures and text have gusto.

Schiller, Barbara. *Audun and His Bear,* il. by Esta Nesbitt. Holt 1968. $3.50; 5–8.

Story, type, layout, and graphics are worth the reader's time.

_____. *The Vinlanders' Saga,* il. by William Bock. Holt 1966. $3.95; 9–12.

This vigorous version of an Icelandic saga is based on *The Vinland Sagas* translated by Magnus Magnusson and Herman Palsson.

Seeger, Elizabeth. *The Ramayana,* il. by Gordon Laite. Scott 1969. $6.95; 11 up.

This retelling of an Indian epic was undertaken with the hope of familiarizing Western children with key elements of Indian culture. The prose is fluid, moving the story forward swiftly and graciously. The rather formal language contributes dignity. Part god, part prince, Rama is exiled from his kingdom for 14 years by his treacherous stepmother. The story follows his adventures and those of his loyal followers during the years in the forest and through the last terrible years of search and war.

Sherlock, Sir Philip. *Anansi, the Spider Man,* il. by Marcia Brown. Crowell 1954. $3.95; 9 up.

In these authentic retellings, the folktales "all Jamaican children like to hear before they go to bed" turn out to be fine stories for American children, too. The swift-moving sketches catch all the fun of the wily spider. By the same author: *West Indian Folk Tales.*

Singer, Isaac Bashevis. *Elijah the Slave,* tr. by the author and Elizabeth Shub, il. by Antonio Frasconi. Farrar 1970. $4.95; 6–10.

In this Hebrew legend an act of charity attests to God's might. Elijah's good deeds are related in vivid and beautifully simple prose, and the magnificent woodcut prints are suggestive of medieval art.

_____. *Joseph and Koza; or The Sacrifice to the Vistula,* il. by Symeon Shimin. Farrar 1970. $4.95; 7–12.

Masterly illustrations and poetic prose are combined in this oversized picture book relating a moving story about Joseph, a wandering goldsmith and a Jew who has to prove God's might by rescuing Kozo, the Mazovian chieftan's daughter, from the threat of sacrifice.

_____. *Mazel and Schlimazel: Or, The Milk of a Lioness,* tr. by the author and Elizabeth Shub, il. by Margot Zemach. Farrar 1967. $4.50; 6–9.

The spirits of good and bad luck battle over a young boy in this Jewish fairy tale. The Eastern European flavor is evident in both text and illustrations.

———. *When Shlemiel Went to Warsaw.* Farrar 1968. $4.50; all ages.

This excellent collection of Jewish tales for children has much the same charming quality as *Fiddler on the Roof* and will be good for the storyteller.

———. *Zlateh the Goat and Other Stories,* il. by Maurice Sendak. Harper 1966. $4.50; 6–12.

Seven tales from European-Jewish folklore retold by a brilliant storyteller with drawings that reflect their humor and pathos.

Spicer, Dorothy Gladys. *Long Ago in Serbia,* il. by Linda Ominsky. Westminster 1968. $3.75; 8–12.

Varied, swiftly told tales about a Tsar's wise peasant wife, twins "beautiful as golden apples," a proud plowman counting his chicks before they were hatched, and a Cinderella with gold slippers. Simple, strong black-and-white pictures.

Stoutenburg, Adrien. *American Tall-Tale Animals,* il. by Glen Rounds. Viking 1968. $3.95; 7–10.

Ten tales that have been handed down through the generations about the feats of strange and wonderful animals, fish, snakes, and insects. This remarkably readable volume has lots of fun and folkloric fancy, pen-and-ink drawings, and much character.

———. *American Tall Tales,* il. by Richard Powers. Viking 1966. $3.50 (P—Viking, $.65); 8–12.

This book of eight tall-tale characters is a reflection of the truly imaginative American spirit and the tall tales Americans impulsively love to spin.

Sturton, Hugh. *Zomo the Rabbit,* il. by Peter Warner. Atheneum 1966. $3.95; 8–12.

This book authentically establishes the wit, humor, and insight of Americans whose ancestors came from Africa. Br'er Rabbit is Zomo's direct descendant.

Sutcliff, Rosemary. *The Hound of Ulster,* il. by Victor Ambrus. Dutton 1964. $4.50; 11–14.

This is a noble retelling of the great saga of Cuchulain, an Irish legendary hero. He is named "the guard hound of all Ulster" when he dashes out the life of a ferocious watchdog against a stone post. His succeeding experiences are equally exciting. By the same author: *The High Deeds of Finn MacCool.*

Tashjian, Virginia A. *Once There Was and Was Not: Armenian Tales Retold,* il. by Nonny Hogrogian. Little 1966. $3.50; 6–9.

An altogether satisfying book in which the stories, illustrations, and design are in full harmony. Based on stories by H. Toumanian.

Tooze, Ruth. *Three Tales of Monkey*, il. by Rosalie Petrash. Day 1967. $4.50; 5–10.

"Did you know it was monkeys who made our first musical instruments? Did you?" With the first line we hear the unforgettable voice of Mrs. Tooze, master storyteller, in this tale she brought from Cambodia. Ornately graceful green and poppy-red illustrations are exactly right.

Tresselt, Alvin and Nancy Cleaver. *The Legend of the Willow Plate*, il. by Joseph Low. Parents 1968. $3.50; 6–10.

A commoner runs away with the betrothed daughter of a nobleman. Instead of living happily ever after, they are hunted by the disappointed suitor; the husband is killed and the wife immolates herself. A goddess intervenes and turns husband and wife into doves. The illustrations catch and hold the essence of the story.

Uchida, Yoshiko. *The Magic Listening Cap*, il. by the author. Harcourt 1954. $3.25 (P—Harcourt, $.75); 9–12.

Ancient folktales from Japan retold with vivid freshness; universal themes with Japanese setting. Most of them will be new to American children. By the same author: *The Dancing Kettle; The Sea of Gold.*

Walker, Barbara. *The Dancing Palm Tree*, il. by Helen Siegl. Parents 1968. $3.95; 9 up.

Sensitive versions of Nigerian folktales.

———. *Once There Was and Twice There Wasn't*, il. by Gordon Kibbee. Follett 1968. $3.50; 8–10.

A delightful introduction to a bald-headed folk character, Keloglan, that everyone should know.

Weisner, William. *Grabbit the Rascal*, il. by the author. Viking 1969. $3.56; 7–9.

A collection of roguish tales based on stories written by Johann Peter Hebel about actual incidents occurring in the late 18th century in Rhineland. Grabbit takes on a couple of promising apprentices and among them they keep the countryside in an uproar. The author adds to the story by telling of the reform of the apprentices and the fate of Grabbit. His puckish two-dimensional drawings carry out the folk quality of the story.

White, Anne Terry. *The Golden Treasury of Myths and Legends*, il. by Alice and Martin Provensen. Golden 1959. $5.95; 9–12.

A wealth of tales from the great mythologies are fresh and dramatic in this collection.

————. *Odysseus Comes Home from the Sea,* il. by Arthur Shilstone. Crowell 1968. $3.95; 9–12.

This version of the Odysseus story is relatively simple but not simple-minded. Avoiding most of the flashbacks of Homer and cutting down the role of Odysseus' son, it tells a straight tale. The pictures have at times a classic calm, at times convey urgency and terror.

Williams, Jay. *The Sword of King Arthur,* il. by Louis Glanzman. Crowell 1968. $3.95; 10–14.

A retelling of the stories from *Le Morte d'Arthur.* Romance and valor intertwine in a tale true to the original.

Williams-Ellis, Amabel. *Round the World Fairy Tales,* il. by William Stobbs. Warne 1963. $4.95; 8–12.

A systematic collection of world literature that now belongs to children. The arrangement, important general background notes, and noteworthy inclusions make this collection an excellent book for home and library.

Withers, Carl. *Painting the Moon,* il. by Adrienne Adams. Dutton 1970. $4.90; 4–9.

A refreshing accounting of why the moon looks as it does today is presented in this version of a folktale from Estonia. The devil, unhappy because the bright moonlight prevents him from doing anything evil, decides to send a man up to the moon to paint it with pitch. Old Father, creator of the world, notices the evil-doer on the moon and as a warning to all who would rob the earth of light he imprisons the man on the moon forever with his pitch, bucket and brush. Illustrations are gouache paintings.

————. *A World of Nonsense: Strange and Humorous Tales from Many Lands,* il. by John E. Johnson. Holt 1968. $4.50; 9–12.

This book is essential to keep alive the absurd tales that may help develop many Gertrude Steins in the coming generations. Anthropologist Carl Withers has both feet and mind in the possible and impossible of generating nonsense with sense.

Yamaguchi, Tohr. *The Golden Crane,* il. by Marianne Yamaguchi. Holt 1962. $3.00; 9–12.

Toshi, a deaf and dumb child, and his stepfather find a wounded golden crane and nurse it to health. The crane attracts much attention; even the emperor wishes to have it. In order to prevent this happening, several cranes appear

and carry Toshi and his stepfather over the ocean horizon.
Beautiful and powerful illustrations. By the same author:
Two Crabs and the Moonlight.

Zemach, Harve. *Awake and Dreaming,* il. by Margot Zemach.
Farrar 1970. $4.95; 8–12.

A memorable fantasy which tells how the young hero
wanders each night into a nightmare world, into delightful
dreams and then, finally, into a never-ending dream which
takes him to the Land of Dreams where he lives happily with
a beautiful lady. Attractive line and wash drawings augment
this hauntingly obscure fantasy based on a Tuscan legend.

BIOGRAPHY

Abodaher, David J. *Warrior on Two Continents.* Messner 1968. $3.50; 11 up.

A stimulating and exciting book about the Polish patriot, General Thaddeus Kosciuszko, who came to America to fight for its freedom with George Washington and who came to know and love such other great Americans as Thomas Jefferson.

Adoff, Arnold. *Malcolm X,* il. by John Wilson. Crowell 1970. $3.75; 6–10.

A brief but effective biography relating how the late Malcolm X became a spokesman of black pride and black anger.

Alderman, Clifford Lindsey. *Retreat to Victory: The Life of Nathanael Greene.* Chilton 1967. $4.50; 12 up.

The stirring story of a general during the years of the Revolutionary War. Greene's retreat drew Cornwallis into a trap that led to his defeat at Yorktown.

Aliki. *The Story of William Penn.* Prentice 1964. $3.95; 5–9.
A picture book about the founder of Philadelphia.

————. *A Weed Is a Flower: The Life of George Washington Carver,* il. by the author. Prentice 1965. $4.50; 5–9.

Born a slave, Carver became a great scientist and advanced the welfare of mankind through his work. Good color illustrations.

Angell, Pauline K. *To the Top of the World: The Story of Peary and Henson,* photos and maps. Rand 1964. $4.95; 10 up.

196

In this unusually well-written story of Peary's discovery of
the North Pole, proper and overdue credit is given to his
remarkable Negro colleague, Henson. The feats of other real
and pseudo-explorers who had the same goal are also
described.

Apsler, Alfred. *Iron Chancellor: Otto Von Bismarck.* Messner
1968. $3.50; 12 up.

A well-written narrative of the life of the man who unified
Germany during the latter half of the 1800's. Interesting
writing style holds the reader to the end. By the same author:
*Fighting Journalist: Horace Greeley; Science Explorer: Roy
Chapman Andrews; World Citizen: Woodrow Wilson.*

Archer, Jules. *The Unpopular Ones.* Crowell-Collier 1968.
$3.95; 12 up.

An interesting and unique presentation of 15 Americans
who were unpopular because of their views and opinions.
Young people can observe that minority views change and
shape American life in important and far-reaching ways.

Arnold, Pauline. *The Young Explorers of the Northwest,* il. by
W. N. Wilson. Criterion 1968. $4.25; 12–14.

The adventures and achievements of five young men, beginning mostly in their teens, are recounted from material from
their journals. They help open the Northwest to exploration
and trade. Bibliography. Index.

Averill, Esther. *Cartier Sails the St. Lawrence,* il. by Feodor
Rojankovsky. Harper 1956. $3.95; 9 up.

The three voyages of Jacques Cartier are retold in a clean
and vivid text based on the explorer's records, including
quotations from them. Illustrations of superior artistic quality. By the same author: *King Philip the Indian Chief; Daniel
Boone.*

Baker, Nina Brown. *Henry Hudson,* il. by George Fulton.
Knopf 1958. $3.44; 10–13.

A convincing story of four years in Hudson's life. From 1607
to 1611, he made four voyages that were troubled by
navigation and human relationship problems. The intrigue
and mutiny that resulted in the explorer's disappearance are
well described.

Banning, Evelyn I. *Mary Lyon of Putnam's Hill.* Vanguard
1965. $3.95; 12 up.

This excellent book tells the success story of Mary Lyon,
founder of Mt. Holyoke College for girls. A poor girl, she
overcomes adversity to become a leading educator of her
day. Many boys as well as teenage girls will like this.

Bernard, Jacqueline. *Journey toward Freedom*, photos and engravings. Norton 1967. $5.50 (P—Dell, $.60); 11 up.

This lengthy, adult-type biography is the dramatic story of Sojourner Truth, born into slavery in New York about 1797 but later an outstanding leader of her people.

Born, Franz. *Jules Verne: The Man Who Invented the Future*, il. by Peter P. Plasencia. Prentice 1964. $3.75; 11–14.

The story of the man whose science fiction books of a century ago hve become facts in the 20th century, from submarines to moon rockets.

Braymer, Marjorie. *The Walls of Windy Troy: A Biography of Heinrich Schliemann*, photos. Harcourt 1960. $3.50 (P—Harcourt, $.60); 11 up.

This is a gripping, though controversial, true account of the amateur archeologist whose all-consuming passion, inspired by reading the *Iliad*, was to find ancient Troy and did so.

Buff, Mary and Conrad. *The Apple and the Arrow*. Houghton 1951. $3.57; 10–14.

The story of William Tell, told from the point of view of the son from whose head Tell shot the apple. Events begin before the revolt against Austria in 1292 and continue through the New Year's Eve bonfires that announced the revolution.

Carter, Bruce. *Nuvolari and the Alfa Romeo*, il. by Raymond Briggs. Coward 1968. $3.29; 8 up.

Nuvolari wins the German Grand Prix with his old-fashioned Italian car, the Alfa Romeo. Refreshing and well written, the story carries a little excitement of the race. By the same author: *Jimmy Murphy and the White Dusenberg*.

Cheney, Cora. *The Incredible Deborah: A Story Based on the Life of Deborah Sampson*. Scribner 1967. $3.95; 12–14.

A lively account of a Massachusetts woman who served two years in the Continental Army disguised as a man.

Coatsworth, Elizabeth, *Bess and the Sphinx*, il. by Bernice Loewenstein. Macmillan 1967. $4.50; 7–11.

Elizabeth Coatsworth's remembrance of her trip to Egypt as a little girl in 1898 is a book for reading aloud, particularly the poems that end many of the chapters.

Coblentz, Catherine Cate. *Martin and Abraham Lincoln*, il. by Trientja. Children 1967. $2.50; 7–9.

Originally published in 1947, this relates an episode in the life of Lincoln and a small boy whose father is a prisoner of war. Based on a true incident.

Coggins, Jack. *Boys in the Revolution,* il. by the author. Stackpole 1967. $4.50; 10 up.

The experiences of three boys in Revolutionary War days are based on their own written accounts. Maps, detailed drawings of ships, and pictures, together with a chronology of the war, add much to the clarity.

Coit, Margaret. *Andrew Jackson,* il. by Milton Johnson. Houghton 1965. $3.50; 11–14.

A beautifully written biography of a colorful and courageous President of the United States.

Commager, Henry Steele. *America's Robert E. Lee,* il. by Lynd Ward. Houghton 1951. $4.25; 10–14.

Emphasizing Lee both as a great general and as a family man, this book gives insight into Civil War times. The portraits and other illustrations are exceptionally good and would prove valuable to history and art students. By the same illustrator in this series: *America's Abraham Lincoln; America's Paul Revere; America's Mark Twain; America's Ethan Allen.*

Coolidge, Olivia. *Edith Wharton: 1862–1937.* Scribner 1964. $3.95 (P—Scribner, $2.75); 11–16.

This tasteful introduction to the American writer Edith Wharton relates her to the times and places in which she lived. By the same author: *Lives of Famous Romans; Men of Athens.*

Cooper, Lettice. *A Hand upon the Time: A Life of Charles Dickens,* prints and photos. Pantheon 1968. $3.95; 12 up.

The popular English novelist and his times, with brief discussions of his best-known works.

Dalgliesh, Alice. *The Columbus Story,* il. by Leo Politi. Scribner 1955. $3.25; 6–9.

A biography only 16 pages in length yet well written and beautifully illustrated in color. While good for reading aloud to second graders, third graders and up will enjoy reading it themselves.

D'Amelio, Dan. *Taller than Bandai Mountain,* il. by Fred Banbery. Viking 1968. $4.50; 12 up.

A fine biography of a Japanese doctor and bacteriologist. The writing is compelling, and the subject matter probably has appeal for many preadolescents.

Daugherty, James H. *Daniel Boone,* il. by the author. Viking 1939. $4.50; 11–15.

A vigorous life story of Daniel Boone. Newbery Award winner in 1940.

———. *Poor Richard,* il. by the author. Viking 1941. $5.95; 10 up.

In Daugherty's first picture, a row of round-faced young Franklins welcome the reader to their family table. From that scene in Ben's father's home to the later one where Ben is jouncing a grandson on his knee, Mr. Daugherty never lets the reader forget the humanity of Ben Franklin; yet the book resounds with joy in Franklin's achievements and with hope for the America Franklin helped to found. By the same author: *Abraham Lincoln; Marcus and Narcissa Whitman; Of Courage Undaunted; Henry David Thoreau: A Man for Our Time.*

d'Aulaire, Ingri and Edgar P. *Abraham Lincoln,* il. by the authors. Doubleday 1939. $3.95; 8–11.

Large, colorful lithographs as well as smaller pictures reinforce the humor and events in the life of Abraham Lincoln. Caldecott Award winner in 1943. By the same authors: *Benjamin Franklin; George Washington; Pocohantas.*

Davis, Russell, and Brent Ashabranner. *Chief Joseph: War Chief of the Nez Perce,* il. by the authors. McGraw 1962. $3.75; 11–14.

An excellent biography of the Indian leader who wanted peace but instead became the greatest fighting chief of the Nez Perce. His slogan was "Whenever white man treats Indians as they treat each other, then we shall have no more wars."

DeGering, Etta. *Christopher Jones: Captain of the Mayflower,* il. by William Ferguson. McKay 1965 $3.95; 11–14.

The stirring, poignant story of the kindly, shrewd man who piloted the *Mayflower* to America and who helped the Pilgrims survive their first dreadful winter at Plymouth.

——— *Gallaudet: Friend of the Deaf,* il. by Emil Weiss. McKay 1964. $3.75; 9–12.

The author's sympathy for and interest in Thomas Gallaudet, pioneer worker for the deaf, are evident in this readable and interesting story. The life and accomplishments of the boy and man are extensively documented.

de Kay, Ormonde, Jr. *The Adventures of Lewis and Clark,* il. by John Powers Severin. Random 1968. $1.95; 8–10.

Much human interest material is given in this simply

written story of the famous Lewis and Clark expedition to the Pacific.

De Treviño, Elizabeth Borton. *I, Juan de Pareja.* Farrar 1965. $3.25; 12 up.

This splendid book relates the story of the black slave, Juan de Pareja, with most of the action centered on his life as assistant to the famous Spanish painter, Diego Velázquez, who eventually became his dear friend. Newbery Award winner in 1966.

Donovan, Frank R., and the editors of *American Heritage* Magazine, illus. *The Many Worlds of Benjamin Franklin.* Harper 1963. $5.95; 9–15.

The illustrations, prints, paintings, and drawings of Franklin's period bring life to the well-written account of his achievements as a diplomat and statesman.

Doss, Helen. *King David,* il. by Norman Kohn. Abingdon 1967. $3.50; 9–12.

This account of major incidents in the life and rule of King David of Judah and Israel shows the strife between his sons and their followers to determine who would be his successor and David's strengths and weaknesses as a man, a father, and a ruler of men.

Douglass, Frederick. *Life and Times of Frederick Douglass,* ed. by Barbara Ritchie. Crowell 1966. $4.50; 12–16.

This skillful abridgment of the 1892 version of his autobiography calls attention to a great Negro who gave his life to the cause of freedom.

Duggan, Alfred. *The Falcon and the Dove: A Life of Thomas Becket of Canterbury.* Pantheon 1966. $4.19; 12 up.

The world of 12th-century Christendom revealed through the life and death of Thomas Becket, chancellor of England and archbishop of Canterbury. By the same author: *Growing Up with the Norman Conquest; Growing Up in the Thirteenth Century.*

Eckert, Allan W. *Blue Jacket.* Little 1969. $4.50; 11 up.

In 1771 a 17-year-old white boy was captured by the Shawnees and later became a famous war chief, Blue Jacket, known throughout the Northwest Territory. Details of Shawnee life and even much of the dialogue are based on historical records. Includes a map.

Fiedler, Jean. *Great American Heroes,* il. by Raymond Burns. Hart 1966. $1.95; 10–14.

Short but stirring biographies of great men in American history. Twenty-six authentic detailed sketches of famous leaders are presented in a style which generates immediate interest. Each chapter is enhanced by a drawing.

Fisher, Aileen, and Olive Rabe. *We Alcotts.* Atheneum 1968. $4.95; 11–15.

An account of the life of the Alcott family of Concord, Massachusetts. Based on journals and letters of the Alcotts and their friends and told from the point of view of Louisa's mother, it vividly depicts the life that served as the basis of much of the fiction of Louisa May Alcott. By the same author: *We Dickinsons.*

Fisk, Nicholas. *Richthofen the Red Baron,* il. by Raymond Briggs. Coward 1968. $3.29; 8 up.

A fast moving action story of Germany's World War I flying ace, the "Red Baron." Richthofen's air battles and victories are included.

Fleming, Thomas J. *First in Their Hearts: A Biography of George Washington,* photos. Norton 1968. $3.95; 10–14.

A well-balanced account of the many-faceted personality and life of George Washington. Direct quotations and reproductions add to the authenticity.

Forbes, Esther. *America's Paul Revere,* il. by Lynd Ward. Houghton 1946. $4.23; 10–14.

A vivid story of the silversmith and his times in the turbulent Boston of pre-Revolutionary days.

Forsee, Aylsea. *Louis Agassiz: Pied Piper of Science,* il. by Winifred Lubell. Viking 1958. $3.77; 10–14.

The determination and drive of a man committed to his work comes through in this biography. Young scientists will sense something of the qualities of a life devoted to science.

Foster, Genevieve. *George Washington,* il. by the author. Scribner 1949. $3.12; 9–11.

A warm biography of Washington from his childhood days to retirement at Mount Vernon. By the same author: *Abraham Lincoln; Andrew Jackson; Theodore Roosevelt.*

Franchere, Ruth. *Cesar Chavez,* il. by Earl Thollander. Crowell 1970. $3.75; 8–14.

The life story to date of Cesar Chavez, leader of the Mexican-American grape pickers' challenge to the grape growers of California. The author ascribes his success in improving labor conditions to three factors: his steadfast commitment to the cause, his dynamic leadership qualities, and the fact that he is one of the people he leads.

Galt, Tom. *Peter Zenger: Fighter for Freedom,* il. by Ralph Ray. Crowell 1951. $4.50; 10–14.

Life of the printer of early Philadelphia who fought for freedom of the press.

Gardner, Jeanne L. *Sky Pioneers,* il. by Douglas Gorsline. Harcourt 1963. $3.25; 5–8.

All children fascinated by feats of flying will like the story of Wilbur and Orville Wright whose experiments, started in childhood with kites, led to the invention of speedy bicycles, fast gliders, motors, and eventually airplanes.

Garnett, Emmeline. *Madame Prime Minister: The Story of Indira Ghandi.* Farrar 1967. $3.50; 12 up.

Biography of the impressive woman who has emerged as a leader of modern India.

Gerson, Noel B. *Passage to the West,* illus. Messner 1968. $3.95; 12 up.

Trying to find the passageway to the Orient, Henry Hudson made four voyages to the new world. His expeditions, discoveries, and eventual abandonment by his crew make an exciting story. Map and drawings.

Gimpel, Herbert J. *Napoleon: Man of Destiny.* Watts 1968. $3.95; 12 up.

A thorough and exciting chronology of Napoleon's rise to fame. The author, Commander Gimpel, has an insight that enhances the military theme of the story.

Gorham, Charles Arson. *The Lion of Judah: A Life of Haile Selassie, Emperor of Ethiopia.* Farrar 1966. $3.25; 12–16.

Not only a biography but an excellent picture of the development of Ethiopia as an independent African nation.

Green, Margaret. *Defender of the Constitution: Andrew Johnson.* Messner 1962. $3.50; 10–14.

An interesting presentation of the life of a neglected President. It contains a notable description of the impeachment proceedings and the restoration of constitutional checks and balances.

Gregor, Arthur S. *Charles Darwin,* illus. Dutton 1966. $4.95; 12 up.

This sympathetic and lucid portrayal of the great scientist is enhanced with photographs and drawings.

Gurko, Leo. *Tom Paine: Freedom's Apostle,* il. by Fritz Kredel Crowell 1957. $4.50; 12 up.

Too few young people in the United States know how much we owe to freedom's apostle, whose "words, not bullets" helped to turn the tide of the American Revolution and to show the world how absurd it was "for an island to govern a continent."

Gurko, Miriam. *Clarence Darrow.* Crowell 1965. $4.50;
11–14.

A fast moving portrait of a brilliant lawyer.

Haines, Charles. *William Shakespeare and His Plays.* Watts
1968. $3.95; 12 up.

An excellent biography, well written, with extensive documentation, and pleasant to read.

Hall, Anna Gertrude. *Nansen,* il. by Boris Artzybasheff. Viking
1940. $4.75; 12 up.

The peaceful strength of the pictures suggests the adventure,
power, and goodness in the life of the man whose ship was
named *Forward* and whose heart went forward into arctic
exploration, aid to war refugees, and the fight for peace.
Distinguished in text, illustrations, and theme.

Hall-Quest, Olga. *Guardians of Liberty: Sam Adams and John
Hancock.* Dutton 1963. $3.75; 10 up.

These two figues come alive and the momentous events in
which they were involved lose their usual awesomeness, but
not their importance, in this exceptional, nonstereotyped
recreation of the period leading up to the American Revolutionary War.

Hardwick, Richard. *Charles Richard Drew: Pioneer in Blood
Research.* Scribner 1967. $3.63; 11–14.

Drew, a Negro born in poverty, rose to international fame in
medicine and was an authority on blood preservation. His
life will be a challenge to Negro youth and interesting to
others. Glossary, bibliography, index. See also Robert Lichello's, *Pioneer in Blood Plasma: Dr. Charles Drew.*

Harrison, Deloris, ed. *We Shall Live in Peace: The Teachings
of Martin Luther King, Jr.,* il. by Ernest Crichlow. Hawthorn
1968. $3.95; 9 up.

Excerpts from the writings and speeches of Martin Luther
King, Jr., including the famous letter to fellow clergymen
from the Birmingham jail and the "I Have a Dream" address
at the Lincoln Memorial in Washington, D. C. Background
information ties together these significant public landmarks
in King's life. Black-and-white sketches have strong emotional impact.

Haviland, Virginia. *William Penn: Founder and Friend,* il. by
Peter Burchard. Abingdon 1952. $2.25; 9–12.

The great Quaker who founded Pennsylvania and Philadelphia is shown as an advocate of religious freedom and a
friend of the Indians.

Hirsch, S. Carl. *On Course!* il. by William Steinel. Viking 1967. $4.50; 10 up.

A history of those who followed the stars to find their ways in sea and space from Pytheas and Prince Henry to today's astronaut. The information is presented with imagination that will hold the attention of the general reader who is not an expert on navigation.

Holbrook, Stewart. *America's Ethan Allen,* il. by Lynd Ward. Houghton 1954. $4.50; 10 up.

Lynd Ward's pictures portray at least as much of the gallant exploits and fierce, independent spirit of Ethan Allen as Mr. Holbrook's vigorous prose about this Revolutionary War hero. They combine well.

Holst, Imogen. *Bach.* Crowell 1965. $4.50; 10–14.

One of the "Great Composers" series, this book will be of particular interest to the young musician, who will enjoy learning how Bach's great compositions were written and the examples of his musical scores. The story of the entire Bach family is sensitively written, recounting their loyalty to each other and their complete commitment to music. By the same author: *Benjamin Britten.*

Hoyt, Edwin P. *Heroes of the Skies,* il. by George J. Zaffo. Doubleday 1963. $2.95; 10–14.

This encyclopedic account of the many great men who have pioneered the air age, written in story form, is a factual reporting of experiments and exploits in the conquest of space from early balloons to jets.

Jablonski, Edward. *Ladybirds: Women in Aviation,* il. by Haris Petie. Hawthorn 1968. $4.95; 11 up.

Excellent accounts of women in aviation. The reading level and writing style are appropriate for adolescents.

Jackson, Robert B. *The Remarkable Ride of the Abernathy Boys,* photos. Walck 1967. $3.75; 8–11.

All youngsters will delight in the exciting adventure of six-year-old Temple and ten-year-old Bud Abernathy, who rode by themselves on horseback to New York City from Oklahoma in 1910. On their return the boys drove a car.

Jacobs, Herbert A. *Frank Lloyd Wright: America's Greatest Architect.* Harcourt 1965. $4.25; 11–14.

Wright's struggles to establish new architectural concepts, conduct his personal endeavors, and achieve financial success are described.

James, Bessie R. and Marquis. *Six Feet Six.* Bobbs 1931. $3.50; 11–16.

Now back in print, this biography pioneered a new trend—
one that reveals to young readers that though a hero may
have had a foot or two of clay, he is still worthy of high
regard. Sam Houston is a classic example of such a person.

Johnson, Gerald W. *Franklin D. Roosevelt: Portrait of a Great
Man,* il. by Leonard Everett Fisher. Morrow 1967. $4.50;
11–15.

This picture of Roosevelt shows the stages of his development and growth as a statesman. Changes in theories of
democratic government during his lifetime are brought out.

Judson, Clara Ingram. *Benjamin Franklin,* il. by Robert Frankenberg. Follett 1958. $3.95; 12 up.

A sensitively written biography of one of America's loving
and industrious citizens. By the same author: *Abraham
Lincoln: Friend of the People; Thomas Jefferson: Champion
of the People; George Washington; Andrew Jackson: Frontier
Statesman; Mr. Justice Holmes; Soldier Doctor; Andrew
Carnegie.*

Kelen, Betty. *Gautama Buddha: In Life and Legend.* Lothrop
1967. $3.95 (P—Avon, $.75); 12 up.

Buddha's life and thought set down for the young.

Kennedy, John F. *Profiles in Courage,* memorial ed., il. by Emil
Weiss. Harper 1964. $2.95 (P—Harper, $.75); 12 up.

Studies of American leaders who during crucial times defied
public opinion to do what they felt was right and best for
their country. Recommended for all library collections, this
edition has a new foreword.

Komroff, Manuel. *Charlemagne.* Messner 1964. $3.50; 12 up.

A chronicle of the achievement of the Frankish king who
became the first ruler of modern Europe. By the same author:
Marie Antoinette.

Kosterina, Nina. *The Diary of Nina Kosterina,* tr. by Mirra
Ginsburg. Crown 1968. $3.95; 12 up.

The actual diary of a 15-year-old Russian girl which begins
in 1936 and ends in November 1941 when she leaves to fight
the Germans. This is a moving account of an adolescent, her
feelings and experiences, and the awareness of personal
frontiers.

Kyle, Elizabeth. *Princess of Orange.* Holt 1966. $3.95; 12–14.

The romantic story of Mary Stuart and William of Orange
who became the rulers of England following the Glorious
Revolution. By the same author: *Girl with a Pen: Charlotte
Brontë; Great Ambitions: A Story of the Early Years of
Charles Dickens.*

Latham, Jean Lee. *Anchor's Aweigh: The Story of David Glasgow Farragut,* il. by Eros Keith. Harper 1968. $4.50; 10–14.

This well-written story of the complete life of Admiral Farragut reviews what little personal life he had outside the Navy but deals chiefly with his naval experiences after he became a midshipman at age ten. Major naval encounters during the War of 1812, the Mexican War, and the Civil War are vividly described.

————. *Carry On, Mr. Bowditch.* Houghton 1955. $3.50; 12 up.

Based on intensive research of mathematical and maritime material, this biography recounts the struggle of a boy apprentice who became a self-taught expert and later wrote a book on navigation that is still used at the U. S. Naval Academy. Human as well as scientific interest. Newbery Award winner in 1956. By the same author: *Medals for Morse; Retreat to Glory; Trail Blazer of the Seas; Young Man in a Hurry.*

Lawrence, Jacob. *Harriet and the Promised Land,* il. by the author. Simon 1968. $5.95; 6–10.

Strong colors and simple rhymes tell the story of Harriet Tubman, the slave who led many of her people North to freedom.

Lichello, Robert. *Pioneer in Blood Plasma: Dr. Charles Drew.* Messner 1968. $3.50; 12 up.

A moving human-interest biography of Charles Drew, a Negro who achieved not only recognition in school and college athletics but also fame in medical science before his accidental death at 46.

McGovern, Ann. *If You Grew Up with Abraham Lincoln,* il. by Brinton Turkle. Four Winds 1966. $2.95 (P—Scholastic, $.60); 6–9.

This fine book depicts what houses, schools, travel, clothes, and other aspects of living were like when Lincoln was a boy and man. Humor is evident in the illustrations. A picture-appendix shows important changes during Lincoln's lifetime.

————. *Runaway Slave: The Story of Harriet Tubman,* il. by R. M. Powers. Four Winds 1965. $2.95 (P—Scholastic, $.60); 6–9.

How an escaped slave led hundreds of others to freedom and attained the name "Moses" is told interestingly and simply.

McKown, Robin. *Thomas Paine.* Putnam 1962. $3.49; 11–14.

Born in England, Paine came to America at the age of 37 in

time to influence, by his thinking and writing, the cause of American independence. He believed in freedom for all mankind; he worked for voting rights for all men, abolition of slavery, emancipation of women, welfare aid, and abolishment of capital punishment.

McNeer, May. *America's Abraham Lincoln,* il. by Lynd Ward. Houghton 1957. $4.00; 10 up.

A splendidly illustrated and written book about Lincoln, done with the careful research and outstanding quality for which this team is famous.

——, and Lynd Ward. *Armed with Courage,* il. by Lynd Ward. Abingdon 1957. $2.50; 10–13.

Biographical sketches of seven great humanitarians: Gandhi, Schweitzer, Nightingale, Grenfell, Carver, Addams, and Father Damien. By the same author and artists: *John Wesley; Martin Luther.*

Meigs, Cornelia. *Invincible Louisa,* photos. Little 1933. (centennial edition, 1968), $4.95; 10–14.

A lively, realistic life of Louisa May Alcott, author of *Little Women,* and her interesting family. Newbery Award winner in 1934.

Meltzer, Milton. *Langston Hughes: A Biography.* Crowell 1968. $4.50; 12 up.

A sensitive portrayal of the Negro poet and playwright written by his longtime friend and collaborator.

Meyer, Edith Patterson. *That Remarkable Man: Justice Oliver Wendell Holmes.* Little 1967. $4.75; 10–14.

Excellent, well-written portrait of a truly remarkable American. The great liberal jurist is sympathetically portrayed.

Meyer, Howard. *Colonel of the Black Regiment: The Life of Thomas Wentworth Higginson.* Norton 1967. $5.50; 14 up.

A lengthy but well-written story of the abolitionist and champion of the rights of women and minority groups. Sidelights on the literary works of the period, including those of Emily Dickinson, are included. This timely work quietly points out the services of many Negroes to the well-being of America.

Miers, Earl Schenck. *Abraham Lincoln in Peace and War,* illus. Harper 1964. $5.95; 10 up.

Beautifully illustrated with paintings and photographs, this book "makes history fascinating." Included are a wealth of interesting anecdotes about the life and times of Lincoln.

Mirsky, Reba Paeff. *Johann Sebastian Bach,* il. by Steele Savage. Follett 1965. $3.95; 10 up.

This sympathetic account of the boy and man who was one of the greatest musical geniuses of all time should appeal to young people whether or not they have a musical background. By the same author: *Balboa: Discoverer of the Pacific; Haydn; Beethoven; Brahms; Mozart.*

Montgomery, Elizabeth Rider. *Hans Christian Andersen: Immortal Storyteller,* il. by Richard Lebenson. Garrard 1968. $2.59; 9–11.

This interesting biography is authentic and sympathetic and clearly reveals Andersen's early life from the cruel taunts of other people, his determination to win fame, the kindness of those who helped him, and his success and recognition even in his homeland. An index and list of famous tales are included.

———. *William C. Handy: Father of the Blues,* il. by David Hodges. Garrard 1968. $2.39; 10–13.

An interesting and authentic account of the great originator of Negro blues. The biography starts with Handy as a 12-year-old boy and continues through his life realistically depicting the biases, prejudices, and problems he encountered. By the same author: *Stories behind Modern Books.*

Mooney, Booth. *General Billy Mitchell,* photos. Follett 1968. $1.95; 10–14.

This fluently and simply written account covers Mitchell's Signal Corps experiences in Cuba, the Philippines, and Alaska and describes his World War I experiences as head of the American Air Force in Europe. His efforts to promote a strong military air service are described, as are the jealousy and opposition of the army and navy, leading to his eventual court-martial and resignation, and at last the vindication of his ideas after death.

Muller, Charles G. *Hero of Two Seas.* McKay 1968. $4.25; 12 up.

The life of an almost forgotten hero of the U. S. Navy, Thomas MacDonough. The writing style is smooth, interesting, and exciting.

Murray, Joan. *The News,* photos by Gwen Krause. McGraw 1968. $1.95; 11 up.

This autobiography of a successful TV newscaster (who, incidentally, is a young Negro woman) depicts the daily life of a woman in this field. She refers to interviews with many celebrities and the coverage of many high-level events, as well as her own flying and participation in the Powder Puff Derby.

Myers, Elisabeth P. *Angel of Appalachia: Martha Berry.* Messner 1968. $3.50; 11 up.

This account reads like fiction. It traces Martha Berry's life from the time when, as a child, she accompanied her father on horseback to help people in the Georgia highlands to the climax of her years when she saw Berry Academy and Berry College providing work and educational opportunities for her "children." Bibliography and index.

————. *Langston Hughes: A Poet of His People,* il. by Russell Hoover and photos. Garrard 1970. $2.79; 11–15.

A factual biography, but a feeling for the humanity of the man himself is missing.

Newman, Shirlee P. *Marian Anderson: Lady from Philadelphia,* photos. Westminster 1966. $3.75; 10–17.

A warm appreciation of the great Negro singer is projected.

North, Sterling. *Young Thomas Edison,* il. by William Barss. Houghton 1958. $2.95; 10–14.

The life of the man of a thousand inventions is recounted in a warm and humane manner. By the same author: *George Washington: Frontier Colonel; Abe Lincoln: Log Cabin to White House.*

O'Connor, Richard. *Sitting Bull,* il. by Eric Von Schmidt. McGraw 1968. $3.95; 11–14.

This sympathetic picture of the leader of the Sioux portrays his skill in battle strategy, his bravery and kindness, and his concern for his people's losing struggle with the white man.

————. *Young Bat Masterson,* il. by A. A. Watson. McGraw 1967. $3.95; 10–12.

The career of a famous lawman—from marshal of Dodge City to sheriff of Manhattan.

Petry, Ann. *Harriet Tubman: Conductor on the Underground Railroad.* Crowell 1955. $3.95 (P—Archway, $.75); 12–15.

The biography of a heroic woman who, having escaped from slavery, personally conducted three hundred other slaves to freedom.

Phelan, Mary Kay. *Midnight Alarm,* il. by Leonard Weisgard. Crowell 1968. $4.50; 11–13.

This thorough account of Paul Revere's life starts with his adult years. His own letters lend authenticity to the text.

Philipson, Morris. *The Count Who Wished He Were a Peasant: A Life of Leo Tolstoy.* Pantheon 1967. $3.95; 12 up.

A very readable account of Tolstoy's genius and the historical and social forces that shaped the Russia of his time.

Randall, Ruth Painter. *I, Jessie.* Little 1963. $3.95; 9–12.

Jessie's own writings furnish material for this sensitive biography of a girl with a fine education and comfortable life at home and in Washington society. Marriage to Lieutenant Fremont took her into pioneer life with exhausting but exciting travels.

Reeder, Colonel "Red." *Dwight David Eisenhower,* il. by Cary. Garrard 1968. $3.15; 10–13.

Much action, fast movement, and ease of reading will attract readers. Eisenhower's biography is short and not a study in depth but is a good introductory book. By the same author: *Medal of Honor Heroes; The Southern Generals.*

Rennert, Vincent Paul. *Western Outlaws.* Crowell-Collier 1968. $3.50; 12–16.

A collection of short biographical sketches of nine men who lived in the latter part of the 19th century. Good portrayal of the rough frontier life of outlaws, train robbers, and rustlers.

Rich, Josephine. *Women behind Men in Medicine.* Messner 1967. $3.50; 11 up.

Twelve little-known women who gave courage and support to leaders in medicine from the 12th to the 20th century are presented against the backgrounds of their worlds. Medical practices during the lifetime of each woman are clearly portrayed. Bibliography.

Richards, Kenneth G. *Harry S. Truman,* photos. Children 1968. $4.50; 13 up.

Thoroughly treats Truman as a man and political leader as well as other roles of his life. The detail of the text and the fine photographs make this a good reference book.

————. *Will Rogers,* photos and sketches. Children 1968. $4.50; 12–16.

This highly interesting biography of the famous cowboy and humorist is liberally sprinkled with examples of his philosophy and wit. Bibliography and index.

Richards, Norman. *Robert Frost,* photos and sketches. Children 1968. $4.50; 12–16.

A well-written account of Robert Frost's life, showing how his experiences produced the deep feelings he expressed in his poems. A few of Frost's poems and lines from others are given. Bibliography and index.

Rink, Paul. *Quest for Freedom: Bolivar and the South American Revolution,* maps and drawings by Barry Martin. Messner 1968. $3.95; 11 up.

Bolivar is portrayed as a self-centered boy who, with hardship and self-denial, develops into the "Great Liberator" of South America. Includes a capsule history of South America from the earliest Indians to the end of Spanish rule and plausible theories for the rise and fall of its unique civilizations.

Ripley, Elizabeth. *Velázquez.* Lippincott 1965. $3.75; 12–14.

A good appraisal of the artist and his times. By the same author: *Botticelli; Gainsborough; Goya; Leonardo da Vinci; Michelangelo; Picasso; Raphael; Rembrandt; Rubens; Titian; Vincent van Gogh.*

Ritchie, Barbara, ed. *The Mind and Heart of Frederick Douglass.* Crowell 1968. $4.50; 12–16.

Contains excerpts from the speeches of the great Negro, for example: "If any man demand of me why I speak, I plead as my apology that abler and more eloquent men have failed to speak."

Rockwell, Anne. *Filippo's Dome.* Atheneum 1967. $3.50; 10 up.

This beautifully written book tells how Filippo Brunelleschi dedicated his life to designing and constructing the dome of the church of St. Mary of the Flower in Florence, Italy, in the 15th century. Effective line drawings.

———. *Paintbrush and Peacepipe: The Story of George Catlin,* il. by the author. Atheneum 1971. $5.25; 8–12.

A factual biographical account of Catlin and his dedicated efforts to help the Indians from North America, South America, and Alaska. Included are numerous illustrations adaptated in sinopia pencil from portraits and sketches Catlin made while living and working among various Indian tribes.

Rollins, Charlemae Hill. *They Showed the Way: Forty American Negro Leaders.* Crowell 1964. $3.50; 9–12.

The brief biographical sketches represent a great variety of occupations and professions in which Negroes have made a great contribution to American life.

Ruskin, Ariane. *Spy for Liberty: The Adventurous Life of Beaumarchais,* illus. Pantheon 1965. $4.19; 10–13.

The daring life of a young apprentice watchmaker who, in addition to being an author, was a fiery advocate for justice and instigated French aid for the colonists during the American Revolution. Reproductions of drawings of famous people of the period add interest.

Sandburg, Carl. *Abe Lincoln Grows Up*, il. by James Daugherty. Harcourt 1940. $3.95; 11–15.

A classic account of Lincoln's boyhood taken from the first volume of *The Prairie Years* and made into a book especially for young people. By the same author: *Prairie Town Boy* (about Sandburg's own boyhood).

Schecter, Betty. *The Dreyfus Affair: A National Scandal.* Houghton 1965. $3.50; 12 up.

A full and objective account of the tragic, complex injustice done to a Jewish army officer and the brave men who fought to correct it in France during the early years of this century.

Schultz, Pearle Henriksen. *Sir Walter Scott: Wizard of the North,* photos. Vanguard 1967. $4.95; 12 up.

Appealingly written, using exciting dialogue to bring the English writer Sir Walter Scott alive.

Severn, Bill. *Mr. Chief Justice: Earl Warren.* McKay 1968. $3.95; 11 up.

Facts and information are blended well with the pleasant writing syle.

Shapiro, William E. *Lenin and Trotsky,* photos. Watts 1967. $2.95; 11 up.

On the 50th anniversary of the Russian Revolution of 1917, the CBS news staff recreated the roles played by Lenin and Trotsky and, thus, the story of their country. A lucid account.

Shapp, Martha and Charles. *Let's Find Out about Daniel Boone,* il. by Vic Donahue. Watts 1967. $2.95; 7–9.

Episodes focus on Daniel Boone's experiences with Indians in Kentucky. Profusely illustrated; large print. Compare James Daugherty's *Daniel Boone.*

Sheehan, Elizabeth Odell. *Good Pope John,* il. by Harry Barton. Farrar 1966. $2.25; 10–14.

An account of a man whose courage, boldness, and love spoke to all the world.

Sims, Bennett B. *Confucius.* Watts 1968. $3.95; 12 up.

In this well-written book, the author exercises great care in presenting true details of Confucius' life and philosophy.

Chinese civilization of the time is clarified. Some selected sayings from Confucius are included, as well as a bibliography.

Sobol, Donald J. *The Strongest Man in the World,* il. by Cliff Schule. Westminster 1967. $3.95; 12 up.

Biographical sketches (factual, fictional, and legendary) about nine people and their feats of strength—John L. Sullivan, Frank Goth, Eugene Sandow, Paul Bunyan, John Henry, and others.

Steele, William O. *Westward Adventure: The True Stories of Six Pioneers,* maps by Kathleen Voute. Harcourt 1962. $3.50; 9–14.

These six stories of early adventurers in the westward push over the Appalachians are well researched and fascinating, with out-of-the-ordinary detail.

Steffens, Lincoln. *Boy on Horseback,* il. by Sanford Tousey. Harcourt 1935. $3.95; 11–15.

Episodes from Steffens' lively childhood in California in the 1870's are taken from his autobiography.

Sterling, Dorothy. *Captain of the Planter.* Doubleday 1958. $3.50 (P—WSP, $.50); 8–12.

The story of Robert Smalls, a slave who bought his freedom, stole a ship from the Confederacy, delivered it to the U. S. Navy, and became a naval officer. Smalls was one of the last southern Negroes to serve in Congress. An exciting and inspiring book.

———. *Lucretia Mott: Gentle Warrior.* Doubleday 1964. $3.50; 11–13.

A swift moving account of one of the most colorful women of the 19th century, a mother of six children, a leader in the women's rights movement, and a preacher in the Society of Friends. This story suggests ideas and ideals for the young reader. By the same author: *Freedom Train: The Story of Harriet Tubman.*

Sterne, Emma Gelders. *Benito Juárez: Builder of a Nation.* Knopf 1967. $3.95; 11 up.

The beginning of the unification of the people of Mexico as a democratic nation is revealed in this life story of the Mexican Indian revolutionary and president. A well-written and interesting presentation.

———. *They Took Their Stand.* Crowell-Collier 1968. $4.50; 12–16.

A collection of sketches of well-known people who stood up

for equal rights. Well written. By the same author: *Mary McLeod Bethune.*

Syme, Ronald. *Bolivar the Liberator,* il. by William Stobbs. Morrow 1968. $3.95; 10–14.

A smoothly written account of the man, of military intrigue and campaigns, and of the development of five South American countries. Large print.

———. *Captain Cook: Pacific Explorer,* il. by William Stobbs. Morrow 1960. $3.36; 8–12.

A readable and realistic account of the English captain and his Pacific explorations.

———. *Captain John Paul Jones: America's Fighting Seaman,* il. by William Stobbs. Morrow 1968. $3.50; 8–12.

Presents a side of John Paul Jones' personality not often described. Along with negative traits, the book shows his great skill and daring as a naval seaman with the Americans during the Revolutionary War and later with the Russian navy.

———. *Nigerian Pioneer: The Story of Mary Slessor,* il. by Jacqueline Tomes. Morrow 1964. $2.95; 10–14.

The life and adventures of a Scottish woman in Africa.

———. *Sir Henry Morgan, Buccaneer,* il. by William Stobbs. Morrow 1965. $3.50; 9–12.

Morgan believed the road to fame and riches in the West Indies was buccaneering. He terrorized the Caribbean, gaining a fierce reputation for wealth and power. In the end he saved Britain's West Indian colonies from Spanish invasion and was knighted in London. Though none of Syme's biographies are written in deathless prose, they are all marked by competent research and sturdy, easy-to-follow style. By the same author: *Francisco Pizarro; Henry Hudson; Cortez of Mexico; Balboa; Cartier; Columbus; Magellan; Vasco da Gama; John Smith of Virginia; De Soto, Finder of the Mississippi.*

Tobias, Tobi. *Maria Tallchief,* il. by Michael Hampshire. Crowell 1970. $3.75; 8–11.

A simply written sketch of Maria Tallchief, an Osage Indian and one of America's finest contemporary ballerinas. Profusely illustrated with brown and orange sketches.

Turk, Midge. *Gordon Parks,* il. by Herbert Danska. Crowell 1971. $3.75; 6–10.

A brief but effective biography of the talented and famous

black novelist, poet, and photographer who heeded his dying mother's message: ". . . if a white boy can do something, so can you. Never give up trying to do your best."

Unstead, R. J. *Royal Adventurers,* il. by William Stobbs. Follett 1967. $2.95; 9–12.

The lives of eight kings and queens display their human characteristics but, generally, also their tragedy and sorrow. Each biography is followed by a page entitled "More About . . . ," which gives details of the historical setting. By the same author: *Some Kings and Queens.*

Veglahn, Nancy. *Peter Cartwright: Pioneer Circuit Rider.* Scribner 1968. $3.95; 12–16.

In the 19th century, Cartwright achieved fame as a lay minister, presiding elder of the Methodist Church, and antislavery legislator.

Vipont, Elfrida. *Weaver of Dreams: The Girlhood of Charlotte Brontë.* Walck 1966. $4.50; 12–14.

A sensitive recreation of the secret world of the young Brontës and especially of Charlotte.

Voight, Virginia Frances. *Mohegan Chief,* il. by Stan Campbell. Funk & Wagnalls 1965. $3.95; 10–16.

An especially interesting story of the life of the modern Mohegan chief, Harold Tantaquidgeon, descendant of Uncas. His knowledge of Indian lore and his part in two Pacific wars will fascinate readers.

———. *Sacajawea,* il. by Erica Merkling. Putnam 1967. $2.68; 8–10.

A basic account of the famous Shoshone princess who guided the Lewis and Clark expedition to the Pacific Ocean in 1805 is well presented. The author has taken care to tie together details in a way that will be satisfying to young readers. Large print.

Webb, Robert N. *Genghis Khan,* il. by Dyno Lowenstein. Watts 1967. $3.95; 12 up.

An exciting account of the unusual life and times of Genghis Khan, ruler of millions of people and perhaps the greatest conqueror in history. By the same author: *Hannibal: Invader from Carthage; Marco Polo: The Great Traveler.*

Wibberley, Leonard. *Man of Liberty.* Farrar 1968. $5.95; 12–16.

A most engaging biography of Thomas Jefferson, emphasizing his life as a family man and a political leader in Virginia and the nation. Much of the human relations and political history of America during his lifetime is encompassed in these pages.

Wilkie, Katherine E. *Teacher of the Blind: Samuel Gridley Howe.* Messner 1965. $3.50; 11 up.

The idealism of a young doctor who in 1824 left Boston to fight in the Greek war of independence, returned to America to practice as a physician, and founded and directed the Perkins Institute for the Blind for some 40 years. His great humanitarian service is described in this well-written but slow paced book.

Williams, Jay, and Charles W. Lightbody. *Joan of Arc,* illus. Harper 1963. $5.95; 10–15.

This carefully detailed chronicle with its rich complement of paintings, illuminations, drawings, and maps should interest more mature elementary readers. The questions raised about the political and religious motives behind Joan's trial and condemnation, and the even more difficult questions about the nature of her inspiration, will naturally concern them less than the drama of the well-written story.

Williams, John A. *The Most Native of Sons.* Doubleday 1970. $3.95; 12 up.

This biography of Richard Wright, author of *Native Son,* tells of his almost unbearably difficult childhood in the Delta country, his move to the false promise of freedom in Chicago, his position of prominence in the American Communist Party and eventual resignation, his fame as a man of letters, and his eventual self-exile to France and death. Readers will gain some understanding of the forces that influence writers.

Winston, Richard, and Harry Bober. *Charlemagne,* illus. Harper 1968. $5.95 (P—Random, $1.95); 12 up.

This biography of the 19th century Frankish emperor, setting forth his many accomplishments, has sentence structure and pictures appropriate for upper elementary and junior high school pupils. Explanations will aid children in interpreting facets of the age in Europe. Splendid illustrations and index.

Wise, Winifred E. *Fray Junípero Serra and the California Conquest.* Scribner 1967. $3.95; 12 up.

To forestall foreign powers wishing to settle the western coast (now California), Spain set Franciscan fathers from Mexico to colonize and convert. The leader was Junípero Serra, founder of the California missions. This carefully researched biography draws from his and his contemporaries' writings, giving many views of life in the 18th century. Compare, for younger children, Leo Politi's, *Song of the Swallows.*

Wojciechowska, Maia. *Odyssey of Courage: The Story of Alvar Nuñez Cabeza De Vaca,* il.by Alvin Smith. Atheneum 1965. $3.75; 10–14.

The life of the Spanish conquistador who, unlike the other Spanish explorers in America during the 16th century, sought to make peace with the Indians rather than to enslave them. His epic overland journey from Florida to Mexico is recounted.

Wood, James Playsted. *The Man Who Hated Sherlock Holmes: A Life of Sir Arthur Conan Doyle.* Pantheon 1965. $3.95; 12–14.

The great energies and varied activities of the English writer who created Sherlock Holmes are presented in relation to the stories the made him famous. By the same author: *Lantern Bearer: A Life of Robert Louis Stevenson; The Snark Was a Boojum: A Life of Lewis Carroll; Sunnyside: A Life of Washington Irving.*

————, and editors of *Country Beautiful* Magazine. *The Life and Words of John F. Kennedy,* photos. Doubleday 1964. $3.95 (P—Scholastic, $.95); 9–12.

A moving portrait of President Kennedy tracing his life from childhood with many photographs and a connecting narrative.

Yates, Elizabeth. *Amos Fortune: Free Man.* Dutton 1950. $3.95; 9–12.

Amos Fortune was captured by slave traders and shipped to Massachusetts. Eventually he learned a trade and bought his freedom. Written with understanding and compassion.

POETRY

Individual Collections

Aiken, Conrad. *Cats and Bats and Things with Wings,* il. by Milton Glaser. Atheneum 1965. $4.50; 6–10.

Sixteen poems and illustrations, all in a modern vein, that explore in a humorous way the natures of animals.

Aldis, Dorothy. *All Together: A Child's Treasury of Verse,* il. by Helen Jameson, Marjorie Flack, and Margaret Freeman. Putnam 1952. $4.50; 4–7.

A collection of 144 simple, rhythmic verses that appeal to young children.

Armour, Richard. *Our Presidents,* il. by Leonard Everett Fisher. Norton 1964. $3.50; 9–13.

Lighthearted verses on each of the presidents, from Washington through Johnson.

Behn, Harry. *The Wizard in the Well,* il. by the author. Harcourt 1956. $3.25; 6 up.

Harry Behn catches the poetic magic of the themes of children's everyday living in verses that are lyric and fresh. Charming sketches reflect the joy and delight of everyday events. By the same author: *A Little Hill; All Kinds of Time; Windy Morning; House beyond the Meadow; Chrysalis: Concerning Children and Poetry.*

Benét, Rosemary and Stephen. *A Book of Americans,* il. by Charles Child. Holt 1933. $3.95; 7 up.

A book of verse about national figures from Christopher Columbus through Woodrow Wilson. Witty and penetrating commentaries cast a new light on historical facts.

Bishop, Elizabeth. *Ballad of the Burglar of Babylon,* il. by Ann Grifalconi. Farrar 1968. $3.95; 10 up.

An exciting account of a fugitive in Rio de Janeiro who runs to the hill of Babylon to await his fate. The story gives an accurate view of a South American village and its occupants.

Blake, William. *A Grain of Sand,* ed. by Rosemary Manning. Watts 1967. $2.95; 10 up.

A well-selected collection of Blake's poems appropriate for children in the upper elementary grades. The selection contains many poems not previously widely anthologized. By the same author: *Songs of Innocence* in two editions, illustrated by Ellen Raskin and Harold Jones.

Brooks, Gwendolyn. *Bronzeville Boys and Girls,* il. by Ronni Solbert. Harper 1956. $3.95; 7–11.

In this small, beautifully illustrated book the author has chosen a broad scope of subjects. While the children are black and the place is Chicago, the place might be anywhere and the children, any children.

Brown, Margaret Wise. *Nibble Nibble.* Scott 1944. $4.50; 4–6.

A collection about bugs, green stems, rabbits, leaves, and many other things in nature. The illustrations are superb—watercolors in shaded greens.

Burgunder, Rose. *From Summer to Summer.* Viking 1965. $3.50; 8–11.

Sensitive poems that express the moods and reflections of a child as a year passes from summer to summer.

Burns, Robert. *Hand in Hand We'll Go,* il. by Nonny Hogrogian. Crowell 1965. $3.75; 9 up.

An attractive book with woodcuts in color that complement the poems.

Caudill, Rebecca. *Come Along!* il. by Ellen Raskin. Holt 1969. $3.59; all ages.

These brief poems speak with polished but simple elegance and contain insights that are fresh and delightfully surprising. The illustrations, done in acrylic paint on colored rice paper, not exactly to scale, achieve moments of nature that complement the word images.

Chute, Marchette. *Around and About,* il. by the author. Dutton 1957. $3.95; 4–8.

Sixty rhymes that previously appeared in three separate volumes. Her silhouettes are drawn and verses written with a true understanding of a child's viewpoint. By the same author: *Innocent Wayfaring; Wonderful Winter.*

Ciardi, John. *The Reason for the Pelican,* il. by Madeleine Gekiere. Lippincott 1959. $3.50; 6–10.

The bizarre, ridiculous, funny, and gay nicely capture a child's point of view in 23 poems. By the same author: *I Met a Man; John J. Plenty and Fiddler Dan; Man Who Sang the Sillies; You Read to Me, I'll Read to You.*

Clifton, Lucile. *Some of the Days of Everett Anderson,* il. by Evaline Ness. Holt 1970. $3.59; 3–7.

Nine poems that reflect nearly all the moods of a sensitive six-year-old. Everett Anderson is black and many of the poems say so in a totally unselfconscious manner.

Coatsworth, Elizabeth. *The Peaceable Kingdom,* il. by Fritz Eichenberg. Pantheon 1958. $3.54; all ages.

In the peaceable kingdom, the child can walk unafraid in beauty and contentment. Gone temporarily are the complexities of modern living, while the child communes with trees, flowers, and beasts in a peaceful forest. The three narrative poems provide a little island of safety and security that may well be a buffer against the great changes and confusions of today's world.

———. *Sparrow Bush,* il. by Stefan Martin. Norton 1966. $3.95; 9–11.

Verses about the world of nature by one of the best-loved children's poets. By the same author: *Down Half the World.*

Cole, William. *What's Good for a Five Year Old?* il. by Edward Sorel. Holt 1969. $3.50; 5.

In slap-dash rhyme, the author expresses what children want their teachers to do and what they don't like them to do.

Dalrymple, Mendoza G. *The Hunter I Might Have Been,* il. by the author. Astor-Honor 1967. $3.50; 12 up.

A poem in graphics and text. After reading, one can't describe the feeling, one just wants others to read it.

de la Mare, Walter. *Bells and Grass,* il. by Dorothy P. Lathrop. Viking 1964. $4.00; 10 up.

These poems exemplify the magic that is uniquely Walter de la Mare's, the gift of seeing again with the heart and senses of childhood. By the same author: *Peacock Pie.*

de Regniers, Beatrice Schenk. *Something Special,* il. by Irene Haas. Harcourt 1958. $2.95; 4–8.

Youngsters will find both the verses and the drawings indeed "something special" because they capture the wonder, the little pleasures, the fun, and the dreams of childhood. The chanting game, "What Did You Put in Your Pocket?" and "What's the Funniest Thing?" will spark young imaginations.

Farjeon, Eleanor. *Eleanor Farjeon's Poems for Children,* il. by Lucinda Wakefield. Lippincott 1951. $3.75; 5–12.

Here are the poems collected from Miss Farjeon's earlier books. Whimsy, everyday happenings, and nature poems sing happily through these pages and provide excellent material for choral speaking.

Field, Rachel. *Poems,* il. by the author. Macmillan 1957. $3.50; 8 up.

A collection of the beloved poet's poems. Her heartwarming interest in children, the sea, flowers, animals, and growing things reveals itself in her delightful reminiscences and friendly sincerity. By the same author: *Calico Bush; Prayer for a Child.*

Fisher, Aileen. *Cricket in a Thicket,* il. by Feodor Rojankovsky. Scribner 1963. $2.95; 4–8.

These nature poems invite young readers to take pleasure in exploring woods and fields. Realistic drawings enliven every page.

_____. *I Wonder How, I Wonder Why,* il. by Carol Barker. Abelard 1962. $2.75; 5–8.

To answer the questions that a child will ask, the poet brings to her verse sensitivity and gaiety, lyricism and a spirit of whimsy.

_____. *We Went Looking,* il. by Marie Angel. Crowell 1968. $3.95; 4–8.

"We went looking for a badger" but found many other animals. The verse and illustrations fit well together. By the same author: *Going Barefoot; Listen, Rabbit!*

Fraser, Kathleen. *Stilts, Somersaults, and Headstands,* il. by Peter Breughel. Atheneum 1968. $3.75; 7–12.

Thirty-seven poems about various children's games, from tug-of-war to piggyback, are accompanied by Breughel's painting "Children's Games."

Frost, Frances. *The Little Whistler,* il. by Roger Duvoisin. McGraw 1966. $3.25; 6–10.

Original verse about nature and the four seasons, sometimes sensitive, sometimes frivolous.

Frost, Robert. *You Come Too: Favorite Poems for Young Readers,* il. by Thomas Nason. Holt 1959. $3.50; 10 up.

Wood engravings and an introduction by Louis Untermeyer make this collection for children especially attractive.

Fyleman, Rose. *Fairies and Chimneys.* Doubleday 1920. $3.25; 7–10.

These gay, lyrical verses about fairies and their ways are a timeless contribution to children's literature.

Hoban, Russell. *The Pedaling Man and Other Poems,* il. by Lillian Hoban. Norton 1968. $3.50; 8 up.

Quiet observations of people and places, animals and objects.

Hopkins, Lee Bennett. *This Street's for Me!* il. by Ann Grifalconi. Crown 1970. $3.35; 4–9.

A collection of poems with inner-city settings, all expressing the hurly-burly movement of the city where there is little quiet or solitude.

Hubbell, Patricia. *The Apple Vendor's Fair,* il. by Julie Maas. Atheneum 1963. $2.75; 5–8.

These poems express a special sensitivity to the commonplace and are spun of dreams and of imagination as well. By the same author: *Catch Me a Wind; Eight* A.M. Shadows.

Hughes, Langston. *The Dream Keeper and Other Poems.* Knopf 1945. $3.24; 12 up.

Many of the poems in this volume will become treasured possessions. The Negro author shows the validity of the blues, as definite a poetic form as haiku.

Jacobs, Leland B. *Alphabet of Girls,* il. by John E. Johnson. Holt 1969. $3.95 (P—Holt, $1.45); 5–9.

Little girls' names, prettily set in clever verse. Jacobs handles poetry well.

———. *Is Somewhere Always Far Away?* il. by John E. Johnson. Holt 1967. $3.95; 4–8.

Lyric verses about city, country, make-believe, and home. By the same author: *Just around the Corner.*

Jordan, June. *Who Look at Me,* il. with paintings. Crowell 1969. $5.95; 10 up.

A collection of poems about the black experience illustrated by reproductions of paintings of Negroes by Americans past and present.

Kredenser, Gail. *The ABC of Bumptious Beasts,* il. by Stanley Mack. Quist 1966. $3.75; all ages.

The wackiest menagerie ever—from an absolutely absurd

aardvark to the zaniest zebras you've never seen! A perfect combination of imaginative poems and two-color illustrations.

Kumin, Maxine W. *No One Writes a Letter to the Snail,* il. by Bean Allen. Putnam 1962. $3.29; 6–10.

A successful adults poet turns her able pen to verse for children.

Langstaff, John. *Ol' Dan Tucker,* il. by Joe Krush. Harcourt 1963. $3.25; 10–14.

Several verses, richly illustrated, of the old song that has served for singing games and square dances for 120 years are provided along with the music. Written by Dan Emmet, a minstrel showman, it has become part of American folklore.

Lear, Edward. *The Complete Nonsense Book,* il. by the author. Dodd 1912, 1958. $5.00 (P—Dover, $2.00); 5–9.

A humorous landmark contribution to literature. The limericks, verses, and line drawings are as fresh and amusing now as when they were first published in the mid-19th century.

————. *The Jumblies,* il. by Edward Gorey. Scott 1968. $2.95; 4 up.

This poem, the first from *The Book of Nonsense,* is well illustrated in black and white. Each Jumbly has distinctly humorous characteristics.

————. *The Pelican Chorus,* il. by Harold Berson. Parents 1967. $3.50; 5–9.

Amusing drawings in color match the nonsense of Lear's poems in this picture book. Music included.

————, and Ogden Nash. *The Scroobius Pip,* il. by Nancy Ekholm Burkert. Harper 1968. $3.95; 8–12.

A handsomely designed and illustrated edition of Lear's melodious and intriguing poem in which all the animals in the world gather around a strange and mysterious creature who calls himself the Scroobius Pip and try to determine whether he is bird, beast, insect, or fish.

Livingston, Myra Cohn. *A Crazy Flight,* il. by James J. Spanfeller. Harcourt 1969. $3.50; 9–12.

Forty-two poems covering a wide range of subjects reflecting childhood experiences and forms of speech.

————. *Whispers and Other Poems,* il. by Jacqueline Chwast. Harcourt 1958. $2.75; 4–9.

One of the few books of poetry since Milne's *When We Were Very Young* that has the same appealing qualities, with all the freshness of the thoughts and expressions of the very young. This is a book adults and children will enjoy together. The illustrations are a fine supplement to the poems. By the same author: *Wide Awake and Other Poems; Old Mrs. Twindly Tart and Other Rhymes.*

McCord, David. *All Day Long: Fifty Rhymes of the Never Was and Always Is,* il. by H. B. Kane. Little 1966. $3.50; 12–14.

Poetry as contemporary as tomorrow and more fun. These witty selections cover nature and childhood experiences and are well matched with appropriate illustrations.

———. *Every Time I Climb a Tree,* il. by Marc Simont. Little 1967. $3.95; 5–9.

Amusing verses by a modern poet. A very attractive format and illustrations enhance this excellent poetry for younger children.

———. *Take Sky,* il. by Henry B. Kane. Little 1961. $3.75; 7 up.

Good humor and a fine sense of words and rhythm pervade these poems. By the same author: *Far and Few.*

Merriam, Eve. *Independent Voices,* il. by Arvis Stewart. Atheneum 1968. $4.25; 10 up.

These portraits in verse present seven men and women and are intended for reading aloud. They are true and interesting glimpses into our history.

———. *It Doesn't Always Have to Rhyme,* il. by Malcolm Spooner. Atheneum 1964. $3.25; 10 up.

Poems in a modern vein, with precise imagery and a playfulness of ideas and patterning.

———. *There Is No Rhyme for Silver,* il. by Joseph Schindelman. Atheneum 1962. $3.25; 7–12.

This author's first book of poetry for children will amuse and delight them and open doors to other poetry.

Milne, A. A. *The World of Christopher Robin,* il. by E. H. Shepard. Dutton 1958. $5.95; 6 up.

These are all the old verses of *When We Were Very Young* and *Now We Are Six* in a beautiful new volume, including all the original drawings of Shepard as well as nine new ones in full color.

Minarik, Else Holmelund. *The Winds that Come from Far Away and Other Poems.* Harper 1964. $2.50; 5–9.

The subject matter of these poems will appeal to many of the younger set.

Moore, Lilian. *I Feel the Same Way*, il. by Robert Quackenbush. Atheneum 1968. $3.25; 3–8.

The feelings and rhythms of childhood are expressed by the
verses in this little book. Each poem is illustrated by its own
picture in delicate pastels.

_____. *I Thought I Heard the City*, il. by Mary Jane Dunton.
Atheneum 1969. $3.75; all ages.

These 17 poems reflect city images not often written
about—television aerials, forsythia bushes, reflections in a
store window. The collage designs both capture and complement the work.

Morgenstern, Christian. *The Three Sparrows and Other Nursery Poems*, tr. by Max Knichg, il. by Nonny Hogrogian.
Scribner 1968. $3.50; 3–8.

Translations from a popular German poet with sensitive
illustrations.

O'Neil, Mary. *Fingers Are Always Bringing Me News*, il. by
Don Bolognese. Doubleday 1969. $3.50; 8 up.

All 14 poems concern fingers. At least one of them should
find a place in nearly every reader's mind and heart. The
collection as a whole seems intended for an older audience
than the author's previous books of verse.

_____. *Hailstones and Halibut Bones*, il. by Leonard Weis-
gard. Doubleday 1961. $3.50; 5–8.

With a compelling sense of rhythm and images that are clear
and fresh, the poet explores the spectrum of colors in 12
poems, from the "show-off shout of red" to the "blueness of
wind over water." By the same author: *People I'd Like to
Keep; Words, Words, Words.*

Richards, Laura. *Tirra Lirra*, il. by Marguerite Davis. Little
1955. $3.75; 5–12.

Brought back into print for the second time by the demand of
teachers and children, these nonsense ditties seem as fresh
and entertaining as ever.

Rieu, E. V. *The Flattered Flying Fish and Other Poems*, il. by E.
H. Shepard. Dutton 1962. $3.50; 9–12.

An amusing collection of poems and nonsense verse by a
distinguished poet and classicist. The poems run the gamut
from humor to pathos.

Roberts, Elizabeth Madox. *Under the Tree*, il. by F. D. Bedford.
Viking 1922. $3.00; 6 up.

This handful of poems that has brought pleasure to the
children and grownups of two generations is back in print
for the delight of a third.

Rossetti, Christina. *Goblin Market,* il. by Ellen Raskin. Dutton 1970. $4.95; 12–16.

Unobtrusively abridged, Christina Rossetti's eerie tale of two sisters and their dire peril from the goblin fruit merchants takes on rich life in Ellen Raskin's exuberant pictures.

Sandburg, Carl. *Early Moon,* il. by James Daugherty. Harcourt 1930. $3.95; 12 up.

A refreshing treatment of familiar people and things in free verse.

————. *Wind Song,* il. by William A. Smith. Harcourt 1960. $3.50 (P—Harcourt, $.45); 10 up.

The poet himself chose these verses, which he thinks are particularly suited to children. Here are humor, the delight in words and sounds, and the imagination that make his poetry outstanding.

Saxe, John Godfrey. *The Blind Men and the Elephant,* il. by Paul Galdone. McGraw 1963. $3.25; 5–8.

Exciting pictures and bright colors bring this old tale to life.

Smith, William J. *Boy Blue's Book of Beasts,* il. by Juliet Kepes. Little 1957. $2.95; 5 up.

Side-splitting nonsense about monkeys, pigs, and unicorns. By the same author: *Laughing Time.*

Snyder, Zilpha Keatley. *Today Is Saturday,* photos by John Arms. Atheneum 1969. $3.62; 8–12.

Twenty-four bright poems explore everyday experiences of suburban children, adding fresh dimensions and reinforcing their fleeting intuitions. Most poems have a narrative quality that will attract children. Some hint at loneliness, unjustified hurt, and the wonder of the universe, but the overall tone is joyous. Black-and-white photographs on almost every page quite specifically express the children of each verse.

Starbird, Kaye. *Don't Ever Cross a Crocodile,* il. by Kit Dalton. Lippincott 1963. $3.95; 5 up.

As in her earlier *Speaking of Cows,* the author manifests humor and understanding of a child's point of view, together with imagination and an ear for rhyme and rhythm. By the same poet: *Snail's a Failure Socially.*

Stevenson, Robert Louis. *A Child's Garden of Verses,* il. by Jessie Wilcox Smith. Scribner 1905. $5.00 (many paperback editions); 5–9.

A classic collection of poems that deal with childhood adventures. Other notable editions illustrated by Brian Wildsmith, Eve Garnett, and Toni Frisell.

Tagore, Rabindranath. *Moon, for What Do You Wait?* ed. by Richard Lewis, il. by Ashley Bryan. Atheneum 1967. $3.50; 5–10.

A fine collection of the Indian poet's works, sensitively illustrated with woodcuts.

Tooze, Ruth. *America,* il. by Valenti Angelo. Viking 1956. $2.00; 5–10.

In this delicately illustrated book, the author sings in beautiful poetic prose of a dream—the dream is America, past, present, and future.

Walsh, John. *The Truants,* il. by Edward Ardizzone. Rand 1968. $2.95; 10 up.

Nineteen poems, all but three short, express varying moods from happiness to sadness, and childhood experiences, such as school days and seashore adventures. The drawings complement the actions and emotions of the poems.

Whitman, Walt. *Overhead the Sun,* il. by Antonio Frasconi. Farrar 1969. $4.95; 10 up.

A compilation of lyrical passages selected from Whitman's *Leaves of Grass* to commemorate the 150th anniversary of his birth. Each poem is illustrated with varicolored woodcut prints.

Anthologies

Adoff, Arnold, comp. *I Am the Darker Brother.* Macmillan 1968. $4.95 (P—Macmillan, $1.25); 9 up.

Although compiled for older readers (15–18), many of these poems can be used successfully with younger children. Poetry on, about, and by American Negroes.

Agee, Rose H., comp. *How to Eat a Poem and Other Morsels: Food Poems for Children,* il. by Peggy Wilson. Pantheon 1967. $3.74; 7–10.

Poems and rhymes about food selected with the advice of children.

Arbuthnot, May Hill, and Shelton L. Root, Jr., comps. *Time for Poetry,* 3rd ed., il. by Arthur Paul. Scott, Foresman 1967. $11.00; 5–13.

A wealth of "reading aloud" poems to challenge children's imagination, combined with a strong section entitled "Keeping Children and Poetry Together."

Association for Childhood Education International, comp. *Sung under the Silver Umbrella,* il. by Dorothy Lathrop. Macmillan 1935. $2.95; 4–14.

Fewer than 200 poems, this is nevertheless an excellent selection for young children and deservedly popular.

Baron, Virginia Olsen, comp. *The Seasons of Time: Tanka Poetry of Ancient Japan,* il. by Yasuhide Kobashi. Dial 1968. $4.50; 12 up.

A book of nature poems in a form that predates haiku, beautifully decorated with brush and ink drawings.

Behn, Harry, tr. *Cricket Songs: Japanese Haiku,* photos. Harcourt 1964. $2.95; 9 up.

The 17-syllable Japanese verse form is presented for children. The requirements for such a form include an aspect of nature, a touch of humor, and a sense of completeness even in the brevity of the verse. Excellent photographic illustrations.

Blishen, Edward, comp. *Oxford Book of Poetry for Children,* il. by Brian Wildsmith. Watts 1964. $7.95; 5–8.

A collection of lively poems about dragons and fairies, humor and nature. The dazzling Wildsmith pictures have strong appeal.

Brewton, Sara and John E., comps. *Laughable Limericks,* il. by Ingrid Fetz. Crowell 1965. $3.75; 8–11.

A hilarious selection of limericks, old and new, prepared specifically for the young reader. By the same compilers: *America Forever New.*

Cole, William, comp. *The Birds and the Beasts Were There,* il. by Helen Siegl. World 1963. $5.95; all ages.

From nonsense, through lyric, to narrative—all kinds of poems about birds and beasts.

_____, comp. *A Book of Nature Poems.* Viking 1969. $5.95; all ages.

A collection of light poems to charm the lover of poetry—in fact a rather heady, rich array of poems for the devotee. The selection is heavily but not exclusively from the English poets and without regard to popularity or balance (there are about as many poems about mushrooms as about mountains).

_____, comp. *Oh, How Silly!* il. by Tomi Ungerer. Viking 1970. $3.37; 8–12.

A balanced collection of humorous verse by English and American poets. Companion volume to *Oh, What Nonsense!*

———, comp. *Oh, What Nonsense!* il. by Tomi Ungerer. Viking 1966. $2.95 (P—Viking, $.65); 5–7.

Ridiculous pictures catch the flavor of nonsense verse.

———, comp. *Poems for Seasons and Celebrations,* il. by Johannes Troyer. World 1961. $3.95; 8 up.

More than 140 traditional and modern poems, selected with discrimination and taste, celebrate the four seasons and 22 important occasions of the year.

———, comp. *Poems of Magic and Spells,* il. by Peggy Bacon. World 1960. $3.95; 9 up.

The 90 poems in this collection, dealing with magical events and strange people, are drawn from the works of more than 60 English and American poets. Not only is this a fine selection, representing a wide range, but it is also a beautiful book in format, with imaginative drawings. By the same compiler: *I Went to the Animal Fair; Story Poems New and Old; Humorous Poetry for Children; Beastly Boys and Ghastly Girls.*

Colum, Padraic, comp. *Roofs of Gold: Poems to Read Aloud.* Macmillan 1964. $3.74; 12 up.

The distinguished Irish author has selected his favorite poems for reading. They range from Shakespeare to Dylan Thomas.

De Forest, Charlotte B., comp. *The Prancing Pony: Nursery Rhymes from Japan,* il. by Keiko Hida. Walker 1968. $3.95; all ages.

These brief verses are from a Japanese educator's collection of anonymous folk poetry and are based on the words of lullabies and children's songs—most of them "very old." De Forest's charming choices have provided inspiration for the illustrations by a famous Japanese collage artist. Although called "nursery rhymes," the poems are not limited to the very young; the combination of words and pictures has an ageless interest.

de la Mare, Walter, comp. *Tom Tiddler's Ground,* il. by Margery Gill. Knopf 1961. $3.89; all ages.

In this volume the poet-collector has written, "Poetry in particular *wears* well. The longer you care for it in itself, the better it gets." Here are poems to care for. By the same compiler: *Come Hither; The Magic Jacket.*

Doob, L. W., comp. *A Crocodile Has Me by the Leg,* il. by S. I. Wangboje. Walker 1968. $2.95; 9–14.

Traditional African verse proves both the unique and the universal quality of the people.

Downie, Mary Alice, and Barbara Robertson, comps. *The Wind Has Wings.* Walck 1968. $6.00; 8–12.

A wide range of moods, patterns, and settings pervades this collection of 77 poems by Canadian writers.

Dunning, Stephen, and others, comps. *Reflections on a Gift of Watermelon Pickle . . . and Other Modern Verse,* photos. Lothrop 1967. $3.95; 12 up.

A collection of modern poetry, with exciting photographs. Beautiful format.

————, ————, comps. *Some Haystacks Don't Even Have Any Needle: and Other Complete Modern Poems.* Lothrop 1969. $4.95; 11 up.

Contains poems selected because of their special relevance for young people. Organized in untitled sections and grouped around underlying themes, the poems are artistically arranged, including appropriate reproductions of modern paintings. There are a few poems of love and delight; many that expose, abrade, tinge gaiety with sarcasm, and leave the reader troubled and disturbed. Teachers willing to explore the darker themes of today's art forms will find the work useful.

Ferris, Helen, comp. *Favorite Poems: Old and New,* il. by Leonard Weisgard. Doubleday 1957. $5.95; all ages.

In this attractive comprehensive volume of 710 poems categorized into 18 interest groups, the greatest poets of yesterday and today are brought together for family and individual enjoyment.

Geismer, Barbara Peck, and Antoinette Brown Suter, comps. *Very Young Verses,* il. by Mildred Bronson. Houghton 1945. $3.50; 4–7.

Over 180 poems dealing with themes (self, animals, weather, etc.) known to interest young children.

Gregory, Horace, and Marya Zaturenska, comps. *The Silver Swan: Poems of Mystery and Romance,* il. by Diana Bloomfield. Holt 1966. $3.95; 12–16.

A fresh and inviting collection for older boys and girls.

Hannum, Sara, and Gwendolyn E. Reed, comps. *Lean Out of the Window,* il. by Ragna Tischler. Atheneum 1965. $3.95; 10 up.

In this anthology of modern poetry there is variety, depth, beauty, and wonder, which offers every reader at least one place for stopping, considering, and returning again.

Hazeltine, Alice, and Elva S. Smith, comps. *The Year Around: Poems for Children,* il. by Paula Hutchinson. Abingdon 1956. $2.50; all ages.

As the seasons change and holidays come and go, the selections, fresh, inspiring, and appealing, reveal a variety of moods and tempos. More than 200 poems are included in this beautiful edition.

Hine, Al, comp. *This Land Is Mine: An Anthology of American Verse,* il. by Leonard Vosburg. Lippincott 1965. $4.95; 10 up.

A collection of over 100 poems, with comments by the compiler tracing the history of the United States from Indian days to the present.

Hopkins, Lee Bennet, comp. *I Think I Saw a Snail: Young Poems for City Seasons,* il. by Harold James. Crown 1969. $3.50; 4–9.

These 19 poems depict seasonal changes and influences in a city. Poets include Langston Hughes, Aileen Fisher, Dorothy Aldis, and Carson McCullers. Each black-and-white sketch definitely relates to the poem and offers identification for the innercity child.

———. *Me! A Book of Poems,* il. by Talivaldis Stubis. Seabury 1970. $3.95; 4–8.

The small child's innocent egotistical world is explored in these 18 short selections written primarily by well-known contemporary poets. Cartoon-like monochromatic illustrations and good overall design make an inviting book.

Huffard, Grace Thompson, Laura Mae Carlisle, and Helen Ferris, comps. *My Poetry Book,* rev. ed., il. by Willy Pogany. Holt 1956. $4.50; all ages.

A revision of the 1934 edition with 20-odd contemporary and classic poems, bringing the total to more than 500. Arranged by subject.

Larrick, Nancy, comp. *On City Streets,* by David Sagarin. Evans 1968. $4.95 (P—Bantam, $.75); 10–13.

An impressive collection of poems about city sights and people compiled by Nancy Larrick with the help of more than 100 youngsters from the innercity. Black-and-white photographs of city scenes add to the effectiveness.

———, comp. *Piper, Pipe that Song Again,* il. by Kelly Oechsli. Random 1965. $2.95; 7–12.

Well-known poets of England and America are represented in this anthology in which melody and movement are accentuated.

————, comp. *Piping down the Valleys Wild: Poetry for the Young of All Ages,* il. by Ellen Raskin. Delacorte 1968. $4.95 (P—Dell, $.95); all ages.

Well selected and categorized, the complete volume would be a valuable resource for any classroom. Black-and-white drawings with distinct lines.

————, comp. *Poetry for Holidays,* il. by Kelly Oechsli. Garrard 1966. $2.39; 7–10.

Well chosen selections for each of much-loved children's holidays throughout the year.

Lewis, Richard, comp. *In a Spring Garden,* il. by Ezra Jack Keats. Dial 1965. $4.50; all ages.

Haiku poetry at its best, demonstrating its ability to speak directly to the heart and imagination.

————, comp. *Miracles: Poems by Children of the English-speaking World.* Simon 1966. $4.95; 7–12.

The children themselves express many moods and thoughts in this collection of original poetry. By the same editor: *Out of the Earth I Sing.*

Livingstone, Myra Cohn, comp. *A Tune beyond Us.* Harcourt 1968. $5.75; 12 up.

Poems from world literatures, freshly chosen and paired with the originals.

Lord, Beman, comp. *The Days of the Week,* il. by Walter Erhard. Walck 1968. $3.25; 3–6.

Traditional verses familiarize the young reader with the seven different days, and a brief explanation tells how each day got its name. Youngsters will love the three-color illustrations.

Love, Katherine, comp. *A Little Laughter,* il. by Walter H. Lorraine. Crowell 1957. $3.50; all ages.

This is a discriminating collection of happy verses. From Edward Lear to Ogden Nash, nonsense verses provide chuckles and hilarious laughter.

McDonald, Gerald D., comp. *A Way of Knowing,* il. by Clare and John Ross. Crowell 1959. $4.95; 9–16.

One of the few anthologies of poetry especially for boys, arranged in nine categories. Most of the poems are short. There are a few lyrical poems, many humorous pieces, several ballads or story poems, a gaggle of puzzles in verse, and a touch of carefully handled inspiration.

McEwen, Catherine Schaefer, comp. *Away We Go: 100 Poems for the Very Young,* il. by Barbara Cooney. Crowell 1956. $3.50; 3–8.

Poetry of quality under such headings as "Me and Mine," "The Outside World," "Nature and Seasons," "Living Creatures," "Special Days," and "Poems for Fun."

McFarland, Wilma, comp. *For a Child: Great Poems Old and New,* il. by Ninon. Westminster 1947. $4.50; 6–10.

A collection of lyrical poems that deal with "close to home" subjects familiar to children.

Morrison, Lillian, comp. *Sprints and Distances: Sports in Poetry and the Poetry in Sport,* il. by Clare and John Ross. Crowell 1965. $4.95; 10 up.

The affinity between sports and poetry is demonstrated in a unique and spirited collection with works ranging from Virgil through Ogden Nash.

Parker, Elinor, comp. *The Singing and the Gold,* il. by Clare Leighton. Crowell 1962. $4.50; 12 up.

Many of these translations, from 30 different lands and from a wide time span, will appeal to older children.

Plotz, Helen, comp. *Imagination's Other Place.* Crowell 1955. $4.50; 12 up.

Poems of science and mathematics. This stimulating book links unexpected sources from the past and present.

————, comp. *Untune the Sky,* il. by Clare Leighton. Crowell 1957. $4.50; 12 up.

Young people who are confirmed lovers of poetry as well as those who have no liking for it will be intrigued by this fascinating collection of poems that range all the way from the Psalms to the works of William Carlos Williams.

Rasmussen, Knud, comp. *Beyond the High Hills: A Book of Eskimo Poems,* photos by Guy Mary-Rousseliere. World 1961. $3.95; all ages.

Spontaneous Eskimo song chants of the hunt, the feast, and the joys and sorrows of living are illustrated by superb full-color photographs.

Read, Herbert, comp. *This Way, Delight: A Book of Poetry for the Young,* il. by Juliet Kepes. Pantheon 1956. $3.50; 5–9.

Intended to set moods and to aid creativity, this collection contains poems by many well-known poets and some who are less so.

Reeves, James, comp. *One's None: Old Rhymes for New Tongues.* Watts 1968. $3.95; 5–12.

A distinctive collection of anonymous rhymes, songs, and chants by a well-known poet. Something for nearly everyone in the elementary grades.

Smith, John, comp. *My Kind of Verse,* il. by Uri Shulevitz. Macmillan 1968. $5.95; 8 up.

Several familiar rhymes are included in this collection, along with one not so well known. Poets include Shakespeare, Keats, Yeats, and Lindsay.

Spier, Peter, comp. *Hurrah, We're Outward Bound!* il. by the compiler. Doubleday 1968. $3.95; 4–8.

In this delightfully illustrated collection of familiar sea songs and rhymes, the pictures follow the maiden voyage in 1830 of a three-masted sailing ship, *La Jeune Française,* from Honfleur to New York and back. A special chant of praise for the soft, colorfully illustrated panoramas of sea and port. From bowsprit to stern, from ship to shore, the details are authentic. By the same artist-editor: *To Market! To Market!; London Bridge Is Falling Down.*

Untermeyer, Louis, comp. *The Golden Treasury of Poetry,* il. by Joan Walsh Anglund. Golden 1959. $2.95; 8 up.

More than 400 poems are in this beautiful anthology, which ranges from light verse to distinguished serious poetry, both traditional and modern.

Weiss, Renee Karol, comp. *A Paper Zoo: A Collection of Animal Poems by Modern American Poets,* il. by Ellen Raskin. Macmillan 1968. $4.50; 5–8.

A slim volume of modern poetry with bright illustrations.

Withers, Carl, comp. *A Rocket in My Pocket,* il. by Susanne Suba. Holt 1948. $4.50; 6–12.

A collection of over 400 rhymes, chants, game songs, tongue twisters, and ear-teasers of youngsters living in many different regions of the United States. All have been authenticated in oral tradition and reflect the language development and social growth of children.

HOLIDAYS

Adshead, Gladys. *Brownies—Hush,* il. by Elizabeth Orton Jones. Walck 1938. $3.75; 4–7.

Brownies will never die if today's children are given a chance to know this wonderful fairy tale with its inimitable format and its Halloween night climax.

Ballian, Lorna. *Humbug Witch,* il. by the author. Abingdon 1965. $2.50; 4–8.

A little witch and her unsuccessful attempts at witchcraft. One evening she wearily takes off piece after piece of comical attire—the last of which proves to be a mask, revealing a hilarious little girl underneath! Too good to miss.

Borten, Helen. *Halloween,* il. by the author. Crowell 1965. $2.95; 6–8.

The origin and history of the holiday are described simply as are the customs of American children today, in this attractive 32-page story in picture book format.

Bright, Robert. *Georgie's Halloween,* il. by the author. Doubleday 1958. $2.95; 4–8.

What's more natural than for Georgie, the most lovable ghost ever created, to have just the right sized Halloween adventure, properly tinged with the mysterious, of course!

Bulla, Clyde R. *The Valentine Cat,* il. by Leonard Weisgard. Crowell 1959. $4.95; 3–8.

A wistful fantasy about a homeless kitten who was all black except for a white heart on his forehead.

236

————. *Washington's Birthday,* il. by Don Bolognese. Crowell 1967. $2.95; 6–9.

Simple words complemented by pleasant illustrations show Washington as a man to be admired. The author also points out Washington's dislike for politics and city life. The present-day celebration of Washington's birthday and the Washington Monument are covered. By the same author: *Lincoln's Birthday.*

Cantwell, Mary. *St. Patrick's Day,* il. by Ursula Arndt. Crowell 1967. $2.95; 6–9.

This spirited book does an admirable job of handling the myths and legends about St. Patrick of Ireland and his miracles, as well as our celebration of St. Patrick's Day. Fact and theory are carefully delineated, and the historical information is particularly vivid.

Dalgliesh, Alice. *The Fourth of July Story,* il. by Marie Nonnast. Scribner 1956. $3.25; 8–12.

A simple narrative of the birthday of the United States which will help children appreciate that Independence Day is something more than fireworks and picnics. Clear and dramatic illustrations are influenced by primitives of the period. By the same author: *The Thanksgiving Story; The Columbus Story.*

Embry, Margaret. *The Blue-Nosed Witch,* il. by Carl Rose. Holiday 1956. $2.95; 6–8.

An engaging tale of broomsticks, a black kitten, and a blue-nosed witch—all entering into the traditional trick-or-treat fun of Halloween.

Flack, Marjorie. *Ask Mr. Bear,* il. by the author. Macmillan 1932. $2.95; 3–6.

Repetition, the opportunity for participation, design, and a charming surprise ending make this picture book a birthday classic.

Harper, Wilhelmina, comp. *Ghosts and Goblins,* il. by William Wiesner. Dutton 1965. $4.95; 7–11.

This attractive newly revised edition of a well-known collection of stories, folktales, and verses from around the world is a rich source of storytelling and reading aloud for the teacher, group leader, or camp counselor.

Heilbroner, Joan. *The Happy Birthday Present,* il. by Mary Chalmers. Harper 1962. $2.50; 4–8.

The experiences of two little boys who decide to buy their mother a birthday present are plainly and amusingly described.

Janice. *Little Bear's Thanksgiving,* il. by Mariana. Lothrop 1967. $3.50; 4–8.

Appealing, winsome Little Bear gets invited to Thanksgiving dinner by his great friend Goldie, and it falls to his forest friends not only to explain the holiday but also to get him there on time.

Mariana. *Miss Flora McFlimsey's Valentine,* il. by the author. Lothrop 1962. $2.50; 6–9.

Miss Flora, a little doll of long ago, makes valentines for her woodland friends. Pookoo Cat, entrusted with delivery, stuffs them into a hollow tree, but when the tree serves as a post office, all turns out well. By the same author: *Miss Flora McFlimsey's Christmas Eve; Miss Flora McFlimsey's Easter Bonnet.*

Milhous, Katherine. *Appolonia's Valentine,* il. by the author. Scribner 1954. $3.31; 5–9.

Appolonia was clumsy but she could draw. Her Pennsylvania Dutch drawings on her valentines make this a good Valentine's Day story. By the same author-artist: *With Bells On,* a Christmas story.

Pannell, Lucile, and Frances Cavanah, eds. *Holiday Round Up,* il. by Manning Lee. Macrae 1950, 1968. $5.50; 10 up.

An anthology of stories for all holidays, birthdays, and the Sabbath. For children of all denominations.

Phelan, Mary Kay. *Election Day,* il. by Robert Quackenbush. Crowell 1967. $2.95; 5–9.

Written in a straightforward manner, this book includes information about how the American system of voting on election day has developed, the importance of this day, and its ancient precedents. Unfortunately missing is the present role of the mass media.

Politi, Leo. *Moy Moy,* il. by the author. Scribner 1960. $3.12; 5–9.

Life in Chinatown is pictured in gay color. The story centers upon the children's part in the Chinese New Year celebration.

Schultz, Gwen. *The Blue Valentine,* il. by Theresa Sherman. Morrow 1965. $3.25; 5–9.

Along with the theme of new girl in the first grade are helpful suggestions on how to make and decorate valentines. Teachers will be able to use this in several different areas.

Showers, Paul. *Columbus Day,* il. by Ed Emberley. Crowell 1965. $2.95; 5–9.

A simple but sprightly text, enhanced by gay pictures, presents in a fair manner the voyage of Columbus and the way October 12 is celebrated today.

Tudor, Tasha. *Becky's Birthday,* il. by the author. Viking 1960. $3.77; 8–11.

Delightful celebration of Becky's tenth birthday—from the moment she awakes until bedtime. A festive evening meal in the woods is climaxed by the unique arrival of a lighted birthday cake floating down a winding stream.

———. *Pumpkin Moonshine,* il. by the author. Walck 1962. $3.75; 4–6.

Sylvie Ann's adventures with the pumpkin are described with enchanting pictures and easy text.

Weisgard, Leonard. *The Plymouth Thanksgiving,* il. by the author. Doubleday 1967. $3.95; 7–11.

Outstanding illustrations and text, based on the known facts about the Pilgrim band, make good history and an excellent visualization of the story.

RELIGION AND HOLY DAYS

Aichinger, Helga. *The Shepherd,* il. by the author. Crowell 1967. $3.75; 3–7.

In strikingly effective pictures and amazingly simple words, this beautiful picture book tells the story of a shepherd's journey to the Christ Child's manger.

Allstrom, Elizabeth. *Truly, I Say to You,* il. by Mel Silverman. Abingdon 1966. $3.00; 10 up.

A magnificent presentation of the Sermon on the Mount, which interprets not only the historical context in which these words were originally spoken by Jesus but also points up their contemporary meaning. Text is selected from the Revised Standard Version of the Bible. The Jewish setting in which Jesus lived is communicated strongly by the illustrations. By the same author and illustrator: *Songs along the Way,* about the Psalms.

Almedingen, E. M. *One Little Tree,* il. by Denise Brown. Norton 1963. $3.50; 8–12.

In Finland, over 50 years ago, a boy summons all his courage to keep a promise and bring Christmas to his family. The slow moving story is appealing with its quaint prose and old-world charm.

Andersen, Hans Christian. *The Little Match Girl,* il. by Blair Lent. Houghton 1968. $3.50; 6–10.

A favorite story, known to evoke thoughtfulness and new awareness, has been given exquisite new treatment by one of the best known children's illustrators. Mr. Lent's fully realized scenes are unforgettable.

240

Anrooy, Frans Van. *The Bird Tree,* il. by Jaap Tol. Harcourt 1967. $3.75; 4–8.

A joyous tale that fills one with a sense of wonder and kindness. Glowing, deep colored illustrations enhance this story of Mark's miraculous Christmas tree.

Armour, Richard. *The Adventures of Egbert the Easter Egg,* il. by Paul Galdone. McGraw 1965. $3.95; 5–8.

In rollicking verse that goes skipping along and rarely loses momentum, this is the story of Egbert, the egg with a face, who finally finds joy and the boy who created him.

Association for Childhood Education International. *Told under the Christmas Tree,* il. by Maud and Miska Petersham. Macmillan 1948, 1962. $2.95; 8–12.

An outstanding collection of Christmas stories plus 14 stories for the Jewish Festival of Lights. Excellent source for storytelling and reading aloud.

Barnhart, Nancy. *The Lord Is My Shepherd, or. Scribner 1949. $6.50; 9 up.*

"An invitation to enter and discover the wonders of the Book of Books." The strength, authenticity, and reverence of the pictures and the fine choice of Bible passages make this book indispensable for "Bible as literature" study.

Barry, Robert. *Mr. Wilowby's Christmas Tree,* il. by the author. McGraw 1963. $3.95; 4–8.

A refreshingly amusing cumulative tale of how the forest animals come to share Mr. Willowby's Christmas tree, which is too tall to stand up straight in his parlor.

Bishop, Claire H. *Martin De Porres, Hero,* il. by Jean Charlot. Houghton 1954. $3.95; 9–12.

A 17th-century Spanish Negro living in Peru experiences great poverty and, through this, develops a great concern for the poor. The third book in Mrs. Bishop's series on the lives of saints.

————. *Yeshu, Called Jesus.* Farrar 1966. $3.50; 9–12.

The boyhood of Jesus of Nazareth recreated in the light of Biblical and archeological scholarship and the development of the Jewish religion. By the same author: *Mozart: Music Magician.*

Bollinger, Max. *Joseph,* il. by Edith Schindler. Delacorte 1969. $3.95; 8–12.

This well-known biblical story of Joseph is retold in a simple, direct narrative. There are insights into the feelings of Joseph and his brothers. Schindler's drawings perfectly suit the story and add to reader appeal.

Branley, Franklyn. *The Christmas Sky,* il. by Blair Lent. Crowell 1966. $3.75; 8–11.

The author carefully follows the scientific method in examining the various possible explanations for the star that appeared in the heavens at the time of Jesus' birth. Stunning woodcuts add to his distinguished presentation, which is based on the story of the star as given each year at the Hayden Planetarium in New York City. Good for reading aloud.

Brewton, Sara and John E. *Christmas Bells Are Ringing,* il. by Decie Merwin. Macmillan 1951. $4.50; 5–12.

An excellent anthology of Christmas poetry, the old and the new, the gay and serious.

Bring a Torch, Jeannette, Isabella, il. by Adrienne Adams. Scribner 1963. $3.25; 4–8.

This lovely 17th-century carol is part of the rich store of Christmas customs belonging to the people of Provence in France. The illustrations reflect warmth and sensitivity.

Broun, Heywood. *A Shepherd,* il. by Gilbert Riswold. Prentice 1967. $4.95; 6 up.

The story of Amos, the shepherd who refused to go with the others to Bethlehem on Christmas Eve. Author and illustrator both skillfully sustain a mood of wonder and majesty.

Brown, Margaret Wise. *The Runaway Bunny,* il. by Clement Hurd. Harper 1942. $2.95; 3–6.

A little bunny with an urge to run away is helped to understand the limits of freedom through his mother's love. Although this book does not mention Easter, it is appropriate for use on that holiday.

Budd, Lillian. *Tekla's Easter,* il. by Genia. Rand 1962. $3.47; 6–8.

While this is a perfect Easter book, evoking the sense of new life that comes with the spring to everyone, everywhere, it is also an authentic portrayal of Swedish life, dress, and customs.

Burch, Robert. *Renfroe's Christmas,* il. by Rocco Negri. Viking 1968. $3.50; 7–10.

Eight-year-old Renfroe, a modern country boy, learns that giving is truly better than receiving. His family's celebration and the local Christmas pageant are the background of this warm, humorous novel, written with flavor and style.

Butler, Suzanne. *Starlight in Tourrone,* il. by Rita Fava Fegiz. Little 1965. $3.50; 7–10.

Six children work to revive the special Christmas march traditional to towns in southern France. Excellent brief characterizations, acceptance of difference, and a promise of positive action for the community make this more than a regional story.

Carlson, Natalie Savage. *Befana's Gift,* il. by Robert Quackenbush. Harper 1969. $3.79; 8–11.

La Befana is a legendary figure who delivers gifts to all good Italian children on Christmas Eve. When she brings a grandson to Cesare, little Gemma is jealous but soon learns that love can be shared. This warm family story is flavored with the rich cultural heritage of Italy.

———. *The Family under the Bridge,* il by Garth Williams. Harper 1958. $3.95; 9 up.

A warmhearted Christmas story of three Parisian children and their mother who live under a bridge and hope Father Christmas will bring them a home. Garth Williams' pictures match the words in which children can share a Christmas Eve pancake supper, the Christmas tree provided by the gypsies, and finally a home.

Caudill, Rebecca. *A Certain Small Shepherd,* il. by William Pène du Bois. Holt 1965. $3.50; 6 up.

Certain to become a Christmas classic! A most poignant and deeply sensitive story tells about a little mute boy from the humblest of homes in Appalachia who conquers all with imagination, courage, and faith.

Chalmers, Mary. *A Christmas Story,* il. by the author. Harper 1956. $1.50; 3–6.

A delightful "tiny" book telling of the search by a small child for a star for the top of the Christmas tree. This is a success story small children will like.

Claxton, Ernest. *A Child's Grace,* photos by Constance Bannister. Dutton 1948. $3.75; 3–6.

Expressed in profound simplicity is this book of gratitude for God's goodness. Line after line is illustrated with full-page photographs involving a child or children. Excellent for Thanksgiving.

Cone, Molly. *The Jewish Sabbath,* il. by Ellen Raskin. Crowell 1966. $2.95; 5–9.

The wonderfully special feeling of the Jewish Sabbath is sensitively portrayed. All Sabbath days serve the same purpose, and this similarity among faiths is brought out. The stunning woodcuts add to a well-crafted text. By the same author: *Purim.*

Cooney, Barbara. *The Little Juggler,* il. by the author. Hastings 1961. $3.25; 8–12.

For this retelling of the ancient legend, the author-artist went to Paris to see the 13th-century manuscript that is its basis and toured France to sketch places where the little juggler might have wandered.

———. *A Little Prayer,* il. by the author. Hastings 1967. $2.25; 5 up.

A short prayer originating long ago in Provence is portrayed in the same expressive style of illustration as *Chanticleer and the Fox.* With simplicity and directness, a petition is made for qualities of spirit to make us "philosophical as the fisherman . . . patient as the spinner . . . merry as the troubadour." The text reflects a zest for life, a quality also evident in the illustrations.

Cunningham, Julia. *Onion Journey,* il. by Lydia Cooley. Pantheon 1967. $3.50; 8–11.

Gilly, who is left alone on the day before Christmas, comes finally to understand his grandmother's mysterious gift of an onion. This is a mood piece with a message, made of a succession of highly evocative scenes and captured in graphic prose.

Daves, Michael. *Young Reader's Book of Christian Symbolism,* il. by Gordon Laite. Abingdon 1967. $3.95; 8–12.

This well-designed book telling the story of major Christian symbols and their relationships to the history and traditions of the Christian church would be especially useful for church schools.

Davis, Katherine, Henry Onorati, and Harry Simeone. *The Little Drummer Boy,* il. by Ezra Jack Keats. Macmillan 1968. $3.95; 4 up.

Pictures in rich color placed on pages that beautifully vary in tone bring warmth to this lovely new Christmas carol. The spare text and rhythmical refrain sing with tenderness. The musical score is included. By the same illustrator as an author: *A Letter to Amy* (birthdays); *Jennie's Hat* (Easter).

de Angeli, Marguerite. *The Old Testament.* Doubleday 1960. $6.95; 6–14.

Moving selections from the King James Version have been arranged and picture after the artist visited the lands of the

Old Testament. It should be read to the youngest. They will
read it for themselves later. By the same author: *Book of
Favorite Hymns.*

de Regniers, Beatrice Schenk. *David and Goliath,* il. by
Richard M. Powers. Viking 1965. $3.75; 6–8.

A powerful portrayal of a favorite Old Testament hero with
strong prose and vivid illustrations that follows biblical
traditions quite faithfully.

Dickens, Charles. *A Christmas Carol,* il. by Philip Reed.
Atheneum 1966. $4.95 (many paperback editions); 8 up.

The text of this wonderful story has preserved the irregulari-
ties of the original printing, and Philip Reed's quaint, softly
colored woodcuts add just the right touch to this small-scale
edition of a beloved classic. Illustrators of other notable
editions are Arthur Rackham and Everett Shinn.

Duvoisin, Roger. *Petunia's Christmas,* il. by the author. Knopf
1952. $3.54; 4–7.

In delightfully simple pictures and text Mr. Duvoisin's
not-so-silly goose Petunia rescues, through hard honest
effort, her love, the gander, from his fate as Christmas
dinner.

Elgin, Kathleen. *The Mormons: The Church of Jesus Christ of
the Latter-Day Saints,* il. by the author. McKay 1969.
$3.95; 9–12.

Starts with the biography of Charles Coulson Rich, a lesser-
known Mormon pioneer, and then establishes the historical
events of the religious sect commencing with Joseph Smith's
vision of God and his Son and ending with the western
colonization. Finally there is a description of present welfare and educational programs of the church. A bibliography, index, organizational chart, and black-and-white
illustrations are provided.

Ets, Marie Hall. *Nine Days to Christmas,* il. by the author.
Viking 1959. $3.50; 4–8.

This lovely picture book reveals the rhythm of a little girl's
life in Mexico City as she waits and helps to prepare for her
Posada, a special Christmas party. Caldecott Award winner
in 1960.

Farjeon, Eleanor. *A Prayer for Little Things,* il. by Elizabeth
Orton Jones. Houghton 1945. $2.50; 5–8.

A prayer for small children asking protection for many
simple treasured things. Interpreted through colored illustrations.

Field, Rachel. *Prayer for a Child,* il. by Elizabeth Orton Jones. Macmillan 1944. $4.95; 5–8.

Poem of prayer showing a child's thankfulness for his material comforts and his faith and trust in his parents and in God. Beautifully illustrated in color. Caldecott Award winner in 1945.

Fisher, Aileen. *Skip around the Year,* il. by Gioia Fiammenghi. Crowell 1967. $3.50; 5–9.

A delightful collection of 38 simple poems about most recognized holidays—civil, Christian, and Jewish. The spirited illustrations help the verses to dance across the pages. By the same author: *Easter.*

Fitch, Florence. *One God,* photos. Lothrop 1944. $3.95; 10 up.

Simple explanations for mutual understanding of the Jewish, Catholic, and Protestant ways of worship. By the same author: *Their Search for God; A Book About God; Allah, the God of Islam.*

Gaer, Joseph. *Holidays Around the World,* il. by Ann Marie Jauss. Little 1953. $4.50; 12 up.

After a good introductory chapter on the origins of holidays, those of the five major religions are discussed. A valuable reference book.

Gilbert, Arthur, and Oscar Tarcov. *Your Neighbor Celebrates,* photos. Ktav 1957. $3.00; 11 up.

An excellent, informative book dealing with the historical background and manner of celebration of Jewish holidays.

Godden, Rumer. *The Story of Holly and Ivy.* Viking 1958. $3.56; 9–12.

The touching story of a little orphan girl, Ivy, in search of a grandmother and a Christmas doll named Holly. By the same author: *The Kitchen Madonna.*

Graham, Lorenz. *Every Man Heart Lay Down,* il. by Colleen Browning. Crowell 1970. $3.75; all ages.

The author has retold the story of the birth of Christ in the idiom of Africans newly come to English speech.

Hale, Linda. *The Glorious Christmas Soup Party,* il. by the author. Viking 1962. $2.50; 4–8.

The durable stone soup motif appears this time in a story of loving and giving. Mrs. Mouse makes do with the humble gifts brought by her guests and provides a Christmas feast.

Harper, Wilhelmina, comp. *Merry Christmas to You,* il. by Fermin Rocker. Dutton 1965. $4.95; 8–12.

A good anthology, newly revised, of Christmas stories and poems, many old favorites, for telling and reading aloud. The wide variety includes miracle, fairy, and modern tales written by many distinguished authors. By the same compiler: *Easter Chimes.*

Hazeltine, Alice. *Easter Book of Legends,* il. by Pamela Bianco. Lothrop 1947. $4.95; 10–12.

Biblical, folk, and modern materials are found in this wide selection of stories and poems for the festival of resurrection and the spring season.

Heyward, Du Bose. *The Country Bunny and the Little Gold Shoes,* il. by Marjorie Flack. Houghton 1939. $3.50; 3–7.

In this modern fairy tale, an ordinary looking bunny is proved kind, wise, and swift enough to be chosen to help in the delivery of Easter eggs. Her appealing adventures are complemented by the illustrations.

Honour, Alan. *Cave of Riches: The Story of the Dead Sea Scrolls,* il. by P. A. Hutchinson. McGraw 1956. $3.51; 8–12.

A simple presentation of the story of the Dead Sea Scrolls including their discovery, their translation, their ultimate destination, and their importance. Unfamiliar terms are explained without breaking the thread of the narrative.

Hood, Flora. *One Luminaria for Antonio,* il. by Ann Kirn. Putnam 1966. $2.68; 6–8.

A simple and sensitive portrayal of how Antonio manages to get the "luminaria" on Christmas Eve, places it at his doorstep, and receives the Christ Child's blessing for the new year. The easy-to-read story introduces the young reader to some Mexican customs.

Hurd, Edith T. *Christmas Eve,* il. by Clement Hurd. Harper 1962. $3.50; 5–9.

Fascinating two-color block prints reflect the simplicity and reverence of the text in this account of the animals on the first Christmas Eve in Bethlehem.

Jones, Elizabeth Orton. *Big Susan,* il. by the author. Macmillan 1947. $3.95; 8–10.

One wonderful night all Susan's dolls come alive. This is a different kind of Christmas book that little girls will love all year.

Jones, Jessie Orton. *This Is the Way,* il. by Elizabeth Orton Jones. Viking 1951. $3.50; 7 up.

Brief verses from the world's religions are directed to the child. The graceful illustrations of children of all races, shown first in their natural environment and then in final assembly, suggest the spiritual unity of mankind. By the same author: *Small Rain.*

Kahl, Virginia. *Plum Pudding for Christmas,* il. by the author. Scribner 1956. $3.12; 4–10.

The king promises to come to Christmas dinner on one condition: that he have plum pudding for dessert. That seems simple until Gunhilde eats the plum. A just-for-fun story with some rollicking situations.

Lexau, Joan M. *More Beautiful than Flowers,* il. by Don Bolognese. Lippincott 1966. $2.95; 4–8.

A beautiful, poetic interpretation of the nature of God as experienced through his creations in the universe. The sparse text and majestic illustrations blend into a harmonious whole. By the same author: *Jose's Christmas Secret.*

Lindgren, Astrid. *Christmas in Noisy Village,* il. by Ilon Wikland. Viking 19–8.

This description of Christmas in Sweden should go straight to the hearts of American children. The simple festivities and the gaiety of it all are portrayed in vivid four-color illustrations.

_____. *Christmas in the Stable,* il. by Harold Wiberg. Coward 1962. $3.75; 4–8.

In a direct and dignified manner, a Swedish mother tells the story of Christmas to her little girl. The child's concepts are masterfully caught in pictures that shine with true radiance.

McGinley, Phyllis. *A Wreath of Christmas Legends,* il. by Leonard Weisgard. Macmillan 1967. $4.95; 9 up.

Here, in a lovely format, are 15 medieval Christmas legends translated into verse with great finesse and artistry. The majority are relatively uncommon.

_____. *The Year without a Santa Claus,* il. by Kurt Werth. Lippincott 1957. $3.00; 5–8.

Delightful fun, written in deft light verse, telling of the year a tired old Santa decided not to make his annual journey. By the same author: *How Mrs. Claus Saved Christmas; Mince Pie and Mistletoe.*

Menotti, Gian Carlo. *Amahl and the Night Visitors,* adapted by Frances Frost, il. by Roger Duvoisin. McGraw 1952. $3.95; 7–10.

Menotti's well known opera adapted in narrative form with no changes in the dialogue. This tale juxtaposes reality and fantasy in an engaging interpretation of faith and human kindness.

Milhous, Katherine. *The Egg Tree,* il. by the author. Scribner 1950. $3.25; 6–8.

An account of the Pennsylvania Dutch custom of decorating a bare tree with painted eggs for Easter. A colorful book. Caldecott Award winner in 1951. By the same author-artist: *With Bells On.*

Monsell, Helen A. *Paddy's Christmas,* il. by Kurt Wiese. Knopf 1942. $3.44; 4–8.

A choice book on the joys of giving. Paddy, a young bear, learns that part of "Christmas is giving something to somebody else and making them happy as well as yourself. It's pretty, and it's loads of fun and it makes you feel good from the inside out!"

Moore, Clement. *The Night Before Christmas,* il. by Leonard Weisgard. Grosset 1949. $1.00; 4–7.

This edition of *A Visit from St. Nicholas* is brimful of the fun and excitement of Christmas Eve. Large print for young readers and large colorful pictures. Illustrators of other notable editions are Grandma Moses and Arthur Rockham.

Nussbaumer, Mares and Paul. *Away in a Manger: A Story of the Nativity,* il. by the authors. Harcourt 1965. $4.25; 5–8.

The story of the birth of the Christ Child retold as though it had occurred in a European winter setting. Full-page illustrations by two Swiss artists are beautiful and luminous. Contains words and music for "Away in a Manger" and "O Come Little Children."

Palmer, Geoffrey. *Quest for the Dead Sea Scrolls,* il. by Peter Forster. Day 1965. $3.49; 8–12.

Tells the story of the finding of the 2,000-year-old manuscripts, the analysis by scholars, and their significance to the Christian church. The story is similar to Honour's *Cave of Riches.*

Pauli, Hertha. *America's First Christmas,* il. by Fritz Kredel. Washburn 1962. $3.89; 10–12.

This is the true story of how Christopher Columbus and the crew of the Santa Maria, including the shipboys, Pedro and Juan, spent Christmas in 1492.

Petersham, Maud. *The Christ Child,* il. by Maud and Miska Petersham. Doubleday 1931. $3.95; 6 up.

This remains a treasured retelling of the Christ Child's birth and childhood taken from the King James Version of the Bible. The stylized watercolors, glowing with beauty, create a memorable world.

Politi, Leo. *Saint Francis and His Animals,* il. by the author. Scribner 1959. $3.63; 5–9.

A simple and dignified retelling of the story of St. Francis as a young man with a love for all life. Incidents are recorded in separate tales, making this a book easily usable to read aloud to younger children.

Potter, Beatrix. *The Tailor of Gloucester,* il. by the author. Warne 1903. $1.50; 7–10.

A longer story from the Beatrix Potter collection of little books. To help the tailor, tiny mice work all night to finish the embroidery on an elegant waistcoat promised for Christmas morning.

Preston, Carol. *A Trilogy of Christmas Plays for Children,* music selected by John Langstaff. Harcourt 1967. $3.95; 10 up.

Nativity plays based on the Bible and oral tradition with complete instructions for staging.

Purdy, Susan. *Festivals for You to Celebrate,* il. by the author Lippincott 1969. $5.95; 5 up.

Here is a real gold mine, usable and interesting—a reference book that contains, in most orderly fashion, background information on many holidays—national, international, and religious; craft activities and recipes, clearly illustrated, range widely in complexity; detailed explanations of procedures and materials; and numerous programing suggestions.

Rappaport, Uriel. *The Story of the Dead Sea Scrolls,* il. by Milka Cizik. Hastings 1968. $4.50; 12 up.

Excellent photographs, drawings, and maps supplement this history. Details of the discovery and deciphering and of the period in which they were written will give the reader a thorough understanding of these important documents. Recommended only for the avid young historian.

Redford, P. E. Gorey. *The Christmas Bower.* Dutton 1967. $3.95; 9–14.

This very amusing story has a department store setting and a cast of out-of-the-ordinary characters. Two eggheads are the protagonists, and it's all so funny that the point comes across very subtly.

Reed, Gwendolyn. *Adam and Eve,* il. by Helen Siegl. Lothrop 1968. $3.75; 4–8.

Taking the Genesis account of creation, the author has elaborated upon the theme of the story and heightened its detail. Poetic prose is accompanied by creative layout and design. Woodblocks in black and white as well as full-page color prints of gold, rust, and black add to the effect.

Reeves, James. *The Christmas Book*, il. by Raymond Briggs Dutton 1968. $4.95; 9 up.

A new anthology with a wide variety of Christmas poetry and stories, selected from the treasure house of English literature and tastefully arranged. There is something for every mood, from the famous classics of Shakespeare, Dickens, Grahame, and Ransome to memories by Dylan Thomas and delightful Paddington by Michael Bond.

Robbins, Ruth. *Baboushka and the Three Kings*, il. by Nicolas Sidiakov. Parnassus 1960. $2.95; 5–9.

This old folktale of Baboushka, the Russian Santa Claus, is made to live again through fascinating colorful lithographs and a pared-to-the-bone text. Together they convey mystery, dignity, and immediacy. Caldecott Award winner in 1961.

Rollins, Charlemae. *Christmas Gif'*, il. by Tom O'Sullivan. Follett 1963. $4.95; 6 up.

An excellent anthology of Christmas poems, stories, and songs written by and about Negroes. There are also many recipes from the "big houses" and from the slave cabins. This collection is a fine contribution to the heritage of the Negro.

Savage, Katherine. *The Story of World Religions*, il. with photos and maps. Walck 1967. $6.00; 12–16.

Historical development and beliefs of Judaism, Hinduism, Buddism, Confucianism, Christianity, and Islam make this a good reference book, which can also serve for recreational reading. Bibliography.

Sawyer, Ruth. *Joy to the World*, il. by Trina Schart Hyman. Little 1966. $3.95; 8–12.

One of America's most famous storytellers uses her unique gift to impart wonder and beauty to six tales of Christmas. A lovely format and warm, richly decorative illustrations are a true complement to its luminous spirit.

————. *The Long Christmas*, il. by Valenti Angelo. Viking 1941. $4.50; 9 up.

All who have been fortunate enough to hear Ruth Sawyer, in person or on a record, telling "The Voyage of the Wee Red Cap" from this book will know that they dare not miss this collection of her Christmas tales from Finland, Austria, Spain, and France. One of the best of American storytellers gives us all these and more to make the 12 days of Christmas "a lighting-up time."

Sechrist, Elizabeth. *Christmas Everywhere.* Macrae 1962. $4.25; 10–16.

The Christmas customs of 20 countries are discussed. Activities, food, and beliefs of the people make this a good resource book for teachers and students.

Sellew, Catherine F. *Adventures with Abraham's Children,* il. by Steele Savage. Little 1964. $3.95; 10 up.

This is a concise, well-written history of the Hebrew people. Children will especially like the stories of adventure and heroism.

Simon, Norma. *Hanukkah,* il. by Symeon Shimin. Crowell 1966. $2.95; 6–9.

The history of the famous battles for religious freedom waged by the Jews long ago in Judea is warmly and plainly told. Traditions surrounding the holiday are included along with its significance today. The glowing pictures complement the text.

Southall, Ivan. *The Curse of Cain,* il. by Joan Kiddell-Monroe. St. Martin 1968. $3.95; 10–12.

The book of Genesis comes alive for the young reader when Adam and Eve emerge as warm, real, sympathetic people, not just "first man" and "first woman." In spite of the length, the time from Creation to the Flood is spanned successfully without detriment to the continuity to the story. Much of the dialogue is in the vernacular of today but does not detract from the atmosphere.

The Thirteen Days of Yule, il. by Nonny Hogrogian. Crowell 1968. $3.95; 5 up.

This is an old Scottish version of the familiar English carol, "The Twelve Days of Christmas." Nonny Hogrogian brings new interest to each page through intriguing groupings, artfully arranged, and the text is fun to read.

Trent, Robbie. *The First Christmas,* il. by Marc Simont. Harper 1948. $2.50; 2–5.

Unexcelled for the very young. Simplicity of text invites conversation about the illustrations. The story ends with "Away in a Manger."

Tresselt, Alvin. *The World in the Candy Egg,* il. by Roger Duvoisin. Lothrop 1967. $3.75; 4–6.

Duvoisin's charming and sparkling collages add immensely to a secret magic world glimpsed through a big glass window in the end of a candy egg. A "child's delight" at Easter time or throughout the year.

Tudor, Tasha. *First Graces,* il. by the author. Walck 1955. $1.95; 6–12.

Some 20 prayers of thanksgiving, easily learned by young children. Special graces for special occasions are included. By the same author: *First Prayers* (two editions, Protestant and Catholic).

———. *Take Joy,* il. by the author. World 1966. $5.95; 6 up.

A collection of Christmas stories, poems, customs, and carols and their music, celebrating both the religious and the secular aspects of the holiday. Included are the particular traditions and recipes of the Tudor family. Lavishly illustrated.

Turner, Philip. *Brian Wildsmith's Illustrated Bible Stories.* Watts 1968. $7.95; 6–12.

Every page is illustrated in full color, and the stories from the two Testaments are retold in simple but lyric prose.

Uchida, Yoshiko. *The Forever Christmas Tree,* il. by Kazue Mizumura. Scribner 1963. $2.95; 5–8.

In a village in Japan, a Christmas tree brings two lonely people, a little boy and an old man, to a new awareness of each other. Quiet, understated, and most successful.

Vipont, Elfrida, comp. *Bless This Day,* il. by Harold Jones. Harcourt 1959. $4.50; 6–12.

A well-selected book of prayers for children. Each page of text is illustrated to relate to the prayers. Each prayer is signed or located in the Bible. A prayer book that avoids sentimentality and speaks to human aspirations and needs.

von Jüchen, Aurel. *The Holy Night,* tr. by Cornelia Schaeffer, il. by Celestino Piatti. Atheneum 1968. $4.95; 5–8.

A simple and graceful free retelling of the story of Jesus' birth as recorded in the Gospel of Luke. Each page opening contains the story set in large clear type surrounded by generous white space giving strength to the overall layout. Accompanied by somber yet luminous illustrations by a distinguished Swiss artist.

Voss, Carl Herman. *In Search of Meaning: Living Religions of the World,* il. by Eric Carle. World 1968. $3.95; 12 up.

Intended as the first of a series, this book gives origins, histories, and comparisons of nine religions.

Wahl, Jan. *Runaway Jonah and Other Tales,* il. by Uri Shulevitz. Macmillan 1968. $3.95; 4–8.

Wahl retells some of his favorite Old Testament stories:
Good Daniel, Captain Noah, Runaway Jonah, Singing David,
and Little Joseph. The illustrations are exciting and gay.

Wenning, Elizabeth. *The Christmas Mouse,* il. by Barbara
Remington. Holt 1959. $3.50; 5–10.

This story of a church mouse who first sang "Silent Night"
will be greatly enjoyed as a read-aloud book.

Winter, Jeanette. *The Christmas Visitors: A Norwegian Folk
Tale,* il. by the author. Pantheon 1968. $3.50; 5–9.

A picture book about greedy trolls, a poor woodsman, and a
large white bear.

Worm, Piet. *Stories from the New Testament,* il. by the author.
Sheed 1958. $3.50; 8–12.

This simple and reverent telling of the life of Christ is
enhanced by pictures and text in the style of the early
illuminated manuscript books.

Wynants, Miche. *Noah's Ark,* il. by the author. Harcourt
1965. $3.25; 5–7.

Striking collage illustrations and simple text retell the Old
Testament story forcefully.

SOCIAL STUDIES

Transportation and Communication

Anderson, William R. *First under the North Pole,* photos and drawings. World 1959. $3.50; 8–12.

The famous voyage of the *Nautilus* is recounted by the man who led the expedition. The reader catches the excitement of the project and learns about an atomic submarine.

Andrist, Ralph K., and Carter Goodrich. *The Erie Canal,* photos and reproductions. American Heritage 1964. $5.95; 11–14.

Many beautiful pastoral photographs and replicas of paintings, with excellent text, describe the purpose, the building, and the use of the Erie Canal.

Asimov, Isaac. *Words from History,* il. by William Barss. Houghton 1968. $5.95; 9 up.

This highly interesting book clearly explains the etymology of 250 words and terms that are derived from history. It may be used as a reference work but is particularly valuable as a delightful source of historical and linguistic tidbits.

————. *Words from the Myths,* il. by William Barss. Houghton 1961. $3.50 (P—NAL, $.60); 10–16.

Familiar words and expressions rooted in Greek mythology are discussed. By the same author: *Words of Science and the History Behind Them.*

Bartlett, Susan. *Books: A Book to Begin On,* il. by Ellen Raskin. Holt 1968. $2.95; 6–8.

"Once upon a time . . . parents told stories to their children.

When the children grew up, they told the same stories to their children." The beginning of bookmaking of which this is a simple but beautiful example is traced from clay tablets and papyrus rolls to modern printing presses.

Batchelor, Julie Forsyth. *Communication: From Cave Writing to Television,* il. by C. C. Batchelor. Harcourt 1953. $3.25; 9–12.

Shows the great variety of communication methods available today and traces the development of some of them. Activities are suggested for those who want to find out more about each type of communication.

Brenner, Barbara. *Barto Takes the Subway,* photos by Sy Katzoff. Knopf 1961. $3.54; 7–11.

A picture story of a Puerto Rican boy taking his first subway ride gears its pictures and descriptive details of subways to children's interests.

Epstein, Sam and Beryl. *The First Book of Printing,* il. by Laszlo Roth. Watts 1955. $2.95; 10–12.

A well-written account of printing from the long-ago invention of movable type in Korea to the huge fast moving presses of today.

————. *The Sacramento: Golden River of California,* photos, maps, and drawings. Garrard 1968. $2.59; 10–12.

The history of the Sacramento River is traced from the early Spanish explorations, through the exciting Gold Rush era, to the important role it plays in contemporary California. An excellent history. By the same authors: *The First Book of Worlds.*

Gordon, George N., and Irving A. Falk. *On the Spot Reporting.* Messner 1967. $3.95; 12 up.

The history of reporting on radio, beginning with the post-World War I years and reaching its dramatic peak during World War II. Names (Graham McNamee, H. V. Kaltenborn, Robert Trout, William L. Shirer, Eric Sevareid, and Edward R. Murrow) and events (the Hauptmann trial, the Hindenberg disaster, the Roosevelt fireside chats) fill this account of the dramatic but numbered days of radio.

Gramet, Charles. *Highways across Waterways: Ferries, Bridges and Tunnels,* photos and diagrams. Abelard 1967. $4.50; 12 up.

Each of these means of crossing water is treated historically, but the bulk of the information is about present constructions that many readers have seen or will be able to see.

Harrison, C. William. *Rivers.* Messner 1967. $3.95; 12 up.

Rivers—cradles of early civilizations; roads for explorers and conquerors; sources of food, power, and water for irrigation; arteries of transportation; carriers of disease and agents of destruction—are viewed with imagination and discussed in smooth professional style.

Helfman, Elizabeth S. *Signs and Symbols around the World.* Lothrop 1967. $4.95; 5 up.

Symbols from picture writing in prehistoric caves to an international sign language of the future are a subject that makes fascinating reading. Alphabets, numerals, signs, and symbols in religion and magic, ownership marks and trademarks, signs for science and industry, trail and road signs, and sign languages of today are organized well into a unified text.

Jackson, Robert B. *The Gasoline Buggy of the Duryea Brothers,* photos. Walck 1968. $3.25; 8–12.

An interesting and well-written account of early automotive history. The story of the Duryeas' efforts and those of other early car makers is related in enough detail to capture the interest of the young car buff. Early photographs add authenticity.

Judson, Clara Ingram. *St. Lawrence Seaway,* il. by Lorence F. Bjorklund and with photos. Follett 1959. $3.95; 10–13.

Children and adults will find this chronological narrative of man's use and development of the waterway fascinating reading. Includes a full historical background as well as the story of the modern project.

Kohn, Bernice. *Secret Codes and Ciphers,* il. by Frank Aloise. Prentice 1968. $3.95; 8–12.

Examples and differences between codes and ciphers will be fun for individuals or small groups to use in studying communication. They will have fun making simple codes and ciphers for others to crack.

McNeer, May. *The Hudson: River of History,* il. by Alfred Watson. Garrard 1962. $2.59; 10–14.

History and legend come alive in this story of the great river that flows both ways. Photographs and maps are supplemented by drawings.

Nathan, Adele Gutman. *The First Transatlantic Cable,* il. by Denver Gillen. Random 1959. $2.95; 10–13.

Communication across the Atlantic Ocean becomes reality

in this story of the men who through belief and perseverance made ocean cables possible.

Ogg, Oscar. *The 26 Letters,* 2nd ed. Crowell 1961. $6.95; 12 up.

How the alphabet evolved from cave drawings to the modern system.

Pei, Mario. *All about Language,* il. by Donat Ivanovsky. Lippincott 1954. $3.50; 12 up.

The fascinating story of the origins, growth, and use of language written for children by a noted linguist.

Popescu, Julian, and others. *Rivers of the World,* vol. I. Walck 1962. $3.00; 9 up.

This volume tells of the Ganges, the Danube, the Amazon, and the Niger, describing the effect of each river on the natives' lives. The second volume, by Geoffrey Whittam and others, deals with the Rhine, the Murray, the Nile, and the St. Lawrence, describing their courses and geographical surroundings and indicating their importance to the natives of their regions.

Rees, Ennis. *The Little Greek Alphabet Book,* il. by George Salter. Prentice 1968. $5.25; all ages.

Light verse and large, handsomely drawn letters give sound, meaning, and image to the Greek alphabet. Design and calligraphy are elegant. Many of the letters will be recognized, and youngsters will see that the modern alphabet is closely related to that of the Greeks.

Roseberry, C. R. *Steamboats and Steamboat Men,* photos. Putnam 1966. $3.49; 10 up.

A highly exciting account of the development of the Hudson River steamboats and the men responsible for their emergence. A fascinating experience with the period of the paddle wheels and floating palaces. Abundant photographs enhance this vivid account.

Ross, Frank, Jr. *Transportation of Tomorrow.* Lothrop 1968. $4.50; 11–16.

Supertrains, hydrofoils, jumbo jets, and whirlybirds are a few among many forms of transportation described in readable text and simple, clear illustrations. Detailed diagrams of interiors and engine parts will delight the buffs.

Saunders, F. Wenderoth. *Building Brooklyn Bridge.* Little 1965. $4.25; 8–12.

A graceful suspension bridge planned by an engineering artist was scientifically constructed to improve transportation for thousands living in a big metropolis. This simple and beautiful book presents an example of what art and science can do to improve the living of many people.

Spier, Peter. *The Erie Canal,* il. by the author. Doubleday 1970. $4.50; 8–12.
Facts, pictures, and songs about the Erie Canal, which opened in 1825 and closed in 1917.

The World's Past

Asimov, Isaac. *The Dark Ages,* maps. Houghton 1968. $4.50; 12 up.
A clear, simple presentation of people and events from 1000 B.C. to 1000 A.D. Dr. Asimov has made the complicated relationships between peoples and countries easily understood and presents facts in a witty and entertaining style.

———. *The Egyptians.* Houghton 1967. $4.50; 12 up.
Delightful presentation of the economic, military, and political history of Egypt from prehistoric times to the Israeli-Egyptian War of 1967 with helpful phonetic pronunciations of the difficult names. By the same author: *Greeks: A Great Adventure; Roman Empire; Races and People.*

———. *The Near East.* Houghton 1968. $4.00; 12 up.
A detailed and interesting account of major developments in the countries of the Near East. Beginning with the earliest known city-states in the area between the Tigris and Euphrates rivers, the author records the rise and fall of civilizations and countries down to the present day.

Baumann, Hans. *The Caves of the Great Hunters,* rev. ed., photos. Pantheon 1962. $3.95; 10–14.
Dramatically true stories of the finding of prehistoric cave paintings by children. Beautifully illustrated.

———. *Lion Gate and Labyrinth,* tr. by Stella Humphries, photos. Random 1967. $4.95; 14 up.
The archeological discoveries of Heinrich Schliemann and Sir Arthur Evans in the late 19th and early 20th centuries provide fascinating documentation for the Greek myths and epics. This book is for the young scholar rather than the general reader. Full-color photographs are exceptionally beautiful. By the same author: *Sons of the Steppe.*

Black, Irma Simonton. *Castle, Abbey and Town*, il. by W. T. Mars. Holiday 1963. $3.50; 10–14.

Alternate chapters of exposition and narration show three ways of life. In black-and-white drawings and colorful end papers picturing knights and ladies, monks and minstrels, serfs and townsmen, the Middle Ages come alive.

Bleeker, Sonia. *The Aztec Indians of Mexico*, il. by Kisa J. Sasaki. Morrow 1963. $3.50; 9 up.

A remarkably complete description of a bloodthirsty people. Though written for nine-year-olds, this examination of the Aztecs and their modern vestigial culture has general appeal. The examples of war, childhood frustration, and class and caste are calculated to sober adult readers. By the same author: *The Incas of the Andes; The Inca; The Maya: Indians of Central America; Ashanti of Ghana; Sioux Indians.*

Bond, Susan McDonald. *Eric, the Tale of a Red-Tempered Viking*, il. by Sally Trinkle. Grove 1968. $3.95; 4–8.

Here is an entertaining and simplified though fairly accurate account of how Eric the Red came to establish the first colony in Greenland. The emphasis is on Eric's temper; it matches his red hair. The humorous illustrations add greatly to the book's appeal.

Brooks, Polly S., and Nancy Z. Walworth. *The World of Walls: The Middle Ages in Western Europe*, drawings, photos, and maps. Lippincott 1966. $6.95; 12 up.

A fascinating book presenting the period through sketches of some of the people who helped shape it.

CBS News Staff. *Trial at Nuremberg*, ed. by William E. Shapiro. Watts 1968. $2.95; 12 up.

The Nuremberg Trials were proceedings without precedent in this century. This book recreates the high drama of the atrocities committed under Adolf Hitler and the decisions reached at these trials. From the Twentieth Century Books series based on the CBS television series.

Chubb, Mary. *An Alphabet of Ancient Egypt*, il. by Jill Wyatt. Watts 1968. $3.95; 8 up.

The Alphabet Books are a new series that describe how men, women, and children worked and played thousands of years ago. The alphabet is used as an outline for exploring the story of each land. Each letter covers a different aspect of the subject—archeologists, boats, cartouches, and so on. The book carefully balances a lightly humorous text with many handsome full-color pictures that capture the style and flavor of the originals. By the same author: *An Alphabet of Ancient Greece.*

Chubb, Thomas Caldecot. *The Byzantines.* World 1959. $4.50; 12–16.

The way of life in the Byzantine Empire more than 760 years ago is revived in a way that will help breathe life into an unknown yesterday. The graphics are stylistically effective.

———. *The Venetians: Merchant Princes.* Viking 1968. $6.95; 12 up.

A very fine look at the power and princes of old Venice. Drawings and illustrations, contemporary to the age, add color and an authentic feeling. This history reads like an exciting novel.

Coolidge, Olivia. *Roman People.* Houghton 1959. $3.75; 10–16.

The author tells it like it was. This should be a basic reading experience for those who want their historical setting straight, without the distortions of the mass communications media.

Cottrell, Leonard. *Digs and Diggers,* photos, drawings, and maps. World 1964. $5.95; 12 up.

This history of the development of methods used by archeologists moves from the well-known Egyptian expeditions to ones in Russia, China, and the Western Hemisphere. By the same author: *Crete: Island of Mystery; Great Leaders of Greece and Rome.*

Daugherty, James. *The Magna Charta,* il. by the author. Random 1956. $2.95; 11–14.

Deals with the historic signing of the Magna Charta and its influence on later documents of freedom and justice. Important concepts are presented in well-written text and artistic illustration.

Denny, Norman, and Josephine Filmer-Sankey. *The Bayeux Tapestry: The Story of the Norman Conquest: 1066.* Atheneum 1966. $7.95; 10–14.

This volume correlates a colorful contemporary work of art with the historical events it portrays, the Battle of Hastings. Details and customs of warfare and transportation are shown and explained by authors who studied and produced colored illustrations of the tapestry. A more nearly complete history of the Norman conquest and its far-flung results in Europe and America, making it an excellent companion volume, is *1066,* by Franklin Hamilton (Dial, 1964). A biography, *William the Conqueror* by Elizabeth Luckock (Putnam, 1966), includes black-and-white illustrations from the "tapestry," really an embroidery.

Dupuy, Trevor N. *The Battle of Austerlitz,* maps, portraits, and drawings. Macmillan 1968. $4.50; 10–14.

After describing the battle setting, the writer gives a brief flashback to Bonaparte's early life. A succinct picture of Napoleon's perfect planning and execution indicates a beginning of the end of the monarchical system in Europe and the beginning of dictatorships. Chronology and index.

Duvoisin, Roger. *They Put Out to Sea,* il. by the author. Knopf 1943. $3.94; 9–12.

Blazing color pictures and vigorous black-and-white sketches bring out the drama of maps and mapmakers. The Greek traders, Marco Polo, Vasco da Gama, and Magellan take their places in this readable expansion of standard geography. Endpaper maps and a bibliography make a substantial contribution.

Edmonds, I. G. *The Khmers of Cambodia: The Story of a Mysterious People,* photos. Bobbs 1970 $5.00; 12 up.

The story of Cambodia and its principal people, the Khmers, from their legendary beginnings until March 19th, 1970, when Prince Sihanouk was deposed as head of state by a military junta. The early history provides the background needed to understand Cambodia's present situation. The last part is a lucid exposition of the effects of big power politics on a small, underdeveloped nation.

Foster, Genevieve. *The World of Columbus and Sons,* il. by the author. Scribner 1965. $5.95; 11–14.

The reader is introduced to the panorama of the world in the time of Columbus as well as to his voyages and discoveries. By the same author: *The World of Captain John Smith.*

Glubok, Shirley. *Discovering Tut-ankh-Amen's Tomb.* Macmillan 1968. $6.95; 10–14.

A step-by-step account of the careful archeological work that went into the discovery of the treasures; a simplified but absorbing retelling of the great *The Tomb of Tut-ankh-Amen,* by Howard Carter and A. C. Mace.

Halliday, E. M. *Russia in Revolution.* Harper 1967. $5.95; 10–15.

The personalities involved and the events of the February Revolution of 1917 come alive in this short, simply written history lavishly illustrated with color and black-and-white reproductions.

Hampden, John, ed. *New Worlds Ahead,* il. by C. Walter Hodges. Farrar 1968. $3.75; 12–16.

Fourteen firsthand accounts of English explorers from Cabot

in 1509 to Bradford in 1620. The style of the originals is maintained, and the book includes footnotes to explain nautical terms and apparent and real discrepancies. Complete index and summary-foreword.

Herold, J. Christopher. *The Battle of Waterloo.* American Heritage 1967. $5.95; 12 up.

An exciting literary experience for the young historian; superbly illustrated, dramatic account of the great battle that ended Napoleon's frantic bid for power. This is the 23rd volume in the Horizon Caravel series of illustrated histories for young readers.

Hodges, C. Walter. *The Norman Conquest,* il. by the author. Coward 1966. $3.69; 9–12.

A noted English historian and illustrator pictures the life of the folk and the Anglo-Saxon lords. Picture book appearance and meaty text combine to interest and satisfy children of varied abilities. The rivalry of Edward and William for succession to the throne and the bloody Battle of Hastings are included. *Magna Carta,* in similar format, is the sequel, a terse picture of feudal life and death in England.

Honour, Alan. *Treasures under the Sand: Woolley's Finds at Ur.* McGraw 1967. $3.95; 12 up.

Wooley's famous find of the city of Ur, once considered legendary, confirmed his early beliefs that the Old Testament was a valid document and that the cradle of civilization was in the Fertile Crescent, not Ancient Egypt. Contains an account of the pre-World War I cooperation between Woolley and the famed Lawrence of Arabia. The reader will gain new insights to the relationships among Bible accounts, ancient myths, and archeology.

Lambie, Beatrice. *The Mackenzie,* maps by Fred Kliem and photos. Garrard 1967. $2.59; 9–12.

An exciting, simple text by a Canadian author concerns early exploration, fur trade, plant and animal life, and modern industry and activities. Well-chosen photographs.

Leacroft, Helen and Richard. *The Buildings of Ancient Greece.* Scott 1966. $3.95; 12 up.

A superb adventure for the young reader interested in architectural heritage. Both text and illustrations allow a highly visual interpretation of the architecture of Greece. An excellent book recommended for selective use with better readers.

Leckie, Robert. *The Story of World War I,* illus. Random 1965. $4.95; 12 up.

An adaptation of the *American Heritage History of World War I.* Photographs, paintings, sketches, maps, and prints combine with a vivid text to bring alive a realistic and stirring account of this first great war of the modern era.

McKown, Robin. *The Story of the Incas,* photos. Putnam 1966. $3.29; 12 up.

A panoramic view of the Inca empire, the mightiest in early South America. Well-selected photographs supplement a readable text, which draws upon the findings of research and archeological expeditions. An index, glossary, and bibliography allow use as a basic reference.

McNeer, May. *The Canadian Story,* il. by Lynd Ward. Farrar 1958. $4.59; 10 up.

A distinctive book in text and illustration portrays the events and people of Canadian history. By the same author: *The Mexican Story.*

Mazar, Amihay, and Alexandra Trone. *Voices from the Past,* il. by Milka Cizik. Hastings 1968. $5.00; 11 up.

Palestine, the land of the Bible, is traced historically through scientific archeological explorations up to the latest investigation of the Dead Sea Scrolls and the excavation of the fortress of Masada. The extreme but accurate detail in text and pictures will narrow appeal to only the committed young historian.

Newman, Robert. *The Japanese: People of the Three Treasures,* il. by Mamoru Funai. Atheneum 1964. $4.25; 10 up.

This artistic book, written with respect and care, shows insight into effects of form of government upon individual personality. The drama comes through in the excellent handling of a vast amount of detail in legend and history.

Nowlan, Nora. *The Tiber: The Roman River,* photos. Garrard 1967. $2.59; 10–12.

The history, geography, and legends of the Tiber River region. The large print, many photographs, and direct style make this an appealing book of ancient and modern Italy.

Pearlman, Moshe. *The Zealots of Masada: Story of a Dig,* photos. Scribner 1967. $5.95; 12 up.

An excellent account of the archeological expedition to excavate and restore Masada and to discover and prove historical facts. The author relates the stories that were the basis for the expedition. More than 50 excellent photographs.

Pine, Tillie S., and Joseph Levine. *The Eskimos Knew,* il. by Ezra Jack Keats. McGraw 1962. $3.95; 7–9.

Science has helped the Eskimos to solve problems of everyday living; in the very same way, it helps us today.

———, *The Incas Knew,* il. by Ann Grifalconi. McGraw 1968. $3.95; 5–9.

An account of the scientific achievements of the ancient Incas, the book cites interesting parallels between Inca science and that of today's world and suggests to the young reader simple experiments he can perform to understand the principles described. By the same authors: *The Chinese Knew; The Egyptians Knew; The Africans Knew; The Indians Knew.*

Priestley, H. E. *Britain under the Romans.* Warne 1967. $5.95; 11–15.

A detailed account of the Roman occupation of Britain from the invasions of Julius Caesar in 55 and 54 B.C. until the withdrawal of the legions early in the fifth century A.D. Much of the description is based on recent archeological discoveries.

Sears, Stephen W. *Desert War in North Africa,* illus. Harper 1967. $5.95; 12 up.

This lively text is well supplemented with drawings, sketches, and photographs to allow the young historian to retrace one of World War II's most dramatic and decisive campaigns. Recommended for better readers with a keen interest in this era of history. From the Horizon Caravel series of illustrated histories.

Snellgrove, L. E. *Franco and the Spanish Civil War,* photos and maps. McGraw 1965. $4.50; 12 up.

"To some Franco was a hero saving Spain from Communism. To some he was a Fascist dictator enslaving his own people." The tragedy of a civil war and the political ideologies it represents are put into perspective by the teacher-author in his frank account of this struggle.

Uden, Grant. *A Dictionary of Chivalry,* il. by Pauline Baynes. Crowell 1968. $10.00; 10 up.

Clear margin sketches, some in color, on a third of each page. The 12th to the 19th centuries are covered in cross-referenced, alphabetized articles of varying length with information about persons, places, battles, and terms of knighthood. A subject index includes 14 broad topics.

Vlahos, Olivia. *African Beginnings,* il. by George Ford. Viking 1967. $6.95; 12 up.

Dedicated to illuminating the past of the Dark Continent, the author has focused on traditional and often prehistoric ties. Good illustrations.

White, Anne Terry. *Lost Worlds,* il. with reprints. Random 1941. $3.95; 12 up.

This is a classic in the field of archeology for young people. The author writes with an absorbing style about the discovery of lost civilizations. By the same author: *All about Archaeology; Prehistoric America; The First Men in the World.*

America's Heritage

Alderman, Clifford Lindsey. *The Devil's Shadow: The Story of Witchcraft in Massachusetts,* il. by Barry Martin. Messner 1967. $3.95 (P—WSP, $.60); 12–16.

Absorbing account of the Salem witchcraft trials of 1692 characterizes in some detail the chief figures, both accusers and victims, and tells what is known about the later lives of the accusers, victims, and judges. By the same author: *The Story of the Thirteen Colonies.*

Andrist, Ralph K. *To the Pacific with Lewis and Clark.* American Heritage 1967. $5.95; 12–16.

An account of the Lewis and Clark expedition of 1804–1806, based largely upon the diaries of the two captains, which tells of the wonders of the unexplored West that the party encountered and shows Lewis and Clark as effective leaders and Sacajawea's vital role as guide.

Arnold, Oren. *The Story of Cattle Ranching,* il. by John M. Floherty, Jr. Harvey 1968. $4.50; 10–14.

A study of western geography, history, folksongs, legends, occupations, and conservation made interesting by relating the history of cattle ranching and cowboys in America up to the scientific development of animal husbandry. The airplane, the computer, the radio, and the "cowtel" are as important as the range and the rodeo. By the same author: *Hidden Treasure in the Wild West.*

Ayars, James Sterling. *The Illinois River,* il. by Lili Rethi. Holt 1968. $4.95; 9–13.

A river and its tributaries cross the state from Chicago on the northeast to Grafton on the southwest. They were a central path for trade when explorers and merchants traveled by water. French, English, Indians, Black Hawk, Abe Lincoln, and preacher Peter Cartwright are among the travelers mentioned.

Baity, Elizabeth. *Americans before Columbus,* photos. Viking 1951. $4.13; 10–14.

Thirty-two pages of photographs precede the text. The author gives a clear account of the settlement of the American continents by wandering hunters from Asia and the development of cultures such as those of the Mayans and the Aztecs. By the same author: *Americans before Man.*

Bauer, Helen. *California Indian Days,* il. by Don Freeman and photos. Doubleday 1963. $3.95; 8–14.

The many excellent photographs, the line drawings, and the simple, well-written text make for a broader appeal than the title indicates.

Berke, Ernest. *The North American Indians,* il. by the author. Doubleday 1963. $4.50; 8 up.

Realistic color paintings and black-and-white sketches complement the text. The life and customs of Indians in various regions of North America are presented in adequate detail.

Blaustein, Albert P., and Robert L. Zangrando, eds. *Civil Rights and the Black American,* il. by the eds. WSP 1970. $1.45; 12–16.

Statutes and legal documents are excerpted, demonstrating the rights of people. Specific references to blacks and firsthand reports of abused civil rights are included; legal interpretation is provided. Good source for black studies course.

Bliven, Bruce, Jr. *The American Revolution,* il. by Albert Orbaan and photos. Random 1958. $1.95; 10–15.

A dramatic account of all phases of the American Revolution including causes, battles, and personages. By the same author: *The Story of D-Day.*

Boorstin, Daniel J. *The Landmark History of the American People from Plymouth to Appomattox.* Random 1965. $3.95; 11–15.

This history of the nation through the Civil War gives clear explanations of the reasons for some of the major developments of the years covered.

Buell, Robert Kingery, and Charlotte N. Skladal. *Sea Otters and the China Trade.* McKay 1968. $4.50; 12 up.

An important bit of American history between 1741 and 1841 during which the West Coast sea otter played a major role in developing that region as well as trade with China. An adventurous account of how many nations greedily tried to corner this valuable fur market, almost causing extinction of the animal.

Buff, Mary and Conrad. *The Colorado: River of Mystery*, il. by the authors. Ritchie 1968. $4.95; 10–14.

An absorbing and detailed account of the history of the Colorado River. Especially exciting is the story of the Powell expedition of 1869 and the first successful navigation of the river. Scenes along the river are vividly illustrated.

Burt, Olive W. *Negroes in the Early West*, il. by Lorence F. Bjorklund. Messner 1969. $3.64; 9–12.

The author tells something of the lives of 17 little-known Negro men and women who contributed to the history of the early Far West. The treatment is straightforward and unsentimental.

Cavanah, Frances. *Our Country's Story*, il. by Janice Holland. Rand 1958. $2.95; 7–9.

A first book for young school children highlights important happenings and famous persons in the story of the country's history. Colorful and attractive illustrations. By the same author: *We Came to America.*

Clagett, John. *These Hallowed Grounds.* Hawthorn 1968. $4.95; 10–14.

Descriptions of some of the great battlefields of American wars are especially interesting because they include brief accounts of the battles fought on each and give the reader information on how best to visit the present-day parks and monuments.

Clifton, Lucille. *The Black BC's*, il. by Don Miller. Dutton 1970. $3.95; 10–14.

Poetry and prose are combined to provide easy-to-read descriptions and interesting information about black history. The organization of topics according to the letters of the alphabet allows a smooth transition from one story to another.

Commager, Henry Steele. *The Great Declaration*, il. by Donald Bolognese and paintings and woodcuts. Bobbs 1958. $3.75; 11–13.

Using the words of men who envisioned a design for freedom and weaving the events of the time into a dramatic narrative, a distinguished historian tells the story of the Declaration of Independence. By the same author: *First Book of American History.*

Coy, Harold. *The First Book of the Supreme Court*, il. by Helen Borten. Watts 1958. $2.95; 10–15.

Appreciation and understanding of our highest court can be

gained from this presentation of its history, judges, and cases. Excellent reference sections. By the same author: *The Americans.*

Cuneo, John R. *The Battles of Saratoga.* Macmillan 1967. $3.50; 10–14.

Detailed but engaging account of the battles that led to the surrender of Burgoyne in the fall of 1777. Included are interesting characterizations of such generals as Arnold, Gates, and Burgoyne. Most of the books in Macmillan's Battle series are well above average.

Dalgliesh, Alice. *America Begins: The Story of the Finding of the New World,* il. by Lois Maloy. Scribner 1958. $3.12; 8–10.

An excellent beginning history of exploration of the New World.

Davis, Burke. *Appomattox: Closing Struggle of the Civil War,* photos and drawings. Harper 1963. $3.95; 10 up.

This is an accurate, gripping, well-organized presentation of the closing days of the Civil War. Prime source material such as diary quotes and contemporary sketches are particularly effective.

Downer, Marion. *Roofs over America.* Lothrop 1967. $3.95; 10–16.

This brief survey of the change in "protection for an interior" from the Cape Cod cottage to the modern A-frame roof is a browsing book.

Fisher, Leonard Everett. *The Doctors,* il. by the author. Watts 1968. $2.95; 8–14.

One of more than a dozen books in the author's Colonial Americans series. There isn't a bad book in the lot—not even a mediocre one. Each volume brings the reader enough appropriate and interesting information so that he can build adequate generalizations of the occupations discussed. One comes away from this book, as from others in the series, with a new respect for this country's ancestors. The black-and-white illustrations, which appear on every other page, are extremely effective in reinforcing and supplementing the text.

———. *The Shoemakers.* Watts 1967. $2.95; 9–11.

One of an attractive and distinguished series useful in middle and junior high years. Trades were carried on privately, but children in large families were often apprenticed to shoemakers in order to learn enough to make more comfortable shoes for the family. Lynn, Massachusetts,

became a shoemaking center, but even soldiers went barefoot in colonial days for lack of footware. The illustrations
and specific trade vocabulary make these supplementary
books attractive. In the same series: *The Schoolmasters; The
Cabinetmakers; The Glassmakers; The Printers;* and others.

Floethe, Louise Lee and Richard. *Sea of Grass,* il. by Richard
Floethe. Scribner 1963. $3.44; 8–12.

Snowy egrets, ospreys, and alligators, water hyacinths and
strangler fig trees are some of the things Billy Panther sees as
he poles his dugout canoe through the Everglades. Beautiful
watercolor illustrations and selective text reveal the beauty
of a little-known area and something of the way of life of the
Seminoles. By the same authors: *Story of Lumber; Fisherman and His Boat; Islands of Hawaii.*

Foster, Genevieve. *Abraham Lincoln's World,* il. by the author.
Scribner 1944. $5.95; 10 up.

Once more Mrs. Foster creates a whole world around a man.
The Charge of the Light Brigade, the Black Hole of Calcutta,
Beethoven, Tecumseh, and Old Ironsides all take their
places around the President until the April day when he
tells his last joke and the carriage rolls away to Ford's
Theatre. "Only then could the people of Abraham Lincoln's
world realize how great he was."

――――. *George Washington's World,* il. by the author. Scribner
1941. $5.95; 10 up.

The world during George Washington's time brought into
focus through selected persons of influence then.

――――. *The World of Captain John Smith, 1580–1631,* il. by
the author. Scribner 1959. $6.95; 12 up.

The book is, said Mrs. Foster, a "slice of history measured by
the lifetime of Captain John Smith, a small courageous
Englishman . . . whose heart had been forever set on adventure." The writer-artist's "horizontal history" method jus-
tifies itself in the first two-page spread, showing "the people
who were living when John Smith was a small boy"—a
shaggy Ivan the Terrible, baby Virginia Dare, and a fierce-
eyed Philip II. Here—as always—Mrs. Foster can help convince young people that "history is people."

Fuller, John. *Our Navy Explores Antarctica,* illus. Abelard
1966. $4.00; 10–14.

An expert on arctic exploration traces its history from 1839
to the present. Pictures are so effective that slow readers
interested in the subject can get a great deal of meaning with
a minimum of reading; expert readers will appreciate the
straight forward, economically worded text and pictures.

Gemming, Elizabeth. *Huckleberry Hill,* il. by the author. Crowell 1968. $4.95; 9 up.

Describes in detail child life in rural New England of the mid-19th century. Season by season, the author chronicles a fascinating and vanished era. The quilting party, maple-sugaring time, muster day, barn-raisings, magniloquent speeches on the Fourth, and frigid schoolhouses are some of the experiences depicted. The book is lavishly illustrated with reproductions of all manner of paintings and drawings as well as with pictures of craft works and everyday objects.

Goodman, Walter. *Black Bondage: The Life of Slaves in the South,* photos. Farrar 1969. $3.75; 10 up.

This book conveys a sense of what it was to be a slave in the American South of before the Civil War. Systematically organized around major topics such as work, play, and family life, the report is concise and comprehensive. It is strengthened by many excerpts from primary sources. The author allows the stark facts to speak for themselves without exaggeration.

Green, Diana Huss. *The Lonely War of William Pinto.* Little 1968. $4.75; 12 up.

An unusual view of the American Revolution is presented in this story of a Jewish family, recreated from records in synagogue archives of New Haven, Connecticut. Fourteen-year-old Will is rejected as a Loyalist by his family and as both a Loyalist and a Jew by his Yale classmates. Today's youth will identify with his struggle to decide whether or not to join the American forces.

Groh, Lynn. *The Pilgrims: Brave Settlers of Plymouth,* il. by Frank Vaughn. Garrard 1968. $2.39; 10 up.

A combination of factual material from Bradford's journal *Of Plimoth Plantation* with a highly appealing literary style allows the Pilgrims to come to life as real people. This account of the Pilgrims and their struggle for survival in a vast wilderness allows young people to see the past through the eyes of the people who lived it. Old prints, engravings, and sketches enhance the text.

Heiderstadt, Dorothy. *Stolen by the Indians,* il. by Carl Kidwell. McKay 1968. $3.50; 9–12.

Twelve true stories about young people who were captured by Indians, how each made out during captivity, and how each survived to tell the tale.

Hiller, Carl E. *From Tepees to Towers,* photos. Little 1967. $4.50; 5 up.

Photographs and a brief text give a chronological view of American architecture.

Hirschfeld, Burt. *A Cloud over Hiroshima.* Messner 1967. $3.95; 12 up.

A suspenseful account of the development and use at Hiroshima of the world's first atomic bomb. This author also examines some of the sensitive problems raised by the development and use of atomic weapons.

Hofsinde, Robert. *The Indian and His Horse,* il. by the author. Morrow 1960. $3.50; 8–12.

The importance of the horse in the life of the North American Indian is told in this interesting little book.

———. *Indian Costumes,* il. by the author. Morrow 1968. $2.95; 8–12.

This latest work by an outstanding authority on Indian culture is a practical guide to the distinctive dress style of ten representative tribes. By the same author: *Indian Sign Language; Indian Picture Writing; The Indian's Secret World.*

Hopkins, Lee Bennet. *Important Dates in Afro-American History,* photos. Watts 1969. $4.95; 10–14.

Adopting the format of "on this date in March of 1891 so-and-so happened," this book is full of interest. Often the statements are extensive enough to give readers more than bare bones of fact. Frequently there is just enough to spur the reader on to further research. Valuable for readers of all ages.

Ingraham, Leonard W. *Slavery in the United States,* il. with drawings and photos. Watts 1968. $2.95; 11 up.

This interesting and concise history opens with an account of the importation of the first blacks. There were 20 of them and, even though they were sold, they were indentured servants and earned their freedom in five to seven years. The economy soon put an end to such a wasteful system. Human beings were needed to work a lifetime, and their children were also needed to work a lifetime. In 1640, blacks ceased being servants by law and became slaves. The author tells the story well, if bluntly. If he errs at all, it is to put the Yankees a bit too much on the side of the angels during the Civil War. The illustrations have been carefully selected and do much to illuminate the text.

Irving, Washington. *A Tour on the Prairies.* Pantheon 1967. $4.95; 12 up.

This book is characterized by the beautiful style found in *Rip Van Winkle, The Sketch Book,* and *Tales of a Traveler.* Washington Irving describes his adventurous trip into the little-known Indian Territory with all proper appreciation due this area then unspoiled by the white man. Recommended only for better readers.

Jackson, Shirley. *The Witchcraft of Salem Village,* il. by Lili Rothi. Random 1956. $2.95; 9–12.

The witchcraft trials of the 1690's are viewed without an attempt to play on the emotions. This well-written book has a good introductory background.

Johnson, Gerald W. *America Grows Up,* il. by Leonard Everett Fisher. Morrow 1960. $4.95; 10–14.

The country's heritage from the Continental Congress to Woodrow Wilson is described in this second volume of a trilogy of United States history for children and youth. Events, accomplishments, and tragedies are recounted in fresh, vital language. Others in the series: *America Is Born; America Moves Forward.*

_____. *Communism: An American's View,* il. by Leonard Everett Fisher. Morrow 1964. $4.25; 12–14.

An analysis of the origin, evolution, and meaning of communism and its history from Karl Marx to Krushchev. Well and simply written, without dramatics, it presents a clear statement of the American citizen's role in the preservation of freedom.

_____. *The Congress.* Morrow 1963. $3.75; 10–14.

A happy combination of literary quality and informational detail results in an outstanding presentation of this branch of government. By the same author: *The Presidency; The Supreme Court.*

Lawson, Robert. *They Were Strong and Good,* il. by the author. Viking 1940. $3.50; 8 up.

More than a picture book, this Caldecott Medal winner tells "the story of the parents and grandparents of most of us who call ourselves American." Lawson's straighforward, irrepressibly humorous and sometimes touching stories and his vigorous pictures of our ancestors should, as the artist hoped, make us "proud of the country that they helped to build."

Lester, Julius. *To Be a Slave,* il. by Tom Feelings. Dial 1968. $3.95 (P—Dell, $.75); 12 up.

A historical sequence of statements, many taken from ex-slaves during the 1930's by the Federal Writers' Project, forms a documentary showing how house servants, accepting their slave owners' point of view, sabotaged the attempts of field workers to escape slavery.

Lincoln, Abraham. *The Gettysburg Address and the Second Inaugural,* il. by Leonard Everett Fisher. Watts 1963. $2.95; 11 up.

Exceptionally beautiful woodcuts illustrate pertinent phrases of two major speeches of the Great Emancipator. The introduction by Carl Sandburg adds to a book appropriate for the basic classroom library.

McCague, James. *Flatboat Days on Frontier Rivers,* il. by Victor Mays. Garrard 1968. $2.69; 9–11.

River transportation by flatboats was vital in the late 1700's and early 1800's. The Mississippi and Ohio rivers were busy with these craft hauling cargo. This exciting historical era is relived in excellent style and illustration. By the same author: *Mississippi Steamboat Days; When Clipper Ships Ruled the Seas.*

McCall, Edith. *Forts in the Wilderness,* il. by Darrell Wiskur. Children 1968. $3.00; 10–14.

This interesting account of the importance of forts in frontier America gives particular attention to the courage involved in building such forts as Kaskaskia and later tells of the heroism of George Rogers Clark in capturing several English forts for his new nation.

McNeer, May. *The American Indian Story,* il. by Lynd Ward. Farrar 1963. $4.95; 10 up.

This is raw stuff for young readers, well calculated to compete with and counteract the inaccurate stereotypes of television. It is a work of art in every way, running the full gamut of tragedy, perfidy, murder, honor, and glory. The 19th-century American attempt at genocide is superbly and honestly presented.

Mandell, Muriel. *The 51 Capitals of the U. S. A.,* photos. Sterling 1965. $3.95; 10 up.

Fascinating photographs and an interesting text combine to give a view of America through its capital cities. Little known events and facts plus the unusual reasons behind the selection of each state capital makes this book appealing to all readers of Americana.

Marcus, Rebecca B. *The First Book of the Cliff Dwellers,* il. by Julio Granda. Watts 1968. $2.95; 9 up.

An excellent collection of interesting black-and-white photographs, drawings, and maps supplement this story about the cliff dwellers of southwestern Colorado. The fascination of these ruins is sure to intrigue most young readers.

Meltzer, Milton. *Bread and Roses.* Knopf 1967. $3.95; 12 up.

The factory, mine, and sweatshop were major sources of employment following the Civil War, and this book traces the struggle of American labor from the beginning of this era to World War I.

_____, ed. *In Their Own Words: A History of the American Negro, 1619–1865.* Crowell 1964. $4.95 (P—Apollo, $1.65); 11 up.

This collection from letters, newspapers, journals, and books showing some of the feelings and thoughts of the Negro people before the Civil War can be considered a valuable recounting of this phase of American history. The other two books in the trilogy cover the years 1865–1916 and 1916–1966.

Miers, Earl Schenk. *Yankee Doodle Dandy,* il. by Anthony D'Adamo. Rand 1963. $3.95; 10 up.

A major writer on the Civil War, turning to the Revolutionary War, makes telling use of basic documents. He develops suspense that holds the reader.

Neal, Harry Edward. *The Protectors: The Story of the Food and Drug Administration,* photos. Messner 1968. $3.95; 10–12.

From its inception in 1931 to the present, this organization has attempted to guard the American public against health hazards ranging from dangerous drugs to adulterated foods. A general overview of several current problems, the book is written in a concise style and objective manner by the former Assistant Chief of the U. S. Secret Service.

Palmer, Bruce. *Chancellorsville,* maps and photos. Macmillan 1967. $3.50; 11 up.

A factual account of the important 1863 battle in northern Virginia involves the reader in a gripping tale of Union General Hooker's "perfect" plans and how General Lee managed a victory against them.

_____. *First Bull Run.* Macmillan 1965. $2.95; 12 up.

An objective, exciting, and well-illustrated account of the first of many battles that ripped the United States during the Civil War. Glimpses into the thinking and military strategy of leaders on both sides of this historical struggle allow the reader close identification.

Phelan, Mary Kay. *Four Days in Philadelphia: 1776,* il. by Charles Walker. Crowell 1967. $4.50; 12 up.

Four days in Philadelphia during the hot summer of 1776 changed the whole future of 13 young colonies. This most important period is vividly traced in a captivating style that gives history a breath of life.

Pratt, Fletcher. *The Civil War,* il. by Lee Ames. Doubleday 1955. $3.95; 9–12.

A short but accurate presentation of the Civil War, its battles, and its leaders. The illustrations are striking. By the same author: *The Monitor and the Merrimac.*

Rounds, Glen. *The Prairie Schooners,* il. by the author. Holiday 1968. $3.75; 10–14.

A fascinating trip, experienced in every detail, from the start to the end of the 2,000-mile Oregon Trail. The established author-illustrator pursues this adventure with his usual talent for details that will catch the attention of readers.

————. *The Treeless Plains,* il. by the author. Holiday 1967. $3.75; 10–14.

Spot drawings add interest to the text, allowing readers to picture life and housing on the middle border of American frontier life in Kansas, Nebraska, and the Dakotas. The child who reads a Laura Ingalls Wilder book will appreciate it more for this introduction.

Russel, Solveig Paulson. *Peanuts, Popcorn, Ice Cream, Candy and Soda Pop: And How They Began,* il. by Ralph J. McDonald. Abingdon 1970. $3.50; 9–11.

Many fascinating tidbits concerning the history and present status of some popular snacks are given. The author is explicit in distinguishing fact from hearsay but unfortunately uses no documentation for either fact or legend.

Sanderlin, George. *Seventeen Seventy-six: Journals of American Independence.* Harper 1968. $5.95; 12 up.

History of the American Revolution as reflected in printed speeches, letters, and other documents of the time.

Schraff, A. E. *Black Courage,* il. by Len Ebert. Macrae 1970. $3.75; 8–12.

Profiles of 21 ordinary people who lived in the early days of the American West—some while that land still belonged to Spain or Mexico. All were black; a few were slaves, but most were free. Some were little more than children. Most were grown men. They all had one characteristic in common—courage.

Silverberg, Robert. *Ghost Towns of the American West,* il. by Lorence Bjorklund. Crowell 1968. $4.50; 12 up.

A fascinating account of the rise and decline of the mining

towns that grew out of America's rush for gold in the middle 19th century. Well researched, the stories make the days of Virginia City, Sutter's Mill, and Denver come to life for the older reader.

Sloane, Eric. *The Sound of Bells,* il. by the author. Doubleday 1966. $2.95; 10–14.

Early Americans celebrated Independence Day with bell ringing, and Mr. Sloane worked with President Kennedy to revive the custom. His text and sketches show the use of bells in many ways: bells on locomotives, on farms—to announce dinner, locate animals, scare crows—and other places. Peace and war have utilized their musical sounds. By the same author-artist: *ABC of Americana; Diary of an American Boy.*

Smith, E. Brooks, and Robert Meredith, eds. *The Coming of the Pilgrims,* il. by Leonard Everett Fisher. Little 1964. $3.50; 10 up.

Original source material from a participant's diary as Governor Bradford records a major historical event. Had his actual words been more clearly identified, the impact of "you were there" would have been even greater. Pictures in bold outline, many vividly colored, are singularly appropriate. By the same editors: *Pilgrim Courage.*

Smith, Howard K. *Washington, D. C.: The Story of Our Nation's Capital,* photos. Random 1967. $3.95; 12 up.

Lively, well-chosen pictures and text trace the history of our nation's capital from an unpromising stretch of farmland in 1791 to the present leading capital of the Western world. This distinguished author presents a vivid history of the city, which is the second home town of every American.

Stearns, Monroe. *The Story of New England,* illus. Random 1967. $3.95; 10–14.

A view of this historic section of the United States with fascinating old prints and paintings as well as maps.

Sterling, Dorothy. *Forever Free: The Story of the Emancipation Proclamation,* il. by Ernest Crichlow. Doubleday 1963. $3.95; 10 up.

Traces efforts of both blacks and whites to end slavery from Colonial times until the Emancipation Proclamation. The dramatic style and accurate background will create better understandings of current integration problems.

Talmadge, Marian, and Iris Gilmore. *Six Great Horse Rides,* il. by Tran Mawicke. Putnam 1968. $3.29; 9–14.

Although most American children are familiar with Paul

Revere's midnight ride, not many have heard of six other courageous patriots whose daring rides saved their countrymen from impending disaster.

Trease, Geoffrey. *This Is Your Century*, photos. Harcourt 1966. $6.95; 9–12.

An exciting history of the 20th century with many well-chosen photographs.

Tunis, Edwin. *Colonial Living*, il. by the author. World 1957. $4.95; 10–16.

All the artifacts and customs of American colonial life are described in detailed and authentic text and pictures. This distinguished book contains a .wealth of information for resource study.

_____. *Indians.* World 1959. $6.95; 9–12.

This book describes the Indians of the entire United States in main groups instead of tribes, depicting their life as it was before they were disturbed and influenced by the Europeans. Exhaustive descriptions of all other phases of Indian life, activities, dress, crafts, weapons, hunting, and farming. By the same author: *Frontier Living; Shaw's Fortune.*

_____. *The Young United States: 1783–1830,* il. by the author. World 1969. $6.95; 10 up.

In great detail, represented in both the text and the illustrations, this social history will give its readers a feel for the period.

Viereck, Phillip. *The New Land,* il. by Ellen Viereck. Day 1967. $12.95; 10 up.

"Discovery, exploration, and early settlement of northeastern United States, from the earliest voyages to 1621, retold in the words of the explorers themselves." Reproductions of original maps are included.

Waltrip, Lila and Rufus. *Cowboys and Cattlemen.* McKay 1967. $3.95; 12 up.

Here are 13 biographical sketches of western cowboys ranging from little known people, such as William Wesley Van Ordset, the cowboy sky-pilot, to such well known figures as Will Rogers. Each account is interesting and often reveals startling bits of information. Together the sketches offer a composite portrait of the Western cowboy as being persevering, self-reliant, law-abiding, optimistic, and rough and ready.

Werstein, Irving. *The Many Faces of the Civil War,* maps. Messner 1961. $3.95 (P—Pflaum, $.60); 12 up.

This book presents tragedy and triumph, revenge and cooperation, and hatred and friendship as parts of the conflict. It presents the heroes and the others behind the scenes, particularly President Lincoln who had to make fearful decisions. An excellent guide for those young readers interested in the Civil War.

Other Lands and Peoples Today

Bernheim, Evelyne and Marc. *From Bush to City: A Look at the New Africa,* rev. ed., photos. Harcourt 1968. $4.50; 12 up.

Many good photographs add dimension to an interesting book about the new Africa.

Bleeker, Sonia. *The Masai,* il. by Kisa J. Sasaki. Morrow 1963. $3.50; 11 up.

A masterful description of a complicated society, some of whose customs are unpalatable to western readers. The author seeks to explain, not justify, certain practices. Excellent for young historians and anthropologists, particularly in the light of sweeping political changes in Africa.

Bowen, David. *Hello Brazil.* Norton 1967. $3.95; 8–12.

An interesting account of Brazil—its geography, its cities, and its people. The book gives a good sense of the diversity of life, custom, and scene to be found in the largest country of Latin America.

Bowles, Cynthia. *At Home in India.* Harcourt 1956. $3.95; 12–15.

This personal account of a visit to India by Chester Bowles' daughter when she was 15 years old is readable and interesting.

Brun, Noelle. *Micias, Boy of the Andes,* tr. by Sandra Greifenstein, photos. Follett 1968. $2.79; 8–10.

Translated from the French, this book, one in a series called Children of the World, offers an accurate, exciting look at the living patterns of Andean Indians.

Clark, Ann Nolan. *Circle of Seasons,* il. by W. T. Mars. Farrar 1970. $3.95; 10 up.

An account of the seasonal cycle of the Pueblo Indian ceremonies as told to and observed by the author: a teacher, friend, and neighbor of the Indians. Recounted in a slow, rhythmic style that matches the ceremonies.

_____. *The Desert People,* il. by Allan Houser. Viking 1962. $3.00; 7 up.

The beautiful phrasing and exquisite word pictures calls for choric speaking or, at least, oral reading. A young Papago Indian tells of his life in the Southwest desert. A child interested in Indians may stay with it for its uniqueness and its richness of information. The casual reader will be less absorbed.

Clayton, Robert, and John Miles. *Scandinavia,* il. by Zena Flax. Golden 1967. $2.95; 9–12.

A geographic approach to Scandinavia with graphic illustrations and yet a factual interesting text. A good source book.

Cooke, David C. *Vietnam: The Country, the People.* Norton 1968. $4.95; 10–14.

The author spent months in this ancient land of contrasts of the old farms and customs and the new cities. From the legend of the dragon and the fairy princess, he goes on to discuss the climate, the many wars, the architecture, and the people and their life, work, and education in old cities and the countryside and villages.

Davenport, William and Roselle. *The Seine,* il. by Roselle Davenport. McGraw 1968. $5.50; 10 up.

Historical points of interest, geographical features, and modern life on and about the meandering river are described in direct style and delicate, beautiful sketches.

Davis, Russell, and Brent Ashabranner. *Land in the Sun,* il. by Robert William Hinds. Little 1963. $4.50; 9–14.

Packed with exciting information and brilliant pictures in four colors, the open format will appeal to young children. High school students and adults will find it a dramatic introduction to the new nations of West Africa.

Flaherty, Robert. *The Story of Comock the Eskimo,* ed. by Edmund Carpenter, il. by Eskimo artists. Simon 1968. $4.50; 10–14.

This is a kind of folk tale-legend based on truth, telling how an Eskimo named Comock, with his wife and several children, survived disaster on the ice of upper Hudson Bay, reached an island, lived there ten years with the most primitive of equipment, and eventually returned to the Quebec mainland. It is a story of human fortitude and tenacity, simply told and enhanced by Eskimo drawings of Eskimo life.

Goldberg, Lea. *Eli Lives in Israel,* photos by Anna Riwkin-Brick. Macmillan 1964. $2.50; 8–10.

Attractive photographs, accompanied by informative text, picture life on a kibbutz in modern Israel. Family relationships are happy.

Grant, Clara Louise and Jane Werner Watson. *Mexico,* il. by Mexican artists. Garrard 1968. $3.25; 9–11.

An interesting introduction to Mexico includes stories, history, and descriptions of contemporary life. It is illustrated by contemporary Mexican artists. Other books in the series (all of them by Jane Werner Watson) are *Canada: Giant Nation of the North; Egypt: Child of the Nile; Greece: Land of the Golden Light.*

Harrington, Lyn. *China and the Chinese,* photos by Richard Harrington. Nelson 1966. $3.95; 12 up.

An introduction to contemporary China. This author has successfully given a human interpretation to the Chinese as they really are. Well-chosen photographs supplement this highly organized text to give the reader a view of all facets of life in modern China.

Herrmanns, Ralph. *River Boy: Adventure on the Amazon,* tr. by Joan Tate, photos. Harcourt 1965. $4.50; 8–13.

Social anthropology beautifully expressed in words and exquisite color photography. A young boy from a primitive tribe living in the far reaches of the Amazon makes an odyssey down the river in search of a long-lost brother. Encounters with strange people from other tribes, the first sight of city life, and wild animals make an exciting story.

Heyerdahl, Thor. *Kon-Tiki,* photos by William Neebe. Rand 1960. $4.95 (several paperback eds.); 9–12.

One of the great true adventure stories of our time. This lavishly illustrated edition of an adult best-seller has lost little of its value through simplification.

Holbrook, Sabra. *Germany, East and West.* Meredith 1968. $5.95; 11–15.

The author tells how the split between the two Germanys occurred and gives the reader some sense of why the wall was built and the difficulties of resolving their status as separate states and unification.

Lifton, Betty Jean. *Return to Hiroshima,* photos by Eikoh Hosoe. Atheneum 1970. $5.95; 11 up.

This book takes the reader back to the City of the Bomb. Twenty-five years later, the city and its people still bear terrible scars of the tragedy. The author, who has lived in Japan for the past 15 years, tells the story of Hiroshima and its people in taut but compassionate prose. The powerful photos provide graphic accents to the account.

Loman, Anna. *Looking at Holland,* photos. Lippincott 1966. $3.25; 9–12.

Crisp, informative text and excellent photographs, many in color, make this both useful and interesting to elementary school students and their teachers. City and country, homes, food, work, and play are characterized.

Manning, Jack. *Young Ireland,* photos. Dodd 1965. $3.25; 9–12.

Charming photographs show children of Ireland at work and play.

Mansfield, John. *Juma, the Little African,* il. by Joseph Escourido. Nelson 1965. $2.50; 6–8.

A small boy is brave when he is trusted by a blind elephant to guide him to the "elephants' graveyard."

Murphy, E. Jefferson. *Understanding Africa,* il. by Louise E. Jefferson. Crowell 1969. $4.95; 12 up.

This comprehensive, well-organized, and understandable introduction to Africa breaks down the continent into seven regions: Northern Africa, Western Africa, Central Africa, Southern Africa, Eastern Africa, Madagascar, and Northeastern Africa. The physical characteristics of the people of each region, topography, and climate are described.

Nakamoto, Hiroko, with Mildred Mastin Pace. *My Japan.* McGraw 1970. $4.95; 11 up.

An autobiography of an upper-class Japanese girl raised in the age-old traditions of her country, whose life was dramatically altered by war.

Pendle, George. *Peru,* photos and map. Macmillan 1966. $3.95; 9–14.

This title in the Lands and Peoples series offers a concise, accurate presentation of a country and its people, customs and folklore, arts and industries, religions and history. It is illustrated with 22 intriguing photographs. Includes a map and an appendix of facts and suggestions for further reading.

Poole, Frederick King. *Southeast Asia,* photos and maps. Watts 1968. $2.95; 10 up.

The political turmoil, the ways of life, and the histories of the modern nations of Southeast Asia are explained in direct style and well-chosen photographs. A complete index and maps of each country add to the utility of this volume.

Sasek, Miroslav. *This Is Hong Kong,* il. by the author. Macmillan 1965. $4.95; 8 up.

By far the most important parts of Mr. Sasek's books are his pictorial maps relating the place to other familiar place names, in this case Saigon, Singapore, and Manila. His closeups and panoramas, in sun-drenched color, of buildings and differing ways of life (housing, food, transportation, clothing) enhance the volume. There is humorous exaggeration of persons and a patterned design of cities and harbors. Though the texts are brief, they will often prove obscure for younger readers. By the same author: *This Is Ireland; This Is Munich; This Is Paris; This Is London; This Is Cape Kennedy; This Is Greece;* and others.

Schloat, G. Warren, Jr. *María and Ramón: A Girl and Boy of Puerto Rico,* photos. Knopf 1966. $2.95; 8–11.

Brief sections on the country, the school, and the town provide some information about Puerto Rico. The story, which centers on a day in the lives of a boy and girl from different families, stresses family unity. Lavishly illustrated with black-and-white photographs, numbered in sequence.

Shirakigawa, Tomiko. *Children of Japan,* photos. Sterling 1967. $3.95; 8–12.

Modern life in rural and urban Japan. Photographs are well placed to illustrate short sections, which include home life, school life, athletics, projects and pastimes, shrines and temples.

Soule, Gardner. *Trail of the Abominable Snowman.* Putnam 1966. $3.49; 8–13.

Factual yet dramatic story of the search for the elusive phantom of the Himalayas.

Spiegelman, Judith M. *Ali of Turkey,* photos. Messner 1969. $3.34; 6–10.

Beautiful photographs and a very simple text make clear to very young readers the problems of a semi-developed country. The work of UNICEF is illustrated very well.

Stein, Mini. *Majola: A Zulu Boy,* photos by Duncan G. Greaves. Messner 1969. $3.50; 7–10.

Excellent photographs and simple narrative make this an outstanding book describing the life of the Zulu. While it is factual in approach, the style is good.

Tooze, Ruth. *Cambodia: Land of Contrasts,* maps and photos. Viking 1962. $3.77; 12 up.

The author's assured and detailed descriptions of Cambodia grow out of firsthand experience and careful study of the country's history. Her sympathetic treatment of the people comes from living for a time among them. Excellent maps and photographs add to the general appeal.

————. *Our Rice Village in Cambodia,* il. by Ezra Jack Keats. Viking 1963. $2.75; 5–9.

With poetic beauty and simplicity of language, a Cambodian boy tells of his family, its work, and its play. The talents of the author and the illustrator blend into an artistic book that exemplifies respect for a people, their culture, and their dignity.

Man and His Problems

Cohen, Robert. *The Color of Man,* photos by K. Heyman. Random 1968. $3.95 (P—Random, $2.60); 10–14.

Excellent photographs and a clear text give some insights into why people prejudge each other on the basis of color.

Colby, C. *Survival Training in Our Armed Forces,* photos. Coward 1965. $2.97; 8 up.

Survival training was initiated during World War II with the expensively trained airmen. In bitter cold, tropic heat, or the jungle, men must learn to live until they rejoin their units. These practical lessons in geography and climate are illustrated with photographs. By the same author: *Cliff Dwellings: Ancient Ruins from America's Past.*

Evans, Eva Knox. *Why We Live Where We Live,* il. by Ursula Koering. Little 1953. $3.75; 9–12.

In simple language the author explains how geological formations and the influence of man on his environment affect how people live and their occupations in different parts of the country. Excellent illustrations. By the same author: *People Are Important; All about Us.*

Heaps, Willard A. *Wandering Workers.* Crown 1968. $4.95; 12 up.

The human side of the migrant worker is sensitively told, and the social issues inherent in this labor force are explored in depth. Taped interviews add to understanding the problems of the migrants.

Holland, John, ed. *The Way It Is,* photos. Harcourt 1969. $3.25; 11 up.

This collection of photographs and accompanying commentary was made by a class of 15 boys from a junior high school in the slums of New York City. These teenagers explore their environment with cameras and record their impressions in writing. It is a realistic testimony, surprisingly well-rounded, frequently poignant, frequently harsh. Middle-class children who read this will learn much of an alien world.

Kelen, Emery. *Peace Is an Adventure.* Meredith 1967. $3.50; 9–12.

Peace is transmitted in numerous ways. This book is an interesting sharing of short stories about the people and agencies that work for the United Nations. An inspiring text shares the dramatic battle for peace the United Nations conducts in all corners of the globe.

Kettlekamp, Larry. *Dreams,* il. by the author. Morrow 1968. $2.95; 10–14.

Dreams have always been of deep interest to mankind. The author tells us that the earliest known record dealing with the subject is an Egyptian papyrus, written about 1350 B.C., which contains interpretations of about 200 dreams. Children seem just as interested in dreams as adults, and they ask questions about them that most adults can't answer. Here is a book that deals in a most fascinating way with the topic. It discusses the importance of dreams, possible interpretations, and some scientific investigations as well as interesting anecdotes. There is even a set of suggestions for studying one's own dreams.

Lewis, Richard. *Journeys,* il. by children. Simon 1969. $4.95; 6–14.

A companion volume to *Miracles,* an anthology of children's poetry, this book includes prose compositions of children, aged 4–14, from English-speaking countries around the world. The compositions have been grouped into nine sections including Beginnings, Days, Animals, Fantasies, Family Life, Other Children, Myself, Nights, and Endings. It is a revealing collection of children's thinking and offers a challenge to teachers to allow children to write freely of their own worlds.

Liston, Robert. *Downtown.* Delacorte 1965. $4.50 (P—Dell, $.60); 13 up.

The only weakness in this informative, personal discussion of contemporary urban problems is the lack of authentic photographs to make indelible the impact of Liston's views.

Mead, Margaret. *People and Places,* il. by W. T. Mars and Jan Fairservis and with photos. World 1959. $6.95 (P—Bantam, $.75); 12 up.

Strong, handsome paintings, clear, lively sketches, and appropriate photographs enrich this notable account of "man's discovery of man," the science of anthropology, by one of its most admired practitioners.

Mendoza, George. *The Hunter I Might Have Been,* photos by De-Wayne Dalrymple. Grosset 1968. $3.95; 9–14.

Stunning black-and-white photographs and eleven spare solemn lines evoke important feelings and ideas. Life or death, violence or nonviolence, man's guilt or responsibility—these are the underlying moral issues. The book has powerful potential for discussion purposes.

BIOLOGICAL SCIENCES

Ancient Living Things

Andrews, Roy Chapman. *All about Strange Beasts of the Past,* il. by Matthew Kalmenoff. Random 1956. $2.95; 10–14.

An excellent discussion of the larger fossils and how larger animals have developed on the earth. By the same author: *All about Whales; All about Dinosaurs; In the Days of the Dinosaurs; Quest in the Desert.*

Armour, Richard. *Odd Old Mammals,* il. by Paul Galdone. McGraw 1968. $3.95; 4–8.

Excellent illustrations are both fearsome and funny. Scientific names used in humorous rhyme are phonetically spelled. About the mammoth's tusks Armour writes: "I wonder, were they natural/or did he have them curled."

Burrell, Roy. *The Early Days of Man,* il. by the author and Tony Dyson. McGraw 1965. $4.95; 11–16.

A modern up-to-date review of the prehistoric past. The most recent scientific techniques for the dating of archeological materials and the contributions of other sciences are all discussed. Line drawings, maps, and a complete index make this an excellent resource.

Darling, Lois and Louis. *Before and after Dinosaurs,* il. by the authors. Morrow 1959. $3.14; 9 up.

A comprehensive study of the development of the first vertebrate land animals for the astute, especially interested young reader. Concepts of adaptation and geographical time are carefully developed. By the same authors: *Kangaroos; Chickens and How to Raise Them; Penguins.*

Ravielli, Anthony. *The Rise and Fall of the Dinosaurs,* il. by the author. Parents 1963. $3.50; 8–12.

Facts about the dinosaurs of 220 million years ago have been checked for accuracy. Excellent illustrations.

Robinson, W. W. *Ancient Animals of America,* il. by Irene B. Robinson. Ritchie 1962. $3.00; 10–14.

This story of life on earth millions of years before man made his appearance describes the giant sharks, the dinosaurs, the winged reptiles, the sea monsters, and the great lizards as they lived ages ago.

Shuttlesworth, Dorothy E. *Dodos and Dinosaurs,* photos. Hastings 1968. $3.25; 8–14.

The home of the largest collection of dinosaur fossils, the American Museum of Natural History, is the subject of the first chapter of this Famous Museum Exhibits series volume. Old photographs complement chapters describing the life of the ancient reptiles and birds.

Sibley, Gretchen. *La Brea Story,* il. by Mary Butler. Ritchie 1968. $3.95; 8–12.

This fascinating story of the California "tar pits" describes how animals, both prey and predator, were caught in the sticky mass. The importance of the asphalt pits to modern scientists is stressed. Excellent illustrations including full-page color pictures and margin drawings recreate the scenes of 40,000 years ago.

Swinton, William Elgin. *The Wonderful World of Prehistoric Animals,* il. by Maurice Wilson. Doubleday 1961. $3.95; 12 up.

This lavishly illustrated history of animal development begins with the one-celled creatures that lived millions of years ago and proceeds to the woolly rhinoceroses and cave bears hunted by Stone Age man. Fossil hunting is presented with a world map of fossil remains.

Zim, Herbert Spencer. *Dinosaurs,* il. by James Gordon Irving. Morrow 1954. $3.25; 8–12.

Giving a brief history of animal development, the author and illustrator present a good introduction to this area of animal life.

Animals

Adamson, Joy. *Elsa and Her Cubs,* photos. Harcourt 1965. $4.95; 6–10.

The lasting affection, trust, and loyalty between animal and human are poignantly portrayed when the famous lioness Elsa brings her three cubs back to the Adamsons' camp to introduce her new family to them. A story every child should have the opportunity of knowing and feeling. Sequel to *Born Free.*

Adrian, Mary. *The North American Bighorn Sheep,* il. by Genevieve Vaughan-Jackson. Hastings 1966. $3.50; 8–11.

The life cycle of the bighorn is presented in story form. Information is accurate and told in an interesting way. The black-and-white drawings have a softness not usually found in this medium. By the same author: *The American Alligator; The North American Wolf.*

Austin, Elizabeth S. *Penguins: The Birds with Flippers,* photos. Random 1968. $1.95; 8–10.

Rockhopper, macaroni, jackass, chinstrap, and emperor are the names of five of the 15 penguin species described. Well-written text accompanies excellent photographs of the penguins' unusual antics.

Bailey, John. *Our Wild Animals,* photos by Leonard Lee Rue. Nelson 1965. $5.95; 10–12.

A factual, comprehensive treatment of many animals ranging from the smallest to the largest. Information on each animal is given concisely, with just enough facts to satisfy the curiosity of the middle elementary child. Black-and-white, and color photographs.

Baker, J. W. *Patterns of Nature,* photos. Doubleday 1967. $3.95; 4–8.

The interdependence of plants and animals, adaptation of living things to their environment, reproduction, and death are the patterns in nature presented. The author's style and range of vocabulary indicate that this book should be read to, and discussed by, younger children. Outstanding photographs.

Balch, Glenn. *The Book of Horses,* photos. Four Winds 1967. $4.95 (P—Scholastic, $.60); 9–14.

All about the various kinds of horses such as the Morgans,

mustangs, Tennessee walkers, and many more, plus information about the origin of the horse, development through the years, and—best of all—easy-to-understand instructions on riding and caring for a horse. Indispensable for the youngster who loves horses. Compare Marguerite Henry's *All about Horses.*

Barker, Will. *Wildlife in America's History,* il. by Howard Jerome Smith. McKay 1962. $3.75; 10–14.

The author has selected significant and interesting facts and stories to show the relationship between animals and people during the development of the United States.

Bauer, Erwin. *My Adventures with African Animals,* photos by the author. Norton 1968. $4.95; 10–16.

Writing in a personal, conversational style, the author explains his own photographs and experiences with the antelopes, elephants, hyenas, giraffes, and 13 other animals. Lack of color photographs detracts from a superb book for African animal enthusiasts.

Beebe, B. F. *Animals South of the Border,* il. by James Ralph Johnson. McKay 1968. $3.95; 9 up.

For those interested in animal life in Mexico, this book offers a map and brief chapters on spider monkeys, collared anteaters, and other lesser known tropical animals. An appendix describing the species and habitat of the animals is supplemented by a complete index. By the same author: *African Elephants; Run, Light Buck, Run!*

Bethell, Jean. *How to Care for Your Dog,* il. by Norman Bridwell. Four Winds 1967. $2.50 (P—Scholastic, $.60); 7 up.

This charming book should be given with every new dog. It covers all aspects of the care that should be given man's best friend. The illustrations add to the charm of the book. Younger children could have it read to them; even mothers could learn from the pointers given.

Bevans, Michael H. *The Book of Reptiles and Amphibians,* il. by the author. Doubleday 1956. $4.50; 8–14.

Colorful pictures of several types of reptiles and amphibians are accompanied by informative text. Old wives' tales are dispelled, and the reader is shown the difference between a poisonous snake and a nonpoisonous one. Instructions are included on the care of these animals as pets. The pictures make this a book for even the young to enjoy.

Bixby, William. *Of Animals and Men.* McKay 1968. $3.95; 10–16.

Inviting chapter titles and detailed, well written information about the scientific study of animal behavior is a must for animal lovers. The behavior of animals is contrasted to that of man, giving the reader a better understanding of his own species.

Bridges, William. *The Bronx Zoo Book of Wild Animals,* photos. Golden 1968. $5.95; 10 up.

A fascinating reference book about more than 2,000 birds, mammals, reptiles, and amphibians of the famous zoo. Well-placed photographs, some full-page and in color, are found on each of the 300 pages. The excellent index and table of contents make this an outstanding family reference book that will be used for many years.

Buck, Margaret Waring. *Along the Seashore,* il. by the author. Abingdon 1964. $3.00 (P—Abingdon, $1.75); 8–12.

Pen drawings depict a great variety of plants and animals along the Atlantic, Pacific, and Gulf coasts of the United States.

———. *Where They Go in Winter,* il. by the author. Abingdon 1968. $3.50 (P—Abingdon, $1.75); 9–14.

Tells what insects, spiders, fishes, amphibians, reptiles, birds, and mammals do when temperatures drop and plant food is gone. The illustrations are detailed enough to be used as identification guides, and maps indicate usual habitat. Detailed index, table of contents, and list of references.

Buff, Mary and Conrad. *Forest Folk,* il. by Conrad Buff. Viking 1962. $3.00; 6–8.

This work conveys the mood, movement, and beauty of forest life through the seasons, during which Dash, a handsome three-year-old buck, wins his place as king of the forest. By the same authors and artist: *Elk Owl; The Big Tree; Dash and Dart.*

Burger, Carl. *All about Cats.* Random 1966. $1.95; 9–12.

A thorough account of cats from the sacred cats of Egypt, through superstitions about cats, to the present image of the friendly Tabby. By the same author: *All about Dogs; All about Elephants.*

Burton, Maurice. *The Sea's Inhabitants,* il. by Eric Thomas. Golden 1968. $2.66; 8–12.

One of the Golden Finding Out about Science series. Excellent color drawings and diagrams illustrate clear, concise text. Good glossary to italicized words in text.

Conklin, Gladys. *I Caught a Lizard,* il. by Arthur Marokvia. Holiday 1967. $3.95; 6–9.

Many small wild creatures are presented in ways that children would naturally discover them. A lizard, a toad, a salamander, and other wild creatures are included. How the animals should be treated and handled are stressed, but most important is the idea that the creatures must be returned to their natural homes. The illustrations are beautiful and delicate in warm, woodsy colors.

_____. *If I Were a Bird,* il. by Arthur Marokvia. Holiday 1965. $3.75; 7–10.
A delightfully written book in free rhythmic verse for the young child who wants to know more about the common birds he sees the year round. The text is accompanied by well-placed real life illustrations of each bird.

Darling, Lois and Louis. *Turtles,* il. by the authors. Morrow 1962. $3.14; 8 up.
Here is excellent informative material about various kinds of turtles, their evolution, where they live, and how they may be cared for as pets.

DeWaard, John. *Plants and Animals in the Air,* il. by Richard Cuffari. Doubleday 1969. $4.50; 8–11.
The principles of flight in various plants, animals, and machines are explained and well illustrated. The process of adaptation to flight and evolutionary changes are detailed in an unusually concise style.

_____. *The Shape of Living Things,* il. by Joan Victor. Doubleday 1969. $4.50; 8–10.
Shows how living things have adapted their shapes to secure food, repel enemies, endure climatic extremes, and perpetuate the species. A large number of plants and animals are described. One of the Living Things of the World series, this book is outsized, with big print, wide margins, colorful illustrations, and an index.

Dodd, Ed. *Chipper the Beaver,* il. by the author. Putnam 1968. $2.68; 7–9.
The life of a young beaver is told simply and well. Chipper's early encounters with natural predators and a man-caused forest fire are superbly illustrated by the creator of *Mark Trail.*

Dugdale, Vera. *Album of North American Animals,* il. by Clark Bronson. Rand 1966. $4.95; 10 up.
Presents 26 large North American animals, many of which have almost vanished; others have adapted to civilization. The present habitat, habits, young, food, and physical char-

acteristics of each animal are described. By the same author: *Album of North American Birds.*

Earle, Olive L. *Strange Fishes of the Sea,* illus. Morrow 1968. $3.25; 8–12.

Clear, straightforward, and concise description of some of the most fascinating oddities of the fish world. Soft pencil drawings add further insight. An index is included for easy reference. Highly readable, highly informative.

Eberle, Irmengarde. *Bears Live Here,* photos. Doubleday 1966. $3.25; 8–11.

Miss Eberle displays her usual good taste and writing style in presenting the story of a big black bear and her two cubs. A highly readable book that seems carefully researched. The photographs are large, clear, and very attractive. By the same author: *A Chipmunk Lives Here.*

Eckert, Allan W. *The King Snake,* il. by Franz Altschuler. Little 1968. $4.75; 10 up.

A biography of a king snake from egg to fully grown eleven-year-old. Eckert tells the story as if he were there and with precise descriptions indicates the feeding, mating, and wandering habits of this North Carolina native.

Fisher, Aileen. *Valley of the Smallest: The Life Story of a Shrew,* il. by Jean Zallinger. Crowell 1966. $3.75; 10–13.

A skillful description of a tiny creature weighing no more than a penny and of the animals who live near the Rocky Mountains. An aesthetic creation.

Fisher, James. *Zoos of the World,* illus. Natural History 1968. $6.95; 10 up.

History and behind-the-scenes information illustrated with many photographs and prints. Published for the American Museum of Natural History.

Gans, Roma. *Birds at Night,* il. by Aliki. Crowell 1968. $3.50; 4–7.

Some general information about the nocturnal habits of common birds. Excellent illustrations and simple text will be of interest to most youngsters. From the usually excellent series for young children, Let's Read and Find Out.

Garelick, May. *What Makes a Bird a Bird?* il. by Leonard Weisgard. Follett 1969. $3.95; 4–8.

Flying and egg-laying characteristics not unique to birds are discussed before the author deals with feathers, the one distinctive characteristic of all birds. The illustrations enrich the book and add much appeal.

George, Jean Craighead. *The Hole in the Tree,* il. by the author. Dutton 1957. $3.75; 6–8.

Many creatures use a hole in a tree as it grows from a tiny size to a large one. An original and appealing book.

————. *"Thirteen Moons" Series,* illus. Crowell 1967–1970. $3.75 ea.; 8 up.

There are 13 "Moon of" books by the same author in this series such as *The Moon of the Bears, The Moon of the Salamanders,* and *The Moon of the Owls.* The information provided is nearly always accurate, but sometimes the story lines and the information conveyed get in each other's way. However, the lyric quality of the text makes the series an unusual one.

Gilbert, Bil. *How Animals Communicate,* il. by Chet Reneson. Pantheon 1966. $3.95; 10 up.

An excellent book on scientific investigations of how and when animals communicate, written in an interesting and informative manner.

Goudey, Alice E. *Here Come the Lions!* il. by Garry MacKenzie. Scribner 1958. $3.63; 8–12.

Interesting information about lions. By the same author: *Here Come the Deer!; Here Come the Bears!; Here Come the Whales!*

Grabianski, Janusz. *Cats,* il. by the author. Watts 1966. $3.95; all ages.

Mr. Grabianski's water colors of all kinds of cats are colorful, subtle, realistic, fanciful—all rolled into one gorgeous book. By the same author: *Horses.*

Hawes, Judy. *Shrimps,* il. by Joseph Low. Crowell 1966. $3.50; 6–8.

Descriptions of the work of marine scientists as well as information about shrimp make for fascinating reading. Attractive color, comparisons, and straightforward language.

Henry, Marguerite. *All about Horses,* il. by Walter D. Osborne. Random 1967. $1.95; 8–12.

Numerous photographs add to the interesting historical information and facts on all breeds and the role horses have played throughout the world. A must for every horse lover.

Hess, Lila. *The Curious Raccoons,* photos. Scribner 1968. $3.50; 7–9.

The lives and habits of a family of inquisitive raccoons.

Holling, Holling C. *Minn of the Mississippi,* il. by the author. Houghton 1951. $4.75; 10–14.

An authentic telling of the life of a snapping turtle who was born in the lake region at the head of the Mississippi River and traveled down the river to the Gulf. There is no personalization of the animal, and present day life as well as historical facts about the river are woven into the story. Exquisite illustrations. By the same author: *Pagoo; Seabird; Paddle to the Sea.*

Hoover, Helen. *Animals at My Doorstep,* il. by Symeon Shimin. Parents 1966. $3.50; 4–8.

Descriptions of forest creatures seen from a cabin buried in the forest wilderness of northern Minnesota. Observations of birds, chipmunks, squirrels, deer, and others are perceptive and beautifully described and illustrated.

Hurd, Edith Thacher. *The Blue Heron Tree,* il. by Clement Hurd. Viking 1968. $3.95; 7–10.

The author describes the life of the herons that come to the Audubon rookery in Marin County, California. Poetic style and excellent two-color illustrations.

Hutchins, Ross E. *The Last Trumpeters,* il. by Jerome P. Connolly. Rand 1967. $3.50; 7–10.

A highly sensitive account of the migratory habits of the trumpeter swan. Written in graceful style, it not only is informative but conveys the author's feeling for nature. The illustrations add detail and beauty.

Jenkins, Alan C. *Kingdom of the Elephants,* il. by Victor G. Ambrus. Follett 1963. $3.25; 13–18.

This is a story of modern India, of the people and the animals who work in the great forests where teak is harvested. Principally it has to do with the training and habits of the great elephants on whose strength the work depends. Their majesty, their loyalty, their treachery, and their intelligence are illustrated in their relations to men and one another.

Jones, Adrienne. *Wild Voyageur,* il. by Lois Darling. Little 1966. $3.95; 9–11.

The story of the life cycle of a Canada goose is told with beauty and accurate knowledge of the birds, their habitat and ways. A distinguished book for all nature lovers.

Kane, Henry B. *Wings, Legs, or Fins,* photos. Knopf 1965. $3.25; 6–9.

Introduces the child to the wonderful and exciting world of animals and how animals transport themselves from place to place by swimming, crawling, leaping, walking, and flying. Simplicity and discovery are the highlights of the text. The photographs are beautifully and delightfully used to reinforce and support the content. There are a number of other attractive and accurate books by the same author.

Kellin, Sally Moffet. *A Book of Snails,* photos by Martin Iger. Scott 1968. $3.50; 7–10.

Fascinating information related in a direct, personal style. The clear photographs can be used to identify snail anatomy and activities. A must for every home or classroom with an aquarium.

Kohn, Bernice. *All Kinds of Seals,* photos. Random 1968. $1.95; 8 up.

Herd life, migration, hunting, and being hunted are parts of the life of the seal that are well told in text and black-and-white photographs.

Lauber, Patricia. *The Story of Dogs,* photos. Random 1966. $2.95; 8–10.

The history of dogs, how they were used, and how they came to be known as man's best friend. The narrative is accurate, informative, and easily read. Print is readable and well spaced. Clear and attractive photographs enhance the text. By the same author: *The Surprising Kangaroos and Other Pouched Animals.*

Liers, Emil E. *A Black Bear's Story,* il. by Ray Sherin. Viking 1962. $3.00; 9–12.

The story of a wise mother's devotion to the education of her cubs is told in a life-cycle style. Illustrations show the seasonal panorama of woodland life and display both the beauty and the harshness of nature. By the same author: *An Otter's Story.*

Lubell, Winifred and Cecil. *In a Running Brook,* il. by Winifred Lubell. Rand 1968. $3.95; 6–9.

The straightforward style will be absorbing to all readers interested in life in fast-moving water. The pictures are beautiful, and the writing has literary quality. By the same authors: *The Tall Grass Zoo; Green Is for Growing.*

McClung, Robert M. *Black Jack: Last of the Big Alligators,* il. by Lloyd Sanford. Morrow 1967. $3.25; 9–12.

Georgia's Okefenokee Swamp is the setting for an alligator's life and environment. Trees, flowers, birds, and animals common to the swamp are described during the various seasons. A story line children will enjoy is woven into the information.

————. *Possum,* il. by the author. Morrow 1963. $3.25; 5–8.

This story accurately and interestingly tells of the life cycle of the United States only pouched animal, the possum. By the same author: *Honker: The Story of a Wild Goose; Horseshoe Crab; The Mighty Bears; The Swift Deer.*

McCoy, J. J. *Swans,* il. by Guilio Maestro. Lothrop 1967. $3.95; 13 up.

The writer's love of birds comes through in this distinguished book about the habits of swans. Conservation needs are emphasized throughout. A glossary of terms is provided as well as a reading list for further study. By the same author: *House Sparrows: Ragamuffins of the City.*

Marchant, R. A. *Man and the Beast.* Macmillan 1966. $4.95; 12–16.

Man must learn to respect and understand animals and animal behavior to better respect and understand himself. Fascinating true stories outline the history of man's relationships with animals. Excellent!

Mason, George Frederick. *The Wildlife of North America,* il. by the author. Hastings 1966. $4.50; 10–13.

The history of wildlife in North America is more than adequately treated. The beginnings of life to the present ways of handling wildlife problems, including the squandering of bird and animal life, are handled factually and realistically. Other aspects of conservation are included. Maps, charts, and black-and-white drawings. By the same author: *Animal Homes.*

Masselink, Ben. *Green: The Story of a Caribbean Turtle's Struggle for Survival,* il. by Maurice Wilson. Little 1969. $4.25; 8–12.

Begins with the laying of eggs on the Yucatan Peninsula by an anonymous turtle, which marks the beginning of Green's life and ends with her return to the same location to lay her own eggs. In between one sees that man is the turtle's worst enemy, for the latter's meat is delicious and the eggs are great delicacies. Facts about the turtle and other sea life are blended into a readable nature story.

Milne, Lorus and Margery. *The Crab that Crawled Out of the Past,* il. by Kenneth Gosner. Atheneum 1965. $3.50; 8–12.

In a concise but lively account, the Milnes describe the crab's appearance, its life cycle, and its history, including the many environments it has been a part of through the millenniums and its importance to the survival of man.

Moore, Shirley. *Biological Clocks and Patterns,* il. by Omar Davis. Criterion 1967. $3.50; 10–14.

Emphasizes animals' sensing powers—the inborn devices that act as clocks, compasses, thermometers, gyroscopes, sonar, radar, and computers. An excellent beginning book for systems analysis in nature. Table of contents, index, and good bibliography.

North, Sterling. *Little Rascal,* il. by Carl Burger. Dutton 1965. $3.75; 8 up.

A "shortened and slightly simplified version of the adult book," which was very popular and won several prizes. The author vividly recalls his own childhood experiences with his pet raccoon in Wisconsin. An often humorous and heartwarming, though slowly paced, story that will appeal to youngsters as will the superb pictures.

O'Neill, Mary. *The White Palace,* il. by Nonny Hogrogian. Crowell 1966. $3.95; 9 up.

The author of *Hailstones and Halibut Bones* tells the story of the life cycle of a Chinook salmon from his emergence from an egg and early life in the skeleton of a larger fish (the "white palace") to the fertilization of his mate's eggs and eventual death. Illustrations are outstanding.

Rau, Margaret. *The Penguin Book,* il. by John Hamberger. Hawthorn 1968. $3.95; 8–11.

Macaroni, rockhopper, emperor, and chinstrap are among the species discussed. Little-known facts are presented in a most fascinating manner. Detailed black-and-white drawings; excellent index.

Rosen, Ellsworth. *Spiders Are Spinners,* il. by Teco Slagboom. Houghton 1968. $3.95; 5–8.

Descriptions of the spider's anatomy, habits, and habitat are told in simple verse form. Appropriately illustrated in black and white, this volume is excellent for its style and information.

Rounds, Glen. *Rain in the Woods and Other Small Matters.* World 1964. $3.00; 9–11.

The descriptions of creatures in a natural setting will develop in the reader a keener sensitivity to his surroundings.

————. *Wild Horses of the Red Desert,* il. by the author. Holiday 1969. $4.95; 6–9.

Well-illustrated account of how the wild horses live throughout the year in the Badlands of South Dakota. The reader is filled with feelings of adventure and can sense the wilderness atmosphere.

Russell, Franklin. *Hawk in the Sky,* il. by Frederic Sweney. Holt 1965. $3.00; 11–14.

This beautiful story of the red-tailed hawk and its constant struggle for survival is sensitively written. The haughtiness, magnificence, and grandeur of the hawk and the elements that it must endure and adjust to are aptly described with real literary quality and splendid illustrations.

Selsam, Millicent E. *Animals as Parents,* il. by J. Kaupmann. Morrow 1965. $3.50; 12–14.

An accurate and interesting account of the birth and care of young fish, reptiles, birds, and mammals.

––––––. *How Animals Tell Time,* il. by J. Kaupmann. Morrow 1967. $3.50; 10–14.

The student who reads this book will find more questions raised than answered. How animals tell time is still shrouded in mystery, and this text challenges the youth of today to find answers for the youth of tomorrow. By the same author: *Courtship of Animals; How Animals Live Together.*

Shapp, Martha and Charles. *Let's Find out about Birds,* il. by Bette J. Davis. Watts 1967. $2.95; 6–9.

An informative book about birds, accurately presented.

Shuttlesworth, Dorothy E. *Animal Camouflage.* Natural History 1966. $3.95; 12–14.

How marine animals, seashore animals, insects, reptiles and amphibians, birds, and mammals hide. Published for the American Museum of Natural History.

Simon, Hilda. *Feathers: Plain and Fancy,* il. by the author. Viking 1969. $4.53; 10–14.

The growth and structure, form, function, color, and patterns of feathers and some unusual feathers and plumes are discussed in lucid detail. Numerous four-color illustrations add to the clarity of the text and the visual enjoyment of the birds.

Stenuit, Robert. *The Dolphin,* photos. Sterling 1968. $5.95; 10–16.

An excellent book on a fascinating subject. A dolphin embryo closely resembles a human embryo. Does this make the dolphin man's long-lost cousin? Black-and-white and color photos and diagrams and exciting incidents explore man's relationships with this mammal.

Stephens, William M. and Peggy. *Octopus Lives in the Ocean,* il. by Anthony D'Attilio. Holiday 1968. $3.50; 6–10.

The life cycle of the common octopus found along the shores of both oceans. Beautiful, detailed illustrations enhance the well-written text.

Steurt, Marjorie Rankin. *Rocky and Sandy,* photos by Bernie and Cynthia Crampton. Ward 1967. $3.50; 4–7.

The life of a tortoise from birth to maturity is told through a series of photographs and simple text. While the text is for younger children, the photographs have an appeal for all ages. Excellent.

Villiard, Paul. *Reptiles as Pets,* photos by the author. Doubleday 1969. $3.95; 9–11.

How to collect reptiles and provide them with proper homes, food, and care are discussed, with details on special requirements of the five major kinds of reptiles.

Weil, Lisl. *Alphabet of Puppy Care,* il. by the author. Abelard 1968. $3.75; 3 up.

In humorous pictures and practical text, Lisl Weil describes some of the things children should know about their dogs and some of the things they should do for them. Illustrations are in three colors and most appealing. Young (and older) dog owners and future dog owners should find this primer both entertaining and informative.

Zistel, Era. *Thistle,* photos by the author. Random 1967. $2.95; 4–7.

An appealing true story about a baby raccoon found by the roadside sick and alone and his friendship with the family's kitten named Chowder.

Conservation and Ecology

Adrian, Mary. *The American Prairie Chicken,* il. by Genevieve Vaughan-Jackson. Hastings 1968. $3.50; 7–10.

Fine black-and-white illustrations and well-written text present aspects of conservation through the story of the Attwater prairie chicken. This volume of the Preserve Our Wildlife series includes exciting information and is well documented.

Archer, Sellers. *Rain, Rivers and Reservoirs: The Challenge of Running Water,* il. with maps and photos. Coward 1963. $2.80; 11–14.

The importance of water conservation, the need for developing new supplies, and how water can be controlled are discussed in this well-illustrated volume.

Atwood, Ann. *New Moon Cove,* photos by the author. Scribner 1969. $3.89; 9 up.

Magnificent photographs merge with brief and lyrical observations. Both camera and pen function to compress in line, color, and sound the essence of one small half circle of the Pacific coastline. No human being is seen nor any animal (except in one small shot), yet within these 30 pages the surge of life and living is intimately felt.

Bauer, Helen. *Water: Riches or Ruin.* Doubleday 1959. $3.95; 9–12.

A detailed discussion of the importance of the relationships between water, soil, and fire. The varied forms of illustration strongly support the plea for conservation of natural resources.

Darling, Lois and Louis. *A Place in the Sun,* il. by the authors. Morrow 1968. $3.95; 12–16.

Major ecological concepts are explored in beautiful illustrations and clear prose. Using the fields and streams of Connecticut as an example, ecological relationships throughout the world are explained.

Fitter, Richard. *Vanishing Wild Animals of the World,* il. by John Leigh-Pemberton. Watts 1968. $7.95; all ages.

Beautifully illustrated British appeal for conservation of endangered species of mammals all over the world. Scholarly appendices are provided on the species involved. Quarto volume with color plates.

Henry, Marguerite. *Mustang, Wild Spirit of the West,* il. by Robert Lougheed. Rand 1966. $3.95; 10–14.

The absorbing story of how Wild Horse Annie Johnson successfully led the recent fight to save the mustangs from virtual extinction. Tells of her lifelong fight, first in Nevada and then on a national level, against the cruel practices of mustangers who hunt their prey in planes and trucks.

Hirsch, S. Carl. *The Living Community,* il. by William Steinel. Viking 1966. $3.75; 11–16.

Ecology is a science of increasing importance to the future of mankind. A captivating text develops the theme that only through a wide understanding of ecological principles can man learn to use his resources wisely for the welfare of all forms of life, including his own.

Kirk, Ruth. *Desert Life,* photos. by Ruth and Louis Kirk. Natural History 1970. $4.50; 5–9.

Emphasizes the importance of rain to plants and animals of the desert and how plants and animals store water to survive. Older children will particularly enjoy the superb color photographs.

Laycock, George. *America's Endangered Wildlife.* Norton 1969. $4.95; 11–13.

Describes over a dozen of the 28 species critically threatened with extinction and records efforts to preserve them. The appendix lists and briefly describes 60 other threatened species. The writing is candid and direct. Similar to Green's earlier *Wildlife in Danger,* although the information here is more complete, more up to date, and for an older child.

———. *Wild Refuge,* photos. Natural History 1969. $3.50; to 12.

A tour of 14 National Wildlife Refuges throughout the United States with information on their wild animals and birds, establishment, and management. Exciting stories of pelicans, wild geese, alligators, otters, and many others are accompanied by close-up photographs.

McCoy, J. J. *The Hunt for the Whooping Cranes: A Natural History Detective Story,* il. by Ray Abruzzi. Lothrop 1966. $4.59; 6–10.

An interesting book recording the efforts of conservationists to save a nearly extinct bird.

Raskin, Edith. *The Pyramid of Living Things,* il. by Joseph Cellini. McGraw 1967. $4.00; 12 up.

The ecological communities of the world are presented in pyramid form. The lower plant life forms the base, and man is at the apex. Effectively written and includes a bibliography for further reading.

Shuttlesworth, Dorothy. *Clean Air, Sparkling Water,* photos. Doubleday 1968. $3.95; 8–10.

The unusually well-chosen photographs show what air and water pollution looks like. The text tells what can be done about it. Youngsters will understand the social issues involved as they read the story of one community's fight against pollution.

Van Dersal, William R. *The Land Renewed: The Story of Soil Conservation,* rev. ed. Walck 1968. $6.00; 12–14.

A new edition of the 1946 book that tells the story of how nearly two billion acres of land in the United States can be saved. Amply illustrated.

Earth Sciences

Atwood, Ann. *The Wild Young Desert,* photos. by the author. Scribner 1970. $4.05; 7–12.

A detailed account of the ways in which various elements of nature act upon the earth to form deserts. Emphasis on the long time-spans involved in this process. Superb color photos.

Bendick, Jeanne. *The Shape of the Earth.* Rand 1965. $2.95; 8–12.

Exciting presentation in word and picture of the origin, composition, and principal features of the earth.

Buehr, Walter. *Water: Our Vital Need,* il. by the author. Norton 1967. $4.25; 10–12.

Historical background combined with presently available knowledge about water: its origin, its uses for transportation, food, irrigation, and recreation, its conservation, and potential sources in the future. Illustrations and diagrams add to the aesthetic as well as to the informative excellence.

Burt, Olive W. *The First Book of Copper.* Watts 1968. $2.95; 9 up.

Information on how copper is found, its uses, and its alloys. May be used by teachers as well as students. An outstanding beginning book.

Carona, Philip B. *Earth through the Ages,* il. by Alex Ebel. Follett 1968. $1.89; 8–12.

Difficult material presented in a concise, direct manner. Time concepts are handled well, and illustrations of theories of earth formation are excellent.

———. *Water,* il. by Phero Thomas. Follett 1967. $1.00; 7–10.

Clear, detailed drawings and simple text with many suggested things to do.

Froman, Robert. *The Science of Salt,* il. by Anne Marie Jauss. McKay 1967. $3.25; 12 up.

An introduction to a career in chemistry through the revelation of fundamental concepts and processes of only two elements, sodium and chlorine: their origins, salt mining, uses of salt in industrial processes, and its role in the human body. This brief, very readable account is in the main trustworthy.

Gans, Roma. *The Wonder of Stones,* il. by Joan Berg. Crowell 1963. $3.50; 5–8.

Charming prose and informative pictures show clearly how stones are formed, how rocks vary, and how the variations are produced.

Goldin, Augusta. *The Bottom of the Sea,* il. by Ed Emberly. Crowell 1966. $3.50; 6–9.

The younger reader can explore the basic geography of the ocean floor through the text as well as through colorful and informative illustrations. Though some concepts may elude the youngest, the book is very readable.

Hogg, Garry. *Deep Down: Great Achievements in Cave Exploration.* Criterion 1962. $3.95; 11–14.

The science of speleology emerges along with the mystery, danger, and excitement of under-earth exploration. Each chapter is a dramatic retelling of a true episode about a famous cave.

Life Magazine Editorial Staff and Lincoln Barnett. *The World We Live in,* photos. Simon 1956. $5.95; 11–16.

Simplified from the adult volume of the same title. Excellent resource book of information for older children.

May, Julian. *They Lived in the Ice Age,* il. by Jean Zallinger. Holiday 1967. $3.75; 6–8.

How glaciers are formed and information on early animals, man included. The soft pictures add a great deal. Much of the text is concerned with scientific theory.

Parker, Bertha Morris. *Golden Treasury of Natural History,* rev. ed. Golden 1968. $6.95; 8 up.

An updated and expanded version of the 1953 volume. The 384 pages are packed with reference materials for all. Detailed, multi-colored illustrations, charts, time lines and diagrams make the use of this reference book a pleasure.

Pough, Frederick H. *All about Volcanoes and Earthquakes,* il. by Kurt Wiese. Random 1953. $2.95; 9–12.

Causes of volcanoes and earthquakes and information about rocks, the earth's interior, and how geological discoveries have been made.

Ravielli, Anthony. *The World Is Round,* il. by the author. Viking 1963. $3.50; 9–12.

Concise text with effective color illustrations show that the world is really round. Basic knowledge about the earth's shape is traced from ancient Greece to modern times.

Reed, W. Maxwell. *The Earth for Sam,* rev. ed., il. by Paul Brandwein. Harcourt 1960. $4.95; 12 up.

A careful, well-illustrated, readable account of the earth from its formation to the beginning of historic times. Organized by geological periods and well indexed. By the same author: *The Sea for Sam; The Stars for Sam,* both similarly expanded and updated.

Shepherd, Walter. *The Earth's Surface,* il. by Laszlo Acs. Golden 1968. $1.99; 8–11.

A basic introduction to the forces that are constantly changing the features of the landscape. The illustrations add generally to the concise text. Only organizational format weakens this as a very useful resource book.

Silverberg, Robert. *The World of the Ocean Depths.* Meredith 1968. $4.95; 10 up.

Includes a brief history of man's exploration of the sea, several fascinating chapters on animal life at increasingly great depths, and a final brief examination of this "last frontier" for its farming and mining possibilities. Bibliography of books and articles. Effectively illustrated and written.

Stephens, William M. *Science beneath the Sea: The Story of Oceanography.* Putnam 1966. $3.64; 10–14.

A good survey of man's growing involvement in the intriguing life under the sea written by the public information officer for the University of Miami's Institute of Marine Science.

Sterling, Dorothy. *Story of Caves,* il. by Winifred Lubell. Doubleday 1956. $3.95; 10–14.

An account of how caves are made, discovered, and explored, and about the things that live in them.

Switzer, George. *Diamonds in Pictures,* photos and diagrams. Sterling 1967. $3.95; 12 up.

Written by the chairman of mineral sciences at the Smithsonian Institution, this book tells about the formation, mining, cutting, and marketing of diamonds, the manufacture of synthetic ones, and industrial uses. The near-exact balance of text and black-and-white photographs and diagrams makes interesting and informative reading.

Human Body

Aliki. *My Five Senses,* il. by the author. Crowell 1962. $3.50;
5–6.

With simple words and sparkling pictures, Aliki captures
the excitement of a child's growing understanding of his
senses, what they are, and what he learns through them
about the world around him.

De Schweinitz, Karl. *Growing Up: How We Become Alive, Are
Born, and Grow,* 4th ed., photos. Macmillan 1965. $3.95;
7–12.

Well written and thoroughly treated, this book explores the
birth process in animals before introducing life and its
beginning in humans. Information is treated honestly, simply, and without awkwardness. The photographs accompanying the text have been carefully selected and are in good
taste.

Elgin, Kathleen. *Read about the Brain.* Watts 1967. $2.95;
9–12.

A truly informative and fascinating account of how man's
brain works is presented simply and accurately. The writing,
which is sequential and developmental in handling the
information, is easily read and understood. By the same
author: *Read about the Ear; Read about the Eye; Read about
the Hand; Read about the Heart.*

Evans, Eva Knox. *All about Us,* il. by Van Earle. Golden 1947,
1965. $3.95 (P—Golden, $.75); 7–11.

One of the earliest books for children on skin color, this can
still be read aloud to children or be read by children. The
combination of humor with a scientific and historical approach and the black-and-white drawings have helped to
keep it from becoming dated.

Froman, Robert. *The Many Human Senses,* il. by Feodor
Rimsky. Little 1966. $4.50; 12–14.

The many complexities of the human senses are described in
a fascinating way. Cross-section diagrams of the sense or-
gans are included.

Goldin, Augusta. *Straight Hair, Curly Hair,* il. by Ed Emberley.
Crowell 1966. $3.50; 6–9.

Readers will be unable to resist directions to experiment
with this subject that is close to everyone. Be prepared to
pull out a few hairs.

Gould, Laurence J., and William Martin. *Think about It: Experiments in Psychology,* il. by Gustave Nebel. Prentice 1968. $3.75; 9–12.

An interesting and lively introduction to basic psychological behavior and methods of investigation. The reader is urged to investigate psychological concepts on his own in an effort to better understand how and why people behave as they do. Well written with the older elementary child in mind.

McGovern, Ann. *The Question and Answer Book about the Human Body,* il. by Lorelle M. Raboni. Random 1965. $1.95; 8–11.

For the child who feeds on small bits of information and enjoys imparting these bits to startled and impressed parents.

Ravielli, Anthony. *Wonders of the Human Body,* il. by the author. Viking 1954. $3.00; 9–12.

Using familiar objects to illustrate the parts of the body, the author tells in text and pictures the story of the machinery of the human being. Vivid, accurate, and readable. By the same author: *From Fins to Hands.*

Schneider, Leo. *Lifeline: The Story of Your Circulatory System,* il. by Jere Donovan. Harcourt 1958. $2.95; 10 up.

The story of blood, its circulation, composition, and function. By the same author: *You and Your Senses.*

Schuman, Benjamin N. *The Human Eye,* il. by Michael K. Meyers. Atheneum 1968. $4.75; 10 up.

The author, an M.D., explains the physiological development of the eye and interprets the phenomenon of sight in terms of the physical action of light. Excellent drawings are invaluable in the step-by-step explanations.

Showers, Paul, and Kay Sperry. *Before You Were a Baby,* il. by Ingrid Fetz. Crowell 1968. $3.50; 6–10.

The beginnings of human life in frank, straightforward language. Excellent illustrations. Also by Paul Showers: *How You Talk; Your Skin and Mine; Hear Your Heart.*

Insects

Conklin, Gladys. *Lucky Ladybugs,* il. by Glenn Rounds. Holiday 1969. $4.50; 4–8.

In simple straightforward language, this book tells the life cycle and habits of ladybugs but fails to mention that there are male ladybugs. Illustrations help to clarify meaning.

———. *We Like Bugs,* il. by Arthur Marokvia. Holiday 1962. $3.95; 4–8.

Writer and artist have treated the six-legged with scientific respect and presented them with beauty. Not too much detail on the kind of insect behavior of interest to the very young observer.

Doering, Harold, and Jo Mary McCormick. *An Ant Is Born,* photos. Sterling 1964. $3.50; 10–16.

A concept-loaded text filled with scientifically accurate facts, presented in an interesting way. Photographs carry much of the load of the information. This fine book is suitable for intensive study.

Goudey, Alice E. *Butterfly Time,* il. by Adrienne Adams. Scribner 1964. $3.25; 5–9.

In poetic text the author captures the wonder and beauty of the gay procession of butterflies "flitting, dancing, chasing one another," through sunny fields and along country roadsides. Many detailed and delicate illustrations help in identifying common butterflies.

Hutchins, Ross E. *Insect Builders and Craftsmen,* photos by the author. Rand 1959. $2.95; 12 up.

Remarkable photographs illustrate the fascinating information about the ant-bee-hornet-wasp group of insects by an authority in the field.

———. *The Travels of Monarch X,* il. by Jerome P. Connolly. Rand 1966. $3.95; 8–11.

The author skillfully creates an imaginary trip taken by a monarch butterfly, which extends over a period of four months and covers a distance of 2,000 miles. Scientific evidence is the basis for the adventures and travels, all treated with accurate facts, lovely color illustrations, and an appreciation for the fragile yet durable monarch butterfly. By the same author: *Caddis Insects: Nature's Carpenters and Stonemasons; Insects: Hunters and Trappers; Strange Plants and Their Ways.*

Knight, David C. *Let's Find out about Insects,* il. by Henry S. Gillette. Watts 1967. $2.95; 6–9.

Excellent introduction to insects discusses the general characteristics of various families of insects, their habits, methods of gathering food, and reproductive processes. Frequent illustrations in black and green clarify the text. Lines are used to point out relationships between text and pictures. For the most part the illustrations are clear and uncluttered by small detail.

Myrick, Mildred. *Ants Are Fun,* il. by Arnold Lobel. Harper 1968. $2.50; 6–10.

Two boys who have tree houses make friends with a new boy who moves into the neighborhood and has an ant house. His ant house is destroyed and the two boys, in helping him rebuild it, learn a great deal about ants.

Selsam, Millicent. *Questions and Answers about Ants.* il. by Arabelle Wheatley. Four Winds 1967. $3.50 (P—Scholastic $.60); 9 up.

The habits of one type of ant are discussed with excellent diagrams accompanying the text. Details are given on how a youngster may construct his own ant farm. The simple language makes it good reading for younger scientists. Highly recommended.

———. *Terry and the Caterpillars,* il. by Arnold Lobel. Harper 1962. $2.50; 4–8.

A little girl learns about the different stages in the life cycle of a moth by caring for three caterpillars found on an apple tree. The caterpillars are kept in glass jars, and Terry is able to observe many fascinating changes. The story is presented simply and is attractively illustrated.

Shuttlesworth, Dorothy E. *All Kinds of Bees,* il. by Su Zan Noguchi Swain. Random 1967. $1.95; 9–12.

This fairly comprehensive study of the bee family relates a short history of bees and their relation to man. While many facts are presented, the reading is enjoyable and the illustrative drawings beautiful. A table of contents and an excellent index make it easy to use.

Sterling, Dorothy. *Caterpillars,* il. by Winifred Lubell. Doubleday 1961. $3.50; 7–9.

Colorful illustrations on every page tell much of the fascinating process by which a caterpillar changes into a butterfly or moth.

Natural Resources and Products

Carr, Albert B. *Islands of the Deep Sea.* Day 1967. $3.29; 12–15.

A well-developed, informational presentation of the knowledge man has of the islands in the Atlantic and Pacific oceans. Life on these dots of land necessitates a closer bond with nature than life on the mainlands. The excitement of the island paradise is often caught by the reader.

Fanning, Leonard. *Over Mountains, Prairies and Seas,* photos and drawings. McGraw 1968. $4.95; 9–11.

The story of the growth of the transportation system that carries oil from its natural home to the places where it is needed is told in very readable language. Excellent photographs add to the story. Unusual incidents are told in this history of oil trade.

Floethe, Louise and Richard. *Farming around the World,* il. by the authors. Scribner 1970. $4.37; 4–8.

Farms and farming are presented in 18 different world settings. The information may be a bit too extensive for the younger reader, but the carefully detailed illustrations will hold his attention.

Howard, Robert West. *Farms,* photos. Watts 1967. $2.95; 9–12.

Many questions about farms, which city children wonder about, are handled succinctly and informatively. Even farm children will profit because the content covers all types of farming throughout the world. Sizes of farms (acreage) are compared to city blocks, and there are black-and-white photographs of children involved in farm chores.

Janes, Edward C. *When Men Panned Gold in the Klondike,* il. by William Hutchinson. Garrard 1968. $2.69; 9 up.

The excitement and heartbreaks that flavored the frantic search for gold in the Klondike region of Canada's Yukon Territory are vividly relayed in this authentic account. Old prints, engravings, and detailed drawings supplement an excellent text.

McCormick, Jo Mary. *Pearls in Pictures.* Sterling 1966. $3.95; 12 up.

The development of the pearl industry is clearly documented in text and illustration. For unusual data on a specific topic this is an excellent reference book.

Meshover, Leonard. *You Visit a Sugar Refinery/Fruit Cannery,* photos by Eve Hoffman. Benefic 1966. $2.00; 7–10.

Clear, modern black-and-white photographs and easy text introduces an American industry, picturing several races among the visiting children. By the same author and photographer: *You Visit a Steamship Airport.*

Milne, Lorus and Margery. *The Phoenix Forest*, il. by Elinor Van Ingen. Atheneum 1968. $3.95; 8–12.

The legend of the phoenix is simply and beautifully told and then applied analogously to a forest after the woods have been consumed by fire. This is an informational book that reads like a novel, but it is doubly interesting because we know the events are true. A must for teachers to read for their own benefit—and to read to children, though selective cutting of long descriptive passages would be appropriate for the latter situation.

Rich, Louise Dickinson. *The First Book of Lumbering*, il. by Victor Mays. Watts 1967. $2.95; 10–14.

The lumbering industry is traced from Colonial times to the present with the emphasis on human needs, way of life, and consumer patterns. Information is accurately presented, and enough illustrations are used to highlight the content. Excellent supplementary book for the social studies program as well as science.

Whitney, David. *Let's Find Out about Milk*, il. by Gloria Gaulke. Watts 1967. $2.95; 5–8.

A highly informative book relating the story of milk from the cow on the farm to the product purchased in the store. The author describes how milk is homogenized and how other food products are made from milk. It will be enjoyed by children in large cities who are not familiar with the process.

Wolfe, Louis. *Drake Drills for Oil*, il. by David Hodges. Putnam 1965. $2.29; 9–11.

Drake's successful drilling for oil in Pennsylvania is told as a short story that classes could dramatize.

Plants

Allen, Gertrude E. *Everyday Trees*, il. by the author. Houghton 1968. $3.25; 6–8.

Develops an appreciation of some common trees and offers basic information about each. Occasionally patronizing to the sincerely interested reader who is reading for depth. Pencil illustrations are simple, clear, and nontechnical.

Beck, Barbara L. *The First Book of Fruits,* il. by Page Cary. Watts 1967. $2.95; 9–12.

An everyday presentation of facts on the 500 varieties of fruit. Accurate information about historical and botanical lines of fruit, what they are, how seeds are formed, improving fruits, and so on. Useful as a reference book.

Butts, David P., and Addison E. Lee. *Watermelon,* il. by Betsy Warren. Steck 1968. $2.25; 8–12.

The detailed study of one plant, its origin, reproductive process, cellular structure, life history, and methods of cultivation and cross pollenization. This excellent presentation has great possibilities for transfering understanding to the life processes of all living things.

Hutchins, Ross E. *This Is a Leaf,* photos by the author. Dodd 1962. $3.75; 10 up.

Fascinating with a highly readable style and striking closeup photographs. By the same author: *This Is a Tree.*

Mannheim, Grete. *Touch Me, Touch Me Not,* photos. Knopf 1965. $3.25; 8–11.

A lively and interesting account of a day spent in a beautiful forest by a group of ten boys who belong to a nature club. The story clips along at an easy and quick pace as each boy discovers for himself the nature of the forest and its inhabitants. The exceptional photography at times overpowers the text.

Milne, Lorus and Margery. *Because of a Tree,* il. by Kenneth Gosner. Atheneum 1963. $3.95; 10 up.

A picture of the cycle of life of trees, using eight varieties as examples. Indirectly this is the story of the interdependence of all living things.

Pomerantz, Charlotte. *Why You Look Like You Whereas I Tend to Look Like Me,* il. by Rosemary Wells and Susan Jeffers. Scott 1969. $3.95; 9–14.

Zany poetry and cartoons explain how Mendel's experiments with garden peas led to the modern theory of heredity. Dry discoveries are made interesting and understandable. A description with supporting diagrams of Mendel's cross pollination process and a short biography of his life supplement the verse.

Selsam, Millicent E. *Milkweed,* photos by Jerome Wexler. Morrow 1967. $3.95; 6–9.

Excellent information presented accurately, simply, and

honestly. The illustrations are beautiful closeups of the various stages of the development of the milkweed and pace the text accurately.

_____. *Play with Seeds,* il. by Helen Ludwig. Morrow 1957. $3.36; 8–12.
Experiences with and information about common seeds and how they are formed. By the same author: *Plants We Eat; Play with Vines; Exploring the Animal Kingdom; See through the Sea; See through the Forest; See through the Jungle; See through the Lake;* and many others.

Weather

Adler, Irving. *Weather in Your Life,* il. by Peggy and Ruth Adler. Day 1959. $3.49; 9 up.
Factors involved in the phenomena of weather are described in such a way that cause and effect relationships are meaningfully developed. Diagrams and photographs are excellent.

Bell, Thelma Harrington. *Thunderstorm,* il. by Corydon Bell. Viking 1960. $3.50; 12 up.
Detailed scientific information about the nature of a thunderstorm. Myths, superstitions, the history of man's discoveries about thunderstorms, and the freakish nature of lightning and man's attempt to protect himself are covered. Technical information is balanced with anecdotes and illustrations to make the book very readable.

Branley, Franklyn M. *Air Is All around You,* il. by Robert Galster. Crowell 1962. $3.50; 6–8.
With simple words and interesting experiments, this book presents to the youngest reader one of the basic principles of our environment: air is everywhere. By the same author: *Rain and Hail; Snow Is Falling; What the Moon Is Like; The Christmas Sky.*

Gallant, Roy A. *Exploring the Weather,* il. by Lowell Hess. Doubleday 1957. $4.50; 10–14.
A concise, well-organized study of weather. Meaningful diagrams and illustrations aid concept development.

Hicks, Clifford B. *The World Above,* il. by Richard Potts. Holt 1965. $3.50; 9–12.

Popular presentation of facts and theories about the weather and the atmosphere.

Sterling, Dorothy. *Fall Is Here,* il. by Winifred Lubell. Doubleday 1966. $3.50; 8–11.

Accurate scientific information is given simply and interestingly on what happens to sunshine, trees, leaves, seeds, birds, and animals in the fall and why. Most of the illustrations are black and white sketches, with a few in color.

PHYSICAL SCIENCE

Astronomy

Asimov, Isaac. *Environments Out There,* photos. Abelard 1967. $3.75 (P—Scholastic, $.60); 10 up.
Starting with the moon, the reader moves farther and farther out into space, discovering what is known about the nature of each planet, and ending with an assessment of problems of space travel. Readably written for the layman and splendidly illustrated.

———. *Galaxies,* il. by Alex Ebel and Denny McMaius. Follett 1968. $1.00; 7–10.
Asimov builds difficult concepts with a sparse, direct style. Though it lacks an organized format for easy reference, this book can be read in its entirety in a single sitting. A fine book for the older reader with weak reading skills.

———. *The Moon,* il. by Alex Ebel. Follett 1966. $1.00; 7–10.
Simply written information on the moon with excellent illustrations.

———. *To the Ends of the Universe.* Walker 1967. $3.95; 12 up.
The story of man's exploration of the universe over 2,500 years. Will be enjoyable for junior high readers and adults.

Bixby, William. *Universe of Galileo and Newton,* photos by Horizon Magazine. Harper 1964. $5.95; 12 up.
Skillful combination of biography and the history of science

as it is influenced by these two men. Concluding material links their influence to contemporary scientific research.

Branley, Franklyn M. *Book of Stars for You,* il. by Leonard Kessler. Crowell 1967. $3.95; 6–10.

An interesting picture book that explains what stars are, where they come from, and how long they last. In the same series: *Book of Satellites for You; Book of Planets for You; A Book of Astronauts for You; A Book of Mars for You; A Book of Moon Rockets for You; A Book of the Milky Way Galaxy for You; A Book of Venus for You.*

_____. *The Moon: Earth's Natural Satellite,* il. by Helmut K. Wimmer. Crowell 1960. $4.50; 10–15.

Technical terminology is balanced with concise, readable writing. Illustrations include a variety of charts, diagrams, and photographs. Contemporary and historical accounts of moon study, myths, and superstitions traditionally associated with the moon.

Dietz, David. *All about the Universe,* il. by John Polgreen. Random 1965. $2.95; 11–14.

Excellent presentation of various theories on the development of the universe, the many kinds of bodies existing in it, and the instruments developed to study it, all illustrated with clear black and white photographs.

Knight, David C. *Comets,* photos. Watts 1968. $2.95; 10 up.

The numerous photographs and the clear, well-organized text make this comprehensive book appropriate to the uninitiated and highly interested students alike. Equal emphasis on technical and historical background. By the same author: *The First Book of the Sun.*

Land, Barbara. *The Telescope Makers,* il. with pictures from Bettmann Archive. Crowell 1968. $4.50; 12–16.

A free-lance writer, using records and experts in the field, tells the story of telescopes from their discovery by Hans Lippershey and their development by Galileo, Newton, and other 19th-century astronomers to Friedman's rocket telescope of today.

Ley, Willy. *Inside the Orbit of the Earth,* il. by Rino Dussi. McGraw 1968. $4.50; 12–16.

The serious student of astronomy will find this book invaluable. Little-known facts of historical and scientific interest about Mercury and Venus are related in Ley's usual lively style and easy-to-use format.

Ronan, Colin. *The Universe,* il. by David A. Hardy. Watts 1966. $4.95; 8–11.

A simple and clearly written introduction to the study of stars, planets, and space travel is very well organized for easy reference. The illustrations and diagrams contribute to the clarity.

Aeronautics and Space

Asimov, Isaac. *ABC's of Space.* Walker 1969. $3.95; 6–12.

A is for Apollo, X is for X-ray. This highly informative text will fascinate children of all ages. By the same author: *Satellites in Outer Space.*

Bruce, Lois. *Space ABC,* photos. Bobbs 1967. $4.00; 7 up.

A is for astronaut; G is for gantry; Q is for quazar—so goes this exciting alphabet book that provides an A to Z exploration of space for today's moon-minded young reader. Dramatic and vibrant.

Coombs, Charles. *Skyhooks: The Story of Helicopters.* Morrow 1967. $3.50; 10 up.

A little history, instructions for operating, and the many uses of helicopters are discussed simply enough to hold the interest of the general reader of any age.

Corbett, Steve. *What Makes a Plane Fly?* il. by L. Darwin. Little 1967. $2.95; 9–12.

An amazingly accurate account of the principles of flight, amply supported by drawings and labeled diagrams.

Dalgliesh, Alice. *Ride on the Wind,* il. by Georges Schreiber. Scribner 1956. $3.12; 8–10.

An interpretation of Lindbergh's *The Spirit of St. Louis* with distinguished illustrations.

Feravolo, Rocco V. *Around the World in Ninety Minutes,* il. by William Steinel. Lothrop 1968. $3.75; 6–9.

Chronicle of a space flight from launch pad to splashdown, told in simple text for the younger reader. The illustrations, while not technical and complex, add to basic understandings about space trips and depict the orbits of two astronauts during the Gemini space flights.

Gallant, Roy A. *Exploring Mars,* rev. ed., il. by Lowell Hess. Doubleday 1968. $3.95; 12–14.

First published in 1956, this very useful oversized volume has been updated with some textual revisions, additional photographs, and an index.

————. *Exploring the Moon,* rev. ed., il. by Lowell Hess. Doubleday 1966. $3.75; 9–14.

A revision of the 1955 science classic to include information from U. S. and Russian space explorations.

Hyde, Margaret. *Exploring Earth and Space,* 4th ed. McGraw 1967. $3.95; 10–14.

Comprehensive survey of exploration as well as possibilities for the scientists of the future.

Kettlekamp, Larry. *Kites,* il. by the author. Morrow 1959. $3.36; 8 up.

Included in this book are directions for building various kinds of kites as well as pertinent information on the scientific aspects of kite-flying. The place of kites in the development of aviation and in the gathering of weather data is also discussed briefly. By the same author: *Singing Strings; The Magic of Sounds; Shadows.*

Liss, Howard. *Unidentified Flying Objects.* Hawthorn 1968. $3.95; 9–12.

This brief book recounts many UFO sightings, both those that have been explained and those still under investigation. The author explores the difficulties and improbabilities of interplanetary flight and the possibility of interplanetary communication to let the reader draw his own conclusion. Well organized and interestingly written.

May, Julian. *Rockets,* il. by Bill Barss. Follett 1967. $1.00; 7–10.

Simple explanation of the principle of rockets with exceptionally attractive and clearly identified illustrations. Suggestions of things to do.

Shippen, Katherine B. *A Bridle for Pegasus,* il. by C. B. Falls. Viking 1951. $3.50; 12 up.

A semi-fictionalized style brings historical facts to life in this record of experiments in flying that include those of Leonardo da Vinci, Samuel Langley, the Wright brothers, Charles Lindbergh, and many others.

Soule, Gardner. *UFO's and IFO's: A Factual Report on Flying Saucers.* Putnam 1967. $3.49; 5–9.

With a brief history of sightings before 1948, this book covers those that have been made since that time. The author includes investigations into the occurrences and possible causes and effects.

Sparks, James C. *Winged Rocketry,* photos. Dodd 1968. $4.50; 10–14.

Rocket pioneers of ancient China, wartime Germany, modern America, and others, interestingly presented by a retired major in the United States Air Force.

Stambler, Irwin. *Supersonic Transport,* photos. Putnam 1965. $3.29; 10 up.

The author speculates about the 1970's, when supersonic transports will be completely operable.

White, Dale. *Is Something Up There? The Story of Flying Saucers.* Doubleday 1968. $3.50 (P—Scholastic, $.60); 8–12.

An extensive account of UFO phenomena. The role of the Air Force in investigating reports shows concern for a reasoned approach to studying reported sightings. The style is vivid and very readable, making this a highly interesting and lively book.

Energy and Machines

Adamson, Gareth. *Mr. Budge Buys a Car.* Chilton 1965. $3.95; 10–16.

A picture book for those who love motor cars, vintage as well as contemporary. Covers some 10,000 years in 32 pages, from prehistoric sleds to Mercedes. Illustrations are plentiful, informative, and amusing; text is written to, not down to, the reader interested in auto mechanics.

Calder, Ritchie. *The Evolution of the Machine,* photos. American Heritage 1968. $4.95; 10–14.

From the wheel to human Orbiter I, this excellent volume scans the history of the development of man's attempt to devise ways to increase his work output. Thorough index, biographical sketches, frequent diagrams, and a straightforward style place the development of the machine in its proper social and historical context. Dramatic photographs.

Cote, Alfred J., Jr. *The Search for the Robots.* Basic 1967. $5.95; 12–16.

The more sophisticated student who seeks applications of the knowledge of biological systems to the solution of man's problems will find information that is related to common experience. A straightforward style.

Fermi, Laura. *The Story of Atomic Energy.* Random 1961. $1.95; 12 up.

The wife of the famous physicist, Enrico Fermi, traces the history of the discoveries that culminated in the release of nuclear energy in 1942; the succeeding, top secret work that culminated in the first atomic explosion in 1945; and the beginnings of peaceful uses of atomic energy.

Freeman, Mae and Ira. *The Story of Electricity,* il. by Rene Martin. Random 1961. $2.95; 10–14.

Invaluable for the average but interested reader, this factual book explains simply and clearly the functioning of electricity in our lives today.

Hirsch, S. Carl. *This Is Automation,* il. by Anthony Ravielli. Viking 1964. $3.75; 12–16.

Automation, what it is, how it grew out of the Industrial Revolution, and the role of the computer are explained. The new skills needed by man to prepare for the changes automation is bringing are pointed out.

Hoke, John. *Solar Energy,* photos and diagrams. Watts 1968. $2.95; 12 up.

The book discusses, in three approximately equal parts, the history of the use of solar energy, present and future uses, and solar energy projects suitable for young people to carry out at home or school. Knowledgeable and well written; includes addresses of companies that sell materials and a bibliography.

Knight, David C. *Let's Find Out about Magnets,* il. by Don Miller. Watts 1967. $2.95; 6–9.

Simple explanation of the principle of the magnet with a few easy experiments.

Schneider, Herman and Nina. *Your Telephone and How It Works,* il. by Jeanne Bendick. McGraw 1952, 1965. $2.75; 8–11.

After describing sound waves, how sound vibrations are turned into electrical currents and detailing the operations of switchboards and the new ways of handling long distance calls, this book explains the use of satellites for transmitting telephone and television communications.

Seeman, Bernard. *The Story of Electricity and Magnetism,* il. by James Barry. Harvey 1967. $4.50; 8–12.

Attractively illustrated account of the history and scientific components of electricity and magnetism as well as easy experiments. A glossary of terms and list of books for further reading included.

Shannon, Terry, and Charles Payzant. *The Sea Searchers,* photos and diagrams. Golden Gate 1968. $4.50; 10–14.

Up-to-date information on new tools, equipment, and vehicles that scientists have developed to explore "the last frontier." Excellent photos and diagrams of present and future undersea efforts are explained in easily understandable terms.

Thompson, Paul D. *Gases and Plasmas,* il. by Mary Lybarger. Lippincott 1966. $4.25; 12–16.

The book deals with the history of discoveries about gases and explores the extension of research on gases into the field of plasmas ("the fourth state of matter") that give promise of harnessing the sun's energy for man's use. Though readably written and well illustrated, this technical discussion is recommended only for the talented, highly informed student of science.

Wilson, Mitchell. *Seesaws to Cosmic Rays,* il. by Eva Cellini. Lothrop 1967. $4.95; 10–14.

The content of physics—force, motion, liquids and gases, light, colors, electricity, electronics, heat, and the quantum theory—are discussed simply, with many graphic illustrations. Format is especially inviting. Two-color drawings explain the text very clearly. Bibliography and index.

GENERAL SCIENCE

Abisch, Roz. *Do You Know What Time It Is?* il. by Boche Kaplan. Prentice 1968. $4.50; 4–8.

This is a colorful picture book that will lead youngsters to an understanding of the concept of time while teaching them to read a clock. Color illustrations and content are expertly combined.

Asimov, Isaac. *Building Blocks of the Universe.* Abelard 1961. $3.50; 12 up.

The story of 102 chemical elements—their discovery, naming, uses, and limitations. Some are discussed separately ("Helium: The Self-Sufficient Element," "Aluminum: The Element of the Kitchen"), and some are discussed in groups ("Copper, Silver, and Gold: The Money Elements"). A heavy subject enlightened by examples the layman is familiar with.

———. *The Clock We Live On,* il. by John Bradford. Abelard 1965. $3.50; 11–16.

The earth itself is the clock we live on. Knowledge of science, geography, and history contributes to understanding the fascinating story of time.

Bendick, Jeanne. *Shapes,* il. by the author. Watts 1968. $2.95; 6–9.

An invitation to young children to observe and experiment with geometric figures. The author's simplicity in writing and illustration and her ability to talk to children without talking down are notable.

_____. *Space and Time.* Watts 1968. $2.95; 6–9.

The everyday world familiar to children is used to help them discover concepts through observing and experimenting.

_____, and Marcia O. Levin. *Take Shapes, Lines, and Letters.* McGraw 1962. $2.95; 9–12.

Demonstrates the relationship of mathematics to art, music, secret codes, shapes in nature, proportions of the human body, space travel—every imaginable area of human interest. So clear are the explanations and so complete the drawings that the reader takes such terms as hyperbola, helix, incosahedron, and golden section in stride.

Branley, Franklyn M. *Floating and Sinking,* il. by Robert Galster. Crowell 1967. $3.50; 6–8.

Invites the young reader to experiment and so to discover why things float and sink. Information for this age group is simplified in the text and attractively and effectively presented in illustrations.

Greene, Carla. *Let's Meet the Chemist,* il. by John J. Floherty, Jr. Harvey 1966. $3.25; 7–9.

Fun for the young reader who would like to go "backstage" with the chemist in various professions—research, chemistry, crime, business, and others.

Irwin, Keith Gordon. *The Romance of Physics,* il. by Anthony Ravielli. Scribner 1966. $4.95; 12 up.

A history of the development of physics from the pioneer work of Archimedes, Galileo, and Newton to that of Einstein and Fermi is mainly biographical in approach. The format, style, and illustration, as well as the quite technical level of treatment, make this book suitable mainly for adults or students already knowledgeable in this field.

Kadesch, Dr. Robert. *The Crazy Cantilever and Other Science Experiments.* Harper 1961. $3.95; 11–14.

Forty fascinating experiments with easily assembled materials that can be performed at home.

Ley, Willy. *The Discovery of the Elements,* il. by the author. Delacorte 1968. $4.95; 12–16.

A truly fascinating account of man's developing understanding of the 104 known chemical elements. Dr. Ley's wry and humorous insights make the history of chemistry, from the ancients to the alchemists to the atomists, immediate and alive to even the most casual reader. A must for any science library.

Lohberg, Rolk, and Theo Lutz. *Electronic Brains,* il. by Fidel Nebehosteny. Sterling 1965. $4.95; 12 up.

Published in Germany in 1963, written in a breezy style with touches of humor, illustrated by many examples, cartoons, and diagrams, and checked for accuracy by a Brown University computer expert, this explanation of computers is elementary for a fairly advanced student of this subject.

Mandell, Muriel. *Physics Experiments for Children,* il. by S. Matsuda. Dover 1968. $1.25 (P); 9–12.

A fascinating book of experiments which are easy to conduct at home or at school. The experiments deal with air, water, mechanical energy and machines, heat, sound, light, magnetism, and electricity. A good introduction to elementary physics; illustrations are excellent in depicting the process involved in each experiment but are, however, a bit crowded on the page.

Raviellei, Anthony. *An Adventure in Geometry,* illus. Viking 1957. $3.75; 9–12.

A comprehensive look at geometry and its place in our world. Concepts are enhanced with fine, explicit illustrations.

Razzell, Arthur G., and K.G.O. Watts. *Three and Shapes of Three,* il. by Ellen Raskin. Doubleday 1969. $2.50; 11 up.

The number three will take on a special significance following this introduction to its place in history and literature. A series of intriguing problems with triangles, polyhedrons, and bases leads the young mathematician through exercises requiring use of materials beyond paper and pencil, including some simple constructions.

Selsam, Millicent E. *Greg's Microscope,* il. by Arnold Lobel. Harper 1963. $2.50; 6–9.

Accurate and interesting information on the use of microscopes. The story revolves around Greg's new microscope, the slides he prepares, the kinds of common household materials he investigates, and the surprising discoveries he makes. The illustrations are attractive.

Stock, Robert. *Natural Wonders of the World.* Parents 1966. $3.95; 9–13.

For the armchair traveler, a fascinating trip through famous natural wonders of the world is illustrated with handsome black-and-white photographs.

Stone, A. Harris, and Bertram Siegel. *The Chemistry of Soap*, il. by Peter P. Plasencia. Prentice 1968. $3.95; 8–12.

Inquiry training and discovery are obvious in this "how-to" book, which emphasizes scientific techniques through the content of the properties of soap. Simple, effective illustrations support such topics as surface tension, emulsification, and evaporation. An excellent glossary is included.

Sullivan, George. *How Do They Make It?* photos. Westminster 1965. $3.95; 8–12.

A fascinating and informative look at the manufacturing process of 20 household products such as salt, soap, and frozen and dehydrated foods. Clear photographs and index make this a good book for browsing as well as reference.

SPORTS AND HOBBIES

Brown, Vinson. *How to Make a Home Nature Museum,* il. by Don G. Kelly. Little 1954. $3.95; 10–12.

An informative book for older boys and girls who like to collect and keep. Collecting, classifying, mounting, and labeling specimens and making models, diagrams, and charts are a few of the activities discussed. In addition there are many suggestions for individual projects that club leaders, campers, and teachers will find helpful.

Bunning, Jim, Whitey Ford, Mickey Mantle, and Willie Mays. *Grand Slam,* photos. Viking 1965. $2.95; 12–16.

Four professional baseball players team up to give important tips on playing the game. The photographs are excellent and numerous.

Colby, C. B. *Early American Crafts Tools, Shops and Products,* photos. Coward 1967. $2.97; 8–12.

Detailed descriptions of the crafts that flourished in the early days of America. Each craft studied is accompanied by outstanding photographs.

Coombs, Charles. *Drag Racing,* photos. Morrow 1970. $3.75; 10–14.

An excellent introduction to hot rods and racing. Information is presented clearly and in an interesting, highly readable manner, and 40 photographs make the sport even more understandable.

Cooper, Elizabeth K. *Science in Your Own Backyard,* il. by the author. Harcourt 1958. $3.50 (P—Harcourt, $.65); 9–12.

An excellent, practical approach to encouraging children to explore their interests in science. This book will be as helpful to teachers and parents who may feel insecure in the science field as it will be challenging to children. Discovery and exploration in his own backyard will spark the imagination of the young scientist.

de Regniers, Beatrice Schenk, and Isabel Gordon. *The Shadow Book,* photos by Isabel Gordon. Harcourt 1960. $2.95; 4–8.

A playful and imaginative exploration in rhythmic prose and sensitive photographs of the things a child and his shadow can do together.

Docherty, Tommy. *Better Soccer for Boys,* photos. Dodd 1968. $3.25; 10–14.

Clear text and many photographs describe the rules and techniques of play.

Durant, John. *Highlights of the World Series,* photos. Hastings 1971. $6.95; 10–16.

Durant has brought information about the world series up-to-date both in text and in pictures. Chances are great for great popularity for the book in September and October and for reference during the rest of the year.

Epstein, Sam and Beryl. *The Game of Baseball,* il. by Hobe Hays. Garrard 1965. $2.59; 8–12.

The Navajo Indians played baseball long before Columbus discovered America. The half-starved soldiers at Valley Forge played ball, trying to keep warm. These are among the surprises found in this, a factual history that comes right down to today's Little Leaguers.

Hano, Arnold. *Greatest Giants of Them All.* Putnam 1967. $3.64; 10 up.

Here is a book that should be owned by every baseball enthusiast. The professional and human side of some of the Giants' greats are spelled out in detail. Most children will want to read it silently and in sections, and this is the recommended approach.

Henry, Marguerite. *Dear Readers and Riders.* Rand 1969. $3.95; 8 up.

The author's stated aim is to provide a "jolly encyclopedia" of information to answer questions of her readers. Based on actual questions asked her, she covers topics ranging from

328 ADVENTURING WITH BOOKS

aspects of her own books to tips on pets, horse riding, and housekeeping. With an index and table of contents, this book will provide an excellent guide to Mrs. Henry's horse stories.

Hobson, Burton. *Coin Collecting as a Hobby.* Sterling 1967. $2.95; 10 up.
Aside from the information for the serious coin collector, there are many interesting and little known facts that will have great appeal to any young person whose interest in money goes no farther than collecting it to spend.

Howard, Elston. *Catching,* il. by Robert Osonitsch. Viking 1966. $2.95; 12–16.
Most young baseball players have little desire to become catchers; the position seems to lack the glamor attributed to other positions. Elston Howard tells how the position should be played, and in the telling he gives the necessary appeal to the position.

Hunt, Douglas and Kari. *The Art of Magic.* Atheneum 1967. $4.95; 9–13.
A discussion of conjuring and magic, historical and modern, with directions for a few easy sleight-of-hand tricks.

Knopf, Mildred O. *Around the World Cookbook for Young People,* il. by Gioia Fiammenghi. Knopf 1966. $3.95; 11 up.
Format is unusual for a cookbook. Each of ten girls from different countries contributes a meal of traditionally favorite dishes from her own country. An introduction preceding each recipe is written in the dialect of its country. The illustrations are warm, personal, and very well done.

Lindsay, Sally. *Figure Skating.* Rand 1963. $2.95; 11–16.
Described are the demanding self-discipline, the harrying mothers, the intense competition, the joy of achievement, and the toll of perfection for those who skate or have interest, aspiration, or hopes in this most demanding of sports.

Lipsyte, Robert. *Assignment: Sports.* Harper 1970. $3.79; 12–16.
New York Times sports columnist Robert Lipsyte writes a series of short, intimate articles about various athletes involved in many different sports. Gives new insights into the sports world and the personalities who make it what it is.

Longman, Harold. *Would You Put Your Money in a Sand Bank?* il. by Abner Grabhoff. Rand 1968. $2.95; 3 up.

Homonyms used in jokes, puns, riddles, and "nonsense conversations" provide amusement and increase word appreciation and language skill with almost effortless ease. Useful with the reluctant reader and reluctant speller, the child for whom English is a second language, and last of all the good reader who enjoys the fun one can have with words. The book is pleasant in itself but also serves as a successful learning tool.

Manners, William. *1 2 3 Go.* Four Winds 1967. $3.50; 10 up.

A good, simple, and practical manual on physical fitness for boys containing an excellent section on the harmful effects that can come from the use of tobacco and alcohol.

Parish, Peggy. *Let's Be Early Settlers with Daniel Boone,* il. by Arnold Lobel. Harper 1967. $3.95; 9–12.

Lively instructions for the would-be pioneer tell how to make everything from clothing to log cabins.

Pickens, Richard. *How to Punt, Pass and Kick,* il. by Fran Chauncy. Random 1965. $1.95; 12–16.

Realistic tips on how to play football are interestingly given by an authority in the field. The black-and-white illustrations give a feeling of motion.

Powers, William K. *Here Is Your Hobby: Indian Dancing and Customs,* photos. Putnam 1966. $3.50; 10–16.

Not only art hobbies but physical education activities can be teamed with the study of American Indians. The cultures of different tribes can be interpreted in a study of their dancing, involving costumes, singing, and history. Photographs illustrate the postures and steps.

Rosenfeld, Sam. *The Story of Coins,* il. by James E. Barry. Harvey 1968. $3.95; 10 up.

This interesting book traces the history of coins and gives practical suggestions and techniques for establishing coin collections. Many illustrations, exhaustive lists on cataloging and terminology, extended readings, and an index make this an authoritative text.

Van Riper, Guernsey, Jr. *The Game of Basketball.* Garrard 1967. $2.59; 8–11.

A history of America's popular sport. The development of this game is traced from its invention in 1891, when peach baskets were goals, up to the present. Young fans will delight in the facts and action-filled accounts presented.

Wilson, Forrest. *Architecture: A Book of Projects for Young Adults,* il. by the author. Reinhold 1968. $6.95; 11 up.

Describes 33 projects "which will lead the reader to an understanding of structural principles, classic symmetry, scale, and space." It will mainly be of interest to those who can follow careful directions and who are interested in a study of architecture. The book is divided into three parts —old architecture, modern architecture, and the language of architecture. Glossary and bibliography.

Wyler, Rose, and Gerald Ames. *Magic Secrets,* il. by Talivaldis Stubis. Harper 1967. $2.50 (P—Scholastic, $.60); 7 up.

A beginning book about tricks that can be done by an amateur, simply written and clearly illustrated for the beginning independent reader who aspires to legerdemain. The text suggests that an audience sees that to which its attention is directed; the small diversionary tactics that add to illusion are shown.

ARTS, CRAFTS, MUSIC, DRAMA, DANCE

Aliki. *Hush Little Baby,* il. by the author. Prentice 1968. $4.25; 3–6.

A sheer delight! The old folk lullaby is wonderfully illustrated and lives again. All children will like this one.

Audsley, James. *The Book of Ballet,* rev.ed., photos. Warne 1968. $2.95; 12–16.

A revised edition of a quality book developed for a specialized interest. Young readers seeking a depth investigation of ballet will not be disappointed with the beautiful photographs that supplement a highly informative text.

Bank-Jensen, Thea. *Play with Paper,* tr. by Virginia Allen Jensen. Macmillan 1962. $3.95; 6–12.

Instructions for making basic forms; encourages the child to create his own figures.

Beaney, Jean. *The Young Embroiderer.* Warne 1967. $3.95; 10–14.

Embroidery is introduced as an exciting art form from which interesting wall hangings, murals, and panels can be created. A highly commendable aspect of the book and one which sets it apart from ordinary how-to-do-it books is the creative element the author invites.

Bennett, Rowena. *Creative Plays and Programs for Holidays.* Plays, Inc. 1966. $6.95; 9–16.

A very complete anthology of plays and programs for the

various holidays as well as the seasons. These royalty-free plays, readings, and poems for children in the middle-elementary grades can easily be used up to early high school. The holidays included are American, with a strong Christian slant.

Berkowitz, Freda Pastor. *On Lutes, Recorders, and Harpsichords,* il. by Malcolm Spooner. Atheneum 1967. $4.75; 10–14.

An interesting introduction makes clear the nature of the Baroque period from the end of the 16th to the 18th century. The dynamic developments in music—as in architecture, painting, and sculpture—contrasted to the serenity of the Renaissance period.

Boni, Margaret Bradford. *Fireside Book of Folk Songs,* arr. for piano by Norman Lloyd, il. by Alice and Martin Provensen. Simon 1947. $6.95; 10–16.

Words, music, and bright pictures are included for 147 favorite songs: ballads, work songs, marching songs, spirituals, hymns, and carols.

Borten, Helen. *Do You Move as I Do?* il. by the author. Abelard 1963. $3.50; 4–8.

This little book should be an effective aid in stimulating dramatic expression and interpretation, especially useful with a shy child. The text invites the reader to express the varying movements of many things.

————. *Do You See What I See?* il. by the author. Abelard 1959. $2.95; 5–8.

An awareness book that raises questions as well as answering them. The author-artist introduces the child to the lines, shapes, and colors around him and to their effects upon his feelings and emotions. The illustrations are rhythmical and lovely.

Brock, Virginia. *Piñatas,* il. by A. M. Jauss. Abingdon 1966. $3.00; 10–14.

A book of holiday piñatas with directions for making 11 of them.

Buckman, Irene. *Twenty Tales from Shakespeare,* photos. Random 1965. $3.95; 10–15.

The great plays of Shakespeare are presented in narrative form. The contents include the comedies, tragedies, and histories and should be valuable to high school students who are trying to grasp the many sides of Shakespeare. Plots are presented with care and taste and should help the student in a painless transition to Shakespearean drama. Foreword by Dame Peggy Ashcroft.

Bulla, Clyde Robert. *Stories of Gilbert and Sullivan Operas,* il. by James and Ruth McCrea. Crowell 1968. $4.95; 10–16.

Bulla has brought 11 Gilbert and Sullivan pieces to children in delightful form. Junior high students can use this to good advantage, too. By the same author: *More Stories of Favorite Operas; The Ring and the Fire: Stories from Wagner's Nibelung Operas.*

Campbell, Ann. *Start to Draw,* il. by the author. Watts 1968. $2.95; 5–9.

Drawing for young children is treated as an imaginative game.

Carlson, Bernice Wells. *Act It Out,* il. by Laszlo Matulay. Abingdon 1956. $2.50 (P—Abingdon, $1.60); 8–12.

A fine source book for ideas and material for dramatic activity—not just plays but games, puppets, pantomime, tableaux, shadow plays, and so on.

Chappell, Warren, adapter. *The Nutcracker,* il. by the adapter. Knopf 1958. $2.95; 8–12.

Little Marie's dreams are the basis for adventures with a handsome young prince (once a nutcracker received as a Christmas gift), the Mouse King, and Princess Pirlipate. Based on Tchaikovsky's world-famous ballet. By the same adapter: *Coppelia, the Girl with Enamel Eyes.*

Chase, Alice Elizabeth. *Famous Artists of the Past,* illus. Platt 1964. $6.95; 9 up.

A large picture book dramatizing important elements in the lives and works of 27 great painters and sculptors.

―――. *Famous Paintings: An Introduction to Art for Young People,* illus. Platt 1962. $6.95; 10 up.

Twelve new pictures have been added to this edition of an attractive picture book of art. Contains 184 plates, including 54 in color.

―――. *Looking at Art,* illus. Crowell 1966. $4.50; 12–14.

More than 100 illustrations in color and black and white in an attractive book.

Chute, Marchette. *Stories from Shakespeare.* World 1956. $3.95 (P—NAL, $.95); 12–16.

Transitional literature of high quality. This book should be no substitute for Shakespeare's plays, but it undoubtedly

will aid many contemporary readers to bridge the time gap
in the dramatic communication form.

Cummings, Richard. *101 Masks,* il. by the author. McKay
1968. $4.25; 8–14.

Excellent and detailed descriptions of how to make all kinds
of masks for fun, drama, and decoration.

Dias, Earl J. *New Comedies for Teenagers.* Plays, Inc. 1967.
$6.95; 12–16.

A good collection of one-act, royalty-free comedies, farces,
and melodramas for older boys and girls, which should be of
value to seventh- and eighth-grade teachers wishing to help
children understand dramatic form.

Dietz, Betty Warner. *Musical Instruments of Africa,* il. by
Richard M. Powers. Day 1965. $5.95; 12 up.

Many photographs, an informative text, and a long-playing
record describe musical instruments of Africa south of the
Sahara.

Downer, Marion. *Discovering Design,* il. by the author.
Lothrop 1947. $3.50; 12–16.

A book that helps train the eye to see design everywhere.
Valuable for both adults and children. By the same author:
The Story of Design, another distinguished volume.

Emberley, Ed. *London Bridge Is Falling Down,* il. by the
author. Little 1967. $3.50; 4–8.

This little song and game book adds fun and flavor to an
age-old song and game universally played by the very young.

———. *Punch and Judy: A Play for Puppets,* il. by the author.
Little 1965. $3.50; 5–9.

The spontaneity and dash of the traditional play are captured in a delightful book.

Freeman, Mae. *Fun with Ballet,* photos. Random 1952. $1.95;
9–12.

Photographs and clear instructive text demonstrate the five
positions and the movements and exercises in ballet dancing.

Fuller, Edmund A. *Pageant of the Theater,* rev. ed., photos.
Crowell 1965. $4.95; 12–16.

This revised edition of the 1941 original is a good historical
panorama of the theatre, covering ancient and modern
theatre in considerable depth. The photographs do not add
to the text.

Gard, Robert E., and David Semmes. *America's Players.* Seabury 1967. $3.95; 10–16.

This history of the American theatre in twenty well-written short stories is good and should be a must for young theatre buffs.

Garson, Eugenia, and Herbert Haufrecht, eds. *The Laura Ingalls Wilder Songbook,* il. by Garth Williams. Harper 1968. $5.95; 9 up.

All the music from the "Little House" books is found in this treasure for any music class. Music is easily played on piano and guitar.

Gilbert, W. S., and Arthur Sullivan. *The Mikado,* retold by Martha Means, il. by Anne and Janet Grahame Johnstone. Watts 1965. $3.50; 8–12.

This is the first in a series called "Curtain Raisers"—the stories of operas, ballets, and the like—and is well worth a look. The illustrations, though flashy, make this almost a twice-told tale. The text, using much of the original libretto, tends to grow confusing. Text and illustrations together do tell a good story.

Glubok, Shirley. *The Art of Africa,* il. arr. by Gerard Nook. Harper 1965. $4.50; 7–10.

An introduction to the simplicity and abstract form of the art work of the African continent, centuries old but generally known only within the last hundred years. Some photos are deceptive because there is no indication of scale; the reader has no way of comparing sizes of objects. By the same author: *The Art of Ancient Mexico; The Art of Ancient Rome; The Art of the North American Indian.*

Green, Carla. *Let's Learn about the Orchestra,* il. by Anne Lewis. Harvey 1967. $3.25; 6 up.

An informative and inspiring book about the modern orchestra, containing the history and development of each group of instruments. Concludes with a tribute to the conductor. Illustrations add much to the high quality of this fine introduction to instruments.

Hark, Mildred, and Noel McQueen. *Special Plays for Special Days.* Plays, Inc. 1947. $5.95; 9–13.

A fine collection of plays for holiday festivals. These plays are well written, easily produced, and worth acting.

Harris, Leon A. *The Great Picture Robbery,* il. by Joseph Schindelman. Atheneum 1963. $3.25; 6–10.

This story approach to art information is surprisingly successful. The book contains significant and beautiful pictures of some of the treasures of the Louvre.

Hart, Tony. *The Young Designer.* Warne 1968. $3.95; 8–12.

The ideas presented here are interestingly described and commendably inclusive. This is the kind of material that could help young children become more sensitive to the good and poor design with which they are constantly confronted.

Hautzig, Esther. *Let's Make Presents,* il. by Ava Morgan. Crowell 1962. $4.50; 9–12.

"How to make 100 gifts for less than a dollar." Stitching and sewing hints and construction directions are well illustrated.

Hawkinson, John. *Pastels Are Great!* il. by the author. Whitman 1968. $3.50; 7–12.

A fine look at the wonders of pastels is a must for any art, hobby, or recreation group. Well illustrated.

Headington, Christopher. *The Orchestra and Its Instruments,* il. by Roy Spencer. World 1967. $3.95; 12–16.

A historical development of the symphony orchestra with full descriptions, photographs, and drawings of the instruments.

Helfman, Harry. *Fun with Your Fingers,* il. by Robert Bartram. Morrow 1968. $3.50; 8–12.

Clever ideas for working with sticks, paper, and string to create toys for amusement, decorations for special occasions, and some inexpensive gifts for friends. Especially valuable if the reader can see the possibilities of extending these ideas into creative enterprises of his own.

Hirsch, S. Carl. *Printing from a Stone: The Story of Lithography,* illus. Viking 1967. $3.75; 10–16.

A history of the craft told through the lives of the men who pioneered in it, with many attractive illustrations.

Hodges, Margaret, ed. *Constellation: A Shakespeare Anthology.* Farrar 1968. $4.50; 12–16.

Outstanding scenes from 26 plays, which include some of the most beautiful poetry in the English language.

Hofsinde, Robert. *Indian Music Makers.* Morrow 1967. $3.50; 7–11.

Again Gray Wolf (Hofsinde) adds to our understanding of American Indians in his 13th book about them. Here he tells not only how much music means in the life of Indians in ceremonial songs, lullabies, victory songs, planting and harvest songs, and love songs but also describes the instruments and how they are made. He closes with examples of old and new songs and their uses.

Holme, Bryan. *Drawings to Live With,* reproductions. Viking 1966. $4.50; 8 up.

Drawing is presented as one of the most intimate and exciting of all art forms. One hundred forty drawings by some of the greatest artists of the world are presented interestingly. Beautiful endpapers are from a drawing by Raoul Dufy.

Hunt, Douglas and Kari. *Pantomime: The Silent Theatre,* photos. Atheneum 1964. $3.95; 12–16.

Contents explore pantomime from various eras and geographic locations. Drama students will enjoy this close look.

Hurd, Michael. *Soldiers' Songs and Marches.* Walck 1966. $4.00; 10–16.

A valuable and enjoyable addition to the Young Reader's Guide to Music series beginning with the ways music was used from earliest times to stir soldiers' spirits or to keep them in step. The author discusses the musical instruments of battle, the drummer boy, military bands, songs, and marches. Fine examples of such songs and marches are included.

Isenstein, Harold. *Creative Claywork,* illus. Sterling 1961. $3.95; 8 up.

An inviting book with clear directions and illustrations.

Jackson, Jacqueline. *Spring Song,* il. by Barbara Morrow. Kent 1969. $3.75; 4–8.

This robust song of spring together with the beautiful color prints make a memorable song and picture book.

Jacobs, David. *Master Builders of the Middle Ages,* illus. American Heritage 1969. $5.95; 10–16.

A study of 400 years of Gothic cathedral architecture, starting from the abbey at Saint-Denis in 1140, introduces artisans, abbots, and the people who shared the beauty of art during the Middle Ages. Sources are a mason's sketchbook, modern photographs, and diagrams. The design, the light, and the development of unity in art are considered symbolic for a house of God.

Jagendorf, Moritz. *Puppets for Beginners,* il. by Jean Michener. Plays, Inc. 1952. $3.95; 6–10.

The whole world of puppets is presented in this colorful little volume, essentially a "how to do it" book on puppets and puppet theatre. Detailed directions are given on how to construct puppets of various kinds and how to produce puppet shows. The illustrations are helpful and attractive. This book should be a welcome addition to any classroom that enjoys creative work with drama. By the same author: *Penny Puppets, Penny Theatre, and Penny Plays.*

Janson, H. W. and Dora J. *The Story of Painting for Young People,* illus. Abrams 1962. $5.95; 12–16.
An illuminating and authoritative study of painting from the days of the caveman to modern times. Illustrated with reproductions in color and black and white.

Johnson, James Weldon and J. Rosamond. *Lift Every Voice and Sing,* il. by Monzelle Thompson. Hawthorn 1970. $3.95; all ages.
Charcoal drawings underscore the dignity and movement of the music and lyrics of this long-time Negro "national anthem."

Kamerman, Sylvia E. *Fifty Plays for Junior Actors.* Plays, Inc. 1966. $8.95; 10–16.
A collection of royalty-free one-act plays for youngsters in upper-elementary and junior high schools. The excellent selections, ranging over a wide interest span, come from classic as well as contemporary sources.

Kapp, Paul. *A Cat Came Fiddling,* il. by Irene Haas. Harcourt 1956. $3.25; 8–12.
Paul Kapp and Irene Haas with new tunes and unforgettable pictures have given children 57 old nonsense rhymes and verses. While the book is modern in every sense, it manages to retain the flavor of the old English songs.

Knudsen, Lynne, comp. *Lullabies from around the World,* arr. by Carl Bosler, il. by Jacquelyn Tomes. Follett 1967. $4.95; 3–8.
The book contains simple lullabies from all around the world, lyrics and music for holidays and every day.

Langstaff, John. *On Christmas Day in the Morning,* il. by Antony Graves-Raines. Harcourt 1959. $3.50; all ages.
An exquisitely illustrated collection of four of our loveliest traditional Christmas carols.

———. *The Swapping Boy,* il. by Beth and Joe Krush. Harcourt 1960. $3.25; 9–12.
The development of a folk song is presented in verse with delightful illustrations. Since each new verse begins with

the same couplet, the book can be used with very young children for sheer enjoyment.

Lewis, Shari, and Lillian Oppenheimer. *Folding Paper Masks,* illus. Dutton 1965. $4.50; 8–10.

Step-by-step instructions are presented with easy-to-follow illustrations for the construction of 21 masks. Most of these projects require little more than a piece of paper.

Love, S. A., and W. D. Cumming. *Plays for Reading and Recording.* Plays, Inc. 1966. $2.95; 12 up.

A collection of plays from standard and classic literary works, designed for oral drama. Sound and music cues and suggestions for characterization are included in the scripts.

Marks, Mickey. *Collage,* photos by David Rosenfeld. Dial 1968. $3.95; 7 up.

Excellent collection of easy-to-do collages. Good photographs enhance the usefulness.

Miller, Irene Preston, and Winifred Lubell. *The Stitchery Book: Embroidery for Beginners,* illus. Doubleday 1965. $4.95; 10–16.

Patterns for embroidery designs and other useful information concerning stitchery in a fascinating book of interest to all ages.

Miller, Louise Helen. *Plays for Living and Learning.* Plays, Inc. 1955. $4.00; 10–16.

An interesting group of plays designed to help the teacher promote various concepts. Their effective use should have interesting and positive results.

Mills, Alan. *The Hungry Goat,* il. by Abner Graboff. Rand 1964. $3.08; all ages.

A well-known Canadian folk singer gives his version of this old folk tale of the goat that ate the shirts right off the line. Abner Graboff's very funny illustrations are perfect for the hilarity of the song. A simple piano and guitar arrangement is given at the end. By the same author: *I Know an Old Lady.*

Mills, John. *The Young Artist,* il. by the author. Sterling 1968. $2.95; 9–14.

A reasonably complete look at art, its history, and the techniques involved in its execution. The writing often falls into a textbook style, but the information will fascinate art enthusiasts.

Moore, Lamont. *The Sculptured Image.* Watts 1967. $2.95; 12–16.

A highly commendable commentary on the sculptor, his

work, and his objectives. Sculptors of note are introduced as
well as some of their works and the elements that have made
them effective.

Moreton, John. *The Love for Three Oranges,* il. by Murray
Tinkleman. Putnam 1966. $3.95; all ages.

One of the Opera Stories for Young People series presented
in cooperation with the Metropolitan Opera Guild. Tinkleman's dramatic colorful illustrations add richly to this
lively retelling of Prince Tartaly's adventures. As in all these
books, only the story is given—no music.

Nuttall, Kenneth. *Play Production for Young People,* il. by N.
S. Hyslop. Plays, Inc. 1966. $4.50; 12–16.

This good introduction for youngsters interested in acting
and play production covers the organization of a drama
group, production ideas, acting, makeup, and costume in a
chatty, informal manner. Line drawings show details of set
construction. A valuable resource book.

Olfson, Lewy. *Dramatized Classics for Radio-Style Reading,*
vol. I and II. Plays, Inc. 1964. $5.00 ea.; 10–17.

Two very fine collections of classics in radio script form,
unique in that sound effects and music are all included in
the scripts. They would be excellent material for the creative
teacher wanting new ways to encourage spoken language
arts with the tape recorder.

Paine, Roberta M. *Looking at Sculpture,* photos and drawings.
Lothrop 1968. $4.95; all ages.

This well-written and well-documented historical look at
the art of sculpture is effectively illustrated.

Price, Christine. *The Story of Moslem Art,* illus. Dutton
1964. $4.95; 10–14.

With the chapters divided by countries, this contains many
illustrations and descriptions. Map, list of sources of illustrations. By the same author: *Made in the Renaissance;
Made in the Middle Ages.*

Priestley, J. B. *The Wonderful World of the Theatre,* rev. ed., il.
by Fermano Facetti. Doubleday 1968. $3.95; 10–16.

One of the better Wonderful World books, this oversized,
colorfully illustrated book presents a fine look at the theatre
from many vantage points. Its history as well as drama from
all parts of the world are handled with imagination and real
knowledge.

Prokofieff, Serge. *Peter and the Wolf,* il. by Frans Haacken.
Watts 1962. $3.84; 5–9.

Prokofieff's musical story, popular ever since its completion in 1936, is turned into a picture book. White lines appear on black background, and a new touch of color is added on each page, until the blue, green, yellow, and red all are included in the procession that marches the bad wolf to his doom. The story is marked by simplicity of plot and language.

Purdy, Susan. *Holiday Cards for You to Make.* Lippincott 1967. $4.95; all ages.

Clear directions for making greeting cards, place cards, and invitations.

Roberts, Cliff. *Start with a Dot,* il. by the author. Watts 1960. $2.95; 5–8.

A fine book for the very young. The creative use of familiar material will be appreciated by child and teacher alike.

Rounds, Glen. *Casey Jones: The Story of a Brave Engineer,* il. by the author. Golden Gate 1968. $3.95; 8 up.

Some simple music accompanies the verses that tell the epic story of Casey's last run on the railroad. Rounds' sympathetic pictures enhance the tale.

_____. comp. *The Strawberry Roan,* il. by the compiler. Golden 1970. $4.27; 8–12.

Even those youngsters who don't like to sing along with the music teacher will enjoy this selection of verses about the classic duel between a bronc buster and the strawberry roan, the meanest horse ever depicted by an artist.

Rublowsky, John. *Music in America.* Crowell-Collier 1967. $3.50; 12–16.

Here is a lively, authentic, well-written account of American music—as a vital area of our artistic life and as one of the country's significant contributions to the 20th-century world. It begins with the sacred and secular music of both Puritans and Moravians and ends with such modern experimentalist composers as Harry Partch and John Cage.

Ruskin, Ariane. *The Pantheon Story of Art for Young People,* il. with reproductions. Pantheon 1964. $6.95; 10–16.

Five thousand years of painting and sculpture from cave painting to the present. A large book with many illustrations in color.

Russell, Solveig Paulson. *Wonderful Stuff: The Story of Clay,* il. by Gray Morrow. Rand 1963. $3.08; 8–12.

This book provides a simple yet highly informative discussion of clay in its practical, artistic, and historical aspects. Fine illustrations add to the effect.

Samson, Anne. *Lines, Spines and Porcupines,* il. by the author. Doubleday 1969. $3.50; 5–9.

A sheer delight! Creative use of lines, circles, and colors opens up a whole new experience for the very young. Imaginations will glow after reading this one.

Sechrist, Elizabeth H., and Janette Woolsey. *New Plays for Red Letter Days,* il. by Guy Fry. Macrae 1955. $4.97; 9–14.

A list of short plays to help celebrate special holidays from Flag Day to Fire Prevention Week. Good and helpful hints are given to actors and directors.

Seeger, Ruth C. *American Folksongs for Children,* il. by Barbara Cooney. Doubleday 1948. $5.50; all ages.

Mrs. Seeger, working with Sandburg, the Lomaxes, and many other lovers and singers of American folksongs, collected these and sang them happily with small children. The range is enormous, and Barbara Cooney's small, droll pictures quietly enliven the pages.

Seidelman, J. E., and Grace Mintoyne. *Creating with Clay.* Crowell-Collier 1967. $3.95; 9–12.

A guide to working with clay that leaves room for the imagination. Equally impressive guides by the same author: *Creating with Mosaics; Creating with Paper; Creating with Paint.*

Severn, William and Sue. *Let's Give a Show,* il. by Carla Kenny. Knopf 1956. $2.75; 9–15.

A topflight source book for youngsters interested in all kinds of theatre activity. The contents are arranged intelligently and written with obvious background knowledge.

Shippen, Katherine B., and A. Seidlova. *The Heritage of Music,* il. by O. V. Ersel. Viking 1963. $6.00; 12 up.

A history of music from primitive times to the modern musician's electronic compositions.

Siegmeister, Elie. *Invitation to Music,* il. by Beatrice Schwartz. Harvey 1961. $4.95; 10–14.

A history to enrich a child's understanding of the music he hears and enjoys.

Slade, Richard. *Modeling in Clay, Plaster and Papier-Mâché,* photos. Lothrop 1968. $3.50; 8 up.

A good guide for young artist who wants to learn more about modeling. Well organized and easy to read.

_____. *You Can Make a String Puppet,* photos by John Watts. Plays, Inc. 1966. $2.95; 8–12.

This is a first American edition of an English volume (1957) on how to make string puppets. It is concise, easy to read, simple to follow, and well illustrated. A valuable addition to any collection on puppetry.

Spilka, Arnold. *Paint All Kinds of Pictures,* il. by the author. Walck 1963. $4.75; 7–12.

The beautiful color-splashed illustrations will inspire the young reader to paint his own ideas, feelings, and thoughts. The uncluttered style of the book, the short sentences, and repetition of key words make for easy reading.

Streatfeild, Noel. *The First Book of the Opera,* il. by Hilary Abraham. Watts 1967. $2.95; 9–14.

Here is a decidedly informal approach to the place of opera in a child's growing experience of the arts. The author reveals what a musical play is and how it may be enjoyed at home on television, radio, or records as well as in the theatre. A brief history of the rise of operas, the operas of Italy and Germany during the 19th and 20th centuries, some of the great singers, the most famous composers, and the producing and costuming of an opera are discussed. By the same author: *The First Book of Ballet.*

Strouse, Susanne. *Candle-Making.* Sterling 1968. $2.95; 7–12.

One of the Little Craft series, this one is translated from the German. All one wants to know about candle-making is contained in this fine little book.

Trease, Geoffrey. *Seven Stages,* photos. Vanguard 1965. $3.95; 12–16.

The great stars of the past are presented in colorful vignettes depicting their lives and the theatre of the day. Seven men and women are presented; censorship and anti-theatre are aspects discussed.

Untermeyer, Louis. *Tales from the Ballet,* il. by A. and M. Provensen. Golden 1968. $5.95; 9–12.

Summaries of the plots of 20 well-known ballets.

Walker, Kathrine Sorley. *Eyes on the Ballet,* photos. Day 1965. $4.29; 10–14.

This careful examination of the world of ballet is well organized, well written, and illustrated with action photographs of some of the world's greatest dancers in their greatest roles. The coverage of the ballet from choreography to costume, from music to mass media should be of great interest to youngsters studying dance or those who have an interest in this aspect of theatre.

Wall, L. V., and G. A. White, eds. *The Puppet Book,* photos and drawings. Plays, Inc. 1967. $6.95; 12 up.

This excellent source book on puppetry comes to America from the Educational Puppetry Association of London. It consists of readings clustered around various aspects of puppetry and its uses, all written by experts in the field. A valuable book for those who wish to engage in puppetry.

Wechsberg, Joseph. *Story of Music,* illus. Pantheon 1958. $4.95; 11–16.

This fine book for the young (and not-so-young) musician or music-lover is most thorough in its coverage. The illustrations are a real asset. Junior high or high school youngsters will like it.

Weik, Mary Hays. *The Scarlet Thread,* il. by Barbara Remington. Atheneum 1968. $4.50; 7–12.

A fine collection of five one-act plays for children. Much production help is included. This is one of the better collections for classroom use.

Weiss, Harvey. *Clay, Wood, and Wire,* il. with classic sculpture selected by the author. Scott 1956. $3.95; 10–14.

A skillful combination of the world's great sculpture and suggestions for stimulating creative experiences. A fine example of a how-to-do-it book in a do-it-yourself age. By the same author: *Paper, Ink, and Rollers; Sticks, Spools, and Feathers.*

Wilson, Erica. *Fun with Crewel Embroidery.* Scribner 1965. $3.95; 7–12.

Concise instructions for stitching with wool on fabric. An inviting book with a distinguished format.

Wirtenberg, Patricia Z. *All-around-the-House Art and Craft.* Houghton 1968. $5.00; 10 up.

A practical, easy-to-follow source book on arts and crafts in a home setting, this would be a good book for the shut-in or home teacher.

Wood, Katherine. *Here's How,* il. by the author. McKay 1968. $3.25; 8–11.

Excellent book has directions for young girls on how to make things out of odds and ends.

FOREIGN LANGUAGE

Cooper, Lee. *Fun with German,* il. by Elizabeth M. Githens. Little 1965. $3.95; 9–12.
Helpful to children learning German for its stories, songs, games, and other entertaining activities.

———. *Fun with Italian,* il. by Ann Atene. Little 1964. $3.95; 9–12.
A collection of stories, games, and songs is used to introduce the reader to Italian pronunciation and grammar. Valuable as supplementary material.

———. *Fun with Spanish,* il. by Ann Atene. Little 1960. $3.95; 9–12.
An amusing volume for the child who reads English and wants to speak Spanish (with a Mexican accent). The illustrations help to teach vocabulary as well as pronunciation.

———, and Clifton McIntosh. *Fun with French,* il. by Ann Atene. Little 1963. $3.95; 9–12.
This important aid in learning French includes short stories, pictures, songs, and activities.

Frasconi, Antonio. *See Again, Say Again,* il. by the author. Harcourt 1964. $3.25; 8–12.
English, Italian, French, and Spanish words are given (with phonetic pronunciation) for a number of familiar items and ideas.

_____. *See and Say: A Picture Book in Four Languages,* il. by the author. Harcourt 1955. $3.25; 5–9.

An introduction to English, Italian, French, and Spanish for young children. The print is color-coded to represent a particular language. Woodcuts are unusual and colorful.

_____. *The Snow and the Sun: La nieve y el sol,* il. by the author. Harcourt 1961. $3.25; 5–8.

Bold woodcuts and striking color distinguish this picture book in which English and Spanish versions are printed side by side. The cumulative folk rhyme from Uruguay suggests European origin in its resemblance to "The Old Woman and Her Pig." The precise repetition encourages language learning.

Hautzig, Esther. *At Home: A Visit in Four Languages,* il. by Aliki. Macmillan 1968. $4.95; 8–10.

Illustrations in bright, strong colors and short text. From one to five everyday words like book, bed, father, potatoes on each of 20 pages are presented in English, French, Spanish, and Russian with accent and stress marks. Recommended for family fun and sharing or for use by individuals.

Joslin, Sesyle. *Baby Elephant's Trunk,* il. by Leonard Weisgard. Harcourt 1961. $2.75; 4 up.

This is an enchanting picture story for the pre-schooler with some exposure to the French language. For the older pupil, it has a gay approach to the French phrases important to travel.

_____. *There Is a Dragon in My Bed,* il. by Irene Haas. Harcourt 1961. $2.95; 8 up.

This gaily illustrated book has French phrases, pronunciation guides, and the English all on the same page. Most phrases have been selected for usefulness, but some are just for fun.

Lear, Edward. *Le hibou et la poussiquette (The Owl and the Pussycat),* tr. by Francis Steegmuller, il. by Barbara Cooney. Little 1961. $2.95; 5–9.

A charming picture book with humorously appropriate illustrations. The English version is appended.

Lenski, Lois. *Papa Petit, Papa Small,* il. by the author. Walck 1963. $3.50; 5–9.

French translation of a nursery classic, with the English version on the same page.

_____. *Vacquero Pequeno: Cowboy Small,* tr. by Donald Worcester. Walck 1960. $3.50; 5–9.

Now children can read a favorite Lenski story in two languages.

Moore, Lilian. *Papa Albert,* il. by Gioia Fiammenghi. Atheneum 1964. $3.95; 5–9.

This delightfully different approach to language learning tells in English of the two little girls who ride around Paris all day with their father in his taxicab. Signs and place names are in French. At the end, a picture dictionary gives the French and English translations of many important words in the story.

Mother Goose in French, tr. by Hugh Latham, il. by Barbara Cooney. Crowell 1964. $3.95; 10–12.

Latham's excellent translation is enhanced by charming illustrations. The sentences are rather long and some of the words are difficult, making this suitable for the student of French.

Politi, Leo. *Rosa,* il. by the author. Scribner 1963. $3.25; 5–9.

Mexican village life and holiday customs are presented delightfully in the story of Rosa, a Mexican girl who wishes for a doll and gets something better.

Rey, H. A. *Jorge el curioso (Curious George),* tr. by Pedro Villa Fernandez, il. by the author. Houghton 1961. $3.90; 5–9.

Curious George, the monkey, has many amusing adventures in the city before going to the zoo. This Spanish translation will prove valuable for youngsters learning the language.

Ritchie, Barbara. *Ramon Makes a Trade,* il. by Earl Thollander. Parnassus 1959. $3.50; 8–11.

This colorful story with Spanish and English versions alternating is written for readers in the intermediate grades, but it is especially useful for those learning Spanish.

————. *To Catch a Mongoose: A Picture Story,* il. by Earl Thollander. Parnassus 1963. $3.95; 7–10.

A boy on the island of Martinique decides to go into business and raise a mongoose for fighting. His sister spoils the plan by raising the mongoose as a pet. The English translation appears at the top of the page, the French at the bottom.

Steegmuller, Francis, and Norbert Guterman. *Papillot, Clignot et Dodo,* il. by Barbara Cooney. Farrar 1964. $3.25; 7–12.

This delightful French version of "Wynken, Blynken and Nod" has important adjuncts—the original poem in English, a brief French-English vocabulary, and a few notes on Eugene Field. Against a blue-black background the figures and properties in the illustrations seem touched with shimmering light.

DIRECTORY OF PUBLISHERS

ABELARD—Abelard-Schuman Limited, 257 Park Ave. South, New York, N.Y. 10010

ABINGDON—Abingdon Press, 201 Eighth Ave. South, Nashville, Tenn. 37202

ABRAMS—Harry N. Abrams, Inc., 110 East 59th St., New York, N.Y. 10022

AIRMONT—Airmont Publishing Co., Inc., 22 East 60th St., New York, N.Y. 10022

AMERICAN HERITAGE—American Heritage Publishing Co., Inc. 551 Fifth Ave., New York, N.Y. 10017

APOLLO—Apollo Editions, Inc., 201 Park Ave. South, New York, N.Y. 10003

APPLETON—Appleton-Century-Crofts, 440 Park Ave. South, New York, N.Y. 10016

ARCHWAY—Archway Books; Distributed by Simon & Schuster

ATHENEUM—Atheneum Publishers, 122 East 42nd St., New York, N.Y. 10017

AVALON—Avalon Press, Box 4083, Washington, D.C. 20015

AVON—Avon Books, 959 Eighth Ave., New York, N.Y. 10019

BALLANTINE—Ballantine Books, Inc., 101 Fifth Ave., New York, N.Y. 10003

BASIC—Basic Books, Inc., 404 Park Ave. South, New York, N.Y. 10016

BENEFIC—Benefic Press, 10300 West Roosevelt Rd., Westchester, Ill, 60153

BERKLEY—Berkley Publishing Corp., 200 Madison Ave., New York, N.Y. 10016

BOBBS—The Bobbs-Merrill Co., Inc., 4300 West 62nd St., Indianapolis, Ind. 46268

BRADBURY—Bradbury Press, Inc., 2 Overhill Rd., Scarsdale, N.Y. 10583

BRAZILLER—George Braziller, Inc., 1 Park Ave., New York, N.Y. 10016

CHILDREN—Childrens Press, 1224 West Van Buren St., Chicago, Ill., 60607

CHILTON—Chilton Book Co., 401 Walnut St., Philadelphia, Pa. 19106

COWARD—Coward, McCann & Geoghegan, Inc., 200 Madison Ave., New York, N.Y. 10016

COWLES—Cowles Book Co., Inc., 488 Madison Ave., New York, N.Y. 10022

CRITERION—Criterion Books, 257 Park Ave. South, New York, N.Y. 10010

CROWELL—Thomas Y. Crowell Co., 201 Park Ave. South, New York, N.Y. 10003

CROWELL-COLLIER—Crowell Collier and Macmillan, Inc. 866 Third Ave., New York, N.Y. 10022

CROWN—Crown Publishers, Inc., 419 Park Ave. South, New York, N.Y. 10016

DAY—The John Day Co., Inc., 257 Park Ave. South, New York, N.Y. 10036

DELACORTE—The Delacorte Press, 750 Third Ave., New York, N.Y. 10017

DELL—Dell Publishing Co., Inc., 750 Third Ave., New York, N.Y. 10017

DIAL—The Dial Press, Inc., 750 Third Ave., New York, N.Y. 10017

DODD—Dodd, Mead and Company, 79 Madison Ave., New York, N.Y. 10016

DONOHUE—M. A. Donohue & Co., 2855 Shermer Rd., Northbrook, Chicago Ill. 60062

DOUBLEDAY—Doubleday & Company, Inc., Garden City, N.Y. 11530

DUELL—Duell, Sloan & Pearce; Distributed by Meredith Corp., 440 Park Ave. South, New York, N.Y. 10016

DUTTON—E. P. Dutton & Co., Inc., 201 Park Ave.,South, New York, N.Y. 10003

EVANS—M. Evans & Company, Inc., 216 East 49th St., New York, N.Y. 10017

FARRAR—Farrar, Straus & Giroux, Inc., 19 Union Square West, New York, N.Y. 10003

FOUR WINDS—Four Winds Press, 50 West 44th St., New York, N.Y. 10036

FUNK & WAGNALLS—Funk & Wagnalls, Inc., 53 East 77th St., New York, N.Y. 10017

GAMBIT—Gambit, Inc., 58 Beacon St., Boston, Mass. 02108

GARRARD—Garrard Publishing Company, 1607 North Market St., Champaign, Ill. 61820

GINN—Ginn and Company, Xerox Education Group, 191 Spring St., Lexington, Mass. 01773

GOLDEN—Golden Press, 1220 Mound Ave., Racine, Wisc. 53404

GOLDEN GATE—Golden Gate Junior Books, 8344 Melrose Ave., Los Angeles, Calif. 90069

GROSSET—Grosset & Dunlap, Inc., 51 Madison Ave., New York, N.Y. 10010

HALE—E. M. Hale and Company, 1201 South Hasting Way, Eau Claire, Wisc. 54701

HARCOURT—Harcourt Brace Jovanovich, 757 Third Ave., New York, N.Y. 10017

HARPER—Harper & Row, Publishers, 10 East 53rd St., New York, N.Y. 10022

HART—Hart Publishing Co., Inc., 719 Broadway, New York, N.Y. 10011

HARVEY—Harvey House, Inc., Irvington-on-Hudson, New York 10533

HASTINGS—Hastings House, Inc. 10 East 40th St., New York, N.Y. 10016

HAWTHORN—Hawthorn Books, Inc., 70 Fifth Ave., New York, N.Y. 10011

HOLIDAY—Holiday House, Inc., 18 East 56th St., New York, N. Y. 10022

HOLT—Holt, Rinehart and Winston, Inc., 383 Madison Ave., New York, N.Y. 10017

HORIZON—Horizon Press, 156 Fifth Ave., New York, N.Y. 10010

HOUGHTON—Houghton Mifflin Company, 2 Park St., Boston, Mass. 02107

HUBBARD—Hubbard Press, 2855 Shermer Rd., Northbrook, Ill. 60062

KENT—Kent State University Press, Kent, Ohio 44242

KNOPF—Alfred A. Knopf, Inc., 201 East 50th St., New York, N.Y. 10022

KTAV—Ktav Publishing House, Inc., 120 East Broadway, New York, N.Y. 10002

LANCELOT—Lancelot Press, 51 West 52nd St., New York, N.Y. 10019

LANTERN—Lantern Press, Inc., 345 Hussey Rd., Mt. Vernon, N.Y. 10552

LIPPINCOTT—J. B. Lippincott Co., East Washington Square, Philadelphia, Pa. 19105

LITTLE—Little, Brown and Company, 34 Beacon St., Boston, Mass. 02106

LOTHROP—Lothrop, Lee & Shepard Co., Inc., 105 Madison, New York, N.Y. 10016

McCALL—McCall Books, 230 Park Ave., New York, N.Y. 10017

McGRAW—McGraw-Hill Book Company, 1221 Ave. of the Americas, New York, N.Y. 10020

McKAY—David McKay Company, Inc., 750 Third Ave., New York, N.Y. 10017

McLOUGHLIN—McLoughlin Brothers; Distributed by Grosset & Dunlap Inc.

MACMILLAN—The Macmillan Company, 866 Third Ave., New York, N.Y. 10022

MACRAE—Macrae Smith Company, 225 South 15th St., Philadelphia, Pa. 19102

MEREDITH—Meredith Corporation, 1716 Locust St., Des Moines, Iowa 50303

MESSNER—Julian Messner, 1 West 39th St., New York, N.Y. 10018

MORROW—William Morrow & Co., Inc., 105 Madison Ave., New York, N.Y. 10016

NAL—New American Library Inc., 1301 Avenue of the Americas, New York, N.Y. 10019

NATURAL HISTORY—Natural History Press, 277 Park Ave., New York, N.Y. 10017

NELSON—Thomas Nelson Inc., Copewood and Davis Sts., Camden, New Jersey 08103

NORTON—W. W. Norton & Company., Inc., 55 Fifth Ave., New York, N.Y. 10003

OBOLENSKY—Obolensky Books, Div. of Astor-Honor, Inc., 67 Southfield Ave., Stamford, Conn. 06904

PANTHEON—Pantheon Books, Inc., 201 East 50th St., New York, N.Y. 10022

PARENTS—Parents' Magazine Press, 52 Vanderbilt Ave., New York, N.Y. 10017

PARNASSUS—Parnassus Press, 2721 Parker St., Berkeley, Calif. 94704

PENGUIN—Penguin Books Inc., 7110 Ambassador Rd., Baltimore Md. 21207

PFLAUM—George A. Pflaum Publisher Inc., 38 West Fifth St., Dayton, Ohio 45402

PHILLIPS—S. G. Phillips Inc., 305 W. 86th St., New York, N.Y. 10024

PLATT—Platt & Munk, 1055 Bronx River Ave., Bronx, N.Y. 10472

PLAYS, INC.—Plays, Inc., 8 Arlington St., Boston, Mass. 02116

PRENTICE—Prentice-Hall Inc., Englewood Cliffs, N.J. 07632

PUTNAM—G. P. Putnam's Sons, 200 Madison Avenue, New York, N.Y. 10016

QUIST—Harlin Quist Books; Distributed by Franklin Watts

RAND—Rand McNally & Co. 8255 Central Park Ave., Skokie, Ill. 60680

RANDOM—Random House, Inc., 201 E. 50th St., New York, N.Y. 10022

REINHOLD—Van Nostrand Reinhold Co., 450 West 33rd St., New York, N.Y. 10001

RITCHIE—The Ward Ritchie Press, 3044 Riverside Drive, Los Angeles, Calif. 90039

ST. MARTIN—St. Martin's Press Inc., 175 Fifth Ave., New York, N.Y. 10010

SCHOCKEN—Schocken Books Inc., 67 Park Ave., New York, N.Y. 10016

SCHOLASTIC—Scholastic Book Services, 50 W. 44th St., New York, N.Y. 10036

SCOTT—Young Scott Books, 333 Avenue of the Americas, New York, N.Y. 10014

SCOTT FORESMAN—Scott, Foresman and Co., 1900 East Lake Ave., Glenview, Ill. 60025

SCRIBNER—Charles Scribner's Sons, 597 Fifth Ave., New York, N.Y. 10017

SEABURY—The Seabury Press, Inc., 815 Second Ave., New York, N.Y. 10017

SHEED—Sheed & Ward, 64 University Place, New York, N.Y. 10003

SIMON—Simon & Schuster, Inc. 630 Fifth Ave., New York, N.Y. 10020

STECK—Steck-Vaughn Company, Box 2028, Austin, Texas 78767

STERLING—Sterling Publishing Co., Inc., 419 Park Ave. South, New York, N.Y. 10016

TRI-OCEAN—Tri-Ocean Books, 62 Townsend St., San Francisco, Calif. 94107

VANGUARD—Vanguard Press, Inc., 424 Madison Ave., New York, N.Y. 10017

VIKING—The Viking Press, Inc., 625 Madison Ave., New York, N.Y. 10022

WALCK—Henry Z. Walch, Inc., 19 Union Square West, New York, N.Y. 10003

WALKER—Walker & Company, 720 Fifth Ave., New York, N.Y. 10019

WARNE—Frederick Warne & Co., Inc., 101 Fifth Ave., New York, N.Y. 10003

WASHBURN—Ives Washburn, Inc., 750 Third Ave., New York, N.Y. 10017

WATTS—Franklin Watts, Inc., 845 Third Ave., New York, N.Y. 10022

WESTMINSTER—The Westminster Press, Witherspoon Bldg., Philadelphia, Pa. 19107

WHEELWRIGHT—The Bond Wheelwright Co., Porter's Landing, Freeport, Maine 04032

WHITE—David White Company, 60 E. 55th St., New York, N.Y. 10022

WHITMAN—Albert Whitman & Co., 560 West Lake St., Chicago, Ill. 60606

WHITMAN PUB.—Whitman Publishing Co., 1220 Mound Ave., Racine, Wisc. 53404

WORLD—World Publishing Co., 110 E. 59th St., New York, N.Y. 10022

WSP—Washington Square Press, 630 Fifth Avenue, New York, N.Y. 10020

AUTHOR INDEX

Abisch, Roz, 322
Abodaher, David, 196
Abrahams, Robert D., 97
Abrashkin, Raymond, 158
Acei, 229, 241
Adams, Samuel Hopkins, 77
Adamson, Gareth, 319
Adamson, Joy, 289
Adler, Irving, 313
Adoff, Arnold, 196, 228
Adrian, Mary, 129, 289, 300
Adshead, Gladys, 236
Aesop, 4
Agee, Rose H., 228
Agle, Nan Hayden, 44
Aichinger, Helga, 240
Aiken, Conrad, 219
Aiken, Joan, 158, 159
Alcott, Louisa May, 77
Alderman, Clifford Lindsey, 196, 266
Aldis, Dorothy, 219
Alexander, Lloyd, 9, 159
Aliki, 9, 196, 306, 331
Allan, Mabel E., 129
Allen, Gertrude E., 311
Allen, Lorenzo, 77
Allfrey, Katherine, 97
Allstrom, Elizabeth, 240
Almedingen, E. M., 97, 175, 240
American Heritage Magazine, 201
Ames, Gerald, 330
Anckarsvard, Karin, 97, 98
Andersen, Hans Christian, 9, 240
Anderson, Lonzo, 77

Anderson, Poul, 175
Anderson, William R., 255
Andrews, Roy Chapman, 287
Andrist, Ralph K., 255, 266
Angell, Pauline, 196
Angelo, Valenti, 44, 144
Angier, Bradford, 129
Anglund, Joan W., 10
Annixter, Jane, 145
Annixter, Paul, 145
Anrooy, Frans Van, 241
Apsler, Alfred, 197
Arbuthnot, May Hill, 175, 228
Archer, Jules, 197
Archer, Sellers, 300
Ardizzone, Edward, 10
Arkhurst, Joyce Cooper, 175
Armour, Richard, 219, 241, 287
Armstrong, Richard, 98
Armstrong, William, 44
Arnold, Elliott, 98
Arnold, Oren, 266
Arnold, Pauline, 197
Arntson, Herbert E., 77
Arora, Shirley L., 98
Arthur, Robert, 129
Arthur, Ruth M., 44, 130
Asbjornsen, Peter C., 10, 175
Asch, Frank, 10
Ashabranner, Brent K., 83, 200, 280
Asimov, Isaac, 255, 259, 315, 317, 322
Atwater, Florence, 45
Atwater, Richard, 45

Atwood, Ann, 301, 303
Audsley, James, 331
Aurembou, Renee, 45
Austin, Elizabeth S., 289
Averill, Esther, 197
Avery, Gillian, 98
Ayars, James Sterling, 14, 266

Bacmeister, Rhoda, 77
Bacon, Martha, 98
Bacon, Peggy, 130
Bailey, Carolyn S., 159
Bailey, John, 289
Baity, Elizabeth, 267
Baker, Betty, 78, 99
Baker, J. W., 289
Baker, Laura Nelson, 176
Baker, Margaret J., 160
Baker, Nina Brown, 197
Balch, Glenn, 289
Baldwin, Anne Norris, 45
Ball, Zachary, 45
Ballard, Martin, 78
Ballian, Lorna, 236
Ballou, Arthur W., 155
Bank-Jensen, Thea, 331
Banning, Evelyn I., 197
Barbeau, Marius, 176
Barker, Will, 290
Barlow, Genevieve, 176
Barne, Kitty, 45
Barnes, Gregory Allen, 99
Barnett, Lincoln, 304
Barnhart, Nancy, 241
Baron, Virginia Olsen, 229
Barrie, J. M., 160
Barringer, D. Moreau, 99
Barry, Robert, 241
Bartlett, Susan, 255
Batchelor, Julie Forsyth, 256
Baudouy, Michel-Aimé, 99, 130
Bauer, Erwin, 290
Bauer, Helen, 267, 301
Baum, Betty, 45
Baumann, Hans, 99, 259
Bawden, Nina, 130
Beale, Will, 45
Beam, Maurice, 46
Beaney, Jean, 331
Beatty, Jerome Jr., 160

Beatty, John, 100
Beatty, Patricia, 46, 78
Beck, Barbara L., 312
Beebe, B. F., 290
Beers, Lorna, 100
Behn, Harry, 219, 229
Bell, Margaret, 100
Bell, Thelma Harrington, 313
Belpré, Pura, 11
Belting, Natalia M., 176
Bemelmans, Ludwig, 11
Benary-Isbert, Margot, 101
Bendick, Jeanne, 303, 322, 323
Benèt, Rosemary, 219
Benèt, Stephen, 219
Bennett, Anna Elizabeth, 160
Bennett, Richard, 160
Bennett, Rowena, 331
Benson, Sally, 176
Berg, Jean Horton, 46
Berg, Joan, 11
Berger, Terry, 176
Berke, Ernest, 267
Berkowitz, Freda Pastor, 332
Berna, Paul, 101, 130, 131
Bernadette, 11
Bernard, Jacqueline, 198
Bernhardsen, Christian, 101
Bernheim, Evelyne, 279
Bernheim, Marc, 279
Berry, Erick, 101
Bethell, Jean, 290
Bevans, Michael H., 290
Beyer, Audrey White, 78
Bianki, Vitali, 145
Bierhorst, John, 176
Bingley, Barbara, 101
Binns, Archie, 145
Binzen, Bill, 46
Biro, Val, 46
Bishop, Ann, 145
Bishop, Claire H., 11, 102, 241
Bishop, Elizabeth, 202
Bixby, William, 290
Black, Irma Simonton, 260
Blake, William, 220
Blaustein, Albert P., 267
Bleeker, Sonia, 260, 279
Blishen, Edward, 229
Bliven, Bruce Jr., 267

Bloch, Marie H., 102
Blume, Judy, 46
Bober, Harry, 217
Boden, Hilda, 102
Bollinger, Max, 241
Bolognese, Don, 12
Bond, Jean Carey, 12
Bond, Michael, 160
Bond, Ruskin, 102
Bond, Susan McDonald, 260
Bonham, Barbara, 78
Bonham, Frank, 47, 131
Boni, Margaret Bradford, 332
Bonne, Rose, 7
Bonsall, Crosby, 131
Bontemps, Arna, 47
Bonzon, Paul-Jacques, 102, 131
Boorstin, Daniel J., 267
Borhegyi, Suzanne de, 131
Born, Franz, 198
Borten, Helen, 236, 332
Boston, Lucy M., 131, 145, 161
Bothwell, Jean, 102 ˙
Bourliaguet, Leonce, 102
Bova, Ben, 47
Bowen, David, 279
Bowen, Robert Sidney, 142
Bower, Louise, 132
Bowles, Cynthia, 279
Braenne, Berit, 102
Brand, Christianna, 161
Brandbury, Bianca, 47
Branley, Franklyn M., 242, 313, 323
Braymer, Marjorie, 198
Brecht, Edith, 132
Brenner, Barbara, 256
Brent, Stuart, 47
Brewton, John E., 229, 242
Brewton, Sara, 229, 242
Bridges, William, 291
Bright, Robert, 236
Brink, Carol Ryrie, 47, 78, 79, 155
Brinley, Bertrand, 155
Brock, Virginia, 332
Brooks, Gwendolyn, 220
Brooks, Polly S., 260
Broun, Heywood, 161, 242
Brown, Marcia, 4, 12, 177
Brown, Margaret Wise, 12, 220
Brown, Pamela, 102

Brown, Vinson, 326
Bruce, Lois, 317
Brun, Noelle, 279
Bryson, Bernarda, 177
Buck, Margaret Waring, 291
Buck, Pearl S., 102, 177
Buckman, Irene, 332
Budd, Lillian, 242
Buehr, Walter, 303
Buell, Robert Kingery, 267
Buff, Conrad, 79, 198, 268, 291
Buff, Mary, 79, 198, 268, 291
Bulla, Clyde Robert, 47, 79, 103, 177, 236, 333
Bunning, Jim, 326
Burch, Robert, 13, 79, 242
Burchard, Peter, 79
Burchardt, Nellie, 48
Burger, Carl, 291
Burgunder, Rose, 202
Burleson, Elizabeth, 103
Burnford, Sheila, 145
Burns, Robert, 220
Burrell, Roy, 287
Burt, Katharine Newlin, 48
Burt, Olive W., 80, 268, 303
Burton, Maurice, 291
Burton, Richard, 177
Burton, Virginia Lee, 13
Butler, Suzanne, 243
Butterworth, Oliver, 161
Butterworth, William E., 48
Butts, David P., 312
Byars, Betsy C., 13, 146
Byers, Irene, 132

Calder, Ritchie, 319
Calhoun, Mary, 48, 177
Cameron, Eleanor, 155, 161
Camp, Paul K., 80
Campbell, Ann, 333
Campbell, Camilla, 177
Campbell, Elizabeth, 80
Campbell, Hope, 48
Cantwell, Mary, 237
Canty, Mary, 48
Carigiet, Alois, 13
Carle, Eric, 2, 14
Carleton, Barbee Oliver, 80
Carlisle, Laura Mae, 232
Carlsen, Ruth Christoffer, 162

Carlson, Bernice Wells, 333
Carlson, Natalie Savage, 48, 49,
    104, 146, 178, 243
Carona, Philip B., 303
Carr, Albert B., 309
Carroll, Lewis, 162
Carter, Bruce, 132, 198
Castex, Pierre, 132
Castle, Frances, 104
Catherall, Arthur, 104, 146
Caudill, Rebecca, 80, 220, 243
Cavanah, Frances, 238, 268
Cavanna, Betty, 49
Cawston, Vee, 105
CBS News Staff, 260
Ceder, Georgiana Dorcas, 80
Chafetz, Henry, 178
Chalmers, Mary, 243
Channel, A. R., 105
Chappell, Warren, 333
Chase, Alice Elizabeth,
Chase, Richard, 178
Chaucer, Geoffrey, 14
Cheney, Cora, 198
Chickering, Marjorie, 81
Christgau, Alice E., 81
Christopher, John, 155, 156
Christopher, Matt, 142
Chubb, Mary, 260
Chubb, Thomas Caldecot, 261
Chute, Marchette, 105, 220,
    330
Ciardi, John, 221
Clagett, John, 268
Clapp, Patricia, 81, 132
Clark, Ann Nolan, 14, 146, 279,
    280
Clark, Margaret Goff, 133
Clarke, Mary Stetson, 81
Clarke, Mollie, 178
Clarke, Pauline, 162
Clarke, Tom E., 81
Claxton, Ernest, 243
Clayton, Barbara, 49
Clayton, Robert, 280
Cleary, Beverly, 49, 81, 146,
    162
Cleaver, Bill, 50
Cleaver, Nancy, 193
Cleaver, Vera, 50
Clifton, Lucile, 221, 268

Clymer, Eleanor, 50, 146
Coatsworth, Elizabeth, 14, 82, 105,
    198, 221
Coblentz, Catherine Cate, 198
Coggins, Jack, 199
Cohen, Peter Zachary, 50
Cohen, Robert, 284
Coit, Margaret, 199
Colby, C. B., 284, 326
Cole, William, 221, 229, 230
Collier, James, 50
Collins, Ruth P., 105
Colum, Padraic, 178, 179, 230
Colver, Anne, 82
Commager, Henry Steele, 199,
    268
Cone, Molly, 50, 51, 146, 243
Conklin, Gladys, 291, 292, 307,
    308
Conrad, Sybil, 51
Constiner, Merle, 82
Cooke, David C., 280
Coolidge, Olivia, 105, 106, 199,
    261
Coombs, Charles, 317, 326
Cooney, Barbara, 244
Cooper, Elizabeth, 327
Cooper, Lee, 345
Cooper, Lettice, 199
Corbett, Scott, 51, 133, 147, 162
Corbett, Steve, 317
Corcoran, Barbara, 52
Cornish, Sam, 52
Cote, Alfred J., Jr., 319
Cottrell, Leonard, 261
Country Beautiful Eds., 218
Courlander, Harold, 179
Coy, Harold, 268
Craig, M. Jean, 162
Crary, Margaret, 133
Credle, Ellis, 106
Cretan, Gladys Y., 52
Cumming, W. D., 339
Cummings, Richard, 334
Cuneo, John R., 269
Cunningham, Julia, 52, 244
Curry, Jane Louise, 179

Dahl, Mary, 82
Dalgliesh, Alice, 82, 83, 199, 237,
    269, 317

Dalrymple, Mendoza G., 221
Daly, Maureen, 147
D'Amelio, Dan, 199
Danska, Herbert, 163
Darling, Lois, 287, 292, 301
Darling, Louis, 287, 292, 301
Daugherty, James H., 200, 261
D'Aulaire, Edgar P., 14, 15, 147, 200
D'Aulaire, Ingri, 14, 15, 147, 200
D'Aulnoy, Mme. La Comtesse, 179
Davenport, Roselle, 280
Davenport, William, 280
Daves, Michael, 244
Davis, Burke, 269
Davis, Katherine,
Davis, Robert, 163
Davis, Russell G., 83, 200, 280
Dayrell, Elphinston, 4
De Angeli, Marguerite, 106, 244
De Forest, Charlotte B., 230
De Jong, Meindert, 52, 106, 147
De Kay, Ormonde, 200
De La Iglesia, Maria Elena, 180
De la Mare, Walter, 180, 221, 230
de Regniers, Beatrice Schenk, 15, 180, 221, 245, 327
de Saint-Exupéry, Antoine, 163
De Schweinitz, Karl, 306
De Trevino, Elizabeth, 201
DeGering, Etta, 200
DeJong, Dola, 133
Denny, Norman, 261
Derleth, August, 134
Deutsch, Babette, 180
DeWaard, John, 292
Dias, Earl J., 334
Dick, Trella Lamson, 53
Dickens, Charles, 245
Dietz, Betty Warner, 334
Dietz, David, 316
Dillon, Eilis, 106, 147
Dixon, Jeanne, 129
Dobrin, Arnold, 147
Docherty, Tommy, 327
Dodd, Ed, 292
Doering, Harold, 308
Domjan, Joseph, 4
Donovan, Frank R., 201
Donovan, John, 53
Doob, L. W., 230

Dorliae, Peter G., 180
Doss, Helen, 201
Douglass, Frederick, 201
Downer, Marion, 269, 334
Downie, Mary Alice, 231
Doyle, Sir Arthur Conan, 134
Drdek, Richard E., 53
Drewery, Mary, 107
Druon, Maurice, 163
Du Mond, Frank, 180
Dugdale, Vera, 292
Duggan, Alfred, 201
Dumas, Gerald, 148
Dunn, Mary Lois, 107
Dunne, Mary Collins, 53
Dunning, Stephen, 231
Dunstan, Maryjane, 109
Dupuy, Trevor N., 262
Durant, John, 327
Durham, Mae, 180
Duvoisin, Roger, 1, 245, 262

Eager, Edward, 163
Earle, Olive L., 293
Eberle, Irmengarde, 293
Eckert, Allan W., 201, 293
Edmonds, I. G., 262
Edmonds, Walter, 83
Eichenberg, Fritz, 1, 2
Eiseman, Alberta, 15
Eisen, Anthony F., 107
Elgin, Kathleen, 245, 306
Elkin, Benjamin, 4
Ellis, Ella Thorp, 107
Ellis, Mel, 53
Emberley, Barbara, 15
Emberley, Ed, 334
Embry, Margaret, 237
Emrich, Duncan, 180
Enright, Elizabeth, 16, 53, 163
Epstein, Beryl, 256, 327
Epstein, Sam, 256, 327
Erwin, Betty K., 54, 156
Estes, Eleanor, 54, 134
Estrada, Doris, 54
Ets, Marie Hall, 16, 245
Evans, Eva Knox, 284, 306
Evernden, Margery, 107

Falk, Irving A., 256
Fall, Thomas, 83

Falls, C. B., 1
Fanning, Leonard, 310
Farjeon, Annabel, 134
Farjeon, Eleanor, 164, 222, 245
Farley, Walter, 148
Fartchen, Max, 107
Faulkner, Nancy, 83, 134
Faulknor, Cliff, 54
Feagles, Anita, 181
Fecher, Constant, 108
Feelings, Muriel L., 108
Feinstein, Joe, 16
Feld, Friedrich, 108
Felton, Harold W., 181
Fenner, Carol, 148
Fenner, Phyllis R., 142
Fenton, Edward, 134
Feravolo, Rocco V., 317
Fermi, Laura, 320
Ferris, Helen, 231, 232
Fiedler, Jean, 201
Field, Rachel, 84, 222, 246
Fillmore, Parker, 181
Filmer-Sankey, Josephine, 261
Finger, Charles J., 181
Finkel, George, 108
Fisher, Aileen, 16, 84, 202, 222,
    246, 293
Fisher, James, 293
Fisher, Laura, 54, 84
Fisher, Leonard Everett, 269
Fisk, Nicholas, 202
Fitch, Florence, 246
Fitter, Richard, 301
Fitzhugh, Louise, 55
Flack, Marjorie, 17, 237
Flaherty, Robert, 280
Fleischmann, Peter, 17
Fleischman, Sid, 17, 84
Fleming, Ian, 164
Fleming, Thomas J., 202
Floethe, Louise Lee, 108, 270, 310
Floethe, Richard, 310
Flory, Jane, 84
Folsom, Franklin, 84
Forbes, Esther, 85, 202
Ford, Whitey, 326
Forman, James, 85, 108, 109
Forsee, Aylsea, 202
Foster, Elizabeth Vincent, 164
Foster, Genevieve, 202, 262, 270

Foster, Joanna, 17
Fox, Paula, 55
Franchere, Ruth, 85, 202
Francis, Dorothy Brenner, 134
Francoise, 2
Frasconi, Antonio, 345, 346
Fraser, Kathleen, 222
Frazier, Neta Lohnes, 85
Freeman, Ira, 320
Freeman, Mae, 320, 334
Frere, Maud, 109
Friedman, Frieda, 55
Friendlich, Dick, 142
Friis-Baastad, Babbis, 55
Friskey, Margaret, 3
Fritz, Jean, 85, 86
Froman, Robert, 303, 306
Frost, Frances, 222
Frost, Robert, 222
Fuller, Edmund A., 334
Fuller, John, 270
Furman, A. L., 55
Fyleman, Rose, 223

Gaer, Joseph, 246
Gág, Flavia, 135
Gág, Wanda, 1, 17, 18
Gage, Wilson, 56, 164
Galdone, Paul, 4, 18
Gallant, Roy A., 313, 318
Galt, Tom, 202
Gans, Roma, 293, 304
Gard, Robert E., 335
Gardner, Jeanne, 203
Garelick, May, 18, 293
Garfield, Leon, 135
Garlan, Patricia Wallace, 109
Garner, Alan, 164
Garnett, Emmeline, 203
Garson, Eugenia, 335
Gates, Doris, 56, 86
Geisert, Arthur, 148
Geismer, Barbara Peck, 231
Gemming, Elizabeth, 271
George, Jean Craighead, 56, 294
Georgiou, Constantine, 148
Gerson, Noel B., 203
Gilbert, Arthur, 246
Gilbert, Bil, 294
Gilbert, Nan, 56
Gilbert, W. S., 335

Gilmore, Iris, 277
Gimpel, Herbert J., 203
Gipson, Fred, 148
Glasgow, Aline, 181
Glubok, Shirley, 335
Godden, Rumer, 109, 246
Goldberg, Lea, 280
Goldin, Augusta, 304, 306
Goodall, John S., 18
Goodman, Walter, 271
Goodrich, Carter, 255
Goolden, Barbara, 135
Gordon, George N., 256
Gordon, Isabel, 327
Gordon, John, 164
Gorham, Charles A., 203
Gottlieb, Robin, 135
Goudey, Alice E., 18, 19, 294, 308
Gould, Laurence J., 307
Grabianski, Janusz, 294
Graham, Lorenz B., 56, 109, 246
Grahame, Kenneth, 164
Gramatky, Hardie, 19
Gramet, Charles, 256
Grant, Clara Louise, 281
Grant, Elisabeth, 135
Graves, Robert, 181, 182
Gray, Elizabeth Janet, 110
Green, Carla, 335
Green, Diana Huss, 271
Green, Margaret, 203
Greenberg, Polly, 19
Greene, Carla, 19, 323
Greenleaf, Margery F., 110
Gregor, Arthur S., 3, 203
Gregory, Horace, 231
Grieder, Walter, 19
Griffiths, Helen, 148
Grimm Brothers, 19–21
Groh, Lynn, 271
Guillot, Rene, 110
Gurko, Leo, 203
Gurko, Miriam, 204
Guterman, Norbert, 347

Hader, Berta, 21
Hader, Elmer, 21
Hagon, Priscilla, 110
Haines, Charles, 204
Hajime, Kijima, 21
Hale, Linda, 246

Hall, Anna Gertrude, 86, 204
Hall, Elvajean, 86
Hall, Marjory, 136
Hall-Quest, Olga, 204
Halliday, E. M., 262
Hamilton, Virginia, 56, 111
Hámori, Lászlo, 111
Hampden, John, 262
Hample, Stuart, 56
Handforth, Thomas, 22
Hannum, Sara, 231
Hano, Arnold, 327
Hardwick, Richard, 204
Hark, Mildred, 335
Harman, Humphrey, 182
Harmon, Lyn, 57
Harper, Wilhelmina, 237, 246
Harrington, Lyn, 281
Harris, Christie, 57, 111
Harris, Joel Chandler, 182
Harris, Leon A., 335
Harris, Marilyn, 57
Harris, Mary K., 57
Harris, Rosemary, 165
Harrison, C. William, 257
Harrison, Deloris, 204
Hart, Tony, 336
Haufrecht, Herbert, 335
Haugaard, Erik, 86, 111
Hautzig, Esther, 336, 346
Haviland, Virginia, 182, 204
Havrevold, Finn, 112
Hawes, Judy, 294
Hawkinson, John, 336
Hayes, William D., 57
Haywood, Carolyn, 57
Hazeltine, Alice, 232, 247
Hazen, Barbara, 5
Headington, Christopher, 336
Heady, Eleanor B., 182
Heaps, Willard A., 284
Heide, Parry, 22
Heiderstadt, Dorothy, 271
Heilbroner, Joan, 237
Heinlein, Robert, 156
Helfman, Elizabeth S., 257
Helfman, Harry, 336
Henry, Marguerite, 112, 149, 301,
  327
Hentoff, Nat, 58
Herbst, Dean Finley, 136

Herold, J. Christopher, 263
Herrmanns, Ralph, 281
Hess, Lila, 294
Heuman, William, 142
Heyerdahl, Thor, 281
Heyward, Du Bose, 247
Hicks, Clifford B., 313
Hieatt, Constance, 182, 183
Hightower, Florence, 58, 149
Hilbert, Peter Paul, 112
Hiller, Carl E., 271
Hine, Al, 232
Hinton, S. E., 58
Hirsch, S. Carl, 205, 301, 320, 336
Hirschfeld, Burt, 272
Hitchcock, Alfred, 136
Hoban, Russell, 22, 223
Hobson, Burton, 328
Hodges, C. Walter, 263
Hodges, Elizabeth Jamison, 183
Hodges, Margaret, 183
Hoff, Syd, 22, 58
Hofsinde, Robert, 272, 336
Hogan, Carol G., 22
Hoge, Dorothy, 183
Hogg, Garry, 304
Hoke, John, 320
Holberg, Ruth Langland, 86
Holbrook, Sabra, 281
Holbrook, Stewart, 205
Holding, James, 183
Holl, Adelaide, 22
Holland, John, 284
Hollander, John, 165
Holling, Holling C., 86, 149, 294
Holm, Anne, 165
Holman, Felice, 58, 136, 165
Holme, Bryan, 337
Holst, Imogen, 205
Honour, Alan, 247, 263
Hood, Flora, 247
Hooker, Ruth, 58
Hoover, Helen, 295
Hopkins, Lee Bennett, 223, 231, 272
Horne, Richard Henry, 112
Hosford, Dorothy, 183
Houston, James, 112, 183, 184
Howard, Elston, 328
Howard, Robert West, 310
Hoyt, Edwin P., 112, 205
Htin Aung, Maung, 184

Hubbell, Patricia, 223
Huber, Ursula, 23
Huffard, Grace Thompson, 232
Hughes, Langston, 223
Hughes, Matilda, 59
Hunt, Douglas, 328, 337
Hunt, Irene, 59, 87
Hunt, Kari, 328
Hunter, Edith Fisher, 59
Hunter, Kristin, 59
Hunter, Mollie, 112, 113, 165
Huntsberry, William, 59
Hurd, Edith T., 247
Hurd, Michael, 337
Huston, Anne, 59
Hutchins, Pat, 23
Hutchins, Ross E., 295, 308, 312
Hyde, Margaret, 318

Ik, Kim Young, 113
Ingraham, Leonard W., 272
Ipcar, Dahlov, 2, 3, 23, 60
Irving, Washington, 272
Irwin, Keith Gordon, 323
Isenstein, Harold, 337
Ishii, Momoko, 113
Ish-Kishor, Sulamith, 87, 113
Iwasaki, Chihiro, 23

Jablonski, Edward, 205
Jablow, Alta, 184
Jablow, Carl, 184
Jackson, C. P., 143
Jackson, Jacqueline, 24, 60, 337
Jackson, Jesse, 60
Jackson, Robert B., 205, 257
Jackson, Shirley, 273
Jacobs, David, 337
Jacobs, Herbert A., 205
Jacobs, Joseph, 24, 184
Jacobs, Leland B., 223
Jagendorf, Moritz, 337
James, Bessie R., 205
James, Marquis, 205
Jane, Mary C., 136
Janes, Edward C., 310
Janeway, Elizabeth, 184
Janice, 238
Janson, Dora J., 338
Janson, H. W., 338
Jansson, Tove, 165

Jarrell, Randall, 165
Jeffries, Roderic, 136
Jenkins, Alan C., 295
Jewett, Eleanore Myers, 185
Jewett, Sarah Orne, 87
Johnson, Annabel, 60, 87
Johnson, Burdetta, 60
Johnson, Edgar, 60, 87
Johnson, Elizabeth, 166
Johnson, Gerald W., 206, 273
Johnson, James Ralph, 149
Johnson, James Weldon, 338
Johnson, LaVerne, 24
Johnson, J. Rosamond, 338
Johnston, Norma, 87
Jones, Adrienne, 60, 295
Jones, Elizabeth Orton, 247
Jones, Jessie Orton, 247
Jones, Liza, 150
Jones, Weyman, 87
Jordan, June, 223
Jorgen, Moe, 175
Joslin, Sesyle, 24, 346
Joutsen, Britta-Lisa, 113
Judson, Clara Ingram, 206, 257
Jupo, Frank, 24
Justus, May, 61

Kadesch, Dr. Robert, 323
Kahl, Virginia, 248
Kalnay, Francis, 150
Kamerman, Sylvia E., 338
Kane, Henry B., 295
Kantrowitz, Mildred, 24
Kapp, Paul, 338
Kassil, Ley, 113
Kästner, Erich, 166
Kaufmann, Alicia, 24
Kay, Helen, 114
Keats, Ezra J., 25, 185
Keith, Eros, 150
Keith, Harold, 88
Kelen, Betty, 206
Kelen, Emery, 285
Kellin, Sally Moffet, 296
Kelsey, Alice Geer, 185
Kendall, Carol, 166
Kendall, Lace, 88
Kennedy, John F., 206
Kenny, Herbert, 166
Kesselman, Wendy Ann, 166
Kettlekamp, Larry, 285, 318

Key, Alexander, 156
Kimishima, Hisako, 185
Kingman, Lee, 114, 136, 150
Kingsley, Charles, 185
Kipling, Rudyard, 166
Kirk, Ruth, 301
Kjelgaard, James A., 150
Klose, Norma Cline, 150
Knight, David C., 308, 316, 320
Knight, Eric, 114
Knight, Ruth A., 151
Knopf, Mildred O., 328
Knott, William C., 156
Knudsen, Lynne, 338
Kohn, Bernice, 257, 296
Komroff, Manuel, 206
Konigsburg, E. L., 61, 143
Koob, Theodora, 61
Kosterina, Nina, 206
Krahn, Fernando, 25
Kredenser, Gail, 223
Kroeber, Theodora, 88
Krum, Charlotte, 25
Krumgold, Joseph, 61, 114
Kumin, Maxine W., 224
Kurkul, Edward, 61
Kyle, Elizabeth, 206

La Farge, Phyllis, 62
La Fontaine, Jean de, 5
Ladd, Elizabeth, 61
Lagerlof, Selma, 167
Lambie, Beatrice, 263
Lamorisse, Albert, 167
Land, Barbara, 316
Lang, Andrew, 185
Langstaff, John, 3, 224, 338
Langton, Jane, 167
Larrick, Nancy, 232
Larson, Jean Russell, 186
Lasell, Fen, 151
Latham, Jean Lee, 88, 207
Lattimore, Eleanor France, 114
Lauber, Patricia, 151, 296
Lawrence, Harriet, 167
Lawrence, Isabelle, 88
Lawrence, Jacob, 207
Lawson, John, 167
Lawson, Robert, 151, 273
Laycock, George, 302
Lazarus, Keo Felker, 89
Leach, Maria, 186

Leacroft, Helen, 263
Leacroft, Richard, 263
Leaf, Munro, 26
Lear, Edward, 224, 346
Leckie, Robert, 263
Lee, Addison E., 312
Lee, Mildred, 62
Lee, Robert C., 143
Leichman, Seymour, 167
Leighton, Margaret, 137
L'Engle, Madeleine, 62, 156
Lenski, Lois, 62, 346
Lester, Julius, 273
Levin, Marcia O., 323
Levine, Joseph, 264
Levine, Rhoda, 168
Levitch, Joel A., 95
Levy, Harry, 89
Lewis, C. S., 168
Lewis, Claudia, 26
Lewis, Gogo, 137
Lewis, Richard, 232, 285
Lewis, Richard W., 62
Lewis, Shari, 339
Lewiton, Mina, 62
Lexau, Joan M., 5, 62, 248,
Ley, Willy, 316, 323
Leydenfrost, Robert, 26
Lichello, Robert, 207
Liers, Emil E., 296
Lifton, Betty J., 186, 281
Lightbody, Charles, 217
Lightner, A. M., 157
Lincoln, Abraham, 274
Lindgren, Astrid, 26, 168, 248
Lindquist, Jennie D., 63
Lindsay, Sally, 328
Lines, Kathleen,
Lionni, Leo, 27
Lipsyte, Robert, 143, 328
Liss, Howard, 318
Liston, Robert, 285
Little, Jane, 169
Little, Jean, 63
Livingstone, Myra Cohn, 224, 233
Lobel, Arnold, 27, 28
Lofgren, Ulf, 28
Lofting, Hugh, 168
Lohberg, Rolk, 324
Loman, Anna, 282
London, Jack, 152
Longman, Harold, 328

Lord, Beman, 143, 233
Love, Katherine, 233
Love, S. A., 339
Low, Alice, 63
Lubell, Cecil, 296
Lund, Doris Herold, 28
Lutz, Theo, 324
Lyon, Elinor, 114, 115

McCague, James, 274
McCall, Edith, 274
McCarthy, Agnes, 63
McCloskey, Robert, 28, 29, 63
McClung, Robert M., 296
McCord, David, 225
McCord, Jean, 64
McCormick, Jo Mary, 308, 310
McCoy, J. J., 297, 302
McDonald, George, 168
McDonald, Gerald D., 233
McEwen, Catherine Schaefer, 234
McFarland, Wilma, 234
McGinley, Phyllis, 248
McGovern, Ann, 186, 207, 307
McGraw, Eloise Jarvis, 89, 115
McGregor, Ellen, 157
McGregor, R. J., 137
McIntosh, Clifton, 344
McKee, David, 29
McKenzie, Ellen Kindt, 186
McKnown, Robin, 207, 264
McNeer, May, 208, 257, 264, 274
McNeill, Mary, 64, 115
McPherson, Margaret, 144
McQueen, Noel, 335
Macintyre, Elizabeth, 115
MacKeller, William, 137, 152
Macken, Walter, 115
Macorlan, Pierre, 115
Maddock, Reginald, 64, 169
Mahon, Julia C., 137
Mahy, Margaret, 29
Maiden, Cecil, 116
Malcomson, Anne, 186, 187
Mandell, Muriel, 274, 324
Manley, Seon, 137
Mann, Peggy, 64
Manners, William, 329
Mannheim, Grete, 64, 312
Manning, Jack, 282
Mansfield, John, 282
Mantle, Mickey, 326

Marchant, R. A., 297
Marcus, Rebecca B., 274
Mariana, 238
Mark, Polly, 116
Marks, Mickey, 339
Martin, Fredric, 137
Martin, Patrica Miles, 64, 116
Martin, William, 307
Masey, Mary Lou, 187
Mason, George Frederick, 297
Masselink, Ben, 297
Matsuno, Masako, 116
May, Julian, 304, 318
Mayne, William, 169
Mays, Willie, 326
Mazar, Amihay, 264
Mead, Margaret, 285
Meader, Stephen W., 89
Meadowcroft, Enid L., 89
Mehdevi, Anne Sinclair, 187
Meigs, Cornelia, 208
Melnikoff, Pamela, 116
Meltzer, Milton, 208, 275
Memling, Carl, 29
Mendoza, Geroge, 138, 169, 286
Menotti, Gian Carlo, 248
Meredith, Robert, 277
Merriam, Eve, 225
Merrill, Jean, 3, 29, 169, 187
Meshover, Leonard, 310
Meyer, Edith P.,
Meyer, Howard, 208
Meyers, Susan, 116
Miers, Earl Schenck, 208, 275
Miles, John, 280
Miles, Miska, 65, 89, 152
Milhous, Katherine, 238, 249
Miller, Irene Preston, 339
Miller, Louise Helen, 339
Mills, Alan, 339
Mills, John, 339
Milne, A. A., 169, 225
Milne, Lorus, 297, 311, 312
Milne, Margery, 297, 311, 312
Minarik, Else Holmelund, 29, 225
Minnton, Janyce L., 187
Mintoyne, Grace, 342
Mirsky, Reba Paeff, 116, 209
Mitchison, Naomi, 117
Moe, Jorgen, 10, 175
Molarsky, Osman, 65

Monjo, F. N., 89, 90
Monsell, Helen A., 249
Montgomery, Elizabeth Rider, 209
Moon, Sheila, 169
Mooney, Booth, 209
Moore, Clement, 249
Moore, Lamont, 339
Moore, Lilian, 226, 347
Moore, Ruth Nulton, 90
Moore, Shirley, 297
Moreton, John, 340
Morey, Walt, 65, 152
Morgenstern, Christian, 226
Morrison, Lillian, 234
Morrison, Lucile, 117
Morrow, Susan Stark, 65
Mosel, Arlene, 29
Moskin, Marietta, 66
Moyes, Patricia, 138
Muehl, Lois, 66
Mukerji, Goapl, 152
Muller, Charles G., 209
Murphy, Barbara, 66
Murphy, E. Jefferson, 282
Murphy, Shirley Roussea, 66
Murray, Joan, 209
Myers, Elisabeth P., 210
Myrick, Mildred, 309

Nahmed, H. M., 187
Nakamoto, Hiroko, 282
Nash, Mary, 138
Nash, Ogden, 224
Nathan, Adele Gutman, 257
Neal, Harry Edward, 275
Neff, Priscilla, 66
Nesbit, E., 67
Nesbitt, Rosemary S., 90
Ness, Evaline, 29, 30, 187
Neufeld, John, 67
Neville, Emily, 67
Newberry, Clare Turlay, 30
Newman, Robert, 188, 264
Newman, Shirlee P., 210
Nic Leodhas, Sorche, 188
Nickless, Will, 170
Nielsen, Jean, 138
Nordstrom, Ursula, 67
Norris, Gunilla B., 67, 117
North, Sterling, 90, 298
Norton, André, 90, 157
Norton, Mary, 170

Nourse, Alan E., 157
Nowlan, Nora, 264
Nussbaumer, Mares, 249
Nussbaumer, Paul, 249
Nuttall, Kenneth, 340
Nyblom, Helena, 188

O'Brien, John S., 152
O'Brien, Robert C., 157
O'Connor, Patrick, 67
O'Connor, Richard, 210
O'Daniel, Janet, 90
O'Dell, Scott, 68, 91, 117
Offit, Sidney, 68
Ogg, Oscar, 258
Olfson, Lewy, 340
Olschewski, Alfred, 30
O'Neill, Mary, 117, 226, 298
Onorati, Henry, 244
Oppenheimer, Lillian, 339
Orgel, Doris, 30, 68
Ormondroyd, Edward, 170
Ottley, Reginald, 117, 153

Pace, Mildred Mastin, 282
Paine, Roberta M., 340
Palmer, Bruce, 275
Palmer, Candida, 68
Palmer, Geoffrey, 249
Pannell, Lucile, 238
Panova, Vera, 118
Parish, Peggy, 329
Parker, Bertha Morris, 304
Parker, Elinor, 234
Parker, K. Langloh, 188
Parkinson, Ethelyn, 68
Pauli, Hertha, 249
Payzant, Charles, 320
Pearce, A. Philippa, 170
Pearlman, Moshe, 264
Pease, Howard, 138
Pedersen, Elsa, 68
Peet, Bill, 30, 170, 171
Pei, Mario, 258
Pendle, George, 282
Pène Du Bois, William, 30, 138, 170, 171
Perez, Norah, 139
Perrault, Charles, 5, 188
Perrine, Mary, 31, 69
Petersham, Maud, 2, 249
Petersham, Miska, 2

Peterson, Hans, 118
Petry, Ann, 91, 210
Peyton, K. M., 118, 139, 153
Phelan, Mary Kay, 210, 238, 275
Philbrook, Clem, 91
Philipson, Morris, 211
Phipson, Joan, 118, 119
Piatti, Celestino, 31
Picard, Barbara L., 119
Pickens, Richard, 329
Pilgrim, Anne, 119
Pine, Tillie S., 264
Pitcher, Marie Elizabeth, 69
Plotz, Helen, 234
Plowman, Stephanie, 119
Poe, Edgar Allan, 139
Politi, Leo, 31, 238, 250, 347
Pollack, Merrill, 189
Pollack, Reginald, 31
Polland, Madeleine, 119, 120
Pomerantz, Charlotte, 312
Poole, Frederick King, 282
Poole, Josephine, 139
Popescu, Julian, 258
Portal, Colette, 31
Potter, Beatrix, 31, 250
Potter, Bronson, 120
Pough, Frederick H., 304
Powers, William K., 329
Pratt, Fletcher, 276
Preston, Carol, 250
Preston, Edna Mitchell, 33
Price, Christine, 340
Priestley, H. E., 265
Priestley, J. B., 340
Prishvin, Mikhail, 120
Prokofieff, Serge, 340
Purdy, Susan, 250, 341
Pyle, Howard, 189

Rabe, Olive, 202
Rabin, Gil, 69
Rand, Ann, 33
Randall, Florence E., 171
Randall, Janet, 91
Randall, Ruth Painter, 211
Rankin, Louise S., 120
Ransome, Arthur, 189
Rappaport, Uriel, 250
Raskin, Edith, 302
Raskin, Ellen, 33, 139, 171

Rasmussen, Knud, 234
Rau, Margaret, 298
Raviellei, Anthony, 288, 304, 307, 324
Raymond, Charles, 69
Razzell, Arthur G., 324
Read, Herbert, 234
Reboul, Antoine, 120
Redford, P. E. Gorey, 250
Reed, Gwendolyn E., 189, 231, 250
Reed, W. Maxwell, 305
Reeder, Colonel "Red", 211
Rees, Ennis, 33, 258
Reesink, Maryke, 33
Reeves, James, 121, 189, 190, 235, 250
Reggiani, Renee, 121
Reidel, Marlene, 33
Renick, Marion, 144
Rennert, Vincent, Paul, 211
Rey, H. A., 34, 347
Reynolds, Marjorie, 153
Rich, Josephine, 211
Rich, Louise Dickinson, 311
Richard, Adrienne, 69
Richards, Kenneth G., 211
Richards, Laura, 226
Richards, Norman, 211
Richardson, Grace, 70
Richter, Conrad, 91
Richter, Hans Peter, 121
Rieu, E. V., 226
Ringi, Kjell, 34
Rink, Paul, 212
Rinkoff, Barbara, 70, 121, 171
Ripley, Elizabeth, 212
Ritchie, Alice, 190
Ritchie, Barbara, 212, 347
Robbins, Ruth, 121, 190, 251
Roberts, Cliff, 341
Roberts, Elizabeth Madox, 226
Robertson, Barbara, 231
Robertson, Dorothy Lewis, 190
Robertson, Keith, 70, 139
Robinson, Barbara, 91
Robinson, Joan, 70
Robinson, Veronica, 70
Robinson, W. W., 288
Rockwell, Anne, 6, 212
Rockwell, Molly, 153
Rockwell, Norman, 153

Rodman, Bella, 71
Rollins, Charlemae Hill, 212, 251
Ronan, Colin, 317
Root, Shelton L., 228
Ropner, Pamela, 71, 121
Rose, Karen, 71
Rose, Mitchell, 34
Rose, Ronald, 34
Roseberry, C. R., 258
Rosen, Ellsworth, 298
Rosenfeld, Sam, 329
Ross, Eulalie S., 190
Ross, Frank Jr., 258
Rossetti, Christina, 227
Rounds, Glen, 153, 276, 298, 341
Rublowsky, John, 341
Ruck-Pauquet, Gina, 171
Rudolph, Marguerita, 190
Rumsey, Marian, 71
Ruskin, Ariane, 212, 341
Russ, Lavinia, 92
Russel, Solveig Paulson, 276, 341
Russell, Franklin, 298
Rydberg, Ernie, 140

Sachs, Marilyn, 71, 92
Salten, Felix, 153
Samson, Anne, 342
Sandburg, Carl, 171, 213, 227
Sanderlin, George, 276
Sandoz, Mari, 92
Sargent, Shirley, 71
Sasek, Miroslav, 283
Sauer, Julia, 172
Saunders, F. Wenderoth, 258
Savage, Katherine, 251
Sawyer, Ruth, 34, 172, 251
Saxe, John Godfrey, 227
Schaefer, Jack, 72
Schatz, Letta, 122
Schecter, Betty, 213
Scheer, George F., 172
Scheer, Julian, 34
Schick, Eleanor, 35
Schiller, Barbara, 190, 191
Schindel, Morton, 17
Schloat, G. Warren, Jr., 283
Schnack, Friedrich, 122
Schneider, Benjamin, 92
Schneider, Herman, 320
Schneider, Leo, 307

Schneider, Nina, 320
Schraff, A. E., 276
Schultz, Gwen, 238
Schultz, Pearle Henriksen, 213
Schuman, Benjamin N., 307
Schweitzer, Byrd Baylor, 35, 172
Scott, Ann Herbert, 35
Sears, Stephen W., 265
Sechrist, Elizabeth, 252, 342
Seed, Jenny, 122
Seeger, Elizabeth, 191
Seeger, Martin L., 122
Seeger, Ruth C., 342
Seeman, Bernard, 321
Segal, Lore, 36
Seidelman, J. E., 342
Seiden, Art, 3
Seidlova, A., 342
Sellew, Catherine F., 252
Selsam, Millicent E., 299, 309, 312, 313, 324
Sendak, Maurice, 36
Seredy, Kate, 36, 122
Seuss, Dr., 36–37
Severn, Bill, 213
Severn, Sue, 342
Severn, William, 342
Shannon, Terry, 321
Shapiro, William E., 213, 260
Shapp, Charles, 213, 299
Shapp, Martha, 213, 299
Sharp, Edith Lambert, 92
Sharp, Margery, 172
Shay, Myrtle, 92
Shearer, John, 72
Sheehan, Elizabeth Odell, 213
Shepherd, Walter, 305
Sherlock, Sir Philip, 191
Shields, Rita, 72
Shippen, Katherine B., 318, 342
Shirakigawa, Tomiko, 283
Shivkumar, K., 6
Sholokhov, Mikhail, 122
Shortall, Leonard, 72
Shotwell, Louisa R., 72
Showers, Paul, 238, 307
Shura, Mary Francis, 72
Shuttlesworth, Dorothy E., 288, 299, 302, 309
Sibley, Gretchen, 288

Siegel, Bertram, 325
Siegmeister, Elie, 342
Silverberg, Robert, 276, 305
Simeone, Harry, 244
Simon, Hilda, 299
Simon, Norma, 252
Sims, Bennett B., 213
Sindall, Marjorie, 122
Singer, Isaac Bashevis, 191, 192
Skladal, Charlotte N., 267
Slade, Richard, 342
Sloane, Eric, 277
Slobodkin, Louis, 37, 157
Smith, E. Brooks, 277
Smith, Elva S., 232
Smith, Emma, 73, 154
Smith, Howard K., 277
Smith, John, 235
Smith, William J., 227
Snellgrove, L. E., 265
Snyder, Zilpha Keatley, 73, 93, 172, 227
Sobol, Donald J., 140, 214
Sonneborn, Ruth A., 73
Sorensen, Virginia, 73
Soule, Gardner, 283, 318
Southall, Ivan, 74, 252
Sparks, James C., 319
Speare, Elizabeth George, 93, 123
Spearing, Judith, 172
Speevack, Yetta, 74
Sperry, Armstrong, 123
Sperry, Kay, 307
Spicer, Dorothy Gladys, 192
Spiegelman, Judith M., 283
Spier, Peter, 235, 259
Spilka, Arnold, 343
St. John, Wylly Folk, 140
Stambler, Irwin, 319
Stapp, Arthur D., 172
Starbird, Kaye, 227
Stauffer, Dwight G., 140
Stearns, Monroe, 277
Steegmuller, Francis, 347
Steele, Mary Q., 173
Steele, William O., 93, 214
Steffens, Lincoln, 214
Steig, William, 37, 173
Stein, Mini, 283
Stenuit, Robert, 299

Stephens, Peggy, 299
Stephens, Peter John, 94
Stephens, William M., 299, 305
Steptoe, John, 38
Sterling, Dorothy, 74, 214, 277, 305, 309, 314
Sterne, Emma Gelders, 214
Steurt, Marjorie Rankin, 300
Stevenson, Robert Louis, 140, 227
Stevenson, William, 123
Stinetorf, Louise A., 123
Stock, Robert, 324
Stockton, Frank R., 94, 173
Stolz, Mary, 74, 123
Stone, A. Harris, 325
Storr, Catherine, 140
Stoutenburg, Adrien, 192
Streatfeild, Noel, 343
Street, James, 154
Strouse, Susanne, 343
Stuart, Morna, 123
Sturton, Hugh, 192
Suba, Suzanne, 38
Sucksdorff, Astrid Bergman, 38
Sullivan, Arthur, 335
Sullivan, George, 325
Sutcliff, Rosemary, 124, 192
Suter, Antoinette, 231
Swarthout, Glendon, 75
Swarthout, Kathryn, 75
Swinton, William Elgin, 288
Switzer, George, 305
Syme, Ronald, 215

Tagore, Rabindrana, 228
Talmadge, Marian, 277
Tamchina, Jürgen, 39
Tarcov, Oscar, 246
Tashjian, Virginia A., 192
Taylor, Don Alonzo, 94
Taylor, Elizabeth, 124
Taylor, Mark, 173
Taylor, Theodore, 75
Teal, Mildred, 173
Thiele, Colin, 154
Thomas, Dawn C., 39
Thompson, Mary Wolfe, 94
Thompson, Paul D., 321
Thompson, Wilma, 75
Thomson, Peter, 75
Thurber, James, 173

Tigue, Ethel, 132
Tobias, Tobi, 215
Toepfer, Ray G., 94
Tolkien, J. R. R., 174
Tooze, Ruth, 124, 193, 228, 283, 284
Townsend, John R., 124
Trager, Helen G., 184
Travers, Pamela, 174
Trease, Geoffrey, 125, 140, 270, 343
Treece, Henry, 125
Trent, Robbie, 252
Tresselt, Alvin, 39, 193, 252
Trone, Alexandra, 264
Tudor, Tasha, 2, 3, 39, 239, 253
Tunis, Edwin, 278
Tunis, John R., 125
Turk, Midge, 215
Turkle, Brinton, 39, 154, 174
Turnbull, Agnes Sligh, 75
Turner, Gerry, 75
Turner, Philip, 253
Twain, Mark, 94

Uchida, Yoshiko, 193, 253
Uden, Grant, 265
Udry, Janice May, 40
Ullman, James R., 144
Ungerer, Tomi, 40
Unkelbach, Kurt, 154
Unrau, Ruth, 95
Unstead, R. J., 216, 235
Untermeyer, Louis, 235, 343

Van Anrooy, Frans, 40
Van Der Loeff, A. Rutgers, 95, 125
Van Dersal, William R., 302
Van Iterson, Siny R., 126
Van Rhijn, Aleid, 126
Van Riper, Guernsey, Jr., 329
Van Stockum, Hilda, 126
Varner, Velma, 40
Vaughan-Jackson, Genevieve, 126
Vavra, Robert, 126
Veglahn, Nancy, 216
Verne, Jules, 127, 158
Viereck, Phillip, 278
Villiard, Paul, 300
Vipont, Elfrida, 216, 253
Vlahos, Olivia, 265

Vlock, Laurel F., 95
Voight, Virginia Frances, 216
Von Jüchen, Aurel, 253
Voss, Carl Herman, 253
Vroman, Mary Elizabeth, 75

Waber, Bernard, 174
Wahl, Jan, 254
Walker, Barbara, 193
Walker, Kathrine Sorley, 343
Wall, L. V., 344
Wallace, Barbara, 95
Walsh, Jill Paton, 127
Walsh, John, 228
Walton, Bryce, 127, 141
Walton, Elizabeth C., 95
Waltrip, Lila, 278
Waltrip, Rufus, 278
Walworth, Nancy Z., 260
Ward, Lynd, 40, 208
Ward, Philip, 75
Ware, Leon, 141
Warner, Gertrude Chandler, 141
Warren, Billy, 154
Warren, Mary Phraner, 76
Watson, Jane Werner, 281
Watson, Sally, 95, 127
Watts, K. G. O., 324
Weaver, Stella, 127
Webb, Robert N., 216
Webster, Jean, 76
Wechsberg, Joseph, 344
Wees, Frances, 141
Weik, Mary Hays, 344
Weil, Ann, 141
Weil, Lisl, 300
Weisgard, Leonard, 239
Weisner, William, 193
Weiss, Harvey, 344
Weiss, Renee Karol, 235
Wellman, Manly Wade, 95
Wells, Robert, 144
Wenning, Elizabeth, 254
Wersba, Barbara, 76
Werstein, Irving, 278
West, Wallace, 76
Westwood, Gwen, 127
White, Anne Terry, 4, 154, 193, 194, 266
White, Dale, 319
White, E. B., 174

White, G. A., 344
Whitman, Walt, 228
Whitney, David, 311
Wibberley, Leonard, 96, 216
Wier, Esther, 76
Wilder, Laura Ingalls, 96
Wildsmith, Brian, 2, 41
Wilkie, Katherine E., 217
Willard, Barbara, 128
Williams, Jay, 128, 158, 194, 217
Williams, John A., 217
Williams, Susan, 128
Williams-Ellis, Amabel, 194
Williamson, Joanne S., 96, 128
Wilson, Erica, 344
Wilson, Forrest, 329
Wilson, Mitchell, 321
Winston, Richard, 217
Winter, Jeanette, 254
Wirtenberg, Patricia Z., 344
Wise, Winifred E., 217
Witheridge, Elizabeth, 76
Withers, Carl, 194, 235
Wojciechowska, Maia, 96, 128, 218
Wolfe, Louis, 311
Wood, James Playsted, 218
Wood, Katherine, 344
Wood, Nancy, 41
Woolsey, Janette, 342
Worm, Piet, 254
Wrightston, Patricia, 158
Wyler, Rose, 330
Wynants, Miche, 254

Yamaguchi, Tohr, 41, 194
Yarmolinsky, Avrahm, 180
Yashima, Taro, 41, 42
Yates, Elizabeth, 96, 218
Yolen, Jane, 6, 42, 59, 174
Young, Patrick, 155

Zangrando, Robert L., 267
Zapf, Marjorie A., 141
Zaturenska, Marya, 231
Zei, Alki, 129
Zemach, Harve, 42, 195
Zim, Herbert Spencer, 288
Zimelman, Nathan, 42
Zion, Gene, 42
Zistel, Era, 300
Zolotow, Charlotte, 43

TITLE INDEX

A for the Ark,   1
A Is for Annabelle,   2
ABC Book,   1
ABC Bunny,   1
ABC of Bumptious Beasts,   223
ABC's of Space,   317
Abe Lincoln Grows Up,   213
About the B'nai Bagels,   143
Abraham Lincoln,   200
Abraham Lincoln in Peace and War,   208
Abraham Lincoln's World,   270
Across Five Aprils,   87
Act It Out,   333
Adam and Eve,   250
Adam and the Golden Cock,   82
Adam Bookout,   72
Adam of the Road,   110
Adventure in Geometry,   324
Adventure in Survival,   46
Adventures of Egbert the Easter Egg,   241
Adventures of Lewis and Clark,   200
Adventures of Paddy Pork,   18
Adventures of Sherlock Holmes,   134
Adventures of Spider,   175
Adventures of Tom Sawyer,   94
Adventures with Abraham's Children,   252
Aesop's Fables,   4
African Beginnings,   265
Air Is All around You,   313
Airfield Man,   132
Akavak: an Eskimo Journey,   112

Album of North American Animals,   292
Aldar the Trickster,   178
Alexander and the Car with a Missing Headlight,   17
Alexander and the Wind-up Mouse,   27
Alfred Hitchcock's Sinister Spies,   136
Ali,   117
Ali of Turkey,   283
Alice's Adventures in Wonderland and Through the Looking Glass,   162
All about Cats,   291
All about Horses,   294
All about Language,   258
All about Strange Beasts of the Past,   287
All about the Universe,   316
All about Us,   306
All about Volcanoes and Earthquakes,   304
All Day Long: Fifty Rhymes of the Never Was and Always Is,   225
All except Sammy,   52
All Kinds of Bees,   309
All Kinds of Seals,   296
All Together: A Child's Treasury of Verse,   219
All-around-the-House Art and Craft,   344
Alley,   134
Alligator Case,   138
Almost Year,   171
Along the Seashore,   291

Alphabet of Ancient Egypt,   260
Alphabet of Girls,   223
Alphabet of Puppy Care,   300
Amahl and the Night
  Visitors,   248
Amazing Inventor from Laurel
  Creek,   76
America,   228
America Begins: The Story of the
  Finding of the New
  World,   269
America Grows Up,   273
American ABC,   2
American Adventures
  1620–1945,   82
American Folksongs for
  Children,   342
American Indian Story,   274
American Prairie Chicken,   300
American Revolution,   267
American Tall Tales,   192
American Tall-Tale
  Animals,   192
Americans before
  Columbus,   267
America's Abraham Lincoln, 208
America's Endangered Wildlife,
  302
America's Ethan Allen, 205
America's First Christmas, 249
America's Paul Revere, 202
America's Players, 335
America's Robert E. Lee, 199
Amigo, 35
Amos and Boris, 37
Amos Fortune: Free Man, 218
Amy and Laura, 92
Anansi, the Spider Man, 191
Anchor of Mercy, 115
Anchors Aweigh: the Story of
  David Glasgow Farragut, 207
Ancient Animals of America, 288
And Now Miguel, 61
And So My Garden Grows, 7
And the Waters Prevailed, 99
And to Think That I Saw It on
  Mulberry Street, 36
Andrew Jackson, 199
Andy Buckram's Tin Men, 155
Angel of Appalachia: Martha
  Berry, 210

Angry Waters, 65
Angus and the Ducks, 17
Animal Camouflage, 299
Animal Doctors: What Do They
  Do?, 19
Animal Family, 165
Animal Frolic, 40
Animals as Parents, 299
Animals at My Doorstep, 295
Animals Mourn for Da Leopard,
  180
Animals South of the Border, 290
Ann Aurelia and Dorothy, 48
Annie Annie, 50
Ant Is Born, 308
Antonio, 120
Ants Are Fun, 309
Ape in a Cape, 1
Apple and the Arrow, 198
Apple Vendor's Fair, 223
Apples Every Day, 70
Appley Dapply's Nursery Rhymes,
  7
Appolonia's Valentine, 238
Appomatox: Closing Struggle of
  the Civil War, 269
Apt 3, 24
Arabian Nights, 185
Architecture: A Book of Products
  for Young Adults, 329
Are You There, God? It's Me,
  Margaret, 46
Ark, 101
Armed with Courage, 208
Armitage, Armitage, Fly Away
  Home, 158
Around and About, 220
Around the World Cookbook for
  Young People, 328
Around the World in Ninety
  Minutes, 317
Around the Year, 39
Art of Africa, 335
Art of Magic, 328
Ask Mr. Bear, 237
Assignment: Sports, 328
At Home: A Visit in Four
  Languages, 336
At Home in India, 279
Attic of the Wind, 28
Audun and His Bear, 190

Aunt Vinnie's Victorious Six, 97
Australian Legendary Tales, 188
Avalanche, 125
Awake and Dreaming, 195
Away in a Manager: A Story of
   the Nativity, 249
Away We Go: 100 Poems for the
   Very Young, 234
Aztec Indians of Mexico, 260

Baboushka and the Three Kings,
   251
Baby Elephant's Trunk, 346
Bach, 205
Backbone of the King: The Story of
   Paka'a and His Son Ku, 177
Ballad of the Burglar of Babylon,
   220
Bambi, 153
Banner in the Sky, 144
Banner over Me, 110
Barbie, 45
Barto Takes the Subway, 256
Bates Family, 117
Bats and Balls, 143
Battle of Austerlitz, 262
Battle of St. George Without, 115
Battle of Waterloo, 263
Battles of Saratoga, 269
Bayeux Tapestry: The Story of the
   Norman Conquest: 1066, 261
Bears' House, 71
Bears Live Here, 293
Bears on Hemlock Mountain, 83
Beast in Holger's Woods, 134
Beast of Monsieur Racine, 40
Because of a Tree, 312
Becky's Birthday, 239
Bedtime for Frances, 22
Befana's Gift, 243
Before and after Dinosaurs, 287
Before You Were a Baby, 307
Behind the Magic Line, 54
Believe in Spring, 51
Bells and Grass, 221
Bells of Bleecker Street, 44
Benito Juarez: Builder of a Nation,
   214
Benjamin Franklin, 206
Benjie's Portion, 78
Benny: The Biography of a Horse,
   150

Beorn the Proud, 119
Beowulf, 124
Bess and the Sphinx, 198
Better Soccer for Boys, 327
Beyond the Frontier, 84
Beyond the High Hills: A Book of
   Eskimo Poems, 234
Big Basketball Prize, 144
Big Blue Island, 56
Big Red, 150
Big Road, 81
Big Snow, 21
Big Susan, 247
Big Wheels, 59
Bigger Than an Elephant, 11
Biggest Bear, 40
Biggest House in the World, 27
Biological Clocks and Patterns, 297
Bird Tree, 241
Birds and the Beasts Were There,
   229
Birds at Night, 293
Black BC's, 268
Black Bear's Story, 296
Black Bondage: The Slaves in the
   South, 271
Black Courage, 276
Black Fiary Tales, 176
Black Fox of Lorne, 106
Black Heart of Indri, 183
Black Jack: Last of the Big
   Alligators, 296
Black Lobo, 154
Black Pearl, 117
Black Tanker, 138
Blackie, the Gorilla, 149
Bless This Day, 253
Blind Colt, 153
Blind Men and the Elephant, 227
Blood for Holly Warner, 56
Blue Canyon Horse, 146
Blue Heron Tree, 295
Blue Jacket, 201
Blue Rose: A Collection of Stories
   for Girls, 190
Blue Valentine, 238
Blue Willow, 56
Blue-Nosed Witch, 237
Blueberries for Sal, 28
Boats on the River, 17
Bola and the Oba's Drummers, 122
Bolivar the Liberator, 215

Bond of the Fire, 107
Bonus of Redonda, 97
Book of Americans, 219
Book of Ballet, 331
Book of Horses, 289
Book of Hugh Flower, 100
Book of Mother Goose and Nursery
  Rhymes, 7
Book of Nature Poems, 229
Book of Reptiles and Amphibians,
  290
Book of Snails, 296
Book of Stars for You, 316
Book of Three, 159
Book of Wishes and Wishmaking,
  180
Book of Wonder Voyages, 184
Books: A Book to Begin on, 255
Borrowed Crown, 116
Borrowers, 170
Bottom of the Sea, 304
Boundary Riders, 118
Boy Alone, 153
Boy Blue's Book of Beasts, 227
Boy of Old Prague, 113
Boy on Horseback, 214
Boy Who Could Sing Pictures, 167
Boy Who Made a Million, 68
Boy Who Played Tiger, 109
Boys in the Revolution, 199
Brady, 85
Brave Cowboy, 10
Bread and Butter Indian, 82
Bread-and-Butter Journey, 82
Bread and Roses, 275
Brian Wildsmith's ABC, 2
Brian Wildsmith's Birds, 41
Brian Wildsmith's Circus, 41
Brian Wildsmith's Illustrated Bible
  Stories, 253
Brian Wildsmith's Mother Goose, 7
Brian Wildsmith's Wild Animals,
  41
Bridge Between, 87
Bridle for Pegasus, 318
Bring a Torch, Jeannette, Isabella,
  242
Bristle Face, 45
Britain under the Romans, 265
Bronx Zoo Book of Wild Animals,
  291
Bronze Bow, 123

Bronzeville Boys and Girls, 220
Brother of the Hero, 113
Brown Cow Farm, 3
Brown Is a Beautiful Color, 12
Brownies—Hush, 236
Buccaneers & Pirates of Our
  Coasts, 94
Building Blocks of the Universe,
  322
Building Brooklyn Bridge, 258
Buildings of Ancient Greece, 263
Bully of Barkham Street, 74
Burnish Me Bright, 52
Burro on the Beach, 53
Burt Dow: Deep-Water Man, 28
Bus Girls, 57
Bushbabies, 123
Butterfly Time, 308
By Secret Railway, 89
By the Great Horn Spoon, 84
Byzantines, 261

Cabin Faced West, 85
Cabin on the Fjord, 116
Caddie Woodlawn, 78
Calico Bush, 84
Calico Captive, 93
California Indian Days, 267
Call It Courage, 123
Call Me Bandicoot, 170
Call of the Valley, 98
Call of the Wild, 152
Cambodia: Land Of Contrasts, 283
Camel Caravan, 104
Canadian Story, 264
Canalboat to Freedom, 83
Candido, 15
Candita's Choice, 62
Candle in Her Room, 130
Candle-Making, 343
Captain Cook: Pacific Explorer, 215
Captain John Paul Jones: America's
  Fighting Seaman, 215
Captain of the Planter, 214
Captured by the Abnakis, 91
Carolina Pirate, 95
Carolina's Courage, 96
Carramore, 126
Carry on, Mr. Bowditch, 207
Cartier Sails the St. Lawrence, 197
Carving on the Tree, 80
Case of the Hungry Stranger, 131

Casey Jones: The Story of a Brave Engineer, 341
Castle, Abbey and Town, 260
Cat Across the Way, 59
Cat and the Mouse and Other Spanish Tales, 180
Cat at Night, 23
Cat Came Fiddling, 338
Catching, 328
Caterpillars, 309
Cathie Runs Wild, 114
Cats, 294
Cats and Bats and Things with Wings, 219
Cave above Delphi, 133
Cave of Danger, 141
Cave of Riches: The Story of the Dead Sea Scrolls, 247
Caves of the Great Hunters, 259
Cay, 75
Certain Small Shepherd, 243
Cesar Chavez, 202
Chalou, 146
Chancellorsville, 275
Chancy and the Grand Rascal, 84
Changeling, 93
Chanticleer, 178
Chanticleer and the Fox, 14
Charlemagne, 206
Charlemagne, 217
Charles Darwin, 203
Charles Richard Drew: Pioneer in Blood Research, 204
Charley, 70
Charlotte's Web, 174
Charm for Paco's Mother, 123
Cheerful Heart, 110
Chemistry of Soap, 325
Chendru: The Boy and the Tiger, 38
Cherokee Animal Tales, 172
Chicken Little, Count to Ten, 3
Chicken Ten Thousand, 24
Chief Joseph: War Chief of the Nez Perce, 200
Children of Japan, 283
Children's Homer: Adventures of Odysseus and the Tales of Troy, 178
Child's Garden of Verses, 227
Child's Grace, 243
China and the Chinese, 281
Chinese Bug, 172

Chingo Smith of the Erie Canal, 77
Chipper the Beaver, 292
Chitty-Chitty-Bang-Bang: The Magical Car, 164
Choctaw Code, 83
Choo Choo: The Story of the Little Engine Who Ran Away, 13
Chris Muldoon, 72
Christ Child, 249
Christmas Bells are Ringing, 242
Christmas Book, 251
Christmas Bower, 250
Christmas Carol, 245
Christmas Eve, 247
Christmas Everywhere, 252
Christmas Gif', 251
Christmas in Noisy Village, 248
Christmas in the Stable, 248
Christmas Mouse, 254
Christmas Sky, 242
Christmas Story, 243
Christmas Visitors: A Norwegian Folk Tale, 254
Christopher Jones: Captain of the Mayflower, 200
Chúcaro, Wild Pony of the Pampa, 150
Cinderella, 5
Circle of Seasons, 279
Circus, 15
City in the Summer, 35
City in the Winter, 35
Civil Rights and the Black American, 267
Civil War, 276
Clarence Darrow, 204
Clarence Turns Sea Dog, 151
Claudia, 95
Clay, Wood, and Wire, 344
Claymore and Kilt, 188
Clean Air, Sparkling Water, 302
Click and the Toyshop, 122
Clock We Live on, 322
Clocks and More Clocks, 23
Cloud over Hiroshima, 272
Clue of the Black Cat, 130
Clyde's Clam Farm, 57
Coin Collecting as a Hobby, 328
Cold Flame, 189
Collage, 339
Colonel of the Black Regiment: The Life of Thomas Wentworth Higginson, 208

Colonial Living, 278
Color of Man, 284
Colorado: River of Mystery, 268
Columbus Day, 238
Columbus Story, 199
Come Along!, 220
Comet in Moominland, 165
Comets, 316
Coming of the Pilgrims, 277
Communication: From Cave
    Writing to Television, 256
Communism: An American's View,
    273
Complete Nonsense Book, 224
Confessions of a Toe-Hanger, 57
Confucius, 213
Congress, 273
Constance: A Story of Early
    Plymouth, 81
Constellation: A Shakespeare
    Anthology, 336
Contender, 143
Contraband of War, 95
Contrary Jenkins, 14
Coriander, 106
Cougar, 75
Count Who Wished He Were a
    Peasant: A Life of Leo Tolstoy,
    211
Country Bunny and the Little Gold
    Shoes, 247
Country Cousin, 49
Country of the Pointed Firs and
    Other Stories, 87
Courage of Sarah Noble, 83
Cowboys and Cattlemen, 278
Crab that Crawled out of the Past,
    297
Crack in The Wall and Other
    Terrible Weird Tales, 138
Crazy Cantilever and Other
    Science Experiments, 323
Crazy Flight, 224
Creating with Clay, 342
Creative Claywork, 337
Creative Plays and Programs for
    Holidays, 331
Cricket in a Thicket, 222
Cricket Songs: Japanese Haiku, 229
Cricket Winter, 165
Crisis at Fort Laramie, 78
Crocodile Has Me by the Leg, 230
Crow Boy, 41

Cruising to Danger, 110
Curious George, 34
Curious Raccoons, 294
Curse of Cain, 252
Cutlass Island, 133
Cyrus Holt and the Civil War, 86

Daddy-Long-Legs, 76
Dancing in the Moon, 2
Dancing Palm Tree, 193
Daniel Boone, 200
Danny Dunn and the Weather
    Machine, 158
Dark Ages, 259
Dark Horse of Woodfield, 149
Dark of the Cave, 140
Dark Venture, 78
Daughter of the Mountains, 120
David and Goliath, 245
David in Silence, 70
Dawn Wind, 124
Day Around the World, 24
Day of the Earthquake, 122
Day We Saw the Sun Come Up, 18
Days of the Week, 233
Dead End Bluff, 76
Dead Man's Light, 133
Dear Dolphin, 166
Dear Readers and Riders, 327
Deep Down: Great Achievements
    in Cave Exploration, 304
Deep Where the Octopi Lie, 64
Defender of the Constitution:
    Andrew Johnson, 203
Depend on Katie John, 48
Desert Life, 301
Desert People, 280
Desert War in North Africa, 265
Devil's Shadow: The Story of
    Witchcraft in Massachusetts, 266
Diamond in the Window, 167
Diamonds in Pictures, 305
Diary of Nina Kosterina, 206
Dictionary of Chivalry, 265
Digs and Diggers, 261
Dinosaurs, 288
Discovering Design, 334
Discovering Tut-Ankh-Amen's
    Tomb, 262
Discovery of the Elements, 323
Do You Know What I'll Do?, 42
Do You Know What Time It Is?,
    322

Do You Move As I Do?, 332
Do You See What I See?, 332
Do You Want to Be My Friend?, 14
Doctors, 269
Doctor's Boy, 97
Dodos and Dinosaurs, 288
Dog for Joey, 56
Dog on Barkham Street, 74
Dog Who Never Knew, 154
Doll's Day for Yoshiko, 113
Dolphin, 299
Dominique and the Dragon, 39
Don't Ever Cross a Crocodile, 227
Don't Take Teddy, 55
Dorp Dead, 52
Down from the Lonely Mountain, 179
Down to Earth, 158
Downtown, 285
Drag Racing, 326
Dragon in the Clock Box, 162
Dragon in the Garden, 169
Dragon Tree, 124
Dragons of the Queen, 74
Drake Drills for Oil, 311
Dramatized Classics for Radio-Style Reading, 340
Drawings to Live with, 337
Dream Hunters, 114
Dream Keeper and Other Poems, 223
Dream Time, 125
Dream Watcher, 76
Dreams, 285
Dreyfus Affair: A National Scandal, 213
Drinking Gourd, 89
Drumbeats in Williamsburg, 88
Drummer Hoff, 15
Durango Street, 46
Dwight David Eisenhower, 211

Eagle Mask: A West Coast Indian Tale, 183
Early American Crafts Tools, Shops and Products, 326
Early Days of Man, 287
Early Moon, 227
Early Thunder, 86
Earth for Sam, 305
Earth Is on a Fish's Back, 176
Earth through the Ages, 303
Earthfasts, 169
Earth's Surface, 305

Easter Book of Legends, 247
Edgar Allan, 67
Edge of Two Worlds, 87
Edith Wharton: 1862–1937, 199
Egg Tree, 249
Egypt Game, 73
Egyptians, 259
Eighteen Cousins, 22
Elbert, the Mind Reader, 171
Elderberry Bush, 86
Eleanor Farjeon's Poems for Children, 222
Election Day, 238
Electronic Brains, 324
Elephant Boy, 128
Elephant's Child, 166
Eli Lives in Israel, 280
Elidor, 164
Elijah the Slave, 191
Elisabeth and the Marsh Mystery, 136
Elisabeth, the Treasure Hunter, 58
Elmer: The Story of a Patchwork Elephant, 29
Elsa and Her Cubs, 289
Elves and the Shoemaker, 19
Emily's Runaway Imagination, 81
Emily's Voyage, 154
Emperor and the Drummer Boy, 121
Emperor and the Kite, 42
Emperor's New Clothes, 9
Empty Schoolhouse, 49
Enchanted Drum, 19
Enchanted Schoolhouse, 172
Encyclopedia Brown: Boy Detective, 140
Enemy at Green Knowe, 131
Enormous Egg, 161
Environments out There, 315
Eric in Alaska, 72
Eric, The Tale of a Red-Tempered Viking, 260
Erie Canal, 255
Erie Canal, 259
Escape, 47
Escape to Witch Mountain, 156
Eskimos Knew, 264
Ever Ride a Dinosaur?, 162
Every Man Heart Lay Down, 246
Every Time I Climb a Tree, 225
Everyday Trees, 311
Everygirls' Companion, 55
Evolution of the Machine, 319

Exploring Earth and Space, 318
Exploring Mars, 318
Exploring the Moon, 318
Exploring the Weather, 313
Eyes on the Ballet, 343

Fabulous Earthworm Deal, 172
Fairies and Chimneys, 223
Fairy Tales from Viet Nam, 190
Fairy Tales of the Orient, 177
Falcon and the Dove: A Life of
    Thomas Becket of Canterbury,
    201
Fall Is Here, 314
False Start, 69
Family Conspiracy, 118
Family under the Bridge, 243
Famous Artists of the Past, 333
Famous Paintings: An Introduction
    to Art for Young People, 333
Far Frontier, 93
Far out the Long Canal, 106
Faraway Dream, 84
Faraway Farm, 102
Faraway Lurs, 100
Farming around the World, 310
Farms, 310
Favorite Fairy Tales Told in
    Czechoslovakia, 182
Favorite Poems: Old and New, 231
Favorite Uncle Remus, 182
Fayerweather Forecast, 58
Feast of Light, 67
Feathers: Plain and Fancy, 299
Felice, 12
Felipe the Bullfighter, 126
Festivals for You to Celebrate, 250
Fiddler of High Lonesome, 174
Fierce and Gentle Warriors, 122
Fifer For the Union, 77
Fifteen, 49
Fifty Plays for Junior Actors, 338
Fifty-First Dragon, 161
51 Capitals of the USA, 274
Fight in the Mountains, 101
Figure Skating, 328
Filippo's Dome, 212
Fingers Are Always Bringing Me
    News, 226
Firefly Named Torchy, 174
Fireside Book of Folk Songs, 332
Fireweed, 127
First Book of Copper, 303
First Book of Fruits, 312

First Book of Lumbering, 311
First Book of Printing, 256
First Book of the Cliff Dwellers,
    274
First Book of the Opera, 343
First Book of the Supreme Court,
    268
First Bull Run, 275
First Christmas, 252
First Graces, 253
First in Their Hearts: A Biography
    of George Washington, 202
First Transatlantic Cable, 257
First under the North Pole, 255
Fisherman's Family, 33
500 Hats of Bartholomew Cubbins,
    37
Five Chinese Brothers, 11
Five-Yard Fuller and the Unlikely
    Knights, 144
Flambards, 118
Flatboat Days on Frontier Rivers,
    274
Flattered Flying Fish and Other
    Poems, 226
Flight of the Doves, 115
Flight of the Kite Merriweather, 173
Flight to Afghanistan, 136
Flight to the Promised Land, 111
Floating and Sinking, 323
Floating Market, 108
Fly Homer Fly, 30
Fly-By-Night, 153
Flying Carpet, 177
Flying Saucer Full of Spaghetti, 25
Fog Magic, 172
Folding Paper Masks, 339
Follow the Wind, 39
Fool of the World and the Flying
    Ship, 189
For a Child: Great Poems Old and
    New, 234
Forbidden Frontier, 111
Forest Folk, 291
Forever Christmas Tree, 253
Forever Free: The Story of the
    Emancipation Proclamation, 277
Forts in the Wilderness, 274
Four Clever Brothers, 19
Four Days in Philadelphia: 1776,
    275
Four Riders, 25
Fourteen Cases of Dynamite, 171
Fourth of July Story, 237

Fox, the Dog, and the Griffin, 175
Fox Went out on a Chilly Night, 6
Foxie the Singing Dog, 147
Franco and the Spanish Civil War, 265
Frank Lloyd Wright: America's Greatest Architect, 205
Franklin D. Roosevelt: Portrait of a Great Man, 206
Franz Tovey and the Rare Animals, 166
Fray Junípero Serra and the California Conquest, 217
Free Souls, 82
Friday Night Is Papa Night, 73
Fiedrich, 121
Friendly Animals, 37
Friends and Enemies, 117
Frog Went A-Courtin', 6
From Bush to City: A Look at the New Africa, 279
From Summer to Summer, 220
From Tepees to Towers, 271
From the Mixed-Up Files of Mrs. Basil E. Frankweiler, 61
Fun with Ballet, 334
Fun with Crewel Embroidery, 344
Fun with French, 345
Fun with German, 345
Fun with Italian, 345
Fun with Spanish, 345
Fun with Your Fingers, 336
Funny Thing, 17

Galaxies, 315
Galinka, the Wild Goose, 145
Gallaudet: Friend of the Deaf, 200
Game Of Baseball, 327
Game of Basketball, 329
Gammage Cup, 166
Garrett's Crossing, 90
Gases and Plasmas, 321
Gasoline Buggy of the Duryea Brothers, 257
Gaudienzia: Pride of the Palio, 149
Gautama Buddha: In Life and Legend, 206
Gay-Neck, 152
General Billy Mitchell, 209
General Felice, 60
General's Boots, 85
Genghis Khan, 216
Gentle Ben, 152
George Washington, 202

George Washington's World, 270
George's Store, 10
Georgie's Halloween, 236
Germany, East and West, 281
Gertrude Kloppenberg, 58
Gettysburg Address and the Second Inaugural, 274
Ghost of Opalina, 130
Ghost of Spirit River, 129
Ghost Towns of the American West, 276
Ghosts and Goblins, 237
Ghosts Go Haunting, 188
Giant Book, 180
Giant John, 27
Giant Story, 15
Giant under the Snow, 164
Gilberto and the Wind, 16
Gilgamesh: Man's First Story, 177
Ginger Horse, 147
Girl in the Witch House, 86
Girl on a Broomstick, 48
Girl Who Sat by the Ashes, 179
Giselle, 117
Glorious Christmas Soup Party, 246
Glorious Conspiracy, 96
Go and Hush the Baby, 13
Goat Boy of Brooklyn, 83
Goblin Market, 227
Goggles, 25
Golden Crane, 194
Golden Egg Book, 12
Golden Goblet, 115
Golden Goose Book, 18
Golden Island, 97
Golden Name Day, 63
Golden Phoenix and Other French-Canadian Fairy Tales, 176
Golden Treasury of Myths and Legends, 193
Golden Treasury of Natural History, 304
Golden Treasury of Poetry, 235
Gone-Away Lake, 53
Good Luck Spider and other Bad Luck Stories, 169
Good Luck to the Rider, 118
Good Master, 122
Good Pope John, 213
Good-Bye, My Lady, 154
Goodbye, Dove Square, 64
Goodbye to the Jungle, 124

Gordon Parks, 215
Grabbit the Rascal, 193
Grain of Sand, 220
Grand Slam, 326
Grandfather Tales, 178
Great American Heroes, 201
Great Dane Thor, 148
Great Declaration, 268
Great Geppy, 171
Great Picture Robbery, 335
Great Rope, 90
Greatest Giants of Them All, 327
Greek Gods and Heroes, 181
Green Gate, 48
Green Grow the Rushes, 115
Green: The Story of a Caribbean
    Turtle's Struggle for Survival,
    297
Greg's Microscope, 324
Grettir the Strong, 188
Greyling, 174
Grimm's Fairy Tales, 20
Grizzly, 60
Growing Up: How We Become
    Alive, Are Born, and Grow, 306
Guardian Angel, 121
Guardians Of Liberty: Sam Adams
    and John Hancock, 204
Gumdrop and the Farmer's Friend,
    46
Gumdrop Necklace, 62
Guy Can Be Wrong, 70
Gypsy, 36

H. Philip Birdsong's ESP, 167
Hah-Nee of the Cliff Dwellers, 79
Hailstones and Halibut Bones, 226
Hakon of Rogen's Saga, 111
Half-Magic, 163
Halfway to Heaven: The Story of
    the St. Bernard, 151
Halloween, 236
Hamid and the Palm Sunday
    Donkey, 107
Hand in Hand We'll Go, 220
Hand upon the Time: A Life Of
    Charles Dickens, 199
Hans Christian Andersen: Immortal
    Storyteller, 209
Hans the Miller Man, 11
Hanukkah, 252
Happy Birthday Present, 237
Happy Orpheline, 104
Happy Owls, 31

Hare and the Tortoise, 5
Harlem Summer, 75
Harpoon Gunner, 127
Harriet and the Promised Land,
    207
Harriet the Spy, 55
Harriet Tubman: Conductor on the
    Underground Railroad, 210
Harry S. Truman, 211
Harry the Dirty Dog, 42
Hawk in the Sky, 298
Headless Cupid, 172
Headlines for Caroline, 59
Hello Brazil, 279
Helter-Skelter, 138
Henny Penny, 18
Henri's Hands for Pablo Picasso,
    114
Henry and the Paper Route, 49
Henry Explores the Jungle, 173
Henry Hudson, 197
Henry Reed's Journey, 70
Herbert Situation, 168
Here Comes the Lions!, 294
Here Comes the Bus!, 57
Here Comes Thursday, 160
Here I Come, Ready or Not, 29
Here Is Your Hobby: Indian
    Dancing and Customs, 329
Here's How, 344
Heritage Of Music, 342
Hero of Two Seas, 209
Heroes, 185
Heroes of the Skies, 205
Hey, What's Wrong With This
    One?, 96
Hidden Year of Devlin Bates, 66
Hide-Out for a Horse, 75
Hiding the Bell, 90
High Country Adventure, 71
High King, 159
High, Wide and Handsome, 187
High-Rise Secret, 62
Highlights of the World Series, 327
Highways Across Waterways:
    Ferries, Bridges and Tunnels,
    256
His Enemy, His Friend, 125
Hoagie's Rifle-Gun, 65
Hobbit, 174
Hole in the Hedge, 137
Hole in the Tree, 294
Holiday Cards for You to Make,
    341

Holiday Round Up, 238
Holidays around the World, 246
Holy Man's Secret, 102
Holy Night, 253
Home Free, 66
Home Is the North, 65
Homer Price, 63
Honey of the Nile, 101
Honor Sands, 62
Horace Higby and the Scientific
    Pitch, 142
Horatio, 146
Horn of Roland, 128
Horse Came Running, 147
Hores in Harry's Room, 22
Horse in the Camel Suit, 138
Horse Without a Head, 101
Horescatcher, 92
Horton Hatches the Egg, 37
Hound of Ulster, 192
House of Dies Drear, 56
House of Sixty Fathers, 106
House of the Bittern, 71
House on Charlton Street, 133
House upon a Rock, 68
Houseboat Mystery, 141
Houses from the Sea, 19
How Animals Communicate, 294
How Animals Tell Time, 299
How Do They Make It?, 325
How Many Kids Are Hiding on My
    Block?, 3
How Many Miles to Babylon?, 54
How the People Sang the
    Mountains up, 186
How to Care for Your Dog, 290
How to Eat a Poem and Other
    Morsels: Food Poems for
    Children, 228
How to Make a Home Nature
    Museum, 326
How to Punt, Pass and Kick, 329
Hubba-Hubba: A Tale of the
    Sahara, 105
Huckleberry Hill, 271
Hudden and Dudden and Donald
    O'Neary, 184
Hudson: River of History, 257
Human Eye, 307
Humbug Witch, 236
Hundred Dresses, 54
Hungry Goat, 339
Hunt for the Whooping Cranes: A

Natural History Detective Story,
    302
Hunter I Might Have Been
    (Dalrymple), 221
Hunter I Might Have Been
    (Mendoza), 286
Hurrah, We're Outward Bound!,
    235
Hush Little Baby, 331

I Am the Darker Brother, 228
I Am Your Misfortune, 190
I Caught a Lizard, 291
I Feel the Same Way, 226
I, Jessie, 211
I, Juan de Pareja, 201
I Know an Old Lady, 7
I Love My Anteater with an A, 2
I Marched with Hannibal, 99
I Think I Saw a Snail: Young
    Poems for City Seasons, 232
I Thought I Heard the City, 226
I Will Adventure, 110
I Wish I Had an Afro, 72
I Wonder How, I Wonder Why,
    222
If I Were a Bird, 292
If You Grew up with Abraham
    Lincoln, 207
Illinois River, 266
Imagination's Other Place, 234
Important Dates in Afro-American
    History, 272
In a Pumpkin Shell, 8
In a Running Brook, 296
In a Spring Garden, 233
In My Mother's House, 14
In Search of Meaning: Living
    Religions of the World, 253
In the Forest, 16
In the Night Kitchen, 36
In Their Own Words: A History of
    the American Negro, 1619–1865,
    275
In-Betweener, 54
Inatuk's Friend, 65
Incas Knew, 265
Inch by Inch, 27
Incredible Deborah: A Story Based
    on the Life of Deborah Sampson,
    198
Incredible Journey, 145
Independent Voices, 225

Indian and His Horse, 272
Indian Costumes, 272
Indian Horse Mystery, 129
Indian Music Makers, 336
Indian Summer, 90
Indians, 278
Innocent Wayfaring, 105
Inoke Sails the South Seas, 34
Insect Builders and Craftsmen, 308
Inside the Orbit of the Earth, 316
Invincible Louisa, 208
Invitation to Music, 342
Iron Arm of Michael Glenn, 143
Iron Chancellor: Otto Von
    Bismarck, 197
Iron Peacock, 81
Ironhead, 53
Irving and Me, 58
Is Something up There? The Story
    of Flying Saucers, 319
Is Somewhere Always Far Away?,
    223
Ishi, Last of His Tribe, 88
Island of Horses, 147
Island of the Blue Dolphins, 91
Islands of the Deep Sea, 309
It All Began with a Drip, Drip,
    Drip, 5
It Doesn't Always Have to Rhyme,
    225
It's Like This, Cat, 67
Ivanov Seven, 184

Jack Tales, 178
Jacob and the Robbers, 33
Jade, 95
Jane-Emily, 132
Janitor's Girl, 55
Japanese: People of the Three
    Treasures, 264
Jayhawker Johnny, 80
Jazz Country, 58
Jeanne-Marie Counts Her Sheep, 2
Jed, 79
Jennifer, Hecate, Macbeth, William
    McKinley and Me, Elizabeth, 61
Jewish Sabbath, 243
Joan of Arc, 217
Joey's Cat, 13
Johann Sebastian Bach, 209
John Billington, Friend of Squanto,
    79
John Henry, 185

John Treegate's Musket, 96
Johnny Tremain, 85
Jonah and the Great Fish, 177
Jorge el curioso (Curious George),
    347
Joseph, 241
Joseph and Koza; Or the Sacrifice
    to the Vistula, 191
Joseph The Dreamer, 177
Josephina February, 29
Journey across the Third Planet,
    156
Journey Cake, Ho!, 34
Journey of Akbar, 181
Journey Outside, 173
Journey to Jericho, 68
Journey toward Freedom, 198
Journeys, 285
Joy to the World, 251
Juan, 123
Jud, 69
Judge, 42
Jules Verne: The Man Who
    Invented the Future, 198
Juma, the Little African, 282
Jumblies, 224
Jungle Book, 166
Jungle Rescue, 105
Junior High Freestyle Swimmer,
    143
Junket, 154

Kallie's Corner, 63
Kap and the Wicked Monkey, 186
Katie Goes to Camp, 35
Keep Your Mouth Closed Dear, 9
Khmers of Cambodia: The Story of
    a Mysterious People, 262
Killer-of-Death, 78
King David, 201
King of the Wind, 149
King Snake, 293
Kingdom Lost for a Drop of Honey
    and Other Burmese Folktales,
    184
Kingdom of the Elephants, 295
King's Choice, 6
King's Fountain, 9
King's Stilts, 37
Kitchen Madonna, 109
Kites, 318
Knee-Deep in Thunder, 169
Knight of the Lion, 182

Kolo the Panda, 150
Komanticia, 88
Kon-Tiki, 281

La Brea Story, 288
Lady Ellen Grae, 50
Ladybirds: Women in Aviation, 205
Lagalág, the Wanderer, 148
Land in the Sun, 280
Land Renewed: The Story of Soil Conservation, 302
Landmark History of the American People from Plymouth to Appomattox, 267
Langston Hughes: A Biography, 208
Langston Hughes: A Poet of his People, 210
Lantern in the Window, 84
Lassie Come Home, 114
Last Battle, 168
Last Trumpeters, 295
Last Viking, 125
Latin American Tales, 176
Laugh Peddler, 81
Laughable Limericks, 229
Laura Ingalls Wilder Songbook, 335
Lavender's Blue, 8
Le hibou et la poussiquette (The Owl and the Pussycat), 346
Lean out of the Window, 231
Lefty's Boy, 53
Legend of the Willow Plate, 193
Legends of King Arthur, 187
Leif the Lucky, 14
Lenin and Trotsky, 213
Leon, 148
Let the Balloon Go, 74
Let's Be Early Settlers with Daniel Boone, 329
Let's Find Out about Birds, 299
Let's Find Out about Daniel Boone, 213
Let's Find Out about Insects, 308
Let's Find Out about Magnets, 320
Let's Find Out about Milk, 311
Let's Give a Show, 342
Let's Learn about the Orchestra, 335
Let's Make Presents, 336
Let's Meet the Chemist, 323
Letter to Amy, 25

Liberty and Corporal Kincaid, 94
Life and Times of Frederick Douglass, 201
Life and Words of John F. Kennedy, 218
Life of a Queen, 31
Life Story, 13
Lifeline: The Story of Your Circulatory System, 307
Lift Every Voice and Sing, 338
Light Princess, 168
Lighthouse Island, 14
Lightning Southpaw, 142
Lillian, 117
Limner's Daughter, 81
Lines, Spines and Porcupines, 342
Lingonberries in the Snow, 113
Lion, 30
Lion and the Rat, 5
Lion Gate and Labyrinth, 259
Lion in the Meadow, 29
Lion of Judah: A Life of Haile Selassie, Emperor of Ethiopia, 203
Lions in the Way, 71
Listen, Rabbit, 16
Litter Knight, 22
Little Bear, 29
Little Bear's Thanksgiving, 238
Little Bookroom, 164
Little Cock, 4
Little Drummer Boy, 244
Little Fishes, 111
Little Fur Family, 12
Little Greek Alphabet Book, 258
Little House, 13
Little House in the Big Woods, 96
Little House of Your Own, 15
Little Is Nice, 24
Little Juggler, 244
Little Laughter, 233
Little Leo, 31
Little Man, 166
Little Match Girl, 240
Little Pear and the Rabbits, 114
Little Pest Pico, 106
Little Plum, 109
Little Prayer, 244
Little Prince, 163
Little Rascal, 298
Little Red, 60
Little Red Riding Hood, 20
Little Sister Tai Mi, 103
Little Thunder, 80

Little Toot, 19
Little Two and the Peachtree, 116
Little Whistler, 222
Little White Hen, 21
Little Witch, 160
Little Women, 77
Little Wrangler, 41
Living Community, 301
London Bridge Is Falling Down, 334
Lone Muskrat, 153
Lone Seal Pup, 146
Lonely War of William Pinto, 271
Loner (Brandbury), 47
Loner (Wier), 76
Lonesome Boy, 47
Long Ago in Serbia, 192
Long Christmas, 251
Long Shot for Paul, 142
Long Vacation, 127
Looking at Art, 333
Looking at Holland, 282
Looking at Sculpture, 340
Lord Is My Shepherd, 241
Lost Half-Hour, 190
Lost John, 119
Lost Queen of Egypt, 117
Lost Worlds, 266
Lotte's Locket, 73
Louis Agassiz: Pied Piper of Science, 202
Love for Three Oranges, 340
Lucky Ladybugs, 307
Lucretia Mott: Gentle Warrior, 214
Lucy, 140
Luigi of the Streets, 104
Lullabies from around the World, 338
Lyrico, the Only Horse of His Kind, 164

Ma Lien and the Magic Brush, 185
Mackenzie, 263
Mad Scientists' Club, 155
Madame Prime Minister: The Story of Indira Ghandi, 203
Madeline, 11
Magic Listening Cap, 193
Magic Michael, 37
Magic Meadow, 15
Magic Secrets, 330
Magician and the Child, 31
Magna Charta, 261
Magnus and the Wagon Horse, 118

Magnus in the Harbor, 118
Mailbox Trick, 51
Majola: A Zulu Boy, 283
Make Way for Ducklings, 28
Malcolm X, 196
Man and the Beast, 297
Man in the Box: A Story from Vietnam, 107
Man in the Moon: Sky Tales from Many Lands, 184
Man of Liberty, 216
Man of the Family, 103
Man Who Hated Sherlock Holmes: A Life of Sir Arthur Conan Doyle, 218
Man Who Talked to Trees, 35
Man with the Bushy Beard and Other Tales, 38
Many Faces of the Civil War, 278
Many Human Senses, 306
Many Moons, 173
Many Worlds of Benjamin Franklin, 201
Maple Street, 44
Marassa and Midnight, 123
Marathon Looks on the Sea, 105
Maria and Ramon: A Girl and Boy of Puerto Rico, 283
Maria Lupin, 134
Maria Tallchief, 215
Marian Anderson: Lady from Philadelphia, 210
Marooned in Orbit, 155
Martin and Abraham Lincoln, 198
Martin de Porres, Hero, 241
Marvelous Misadventures of Sebastian, 159
Mary Jane, 74
Mary Lyon of Putnam's Hill, 197
Mary Poppins, 174
Masai, 279
Master Builders of the Middle Ages, 337
Matchlock Gun, 83
Matthew, Mark, Luke and John, 103
Matuk, the Eskimo Boy, 105
Mavericks, 72
Maxie, 24
May I Bring a Friend?, 15
Mazel and Schlimazel: Or the Milk of a Lioness, 191
McBroom's Ear, 17
Me! A Book of Poems, 232

Mei Li, 22
Melon Patch Mystery, 135
Member of the Gang, 70
Memoirs of a London Doll, 112
Merry Christmas to You, 246
Message to Hadrian, 125
Mexico, 281
Michael Grows a Wish, 151
Micias, Boy of the Andes, 279
Midget League Catcher, 143
Midnight Alarm, 210
Midnight Fox, 146
Mighty Hunter, 21
Miguel's Mountain, 46
Mikado, 335
Mika's Apple Tree, 103
Mike Mulligan and His Steam
   Shovel, 13
Mike's Toads, 164
Milkweed, 312
Miller, the Boy and the Donkey, 6
Millions of Cats, 18
Mimosa Tree, 50
Mind and Heart of Frederick
   Douglass, 212
Mine for Keeps, 63
Minn of the Mississippi, 294
Mira! Mira!, 39
Miracles on Maple Hill, 73
Miracles: Poems by Children of the
   English-Speaking World, 233
Mishmash, 147
Miss Bianca: A Fantasy, 172
Miss Flora McFlimsey's Valentine,
   238
Miss Happiness and Miss Flower,
   109
Miss Hickory, 159
Miss Kirby's Room, 46
Miss Pickerell Goes Undersea,
   157
Mississippi Possum, 152
Mister Corbett's Ghost, 135
Moccasin Trail, 89
Modeling in Clay, Plaster and
   Paper-Mâché, 342
Mogo's Flute, 126
Mohegan Chief, 216
Mommy, Buy Me a China Doll, 7
Momolu, 109
Momotáro, 178
Money Machine, 139
Monkeys and the Pedlar, 38
Moon, 315

Moon: Earth's Natural Satellite,
   316
Moon Eyes, 139
Moon, for What Do You Wait?, 228
Moon Jumpers, 40
Moon Man, 40
Moon Mouse, 22
More Beautiful than Flowers, 248
More Tales of Faraway Folk, 180
More than Courage, 99
Mormons: The Church of Jesus
   Christ of the Latter-Day Saints,
   245
Mossy Trotter, 124
Most Native of Sons, 217
Most Terrible Turk, 114
Mother Goose, 8
Mother Goose and Nursery
   Rhymes, 8
Mother Goose in French, 347
Moy Moy, 238
Mr. Budge Buys a Car, 319
Mr. Chief Justice Earl Warren, 213
Mr. Miacca, 24
Mr. Miacca: An English Folk Tale,
   187
Mr. Popper's Penguins, 45
Mr. Revere and I, 151
Mr. Toast and the Woolly
   Mammoth, 47
Mr. Wilowby's Christmas Tree, 241
Mrs. Coverlet's Detectives, 138
Muddy Road to Glory, 89
Mukhtar's Children, 127
Museum House Ghosts, 172
Music in America, 341
Musical Instruments of Africa, 334
Muskie Hook, 50
Mustang, Wild Spirit of the West,
   301
Mutineers, 98
My Adventures with African
   Animals, 290
My Brother Stevie, 50
My Five Senses, 306
My Japan, 282
My Kind of Verse, 235
My Kingdom for a Grave, 119
My Poetry Book, 232
My Side of the Mountain, 56
Mysterious Disappearance of Leon
   (I Mean Noel), 139
Mystery aboard the Ocean
   Princess, 135

Mystery and More Mystery, 129
Mystery at Blackstone Lake, 140
Mystery at Lion's Gate, 136
Mystery at Long Barrow House, 134
Mystery at Mappins, 132
Mystery at Monkey Run, 137
Mystery at Old Sturbridge Village, 137
Mystery at the Old Forge, 132
Mystery in Newfoundland, 141
Mystery of the Fat Cat, 131
Mystery of the Forgotten Map, 134
Mystery of the Great Swamp, 141
Mystery of the Jittery Dog-Walker, 135
Mystery of the Missing Stamps, 133
Mystery of the Ski Slopes, 129
Mystery of 22 East, 141
Mystery on Nine-Mile Marsh, 136

Nannabah's Friend, 69
Nansen, 204
Napoleon: Man of Destiny, 203
Narni of the Desert, 127
Natural Wonders of the World, 324
Near East, 259
Negroes in the Early West, 268
Never Try Nathaniel, 84
New Comedies for Teenagers, 334
New Day, 12
New Friend, 43
New Home for Billy, 61
New Land, 278
New Moon Cove, 301
New Plays for Red Letter Days, 342
New Tall Tales of Pecos Bill, 181
New Worlds Ahead, 262
News, 209
Next Door to Zanadu, 68
Ngari the Hunter, 34
Nibble Nibble, 220
Nibble Nibble Mousekin: A Tale of Hansel and Gretel, 20
Nicole, a Little French School Girl, 109
Nigerian Pioneer: The Story of Mary Slessor, 215
Night before Christmas, 249
Night Noises, 24
Night of the Black Frost, 104
Nightbirds on Nantucket, 158
Nightingale, 9

Nine Days to Christmas, 245
Ninji's Magic, 115
Nkwala, 92
No Boats on Bannermere, 140
No One Writes a Letter to the Snail, 224
No Sleep for Angus, 135
Noah Riddle?, 145
Noah's Ark, 254
Nock Family Circus, 23
Nomusa and the New Magic, 116
Noodles, Nitwits, and Numskulls, 186
Norman, 34
Norman Conquest, 263
North American Bighorn Sheep, 289
North American Indians, 267
North Town, 56
North Wind and the Sun, 5
Norwegian Folk Tales, 175
Not over Ten Inches High, 89
Nurse Matilda Goes to Town, 161
Nutcracker, 333
Nutshell Library, 36
Nuvolari and the Alfa Romeo, 198

O Children of the Wind and Pines, 176
Octopus Lives in the Ocean, 299
Odd Old Mammals, 287
Odysseus Comes Home from the Sea, 194
Odyssey of Courage: The Story of Álvar Nuñez Cabeza de Vaca, 218
Of Animals and Men, 290
Oh, How Silly!, 229
Oh Lord, I Wish I Was a Buzzard, 19
Oh, What Nonsense!, 230
Ol' Dan Tucker, 224
Old Abe: The Eagle Hero, 155
Old Sam and the Horse Thieves, 94
Old Testament, 244
Old Yeller, 148
Olode the Hunter and Other Tales from Nigeria, 179
On Christmas Day in the Morning, 338
On City Streets, 232
On Course!, 205
On Faraway Street, 118

On Lutes, Recorders, and
    Harpsichords, 332
On the Sand Dune, 68
On the Spot Reporting, 256
Once a Mouse, 4
Once the Hodja, 185
Once There Was and Twice There
    Wasn't, 193
Once There Was and Was Not:
    Armenian Tales Retold, 192
One God, 246
101 Masks, 334
1 Is One, 3
One Is One, 119
One Little Tree, 240
One Luminaria for Antonio, 247
One Morning in Maine, 28
One Small Blue Bead, 35
One Special Summer, 49
1 2 3 Board Book, 3
1 2 3 4 5, 3
1 2 3 Go, 329
1 2 3 to the Zoo, 2
One's None: Old Rhymes for New
    Tongues, 235
Onion Journey, 244
Operation Time Search, 157
Orange Scarf, 148
Orchestra and Its Instruments, 336
Orders to Vietnam: A Novel of
    Helicopter Warfare, 48
Oregon at Last!, 95
Orphans of Simitra, 102
Orphans of the Wind, 86
Other Side of the Fence, 51
Other Side of the Mountain, 26
Other Side of the Street, 103
Our Country's Story, 268
Our Eddie, 87
Our Navy Explores Antarctica, 270
Our Presidents, 219
Our Rice Village in Cambodia, 284
Our Wild Animals, 289
Out of Hand, 73
Outlaw Red: Son of Big Red, 150
Outsiders, 58
Over and Over, 43
Over in the Meadow, 3
Over Mountains: Prairies and Seas,
    310
Over the Blue Mountain, 91
Over the Hills and Far Away, 92
Overhead the Sun, 228
Owlglass, 170

Oxford Book of Poetry for Children,
    229

Packy, 132
Paddington at Work, 160
Paddle-to-the-Sea, 86
Paddy's Christmas, 249
Padre Porko: The Gentlemanly Pig,
    163
Pageant of the Theater, 334
Pagoo, 149
Paint All Kinds of Pictures, 343
Paintbrush and Peacepipe: The
    Story of George Catlin, 212
Painting the Moon, 194
Paleface Redskins, 60
Pantheon Story of Art for Young
    People, 341
Panther's Moon, 102
Pantomime: The Silent Theatre,
    337
Papa Albert, 347
Papa Petit, Papa Small, 346
Paper Dragon, 66
Paper Zoo: A Collection of Animal
    Poems by Modern American
    Poets, 235
Papillot, Clignot et Dodo, 347
Parrot of Isfahan, 108
Parsley, 11
Passage to the West, 203
Pastels Are Great!, 336
Patricia Crosses Town, 45
Patrol Car, 136
Patterns of Nature, 289
Peace Is an Adventure, 285
Peaceable Kingdom, 221
Peanuts, Popcorn, Ice Cream,
    Candy and Soda Pop: And How
    They Began, 276
Pear Tree, the Birch Tree, and The
    Barberry Bush, 13
Pearls in Pictures, 310
Peasant and the Donkey: Tales of
    the Near and Middle East, 187
Pedaling Man and Other Poems,
    223
Pelican Chorus, 224
Penguin Book, 298
Penguins: The Birds with Flippers,
    289
People and Places, 285
People in Palestine, 106
Peppersalt Land, 57

Percy, Polly, and Pete, 30
Perilous Road, 93
Periwinkle Jones, 54
Persian Folk and Fairy Tales, 187
Peru, 282
Peter, 165
Peter and Butch, 119
Peter and the Wolf, 340
Peter Cartwright: Pioneer Circuit
   Rider, 216
Peter Pan, 160
Peter Zenger: Fighter for Freedom,
   202
Peter's Chair, 25
Pete's Puddle, 17
Petunia's Christmas, 245
Phaethon, 189
Phantom of Walkaway Hill, 134
Phantom Palomino, 138
Phoenix Forest, 311
Physics Experiments for Children,
   324
Piece of Fire and Other Haitian
   Tales, 179
Pieces of Home, 89
Pilgrim Neighbors, 86
Pilgrims: Brave Settlers of
   Plymouth, 271
Piñatas, 332
Pioneer in Blood Plasma: Dr.
   Charles Drew, 207
Piper, Pipe That Song Again, 232
Piping down the Valleys Wild:
   Poetry for the Young of All Ages,
   233
Pippa Passes, 51
Pippi Longstocking, 168
Pirate's Island, 124
Pistol, 69
Pistol in Greenyards, 112
Pit, 64
Pizorro, 126
Place, 105
Place in the Sun, 301
Plants and Animals in the Air, 292
Play Production For Young People,
   340
Play with Me, 16
Play with Paper, 331
Play with Seeds, 313
Plays for Living and Learning, 339
Plays for Reading and Recording,
   339
Plum Pudding for Christmas, 248

Plymouth Thanksgiving, 239
Poems, 222
Poems for Seasons and
   Celebrations, 230
Poems of Magic and Spells, 230
Poetry for Holidays, 233
Pool of Fire, 155
Poor Richard, 200
Pop Corn and Ma Goodness, 33
Poppy in the Corn, 127
Porterhouse Major, 160
Portrait of Margarita, 44
Possum, 296
Potato Talk, 33
Prarie Schooners, 276
Prancing Pony: Nursery Rhymes
   from Japan, 230
Prayer for a Child, 246
Prayer for Little Things, 245
Pretzel Hero: A Story of Old
   Vienna, 121
Prince Bertram the Bad, 28
Prince in Waiting, 156
Princess of Orange, 206
Printing from a Stone: The Story of
   Lithography, 336
Prisoners in the Snow, 104
Profiles in Courage, 206
Project: Scoop, 57
Promise Is a Promise, 51
Proserpina, the Duck That Came to
   School, 148
Protectors: The Story of the Food
   and Drug Administration, 275
Pulga, 126
Pumpkin Moonshine, 239
Punch and Judy: A Play for
   Puppets, 334
Puppet Book, 344
Puppets for Beginners, 337
Purloined Letter and the Murders
   in the Rue Morgue, 139
Pursuit, 131
Pushcart War, 169
Puss in Boots, 5
Pyramid of Living Things, 302

Queenie Peavy, 79
Queen's Own Grove, 78
Queen's Wizard, 100
Quest for Freedom: Bolivar and the
   South American Revolution, 212
Quest for the Dead Sea Scrolls, 249
Quest of the Gole, 165

Question and Answer Book about the Human Body, 307
Questions and Answers about Ants, 309
Quick Pivot: Stories of Basketball, 142

Rabbit Hill, 151
Rabbits Rafferty, 148
Rain Boat, 88
Rain Drop Splash, 39
Rain in the Woods and Other Small Matters, 298
Rain Makes Applesauce, 34
Rain, Rivers and Reservoirs: The Challenge of Running Water, 300
Rainbow Book of American Folk Tales and Legends, 186
Rama the Gypsy Cat, 146
Ramayana, 191
Ramon Makes a Trade, 347
Ramona the Pest, 49
Rani, Queen of the Jungle, 148
Rapunzel, 20
Rattlesnake Run, 89
Raven's Cry, 111
Reach Out, Ricardo, 53
Read about the Brain, 306
Reason for the Pelican, 221
Rebel Courier and the Redcoats, 82
Red Balloon, 167
Red Fairy Book, 185
Red Sails to Capri, 141
Reflections on a Gift of Watermelon Pickle . . . and Other Complete Modern Poems, 231
Reggie's No-Good Bird, 48
Remarkable Ride of the Abernathy Boys, 205
Renfroe's Christmas, 242
Reptiles as Pets, 300
Retreat to Victory: The Life of Nathaniel Greene, 196
Return of the Twelves, 162
Return to Hiroshima, 281
Rhyming Will, 121
Ribsy, 146
Rich Man and the Shoemaker, 5
Richthofen the Red Baron, 202
Ricky in the World of Sport, 144
Ride on High, 68
Ride on the Wind, 317
Ride Proud, Rebel!, 90

Ride the Wild Storm, 153
Rider and His Horse, 111
Rifles for Watie, 88
Ring in the Prairie: A Shawnee Legend, 176
Ring O'Roses, 8
Ring the Judas Bell, 108
Ringtail, 149
Rise and Fall of the Dinosaurs, 288
River at Green Knowe, 161
River Boy, 77
River Boy: Adventure on the Amazon, 281
River Kings, 107
Rivers, 257
Rivers of the World, 258
Roam the Wild Country, 107
Roan Colt, 153
Robert Frost, 211
Robin Hood of Sherwood Forest, 186
Rocket in My Pocket, 235
Rockets, 318
Rocky and Sandy, 300
Roly-Poly Pudding, 31
Roman People, 261
Romance of Physics, 323
Roofs of Gold: Poems to Read Aloud, 230
Roofs over America, 269
Room 10, 63
Roosevelt Grady, 72
Rootabaga Stories, 171
Rosa, 347
Rosie's Walk, 23
Rough Ice, 143
Round the World Fairy Tales, 194
Round Trip Space Ship, 157
Rowan Farm, 101
Royal Adventurers, 216
Rrra-ah, 150
Runaway Bunny, 242
Runaway Home, 72
Runaway Jonah and Other Tales, 254
Runaway Ralph, 162
Runaway Slave: The Story of Harriet Tubman, 207
Russia in Revolution, 262

Sacajawea, 216
Sacramento: Golden River of California, 256
Sail, Calypso!, 60

Saint Francis and His Animals, 250
Salt Boy, 31
Sam (Corcoran), 52
Sam (Scott), 35
Sam Bangs, and Moonshine, 30
Sam Bottleby, 162
Sand Ponies, 66
Santiago, 11
Saturday Gang, 136
Scandinavia, 280
Scarlet Thread, 344
Science beneath the Sea: The Story of Oceanography, 305
Science in Your Own Backyard, 327
Science of Salt, 303
Scroobius Pip, 224
Sculptured Image, 339
Sea Egg, 161
Sea Horse, 40
Sea of Grass, 270
Sea Otters and the China Trade, 267
Sea Pair, 46
Sea Pup, 145
Sea Searchers, 321
Sea Wall, 106
Seapiece, 45
Search for the Robots, 319
Sea's Inhabitants, 291
Seashore Story, 42
Seasons of Time: Tanka Poetry of Ancient Japan, 229
Secret Codes and Ciphers, 257
Secret Journey of the Silver Reindeer, 114
Secret Kind of Weapon, 98
Secret Language, 67
Secret of the Dark Tower, 137
Secret of the Hidden Painting, 130
Secret of the Missing Boat, 131
Secret of the Sacred Lake, 131
Secret of the Unknown Fifteen, 133
Secret Shoemakers and Other Stories, 190
Secrets of Hidden Creek, 140
See Again, Say Again, 345
See and Say: A Picture Book in Four Languages, 346
Seesaws to Cosmic Rays, 321
Seine, 280
Selina's New Family, 119

Serendipity Tales, 183
Seven Ravens, 20
Seven Stages, 343
Seven Tales, 9
Seventeen Seventy-Six: Journals of American Independence, 276
Seventh Mandarin, 6
Shadow Book, 327
Shadow of a Bull, 128
Shadow of a Crow, 69
Shadow on the Sun, 165
Shanty-Boat Bill, 80
Shape of Living Things, 292
Shape of the Earth, 303
Shapes, 322
Shawneen and the Gander, 160
Shepherd (Aichinger), 240
Shepherd (Broun), 242
Shepherds Nosegay Stories from Finland and Czechoslovakia, 181
Sheriff Stonehead and the Teenage Termites, 160
Shinty Boys, 144
Shoemakers, 269
Shoes from Yang San Valley, 113
Shrimps, 294
Siege and Fall of Troy, 182
Signs and Symbols around the World, 257
Silkspinners, 186
Silly Little Kid, 16
Silver Chief: Dog of the North, 152
Silver Crown, 157
Silver Curlew, 164
Silver Swan: Poems of Mystery and Romance, 231
Simon, 51
Simon's Way, 107
Sing down the Moon, 91
Sing Little Mouse, 16
Sing Mother Goose, 8
Singing and the Gold, 234
Singing Hill, 52
Single Light, 128
Single Trail, 71
Sir Gawain and the Green Knight, 183
Sir Henry Morgan, Buccaneer, 215
Sir Walter Scott: Wizard of the North, 213
Sister's Tale, 104
Sitting Bull, 210
Six Feet Six, 205
Six Great Horse Rides, 277

Six Who Were Left in a Shoe, 179
Skip around the Year, 246
Sky Dog, 39
Sky Pioneers, 203
Sky-Eater and Other South Sea
  Tales, 183
Skyhooks: The Story of
  Helicopters, 317
Slavery in the United States, 272
Sleep Baby Sleep, 7
Sleeping Beauty, 20
Sleeping Beauty, 188
Sneaker Hill, 168
Snow and the Sun: La nieve y el
  sol, 346
Snowbound, 45
Snowy Day, 25
So Dear to My Heart, 90
So Ends This Day, 85
Solar Energy, 320
Soldiers' Songs and Marches, 337
Some Haystacks Don't Even Have
  Any Needle, 231
Some of the Days of Everett
  Anderson, 221
Something Special, 221
Sometime Island, 45
Song of Robin Hood, 186
Song of the Empty Bottles, 65
Song of the Swallows, 31
Sons of the Steppe, 99
Sophia Scrooby Preserved, 98
Sorcerer's Apprentice, 5
Soul Brothers and Sister Lou, 59
Sound of Bells, 277
Sound of Sunshine, Sound of Rain,
  21
Sounder, 44
South Swell, 67
Southeast Asia, 282
Space ABC, 317
Space and Time, 323
Space Olympics, 157
Spanish Letters, 113
Sparkle and Spin: A Book about
  Words, 33
Sparrow Bush, 221
Special Plays for Special Days, 335
Spectacles, 171
Spider Plant, 74
Spiders Are Spinners, 298
Spring Begins in March, 63
Spring Rider, 167
Spring Song, 337

Sprints and Distances: Sports in
  Poetry and the Poetry in Sport,
  234
Spy for Liberty: The Adventurous
  Life of Beaumarchais, 212
St. Lawrence Seaway, 257
St. Patrick's Day, 237
Stampede North, 85
Star and the Sword, 116
Star Mountain, 177
Starlight in Tourrone, 243
Start to Draw, 333
Start with a Dot, 341
Staying Home Alone on a Rainy
  Day, 23
Steadfast Tin Soldier, 9
Steamboats and Steamboat Men,
  258
Stevie, 38
Stilts, Somersaults and
  Headstands, 222
Stitchery Book: Embroidery for
  Beginners, 339
Stolen by the Indians, 271
Stone of Victory and Other Tales,
  179
Stone-Faced Boy, 55
Stories from Shakespeare, 333
Stories from the New Testament,
  254
Stories of Gilbert and Sullivan
  Operas, 333
Stories of the Gods and Heroes,
  176
Stories of the Steppes, 187
Storm Boy, 154
Storm from the West, 128
Stormy, Misty's Foal, 149
Story about Ping, 17
Story of Atomic Energy, 320
Story of Cattle Ranching, 266
Story of Caves, 305
Story of Coins, 329
Story of Comock the Eskimo, 280
Story of Dogs, 296
Story of Electricity, 320
Story of Electricity and Magnetism,
  321
Story of Ferdinand, 26
Story of Holly and Ivy, 246
Story of King Arthur and His
  Knights, 189
Story of Moslem Art, 340
Story of Music, 344

Story of New England, 277
Story of Painting for Young People, 338
Story of the Dead Sea Scrolls, 250
Story of the Incas, 264
Story of William Penn, 196
Story of World Religions, 251
Story of World War I, 263
Storyteller's Pack, 173
Stowaway to the Mushroom Planet, 155
Straight Hair, Curly Hair, 306
Stranded: A Story of New York in 1875, 79
Strange Case of Dr. Jekyll and Mr. Hyde, 140
Strange Fishes of the Sea, 293
Strange Summer in Stratford, 139
Stranger at Green Knowe, 145
Strawberry Roan, 341
Street Kids, 163
Street of the Flower Boxes, 64
Striped Ice Cream, 62
Stripes and Spots, 23
Strongest Man in the World, 214
Struggle at Soltuna, 98
Stuck with Luck, 166
Such Is the Way of the World, 4
Sue Ellen, 59
Summer Adventure, 62
Summer Sleigh Ride, 156
Sun Is a Golden Earring, 176
Sun Train, 121
Sung under the Silver Umbrella, 229
Superlative Horse, 169
Supersonic Transport, 319
Survival Training in Our Armed Forces, 284
Suspense: A Treasury for Young Adults, 137
Suzie Mariar, 38
Swan of the East: The Life and Death of the German Cruiser Emden in World War I, 112
Swans, 297
Swapping Boy, 338
Swimmy, 27
Sword of King Arthur, 194
Sword to Slice Through Mountains and Other Stories, 103
Sylvester and the Magic Pebble, 173

Taash and the Jesters, 186
Tacky Little Icicle Shack, 61
Tailor of Gloucester, 250
Take Joy, 253
Take My Waking Slow, 67
Take Shapes, Lines, and Letters, 323
Take Sky, 225
Tales from Grimm, 21
Tale of a Donkey, 144
Tale of Jemima Puddle-Duck, 32
Tale of Mr. Jeremy Fisher, 32
Tale of Mr. Tod, 32
Tale of Mrs. Tittlemouse, 32
Tale of Peter Rabbit, 32
Tale of the Flopsy Bunnies, 32
Tale of Tom Kitten, 32
Tale of Two Bad Mice, 33
Tales from Silver Lands, 181
Tales from the Ballet, 343
Tales Told Again, 180
Tales Told near a Crocodile, 182
Taliesin and King Arthur, 190
Talkative Beasts: Myths, Fables and Poems of India, 189
Talking Cat and Other Stories of French Canada, 178
Tall Book of Mother Goose, 8
Tall Tales of the Catskills, 180
Taller than Bandai Mountain, 199
Tani, 116
Taro and the Sea Turtles, 147
Taro and the Tofu, 116
Taste of Spruce Gum, 60
Tatsinda, 163
Teacher of the Blind: Samuel Gridley Howe, 217
Teacher's Pet, 65
Teddy Bear Habit, 50
Tekla's Easter, 242
Telescope Makers, 316
Tell Me a Mitzi, 36
Terrible Churnadryne, 161
Terry and the Caterpillars, 309
Tessie, 60
That Barbara!, 75
That Remarkable Man: Justice Oliver Wendell Holmes, 208
There Is a Dragon in My Bed, 346
There Is No Rhyme for Silver, 225
These Hallowed Grounds, 268
They Lived in the Ice Age, 304
They Put out to Sea, 262

They Showed the Way: Forty
    American Negro Leaders, 212
They Took Their Stand, 214
They Were Strong and Good,
    273
Thieving Dwarfs, 177
Think about It: Experiments in
    Psychology, 307
Thirteen Days of Yule, 252
Thirteen Moons Series, 294
This Dear-Bought Land, 88
This Is a Leaf, 312
This Is a Recording, 52
This Is Automation, 320
This Is Hong Kong, 283
This Is the Way, 247
This Is Your Century, 278
This Land Is Mine: An Anthology
    of American Verse, 232
This Street's for Me!, 223
This Way Delight: A Book of
    Poetry for the Young, 234
Thistle, 300
Thomas Paine, 207
Thor and the Giants, 181
Thou Shalt Not Kill, 120
Threat to the Barkers, 119
Three and Shapes of Three, 324
Three Billy Goats Gruff, 10
Three Cheers for Charlie, 122
Three Robbers, 40
Three Sparrows and Other Nursery
    Poems, 226
Three Tales of Monkey, 193
Thumbelina, 10
Thunder in the Sky, 139
Thunder of the Gods, 183
Thunderstorm, 313
Thy Friend, Obadiah, 154
Tiber: The Roman River, 264
Tico and the Golden Wings, 27
Tide in the Attic, 126
Tiger in the Lake, 61
Tiger's Whisker and Other Tales
    and Legends from Asia and the
    Pacific, 179
Tikki Tikki Tembo, 29
Tiktá 'Liktak, 184
Tim to the Lighthouse, 10
Time at the Top, 170
Time Cat, 159
Time for Fairy Tales Old and New,
    175
Time for Poetry, 228

Time for the Stars, 156
Time Garden, 163
Time of Wonder, 29
Time-Ago Tales of Jahdu, 111
Tiny Seed, 14
Tirra Lirra, 226
Tistou of the Green Thumb, 163
Tit for Tat and Other Latvian Folk
    Tales, 180
Tituba of Salem Village, 91
To Be a Slave, 273
To Catch a Mongoose: A Picture
    Story, 347
To Dream upon a Crown, 128
To Tell My People, 120
To the Ends of the Universe,
    315
To the Pacific with Lewis and
    Clark, 266
To the Top of the World: The
    Story of Peary and Henson, 196
Today I Am a Ham, 68
Today Is Saturday, 227
Told Under the Christmas Tree,
    241
Tom Paine: Freedom's Apostle,
    203
Tom Tiddler's Ground, 230
Tomahawk Border, 93
Tomahawk Shadow, 83
Tombi's Song, 122
Tom's Midnight Garden, 170
Tomten, 26
Tony's Steamer, 75
Topi Forever, 91
Torrie, 87
Touch Me, Touch Me Not, 312
Touchdown Maker, 142
Tough Winter, 151
Tour on the Prairies, 272
Towappu: Puritan Renegade, 94
Trace through the Forest, 91
Trail of the Abominable Snowman,
    283
Train Ride, 38
Traitors, 109
Transportation of Tomorrow, 258
Traveling Musicians, 21
Travels of Monarch X, 308
Treasure of Green Knowe, 161
Treasure of Li-po, 190
Treasure of Siegfried, 175
Treasure on Heron's Neck, 61
Treasure Trove of the Sun, 120

Treasures under the Sand:
    Wolley's Finds at Ur, 263
Tree of Freedom, 80
Treeless Plains, 276
Tressa's Dream, 66
Trail at Nuremberg, 260
Trilogy of Christmas Plays for
    Children, 250
Trina's Boxcar, 64
Troubadour, 110
Trouble for the Tabors, 135
Trouble with Gus, 69
Truants, 228
True Tall Tales of Stormalong, 181
Truly, I Say to You, 240
Trust a City Kid, 59
Tune beyond Us, 233
Tunnel in the Sky, 156
Turnabout Trick, 147
Turtles, 292
Twenty and Ten, 102
Twenty Tales from Shakespeare,
    332
Twenty Thousand Leagues under
    the Sea, 158
Twenty-One Balloons, 171
26 Letters, 258
Twilight of Magic, 168
Two Are Better than One, 79
Two Crabs and the Moonlight, 41
Two Friends, 64
Two on the Trail, 92
Two Uncles of Pablo, 100
Two Worlds of Damyan, 102
Tyler, Wilkin and Skee, 79

UFO's and IFO's: A Factual Report
    on Flying Saucers, 318
Umbrella, 42
Uncle Fonzo's Ford, 65
Under the Tree, 226
Understanding Africa, 282
Undertow, 112
Unidentified Flying Objects, 318
Universe, 317
Universe Between, 157
Universe of Galileo and Newton,
    315
Unpopular Ones, 197
Untune the Sky, 234
Up a Road Slowly, 59
Uproar, 30
Uptown, 38
Uranium Pirates, 132

Vacquero Pequeno: Cowboy Small,
    346
Valentine Cat, 236
Valley of the Smallest: The Life
    Story of a Shrew, 293
Vanishing Wild Animals of the
    World, 301
Vassilis on the Run, 125
Velázquez, 212
Velvet Room, 73
Venetians: Merchant Princes, 261
Venture for a Crown, 108
Veronica Ganz, 71
Very Small Miracle, 152
Very Young Verses, 231
Vicky and the Monkey People, 101
Vietnam: The Country, the People,
    280
Vikan the Mighty, 145
Viking Adventure, 103
Vinlander's Saga, 191
Viva Chicano, 46
Voices from the Past, 264
Voices in the Fog, 95
Voices in the Night, 77
Voyages of Doctor Dolittle, 168

Wait Till the Moon is Full, 12
Walk in My Moccasins, 76
Walk the World's Rim, 99
Walking Stones, 165
Walls of Windy Troy: A Biography
    of Heinrich Schliemann, 198
Wandering Workers, 284
Warrior on Two Continents, 196
Warrior Scarlet, 124
Washington D. C.: The Story of
    Our Nation's Capital, 277
Washington's Birthday, 237
Watch Fires to the North, 108
Watch for a Tall White Sail, 100
Water, 303
Water: Our Vital Need, 303
Water: Riches or Ruin, 301
Watermelon, 312
Wave, 183
Way It Is, 284
Way of Knowing, 233
We Alcotts, 202
We Like Bugs, 308
We Lived in the Almont, 50
We Shall Live in Peace: The
    Teachings of Martin Luther King,
    Jr., 204

We Went Looking, 222
Weather in Your Life, 313
Weaver of Dreams: The Girlhood of
  Charlotte Brontë, 216
Wee Gillis, 26
Wee Joseph, 152
Weed Is a Flower: The Life of
  George Washington Carver, 196
Western Outlaws, 211
Westward Adventure: The True
  Stories of Six Pioneers, 214
What Do You Say, Dear?, 24
What Makes a Bird a Bird?, 293
What Makes a Plane Fly?, 317
What Shall We Have for
  Breakfast?, 42
What Then, Raman?, 98
What's Good for a Five Year Old?,
  221
What's in the Dark?, 29
When I Go to the Moon, 26
When Men Panned Gold in the
  Klondike, 310
When Shlemiel Went to Warsaw,
  192
When the Stones Were Soft: East
  African Fireside Tales, 182
Where Does the Butterfly Go When
  It Rains?, 18
Where Have You Been?, 12
Where the Lilies Bloom, 50
Where the Wild Things Are, 36
Where They Go in Winter, 291
Which Was Witch: Tales of Ghosts
  and Magic from Korea, 185
Whichaway, 75
Whingdingdilly, 30
Whispering Mountain, 158
Whispers and Other Poems, 224
White Archer: An Eskimo Legend,
  184
White Bird, 47
White Cat and Other Old French
  Fairy Tales, 180
White Horse Gang, 130
White Land, 9
White Lark, 75
White Palace, 298
White Snow, Bright Snow, 39
White Stag, 122
White Stallion of Lipizza, 112
White Twilight, 120
Who Look at Me, 223
Who Needs an Oil Well?, 95

Whose Town, 56
Why Not Join the Giraffes?, 48
Why the Sun and the Moon Live
  in the Sky: An African Folk-
  tale, 4
Why We Live Where We Live, 284
Why You Look Like You Whereas I
  Tend To Look Like Me, 312
Wild Horses of the Red Desert, 298
Wild in the World, 53
Wild Refuge, 302
Wild Voyageur, 295
Wild Young Desert, 303
Wildcat under Glass, 129
Wilderness Winter, 94
Wildlife in America's History, 290
Wildlife of North America, 297
Will Rogers, 211
William C. Handy: Father of the
  Blues, 209
William Penn: Founder and
  Friend, 204
William Shakespeare and His
  Plays, 204
Willie Was Different the Tale of an
  Ugly Thrushling, 153
Wind Has Wings, 231
Wind in the Willows, 164
Wind of Change, 99
Wind Song, 227
Winds That Come from Far Away
  and Other Poems, 225
Winged Rocketry, 319
Winged Watchman, 126
Wings, Legs or Fins, 295
Winner, 34
Winners, 76
Winnie the Pooh, 169
Winter Cottage, 47
Winter Danger, 93
Winter Patriot, 92
Winterbird, 29
Wise Fool, 4
Witch Dog, 100
Witch of Blackbird Pond, 93
Witch of the Woods: Fairy Tales
  from Sweden, 188
Witchcraft of Salem Village, 273
Witches' Bridge, 80
Witch's Daughter, 130
With an Open Hand, 66
Wizard in the Well, 219
Wolf and the Seven Little Kids, 21
Wolves of Willoughby Chase, 159

Women behind Men in Medicine, 211
Wonder Clock, 189
Wonder of Stones, 304
Wonderful Adventures of Nils, 167
Wonderful Egg, 23
Wonderful Eggs of Furicchia, 6
Wonderful Stuff: The Story of Clay, 341
Wonderful Terrible Time, 74
Wonderful Tree, 28
Wonderful World of Prehistoric Animals, 288
Wonderful World of the Theatre, 340
Wonders of the Human Body, 307
Words from History, 255
Words from the Myths, 255
World above, 313
World in the Candy Egg, 252
World Is Round, 304
World of Captain John Smith, 1580–1631, 270
World of Christopher Robin, 225
World of Columbus and Sons, 262
World of Nonsense: Strange and Humorous Tales from Many Lands, 194
World of the Ocean Depths, 305
World of Walls: The Middle Ages in Western Europe, 260
World We Live in, 304
World's Greatest Freak Show, 33
Would You Put Your Money in a Sand Bank?, 328
Would-Be-Goods, 67
Wreath of Christmas Legends, 248
Wrinkle in Time, 156
Wump World, 170

Yankee Doodle Dandy, 275
Yankee Doodle's Cousins, 187
Yankee Trader: Ben Tanner-1779, 81
Year Around: Poems for Children, 232
Year Mom Won the Pennant, 142

Year of the Jeep, 70
Year of the Raccoon, 150
Year to Grow, 58
Year without a Santa Claus, 248
Yeshu, Called Jesus, 241
Yosemite Tomboy, 71
You Better Come Home with Me, 167
You Can Make a String Puppet, 342
You Come Too: Favorite Poems for Young Readers, 222
You Visit a Sugar Refinery/Fruit Cannery, 310
You Were Princess Last Time, 54
Young Artist, 339
Young Bat Masterson, 210
Young Designer, 336
Young Detectives, 137
Young Embroiderer, 331
Young Explorers of the Northwest, 197
Young Ireland, 282
Young Mark, 97
Young Reader's Book of Christian Symbolism, 244
Young Thomas Edison, 210
Young Unicorns, 62
Young United States: 1783–1830, 278
Young Hand in Mine, 52
Your Neighbor Celebrates, 246
Your Telephone and How It Works, 320

Zamani Goes to Market, 108
Zealots of Masada: Story of a Dig, 264
Zeb, 77
Zebra Came to Drink, 146
Zeee, 16
Zero Stone, 157
Zlateh the Goat and Other Stories, 192
Zomo the Rabbit, 192
Zoo on the First Floor, 112
Zoos of the World, 293